WITHDRAWN

This book may be kept

FOURTEEN DAYS

A fine of TWO CENTS will be charged for each day
the book is kept over time.

May 21'52	Jan 5 65		
Jun 17'53	May 12 66		
May 8 '54	Apr 8'69		
May 26 54	Dec 16 70		
Apr 30 55	Aug 8 '75		
May 24'55			
930			
Apr 23'57			
Apr 24'57			
Jul 30'57			
May 2'58	pd		
May 5'59			
Aug 19 '59			
May 20'60			
May 23'61			
Aug 5'61			
Mar 19'64			

THE CENTURY HISTORICAL SERIES
WILLIAM E. LINGELBACH, *Editor*

WORLD WARS AND REVOLUTIONS

World Wars and Revolutions

THE COURSE OF EUROPE SINCE 1900

by

WALTER PHELPS HALL, Ph.D.

Dodge Professor of History
Princeton University

D. APPLETON-CENTURY COMPANY

INCORPORATED

NEW YORK   LONDON

Copyright, 1943, by

D. APPLETON-CENTURY COMPANY, INC.

4113

Copyright, 1926, by The Century Co.

Copyright, 1941, by D. Appleton-Century Company, Inc.

PRINTED IN THE UNITED STATES OF AMERICA

PREFACE

Since the events herein described have taken place within the memory of living men, this book may be regarded as contemporary history. To some historians such a description in itself is sufficient reason to read no further; others, sensitive to the momentous character of these years of turmoil, believe it not only permissible but desirable to chronicle the present, and even to dub what they have written, "history." The writer, it is evident, is sympathetic to their point of view. He is, of course, aware that much which he has written is not definitive. On the other hand, the revolutionary tempo of this present hour and the bitter death of young men everywhere in this global maelstrom are facts which need recording by one who breathes the atmosphere of 1943.

The larger part of this book is taken from the last eleven chapters of *The Course of Europe Since Waterloo*, in which the late Professor William Stearns Davis was co-author. Acknowledgment is due him for the material in Chapters II and III. Acknowledgment is also due Henry Holt and Company for kind permission to reprint in Chapter VIII a number of pages taken from the author's *Empire to Commonwealth*, which they published.

WALTER PHELPS HALL,
PRINCETON, N. J.

CONTENTS

vii

LIST OF MAPS AND GRAPHS

LIST OF ILLUSTRATIONS

(Superior numbers refer to explanatory notes on pages xv and xvi.)

EXPLANATORY NOTES

[1] Lord John Fisher (1841-1920), first sea lord of the admiralty at the commencement of the First World War, was a famous British sea-dog to whom should go much credit for England's naval preparedness in that conflict. Fisher was an intimate friend of King Edward VII and was said to have asked permission of that monarch "to Copenhagen the German fleet," in other words, to attack it without declaration of war. Fisher, disapproving of the continued efforts to force the Dardanelles, resigned in 1915.

[2] The General Secretary of the Communist Party in the U.S.S.R. is here shown flanked by two Communist leaders who have, up to this present writing, (1943), continued in the favor of the Russian dictator. Voroshilov, on Stalin's right, is Vice-Premier of the U.S.S.R. and chairman of its committee of defense. Kalinin, on Stalin's left, is chairman of the Presidium, an important body charged with the execution of the laws and theoretically elected by the two Soviet congresses.

[3] The character of the crop being cultivated and the costumes and faces of the cultivators are indicative of the widespread area of Soviet rule. Cotton is grown in the Azerbaijan Soviet Republic between the Black Sea and the Caspian and also in the Uzbek Soviet Republic in Central Asia.

[4] The picture illustrates in graphic fashion the inculcation of fascism, beginning at the cradle. The honor guard of bambinos are wearing their first uniforms. Step by step they will graduate through various organizations until they become fascist militiamen.

[5] The city of Victoria, on the island of Hongkong, lies in the foreground. Aside from Singapore, the island was Britain's most cherished possession in Asiatic waters. When annexed in 1841, it was occupied by a few scattered fishing folk. Now Victoria has nearly 400,000 people. Defensively the island is strong, but the large civilian population makes provision for food difficult, for the island is only thirty-two square miles in area.

[6] A close look at the photograph will show that these Japanese sampans more closely resemble United States river barges than the tiny overcrowded craft in Chinese rivers and harbors upon which large families cluster. At Yokohama these barges are used for unloading freight from ships which can not dock conveniently. Yokohama is one of the five largest cities in Japan. Almost completely destroyed by earthquake in 1923, its rebuilding was completed in six years.

[7] The picture was taken several years ago, before the General became engaged in open hostilities with the Japanese. A favorite disciple of Dr. Sun Yat-sen and married to one of the famous Soong sisters (one of whom is the widow of Sun Yat-sen) the General was the natural choice for the headship of the Kuomintang party (Chinese Nationalists) who control the government of China.

[8] Chungking, capital of the Chinese Nationalists, is in western China. As Nanking was about to be captured by the Japanese, the Chinese moved their capital

farther up the Yangtse to Hankow. Pursued there by the men of Nippon, they retreated farther up the valley to Chungking. This picture was taken from the south bank of the Yangtse and illustrates not only the ruthlessness of modern war but also the inrush of modern culture on ancient China, as one may judge from the Western style of architecture in vogue even in the far interior of China.

[9] Churchill is accompanied by Sir Dudley Pound, first sea lord of the admiralty, a post always held by a professional naval officer and in importance second only to first lord of the admiralty, customarily held by a civilian, and held by Churchill in both of the World Wars of the twentieth century. This is a picture of the British Prime Minister upon his return from a conference with Premier Reynaud before the fall of France.

[10] This unusual view of "The Rock" is taken from the northwest. Britain has held Gibraltar ever since the Treaty of Utrecht in 1713. The military and naval importance of the Rock is not as great as in past centuries, but nevertheless its loss would be keenly felt. To what extent it is prepared to stand a lengthy siege is a military secret. There is no fresh water on the Rock except that gathered in cisterns from rain-water.

[11] The old and ornate Reichstag building was destroyed by fire in the early days of Nazi terrorism, and such infrequent sessions as the Reichstag has held since have convened in the Kroll Opera House. There are never any debates at such sessions; they are simply sounding-boards for a speech by Hitler. Sitting in the chair behind the speaker is the number two Nazi, Hermann Goering, President of the Reichstag.

[12] At an unnamed Canadian port, presumably Halifax, three British flags may be seen hoisted over three of the fifty over-age destroyers traded by the American government in the late summer of 1940 for naval stations in the British West Indies. The fifty destroyers are small but efficient craft, and they were turned over to the British tars with their food lockers well stocked with fresh oranges and other delicacies much appreciated by their new crews.

WORLD WARS AND REVOLUTIONS

CHAPTER I

ANTECEDENTS OF THE FIRST WORLD WAR

ON JUNE 28, 1914, an Austrian archduke was shot at Sarajevo in the Balkans and within five weeks the greater part of Europe was at war. Four years later the German Reich, hampered by impotent allies, lamed by empty stomachs, hammered by Foch's armies, ceased to be. The German High Command had lost their war; and many, blinded by victory and confused by rejoicing well-nigh universal, believed all war banished from the world. Instead within one generation, in a short twenty years, a murkier and more murderous hurricane than that of 1914 came roaring out of Central Europe, to sweep every ocean, to engulf continents.

The war of 1914-18, the first World War, burst on a relatively unsuspecting world. Few even of the statesmen of that day were convinced of its coming. True, in 1911, 1912, and in 1913 there had been little wars involving European countries. But all these, properly speaking, had been periphery affairs. That trifling and semi-comic conflict between Italians and Turks in 1911, involving Libyan oases, did not really threaten Europe's peace; and the two Balkan wars of 1912 and 1913, though bloody enough to satisfy Tamerlane, seemed far away from the main currents of European civilization. Certain savants held that these might even be considered harbingers of coming world peace, since in less enlightened times such frontier wars might well have involved one or more of the great powers, all of whom were now too sagacious to draw the sword.

WHY WAR WAS THOUGHT OUTMODED

These optimistic fancies were not without foundation. The century which had passed since Waterloo had done more to improve the material welfare of the average European than any other such period in history. Man at last was regarded as the conqueror of his environment. Prosperity was widespread and rapidly becoming more so; so likewise were general intelligence and specialized scientific knowledge. Measured in terms either of dollars, literacy, or health, the advances of the age were unparalleled; and progress was its watchword, an especially beneficent progress that in and of itself tended to increase at an ever-accelerated momentum. So the wise men held.

Particularly notable was the increase in economic wealth. In almost every industry new inventions enlarged the volume of production. The cost of steel dropped steadily after Bessemer converters came into use, and dropped still more after the open hearth process of manufacture was developed. Cheap steel led to the invention and perfection of many new machines, from hydraulic cranes to Otis elevators. In agriculture the use of new fertilizers grew apace, and the breeding of live stock on scientific lines developed with rapidity—hens laid more eggs and cows gave more milk in 1914 than in 1814. Coal tar, as a source for dyes, cheapened and improved textiles. Hydroelectric power had already displaced steam in certain industries; Diesel and gasoline engines no longer were toys. The world looked forward to a new and peculiarly promising Industrial Revolution.

Improvements in distribution did not lag far behind. One by one came the great transcontinental railroads, the Union Pacific in the United States, following hard upon the close of the Civil War; the Canadian Pacific, opening up the wheat lands of the Prairie Provinces; the Trans-Caucasian, already by 1888 reaching the fabled city of Samarkand; the Trans-Siberian, begun in 1890 and diverting in part the trade routes of the Orient; the Berlin, Byzantium, Bagdad Intercontinental, in process of construction; the Cape to Cairo inspiration of Cecil Rhodes, already stretching from Egypt to the Sudan and from Cape Town to the Zambesi.

Just as noteworthy were improved transportation facilities within Europe. At the Simplon and St. Gotthard passes, railway tunnels pierced the Alps. From the Ukraine wheat now reached Europe overland through Germany and Austria. Light railways, such as Belgium specialized in, were laid down near commercial centers, and interior canalization also, in which Germany excelled, was developed. In consequence, freight rates dropped, and the volume of commerce grew in proportion.

In ocean transportation the advance was even more marked. The eighteen-eighties saw steel supplanting iron in the construction of ships —nearly as substantial an improvement over the iron ships of the 'sixties as the latter were over their wooden predecessors. The turbine engine, although invented, had not as yet made clear its usefulness; but on the other hand, the triple expansion engine of the end of the century had enormously economized ship space, while the installation of twin screws and of water-tight compartments diminished largely the danger of disaster in mid-ocean. On all the seven seas the tramp cargo carriers of England, Norway, and Germany competed fiercely with each other; while on the Atlantic, the phenomenal success of the Hamburg-American Line, rapidly rising to first place among the steamship companies of the world, gave constant proof of marine progress undreamed of fifty years before.

Increased production, without new markets, then meant overproduction, and new markets were speedily forthcoming. To a great extent, Europe and the Americas provided them, but not solely. Asia proved to be a quick absorber of the surplus production of Europe and, somewhat less so, Africa. As early as the 'sixties, Karl Marx had noted the extent to which machine-made cotton cloth had depressed the hand loom weaving of India. Now Germany, as well as England, was discovering in India an ever-increasing market for her manufactured goods before the twentieth century was even under way. Guns, munitions of war, clocks, cloth, sewing machines, hardware, steel rails, linoleum, an endless list of articles from European workshops began to flood the undeveloped continents. Peasants in Syria began to clamor for the red-tiled roofing of France; the cheap agricultural implements of Germany found a ready market in distant Java as well as in the nearer Balkans. On the banks of the Irrawaddy English cutlery was sold, and black maidens of Nyasaland clothed themselves in Lancashire cottons.

Nor did the cargo boats return empty. Tea and coffee, raw silk, tobacco, ivory, tin, peanuts, gold, diamonds, rubber, spices, all of these commodities entered Europe in ever-increasing volume. By 1914, many luxuries of 1814 had become daily necessities.

In scientific progress, as distinct from economic, there was even greater cause for rejoicing. Let us make clean and wholesome the world in which we live, cried the late nineteenth and early twentieth centuries, and all will be well with man.

In medicine, for instance, and in the general understanding and control of public health striking advances were recorded. Although the industrial cities in Europe grew rapidly in population and became yearly more congested, the death rate in many of them decreased during the hundred years after Waterloo by more than fifty per cent. Typhus fever in Western Europe during the same period was eliminated and other terrifying diseases brought under control.

In bacteriology the advance was noteworthy. The bacilli of malaria, of tuberculosis, and of diphtheria were discovered and studied, their final defeat plotted. Proper treatment began for pneumonia. Biological chemistry brought new light to bear on the digestive functions, and the complexities of human metabolism were, for the first time, partially understood—physiology was becoming a new science. German research taught us how to understand neurology and in German laboratories the germ of syphilis was isolated and a cure found for that dread disease.

An Englishman and an Italian shared the honor of tracing malaria to
its source. Pasteur in France became famous through his knowledge of
toxins and anti-toxins, culminating his long career of usefulness with
his discovery of a sure cure for hydrophobia. The Institut Pasteur
was organized by him to combat this dreaded disease in 1888, and soon
afterward the death-rate from it sank to less than one per cent. It is
with pardonable pride that the great Frenchman, enthralled by the
growth of science, somewhat naïvely remarked: "But of this we may
be sure, that science, in obeying the laws of humanity, will always
labor to enlarge the frontier of human life."

THE BOURGEOISIE

These economic and scientific accomplishments ran parallel with the
advance in influence and power of the bourgeoisie or middle class.
Dominant by 1914 in western Europe, and year by year acquiring more
influence in such conservative countries as Germany, Austria-Hungary,
and Russia, the bourgeoisie placed their imprimatur firmly on the nineteenth century. The bourgeoisie as a class were optimistic; how could
they be otherwise since the Industrial Revolution and the capitalistic
system which had brought them to the fore continued to pour new
wealth into their lap, railroads, steamship lines, plantations in Malaya,
sheep ranches in Australia and the Argentine, factories in the Ruhr, in
North Italy, in the Rhône valley, in the British midlands. The bourgeoisie were devotees of progress; how could it be otherwise in view of
the scientific and technological advances made under their patronage?
Never had there been a time when man knew so much; never had there
been a time when he was so inventive. Within the span of one hundred
years he had invented the steamship and the locomotive, the camera,
the telephone, the telegraph, the sewing machine, the bicycle, the phono-
graph, the cinematograph, automobile, and airplane. Was it beyond
his powers to invent a plan whereby war might be done away with?
The bourgeoisie, as good Darwinians, subscribed heartily to progressive
evolution and to the idea that war was an outmoded relic of the barbaric past. If man had risen from primeval slime through countless
aeons of biological adaptation to the rank of a nineteenth-century
bourgeois, to what greater elevation might he not yet ascend?

This progress the bourgeoisie interpreted in terms of politics, education, labor legislation and growing international good-will. In politics
they could point to the map of Europe and show how it had been sim-
plified and made more intelligible. Thanks to Cavour that "geographical expression," Italy, had become a nation; thanks to Bismarck the
thirty-nine Germanies of 1815 had been united. By 1914 every state in

Europe, not excluding Russia and Turkey, had some kind of constitution guaranteeing civil liberties and providing legal remedies against arbitrary personal government. Political democracy, too, was held a sign of progress. Popularly elected lower houses of legislature clamored for more power and frequently obtained it, as for instance in 1911 when the veto power of the House of Lords was reduced to almost a nullity. Since economics and politics were in general considered separate, the bourgeoisie once having obtained the vote for themselves were willing enough to have the franchise extended to other classes. In England both Disraeli and Gladstone urged that it be broadened; in the North German Confederation universal manhood suffrage was introduced by Bismarck as early as 1866; Republican France gave the vote to all adult males; and in the small Scandinavian states it was even presented to women. On the continent liberal suffrage requirements became the rule rather than the exception. True, there were certain noticeable restrictions, in Germany (as far as Prussia was concerned, and Prussia was three-fifths of the Reich), and in Russia where the electoral laws were manipulated in favor of rich landlords; true, also, neither the popularly elected Reichstag in Germany nor the Russian Duma possessed sovereign authority. Nevertheless, even in those two countries democratic practices were far more prevalent than a hundred years earlier. The bourgeoisie were enlightened folk; they were willing to help the workingman obtain the vote, partly because they were happy themselves and wanted to make others happy, partly because they believed in progressively raising the standard of living for all classes.

Since they were enlightened and benevolent they thought highly of popular education, and surely in that matter the nineteenth was the most progressive of all centuries! Illiteracy, outside of Russia, was everywhere on the wane, and in most of Europe new schools, both elementary and advanced, were paid for and operated by public funds. This advance was paralleled by a striking improvement in public health, as sanitary inspection, water works, tuberculosis sanatoria, and a lowered death-rate proved. In labor legislation the record was equally admirable, as witnessed by the passage of workmen's compensation acts, old-age pensions, child-labor laws, the opening of labor exchanges, and provisions for compulsory insurance against industrial accidents, sickness, and unemployment.

Superficially the late nineteenth century was a most civilized era, certainly in comparison with the past, certainly in comparison with the present, as far as travel, the interchange of ideas, and the development of international good-will was concerned. Toward its end one could travel all over Europe without a passport (except in Turkey and

Russia) and everywhere feel safe from molestation. The rate of exchange between countries seldom varied, and the traveller could at all times know approximately what his money would be worth. By international agreement intercommunication by letter and by telegraph was practically immune from censorship. From Waterloo to 1914 there had been no widespread European war. Such wars as did occur had been brief in duration, like the Franco-Prussian War of 1870-71; and since the Russo-Turkish War of 1877 there was no war at all within Europe, if we except the Balkans. A truly international spirit was something more than a figment of the imagination. International socialism, international finance, and international culture (such as came from international studies and travel, exchange professorships, musical festivals, Olympic Games, etc.), many said, would banish wars altogether.

The world, indeed, was a pleasant place for entrepreneur and capitalist, intent on new enterprises or eager to enlarge old ones, for those skilled artisans who belonged to trade unions and whose standard of living had risen steadily, for the majority of public officials and lawyers, for those who possessed private property and for those who ministered to their wants, for many scholars and scientists modestly endowed, and for those clergymen, writers, and publicists with faith rooted firmly in orderly evolution, regarding this if not the best of all possible worlds at least as one growing steadily better.

LIBERALISM AND NATIONALISM

The majority held this true not simply of the physical environment in which they lived and moved but also of those social ideals which they had long cherished. Nationalism and liberalism, twin sisters of the bourgeois epoch, still were regarded by broadminded and progressive thinkers as beacons of progress for all mankind. Was it not evident that nationalism was making headway in the Balkan peninsula where Macedonia still remained to be redeemed from Turkish misrule, and that a moral obligation rested upon the civilized world to help the various Greeks, Bulgars, and Serbs domiciled there to join their own nationalities under their respective national flags? Could not the same forward drift in Ireland be noted where concession after concession in both the economic and the political sphere almost inevitably implied a successful resurgence of Irish nationalism? The difficulties which impeded the growth of nationalism in the Austro-Hungarian empire seemed almost beyond solution: but men of good-will did not despair of progress. Had not the heir to the Hapsburg throne suggested the possibility of a triple instead of a dual monarchy, a triple monarchy of

Germans, Austrians, and Slavs whereby the nationalistic dreams of the latter might be realized?

So, too, was it in regard to liberalism. The meaning of the word changed; but so did the whole realm of ideas in a Darwinian universe, and one did not have to worry about that. It had now become the fashion to conceive of liberalism as a doctrine whereby the state might "liberate" various groups of people from unnecessary hardship by guarantees of minimum wages, of decent living conditions, guarantees that all members of society would have an equal chance to make the most of their own abilities. Granted that this was anomalous, that it gave the word "liberal" a different connotation in 1914 from what it had had in 1830, when it stood for straight laissez-faire and the least government the better; nevertheless liberalism in its political sense, as a doctrine favoring constitutional government and an enlarged suffrage, was, as we have noted, progressing steadily. And liberalism as a philosophic concept still remained what it always had been: liberating the individual from the fetters of inherited modes of thought and ancient prescripts of old-time authority. As such it had always been a "suspect" word to ecclesiastical authority, and in his famous Syllabus of Errors the Pope himself had denounced liberalism (1864). But there were many liberal Roman Catholics for all of that, and the vogue of liberalism tended to increase rather than diminish as the century grew older. It was a good umbrella word, insofar as under its sheltering canopy so many varied types could take shelter. In it were summed up those major tendencies in economics, politics and religion which made man quite confident in 1914 of the forward march of humanity.

DANGER SIGNALS IN 1914: ECONOMIC BACKGROUND

The foundations, however, of European peace were far more shaky than the optimistic bourgeoisie realized. In both the world of material fact (economics) and in that of ideals (religion), danger lurked. Strange fluctuations in trade and commerce which nobody understood very well caused trouble. Alternative cycles of expansion and depression made business something of a gamble, always threatening and sometimes causing acute unemployment. Increased comforts due to power machinery did not necessarily make people happier. Real income rose steadily for almost everyone; but psychic income grew at a more laggard pace; and some there were who questioned whether it grew at all. Meanwhile, decade by decade social unrest mounted; how could it be otherwise with this new-sprung urban proletariat so recently footloose from the old restraints of rural living and constantly uncertain of the morrow? Then, too, competition between individuals gave certain disquieting evidences of turning into competition between states, which, if carried to the logical conclusion, meant war. And as this occurred, Christianity as a mystical belief in a risen savior dying for all men irrespective of color, race, or nationality lost much of its hold on the European imagination, thus encouraging the growth of more narrow and more chauvinistic ideals which boded little good for civilization's tomorrow.

Karl Marx's indictment of the nineteenth century bourgeoisie in the *Communist Manifesto* of 1849 was both brutal and jaundiced but it did, nevertheless, sound one justifiable warning—that the capitalistic world of the open market had within it the seeds of its own destruction. Production did tend to outstrip consumption, and the big man of business did tend to force the little fellow to the wall. The powerful and successful did not dare to stop even if they wished; they must secure bigger and yet bigger victories or else go down in the never-ending struggle for gain. Surplus capital which constantly piled higher and higher led to panics and to resultant economic depression unless somewhere or somehow new markets were found. Since domestic markets were soon saturated with goods which could not be sold there was inevitable pressure for markets overseas, particularly in undeveloped lands. The rate of interest declined steadily in the late nineteenth century and the possessors of new wealth, always eager to invest it to good advantage, were mainly responsible for the international scramble which occurred for territorial acquisitions in Africa and for economic and political privilege in Asia. What then could be more logical than for these economic tycoons to drape themselves in their respective national flags and in the sacred name of patriotism to continue (oftentimes subjectively and unconsciously) their competition until it crystallized in imperialistic war?

This, in essence, was the Marxian explanation of the first World War. And there was a good deal to be said for it. The partitioning of Africa toward the end of the nineteenth century was brought about by many causes but foremost among them, it must be conceded, was a search for raw materials and for markets for manufactured goods. The exploitation of eastern Asia by western nations was similarly motivated. French and British economic interests did clash in Egypt and Anglo-German economic rivalries had much to do with hoisting the British Union Jack over Uganda, and the White, Black, and Red of Imperial Germany over Togo and Kamerun. The scramble for concessions in China was more economic than political in character, and in all that had to do with the presumptive Bagdad railway bankers played as important a part as did statesmen, possible more important.

The imperialistic adventures of the great powers in the half century before 1914, their rivalries, their threats and counterthreats, annexations, compromises, all were colored by economic competition. And insofar as the latter brought about louder and louder demands for more and bigger warships, for larger and costlier armies, it did lead directly to the first of the two World Wars.

But we must be careful not to read too much into this explanation. It was not simply economic jealousy of Russia which led Britain to lease the port of Weihaiwei on the southern shores of the Gulf of Pechili; it was also political and naval prestige. Nor did France extend her empire in every direction in Northwest Africa simply to satisfy French entrepreneurs; more important than that were the fighting Senegalese who would form a black watch on the Rhine in any future German war. Colonial squabbles were numerous among the great powers in the decades immediately antecedent to 1914; but it must be remembered that almost all of these were amicably settled, or were about to be settled, before the outbreak of the great war. Thus England and France compounded their colonial differences in 1904, England and Russia in 1907, England and Germany at different dates from 1885 down to the eve of the world conflict, a final agreement concerning the Bagdad railway being initialed just at the time the two countries became involved in war over an entirely different controversy.

Marxian explanations as to the causes of war are always plausible but to sustain them by proof is not easy. To point out, for instance, that Germany was outstripping Britain in economic progress at the commencement of the twentieth century is a simple matter of statistics; but that did not mean that war between the two countries was inevitable. It is quite true that German steel production forged ahead of Britain's, that certain South American markets hitherto almost a British monopoly were won over by the German commercial traveller, that German firms got British contracts for work done in Britain, that British public opinion was irritated thereby, and that German boastfulness was resented. But that did not mean that war would follow. The argument would be much stronger had British trade and commerce actually declined. The reverse was the truth; British trade continued to expand. The difference lay in the respective rates of increase.

Economic rivalry between Britain and Germany was keen, but it was also profitable to both countries. The leading steamship company navigating the Nile River flew the flag of the North German Lloyd, but that did not diminish Britain's trade with Germany; the tariff laid on imports in India was the same for both German and British importers, but that did not cause a decline of British trade with India. Trade did not necessarily follow the flag. It might be and was a source of annoyance to ambitious Germans that the Union Jack flew over so large a surface of the globe, but it was a political and not an economic annoyance. The British colonial market lay open to the German trader on equal terms with his British competitor. Only in Canada was there then a slight preferential tariff in favor of Britain.

RELIGIOUS BACKGROUND

A distinguished American historian has entitled the last quarter of the nineteenth century *The Age of Materialism*. This imputation is somewhat unfair to the benevolent bourgeoisie who dominated that period and the first fourteen years of the twentieth century, but it is true that the idea of the advance of humanity via the media of improved external circumstances permeated human thought and activity, so much so that ethics tended to take the place of religion; and "other-worldliness," as it was called, went largely out of fashion. The Christian church, statistically, did not decline. The money of professed Christians was poured out bounteously for schools, colleges, hospitals, homes for orphans and asylums for the aged. But many felt then, and more have felt since, that this stressing of the social message of Christianity, combined with unprecedented material and scientific progress, focussed man's attention so closely on the earthly and the tangible as to distort his vision and to lessen his faith in such eternal verities as sin and redemption, sacrifice and salvation.

Others, more scientifically minded, decried that point of view and tried to prove that man had failed to avoid catastrophe in the past not because he had become too engrossed in new knowledge but because the new knowledge was insufficient in scope and insufficiently related to the genus homo. They regarded the study of such subjects as anthropology, economics, psychology, sociology, and comparative religion as offering us our best hope for an orderly and humane society in years to come, and they advocated not a greater but a less emphasis upon revealed religion. The fact that the sciences upon which they relied had already been the subject of much detailed study, analysis, and research for many years, without as yet doing much of anything to check revolutionary and social chaos, troubled them not a whit. What was significant in their eyes was that these sciences might still be considered in their infancy, and that if man would only devote himself as wholeheartedly to their pursuit as he had devoted himself to technology and to the chemical laboratory, then he might have a chance to become master not only of the earth but also of himself; and perhaps ultimately of the very stars.

The majority of those who thought thus might be described as tending toward agnosticism; and somewhere between them and the orthodox upholders of the historic church creeds were to be found, one suspects, a majority of the folk in western Europe and the United States. That majority would have resented, and perhaps justly, the appellation *agnostic*. Nominally it was Christian; but its faith could not be said to be very warm. It did not so much disbelieve in historic Christianity as it was indifferent to it. To what extent this religious apathy was due to sheer accumulation of more and more goods, commodities, and luxuries, to what extent it was caused by overweening conceit in the more recent miracles of science, and how far biblical criticism and Catholic modernism were responsible for its growth it is impossible to say. But this may be affirmed: Teutonic glorification of race, French exaltation of an exclusive Gallic culture, British conceit in imperial conquest, and our own American pride in economic production tended to crowd out of men's hearts not only those more gentle precepts of Christ which lay emphasis on the loving-kindness of God, but also any overwhelming conviction of moral obligation and duty sealed by the Blood of the Everlasting Covenant. The sense of sin was fading fast from the western world. The Kingdom of God on earth took precedence both over the Kingdom of God within and the Kingdom of God after death, and that which was mystical and trans-cedental in our religious heritage was threatened with extinction. The medieval concept of pride as the worst of the seven deadly sins did not thrive in the essentially lay atmosphere of the twentieth century, for rationalism, armored in applied science, guarded the fortress of our intellectual pride.

POLITICAL BACKGROUND

Economic instability and religious uncertainty led to irritability and neuroses. But these were not the only causes of discontent. Other factors, essentially political in character, added their full quota to the danger of a European conflagration.

The political roots of the first World War were many, but probably the most important was the old quarrel between Austria and Russia as to who should control the Balkan peninsula. That quarrel came to a head with the diplomatic defeat of Russia at the Congress of Berlin in 1878, and smouldered and festered until it broke in 1914, the immediate cause of World War I. The ramifications of this particular contest were, as we shall note, varied and important. What was originally a relatively simple problem in international relations involving just two countries grew into a headlong conflict between Pan-German agitation on the one hand and Pan-Slavism on the other, the mighty German empire of Bismarck aligning herself on the side of Austria as

Russia hastened to the assistance of her little Slavic brethren in the Balkans.

France, which had no interests in the Balkans, ultimately was drawn into the controversy as a result of losing Alsace-Lorraine. Beaten and humiliated by Prussia in 1870, France did not forget her two lost provinces. True, the pang of losing them slowly dimmed; but the desire for revenge did not die, and when France saw her chance to ally herself with Russia in the 'nineties she did so. From then on, the division of Europe into two armed camps became a sinister fact. Germany, Austria, Italy in one camp; France and Russia in the other.

Meanwhile England's traditional policy of voluntary aloofness from continental broils became more and more difficult to maintain. Fear for her own safety, due to French threats in Africa and to Russian threats in Asia, led her to approach Berlin, and when she was treated with indifference by the Kaiser's diplomatists, to listen to the siren invitation emanating from the French encampment (1904). This she finally entered (1912), having in the interim made friendly gestures toward the Russian bear (1907). The delicate balance of power now was dangerously unstable indeed, and when Austria annexed Bosnia (1908), Germany thought it necessary to support her militant ally to the limit lest she herself be involved in war without allies or friends. If history is to be considered purely from the diplomatic angle, which would be an error, the first World War might possibly be considered inevitable after Britain tied herself (loosely, it is true) to the chariot wheels of Franco-Russian imperialism. That the Italo-Austro-German imperialism was no more enlightened or benign may be conceded. The fact remains that when England swung toward France and Russia a true balance no longer held. The ties which bound England to her two new friends were not tightly drawn, and the British lion might possibly have loosed himself even after Sarajevo and the murder of the Austrian archduke in 1914. But by that time it was difficult for even a lion to disentangle himself from the network of agreements and understandings in which he had thus become involved. In theory European alliances and counteralliances were all defensive in character; but so complicated had they become by 1914 that escape from them in that fatal year proved impossible.

THE BISMARCK ERA

To tell the story in somewhat more detail as to how and why these tangled alliances were made, and to analyze with some care the bungling diplomacy of the late Kaiser, the swift onrush of naval rivalry between Germany and Britain, and the inevitable nemesis which over-

THE PEOPLES OF
SOUTHEASTERN EUROPE
1878-1885

Scale of Miles
0   50   100   150   200   250

Turks

Rumanians

Bulgarians

Croats and
Serbs

Greeks

Albanians

RUSSIA

HUNGARY

Drave
Funfkirchen
Save R.
Danube R.

Dniester R.
Bug R.
Buko-
vina
Transylvania
Jassy
Moldavia
Kishinev
Bessarabia
Prut R.
Akkerman

Temesvár
Kronstadt
Galatz

BOSNIA
Administered by
Austria-Hungary
Sarajevo
since 1878
Herze-
govina
Cattaro
NOVI
BAZAR
MONTE-
NEGRO

Belgrade
Wallachia
RUMANIA
Iron Gate
Bucharest
Dobruja
Constantsa

SERBIA
Vidin
Danube
Silistria
Rustchuk
Shumla
Varna

Morava R.
Nish
BULGARIA
Sofia
Eastern Rumelia
Philippopolis
Maritza
Burgas
Adrianople

ADRIATIC SEA

ITALY
Brindisi

Strait of Otranto

Ionian Islands

Corfu

Uskub
(Skoplje)

Monastir
(Bitolia)

TURKEY EMPIRE

Salonika

Larissa

Patras
Morea
Athens
GREECE
Cyclades

Lemnos
Gallipoli
Dardanelles
Mytilene

San Stefano
Marmara
Sea

Constantinople
Bosporus
Scutari

Asia Minor

Chios
Smyrna

Samos

Rhodes

BLACK SEA

AEGEAN SEA

Brusa

Crete

MEDITERRANEAN   SEA

Longitude   East   from   Greenwich

© The Century Co., 1932

took Europe in the summer of 1914, let us go back to the victorious Bismarck of 1871.

At that time France lay helpless and Bismarck wanted her to remain so. Without allies the Gallic foe could not hope to cross swords with him again and for precaution's sake he deemed it wise that Germany not France secure allies. Therefore in 1873 he organized the *Dreikaiserbund,* or Three Emperors League—Austria, Russia, and Germany being the signatories.

This *Dreikaiserbund* was no hard and fast military alliance; there were no mutual pledges given or taken for armed assistance. All that the three emperors agreed to do was to assist one another in maintaining the status quo and to consult should it be endangered. The *Dreikaiserbund* came to grief as a result of the Congress of Berlin. After its sessions Russia felt convinced that her old traditional friendship with Prussia had been betrayed by Bismarck. The Chancellor of Germany insisted that he only played the honest broker but Russia believed herself double-crossed. What she saw was the double-eagle of Austria-Hungary in Bosnia and herself defrauded of Balkan gains. Her annexation of Bessarabia and her territorial gains east of the Black Sea hardly seemed compensation for the annulment of the treaty of San Stefano. From this time forward Russia never again quite trusted Germany.

Bismarck may not have been responsible for Russia's failure to gain more in 1878, but he knew that Berlin had been the place where Russia's defeat had been recorded and that he had presided over the congress held there. Immediately, therefore, he sought to repair his diplomatic fences by tying up as closely with Austria as that country would permit. If he had to make a choice between Austria and Russia he preferred the former country. Her frontier marched more closely with that of Germany; her armies held the bastions of the Carpathian Mountains whence they could debouch upon advancing Russians; and furthermore, within Austria-Hungary were over 10,000,000 Germans who might yet be incorporated into a greater Reich.

Consequently Bismarck betook himself to Vienna. What he hoped to obtain was a hard and fast military alliance whereby Austria and Germany bound themselves to resist with all their forces a renovated French army attacking Germany or a Russian army attacking Austria; what he did obtain was an agreement concerning Russia alone. In case of war provoked by Russia upon either signatory the other agreed to march to the defense of its ally. This was the celebrated Dual Alliance between Austria and Germany, signed in 1879 and destined to become the nucleus of a most intricate network of alliances and counter-alliances between various European states.

The Austro-German alliance worried the Czar. He began to think more kindly of his old ally, Germany, and Bismarck with an eye toward placating Russia (a characteristic of his diplomacy throughout a long lifetime) cheerfully consented in 1881 to a renewal of the *Dreikaiserbund*. The terms were more specific than those of the old agreement. All three emperors agreed to remain neutral in case one of their three countries was attacked by a fourth. In the event of Turkey in Europe being divided they were to agree in advance upon the spoils. Austria was to be permitted to annex Bosnia outright, provided she raised no objection to the union of Bulgaria with Eastern Rumelia.

The second *Dreikaiserbund* was to be wrecked, as was the first, by a renewal of Austro-Russian jealousy concerning the Balkans. This time it was Bulgaria which caused the trouble. That country (1885-87) objected vigorously to the tutelage of Russia, drove Russian officers out of her army, annexed Eastern Rumelia to Bulgaria without Russian permission. The Czar, infuriated, took steps to punish Bulgaria, Austria objecting. Bismarck cared nothing about the Balkans; what he wanted above everything else was to prevent his two allies from quarreling. Fortunately for him, a very definite stand was made unnecessary by England and Italy joining Austria in a Mediterranean agreement (1887) preserving the status quo in that sea and in the Near East.

Russia was now thoroughly angry at Austria and more suspicious than ever of Germany whom, despite professions of friendship, she suspected of conniving at her Balkan defeat. Therefore she would have no more to do with the *Dreikaiserbund*.

Bismarck's years of service were now nearly over but before retiring he made one more desperate and successful effort to insure the eastern marches of his fatherland against Muscovite invasion. In 1887 he made a curious treaty with Russia. He called it a "reinsurance treaty" and it was to run for three years. Its provisos were three: (*a*) Germany and Russia to be neutral if either country became involved in war; (*b*) the above not to apply to a war "against Austria or France resulting from an attack upon one of these two Powers by one of the contracting powers"; (*c*) Germany "to recognize rights historically acquired by Russia in the Balkans."

A curious treaty this! Did it mean that Bismarck was double-crossing his ally, Austria? Technically, of course, the answer was in the negative. He was still pledged to assist Austria by force of arms if Russia attacked her; only in case of Austria attacking Russia was Germany to remain neutral. On the other hand it is difficult to draw a line between offensive and defensive war. Suppose Russia should mobilize her huge strength against Austria in order to prod the latter country into fighting. Who then could be said to have started the war? Bismarck was skating on thin ice by this treaty; but all of his life he had kept some line to Russia open and he did not want to tempt the Czar into a possible French alliance, always a nightmare to him.

Meanwhile, to the dual alliance with Austria-Hungary there came in 1882 an accession of strength—or of weakness—Italy. That nation had been consumed with anger at the French occupation of Tunis one year earlier. Bismarck was largely responsible for that Gallic advance, since he had suggested after the Franco-Prussian War that the French seek compensation for the loss of Alsace-Lorraine in Africa. Then when Britain annexed Cyprus after the Congress of Berlin, Disraeli had added his advice to that of Bismarck and suggested Tunis as a proper field for French exploitation. But Tunis was less than 100 miles from Sicily and the European population there was largely Italian in blood. Nobody had offered Italy anything after the Berlin congress and the Italians were bitter at this French coup. Therefore they came knocking at the Berlin gate seeking allies.

Bismarck did not trust the Italians and he was not anxious to have them included in his alliance system. If a refusal, however, meant that the Italians might sign up with another group, that was another matter. Thereupon Bismarck suggested to the Italians that they approach Austria first, for owing to the inclusion of many Italians within the boundaries of Austria there had been friction between the two countries. Austria proved willing to admit Italy to the Austro-German fold, for she did not want a potential foe at her back door should she engage in war with Russia, and Bismarck was willing to have still another guarantee against France. Consequently, in 1882 the Dual Alliance between Germany and Austria was superseded by the new Triple Alliance, of Germany, Austria, and Italy.

With Italy in the bag, with Rumania part way in (that country had an alliance with Austria but not with Germany), and with his Russian reinsurance treaty, Bismarck left Germany in a secure position at the date of his retirement (1890).

WILLIAM II RUINS THE WORK OF BISMARCK

She was not to stay there. One of the first acts of the melodramatic young Kaiser after forcing Bismarck's resignation was to wreak havoc with the latter's diplomacy by refusing to renew the reinsurance treaty in 1890. This act inevitably drove France and Russia together. In some respects the alliance between these two countries, the new dual alliance, was not natural. Republican France had never forgotten

Alsace-Lorraine but to autocratic Russia it made no difference who ruled those two provinces; vice versa, the Balkan jealousies of Austria and Russia in the Balkans did not interest Paris. Both France and Russia held grievances against England, the former in Egypt and the Upper Nile, the latter on the Afghan border. But it is doubtful if these alone would have brought France and Russia into an alliance. It was Germany in conjunction with England that cemented it. In the 'nineties there was a goodly possibility that England might become a fourth partner in the Triple Alliance, leaving France and Russia isolated and alone. In 1890 Germany and England signed a treaty liquidating certain colonial disputes, England assuming a protectorate over Zanzibar, Germany annexing Heligoland, and more agreements might follow. St. Petersburg and Paris took alarm. The Russians needed French money, the French, Russian warpower. And so in 1894 they became allied. "If France is attacked by Germany, or by Italy supported by Germany," the treaty read, "Russia shall employ all her available forces to attack Germany. If Russia is attacked by Germany or by Austria supported by Germany, France shall employ all her available forces to fight Germany." And lest there be any doubt as to just what that meant, the commitments were made quite specific. According to clause three: "The forces to be employed against Germany will be, on the part of France, 1,300,000 men, on the part of Russia 700,000 to 800,000. These forces will engage with all their might, so that Germany has to fight both on the East and West."

Thus were the rival camps established, the new dual alliance against Bismarck's Triple Alliance. The bad dreams of the Iron Chancellor had come to pass; Germany had potential foes on either flank.

There was as yet no immediate danger of war. All the alliances were said to be defensive and the two rival camps balanced off neatly against one another. The triplice had, to be sure, the advantage of interior lines, if it came to a fight; but on the other hand the nationalistic divergencies of the Austro-Hungarian peoples were a drawback and the potential manpower of Russia was enormous.

Possibly there might not have been any international war at all had it not been for Anglo-German rivalry and misunderstanding. For many decades the Germans and the British had been drifting apart. The British thought the Germans were a misguided folk who had not shown the intelligence to plan their national development along British constitutional lines. They had not forgotten that Bismarck carried through his increase in the Prussian army without popular consent once before, and they remembered the annexation of Schleswig-Holstein without British consent and the fact that Queen Alexandra, wife of Edward VII, was a Danish princess. They also viewed with disfavor the German tariff system, the embryonic German navy, the Teutonic demands for colonies, and the commencement of German competition overseas in steel and iron products. Always, too, the hardness of tone and vulgarity of manners of the new Germany jarred the sensibilities of the British.

Germans, on the other hand, chafed under what they considered British patronage. The complacent universality and self-assured superiority of their island neighbors in their opinion was without justification. The Germans regarded the British as a retired robber turned pious, desirous of spending his declining years in luxury without anyone inquiring into the sources of his wealth. Von Treitschke, Germany's great historian, taught the German youth that the day of England's greatness was past, and most Germans believed him.

Nevertheless, despite these facts there seemed more reason for Britain to ally herself with Germany than with any other country— if an alliance became necessary for national safety and if reliance no longer could be put on "splendid isolation," England's great tradition. To begin with there were as yet no such specific grounds for disagreement between England and Germany as existed between the latter country and France, or England and France, or England and Russia. The open sore of Alsace-Lorraine still remained unhealed. The Third Republic and the British Empire clashed at many points: in Siam, in Egypt, in Oceania, north of the Gulf of Guinea, and along the headwaters of the Nile. The British lion and the Russian bear growled at one another across half a dozen Asiatic frontiers, and the Trans-Caucasian Railway had brought Russian Cossacks within striking distance of the Khyber Pass. Furthermore the Trans-Siberian Railway threatened to bring all North China under Russian influence, a thought most distasteful to British diplomats.

Consequently, the British toyed in the eighteen-nineties with the idea of a German-British alliance and so, too, did German statesmen. In fact, one might well have eventuated had it not been for three factors: (*a*) the personality of the Kaiser, (*b*) the belief of German diplomats that Britain ultimately would have to join the triplice, thus making it a quadruple alliance, and (*c*) the South African war of 1899-1902.

Kaiser William II never was able to view objectively the homeland of his mother, the British princess Victoria, favored daughter of the old British queen. This nervous, neurotic, yet frequently brilliant ruler of Germany blamed his mother for the withered arm with which he was born, hated her violently, and, through her, England. Great predecessors of his on the Prussian throne had become famous for their armies; why should he not be enrolled among the famous of

Valhalla as the founder of German sea power? British newspapers mocked at his country and at him and he resented it—yet curiously enough, with all his Anglophobia there was mixed much admiration for England and what he would say about that country never could be predicted. If he had only kept silent... but that was one thing William II could not do. He was determined that "the old peacock," his uncle, Edward VII, should be put in his place; he always wanted to show off before the British, who became alarmed that one possessed of such unquestionable power should be so irresponsible.

The German diplomats, meanwhile, overplayed their cards. They had an idea that England would come to them cap in hand and that they had only to wait long enough and England would beg to be admitted to the Triple Alliance. Now many influential British statesmen were quite willing to make a defensive treaty with Germany alone, the two countries to stand shoulder to shoulder if attacked; but they were unwilling to commit their country to any Austro-German policy in the Balkans which might be the case if they joined hands with Italy and Austria. Consequently, there was a great deal of smoke and but very little fire in regard to the projected alliance.

Then, too, there was the South African problem which culminated in the Boer War. The Germans were accustomed to consider the Boers as racial cousins who might form the nucleus of a potentially Teutonic nation in South Africa. German Southwest Africa was only separated from the Transvaal by the thinly populated Bechuanaland; and furthermore the Transvaal abutted on Portuguese East Africa, through which ran the railway from Pretoria. Suppose that Delagoa Bay were some day to fall to Germany, or perhaps Bechuanaland? German influence was felt at Pretoria and the Germans were keenly alive to the advantages which might accrue to themselves if the two Boer republics remained independent long enough. When the Jameson Raid occurred in 1895 the Kaiser was wildly excited and insisted upon telegraphing his congratulations to Kruger, a fact which added to his unpopularity in Britain.

The advent of the South African war found German public opinion heavily Anglophobe, and when the British illegally stopped a German merchant ship bound for Delagoa Bay, relations between the two countries became very strained. Germany preserved neutrality throughout the war, and the Kaiser discouraged the Russians when they suggested a continental front against England; but this did not discourage the German press from attacking England. Chamberlain, England's spokesman, did, it is true, continue to hold out the olive branch to Germany, suggesting an Anglo-Saxon alliance of Germany, England, and the United States; but his appeal fell upon deaf ears. The Colonial

Secretary was not a tactful man. Somewhat later in the war, in defending the conduct of the British troops, he implied that their behavior was at least more exemplary than that of the Prussians in 1870-71, and as he did so the newspapers of Germany took up the challenge in no peaceful strain. Echoes of the Boer War were to continue for a good many years and as late as 1908 the Kaiser added greatly to his unpopularity in England by an interview granted to the London *Daily Telegraph* wherein he boasted that the plans of campaign used by the British armies in South Africa had been drawn up by his imperial self.

The growing animosity, however, between England and Germany did not mean that the former country was prepared to enter the Franco-Russian camp—not yet. The tradition of isolation was still strong in England, even if the Boer War did make the British feel that they were without friends on the continent. And therefore Lord Lansdowne, foreign secretary in the Balfour government, 1902-05, contented himself with striking an alliance with Japan in 1902 whereby that distant Asiatic empire exchanged mutual guarantees with Britain, the alliance to be invoked in case either country got into a war in Far Eastern waters (1902).

Ultimately, Britain was to veer into alignment with France and Russia, but her doing so was a long and slow process. She never got all the way into the Franco-Russian tent, one foot, perhaps, being outside the flap as late as 1914. When the World War broke, the alignment of Powers quite properly was called the Triple Alliance and the Triple Entente, but even the word *entente* is a little too strong to imply Anglo-Russian relations. France and Russia were very closely allied but England was allied with neither. The truth then was that she was on something more than good terms with Russia and under very definite obligations to France.

The Entente Cordiale

The story of how that came about relates more properly to France than to England. In the former country at the turn of the century was one of Europe's cleverest diplomats, Delcassé. He had been a bitter enemy of England and at the time of Kitchener's bloodless victory at Fashoda on the Upper Nile over the Frenchman, Marchand, Delcassé raged. But the Frenchman was a realist; he knew that overseas it was impossible to defy Britain. Why not therefore come to terms with her and extend the French colonial empire in those regions (if there were any such) to which the British laid no claims? What Delcassé had his eye on was Morocco; if the British would but give

him a free hand there he felt it quite worth while to surrender French
claims in the Upper Nile valley (unenforceable anyway) and in Egypt
where they possessed a nuisance value only. Other outstanding rivalries
in the colonial world might be compounded also, fishing disputes off
the Newfoundland coast, islands in Oceania, the island of Madagascar,
boundary lines and frontiers still in dispute between France and England in tropical Africa north of the Gulf of Guinea, and also in Siam,
which little country was most unfortunately situated, indeed, with
British Burma on the west and French Indo-China on the east.

Cautiously, Delcassé approached Lansdowne; would his lordship
be agreeable to a general colonial settlement? The French suggested
terms, the British counter terms, and a protracted bargain in colonial
frontiers was under way. The result was almost a diplomatic revolution. Britain abandoned at this time (1904) not only her traditional
anti-French policy in respect to colonial expansion but also the time-
honored policy of abstention from continental commitments sponsored
by Canning, Palmerston, and Salisbury, and only slightly compromised
by her participation in the Crimean War. It proved the beginning of
what was to England an insurance policy against an unpredictable
Kaiser and an aggressive Germany, and what was to Germany the
commencement of a policy of encirclement initiated by the jealous
British who sought to surround Germany with an iron ring.

The Anglo-French accord looked harmless. In the more important
of the treaties now signed, France acknowledged the priority of
Britain's position in Egypt, the British in return recognizing that
French interests in Morocco were more important than their own. But
the Germans suspected secret clauses and were justified in so doing,
clauses which stated that if England in the future decided to change
the status quo as to Egypt, France would support her in so doing,
and that if France found it necessary to change the status quo in
Morocco, Britain would support her, in the latter eventuality provision
being made for Spanish annexations in Morocco, since England did not
want a powerful France opposite Gibraltar.

The treaty said nothing about Italy; it did not need to, since four
years earlier (1900) France had made a bargain with Italy which
provided for Italian compensation in Tripoli should France decide to
push westward from Algeria to Morocco. The treaty said nothing
about Germany; but after all why should she be invited to share in
the exploitation of Morocco; did not that region lie adjacent to
French territory (Algeria), and was there not much more French
money invested in Morocco than there was German?

Nevertheless, Morocco was supposed to be independent; there were
German merchants there; and somewhat earlier when ambiguous

Anglo-German negotiations were afoot there had been British suggestions that England would not oppose Germany's gaining a foothold in Morocco. The German foreign office was indignant at this disregard of German colonial ambitions and brought pressure to bear on a very reluctant Kaiser to land at Tangier and to make a provocative speech in which he congratulated the Sultan of Morocco upon retaining his independence and assured him of German friendship.

With one of those flares of real insight which occasionally came to him the German ruler scented trouble and he found it. The French were furious at this German intervention and the British, although more calm, aligned themselves with the French. Delcassé talked too much and too belligerently, and the French, not eager for war, dismissed him. The Germans, however, not content with getting rid of Delcassé, demanded that an international conference be held to decide Morocco's future.

The proposal was an unfortunate one for Germany since the conference of 1906 which met at Algeciras proved a great setback for her. England supported France, as of course did Russia. But Italy supported France, too, since owing to her treaty of 1900 with that country, Tripoli was earmarked for Italy if France gained control over Morocco. The Italians now had their feet in both camps and the Germans realized as never before what an insecure hold they had on Italy. Spain also joined the anti-German group, owing to the promise of enlarged territory opposite Gibraltar, and even the United States threw the weight of her influence against Germany.

Two questions were in the foreground at Algeciras—finance and police. The finances of Morocco were as hopelessly muddled as those of Egypt in 1878, and since French bankers had loaned most of the money borrowed by the Sultan, France demanded a Bank of Morocco under a French president. This French claim was not sustained; nevertheless, the French won an indirect victory, since the international bank that was established was largely controlled by the Bank of France, the Bank of England, the Bank of Spain, and the German Imperial Bank, and the French knew that the Spaniards and the English were on their side.

But how was order to be maintained in Morocco, particularly in the seaports and along the frontier? The Germans demanded a share in policing this unruly country and they did not succeed in obtaining it. In this lay their major defeat. The conference voted that France, assisted by Spain, should officer the police, and to give an international appearance to this decision a Swiss inspector-general was appointed. Thus ended 1906. The Kaiser's intuition of the preceding year had been a good one.

In 1907 Germany was to receive a further shock in the announcement of an Anglo-Russian treaty. Like the Anglo-French treaties of
1904, it looked innocent enough, but the Germans wondered what might
be behind it.

Russo-German relations since the non-renewal of Bismarck's reinsurance treaty had been unstable. When Russia and Japan fought it
out in 1904-05 to a finish, the Kaiser had been violently pro-Russian.
To his heated imagination it was a war of East against West, of Asiatic
paganism against Christian culture. He bombarded the Czar with
advice as to how the war might be won; he took an active part in
assisting the coaling of the Russian fleet bound to Asiatic waters; and
he sent the draft of a projected treaty of alliance between Germany
and Russia to the Czar for approval. Shortly after in 1905 he met the
Czar off the coast of Finland and persuaded that weak monarch to
sign the treaty of Björko, definitely committing himself to an alliance
with Germany. The Russian foreign office was horrified; France had
not been consulted. When that country resolutely refused to enter into
any alliance in which Germany was a partner as long as Alsace-Lorraine
remained German, the Czar backed out of the Björko treaty with
what grace he could. A year later, at Algeciras, Russia voted with
France against Germany and the Kaiser and everybody else who knew
anything about it realized that Björko was meaningless.

Meanwhile, Anglo-Russian relations during this same period were
more unfriendly than in several decades. The Anglo-Japanese treaty
of 1902 angered the Russians and prevented any hope they might
have of allies in their Far Eastern adventure; and an accidental firing
upon British trawlers in the North Sea by Russian warships made
British public opinion even more Russophobe than it had ever been
in more recent years.

It had been sufficiently so before. During the Boer War the Russians
steadily encroached on the independence of Persia and endeavored as
well to obtain a coaling station adjacent to the Persian Gulf over
the waters of which, according to Lord Curzon, Britain exercised a
kind of Monroe Doctrine. In Tibet and in Afghanistan there were
Russian intrigues afoot, and any rapprochement between England and
Russia seemed as remote in 1905 as one between England and France
in 1904.

Nevertheless, that rapprochement took place. The treaty of 1907
between England and Russia related, it is true, entirely to Asia. By
it the paramount interest of Britain in Afghanistan was recognized,
Tibet was guaranteed as a no-man's land, and Persia was divided by
the two signatories into three zones. The first of these, the northern
and most important, containing the cities of Tabriz and Teheran,

went to Russia. Then came an intermediate zone in which neither Britain nor Russia claimed influence. The third zone, to the south and east, was given to Britain. These zones in theory simply marked off spheres of economic influence. Persia's independence solemnly was recognized, as was customary in treaties of this ilk.

The treaty was a blow to the Germans. England now was the friend of both Russia and France; Russia, although not anti-German, was the foe of Austria, Germany's sole dependable ally in the Balkans; Russia also was the close ally of France, still hostile to Germany because of Alsace-Lorraine. The Germans were worried and felt more need than ever of Austria.

Because of this fact Germany felt it very necessary to take a firm stand at the next international crisis which arose in the Balkans in 1908. Behind it lay the somewhat unsavory machinations of the Russian foreign secretary, Isvolsky, and the Austrian foreign minister, Aerenthal. These two men concocted a secret agreement at Buchlau whereby the straits which connected the Black Sea with the Mediterranean should become open for Russian warships in return for which the Austrians should be permitted to annex Bosnia and Herzegovina, which they had been administering since 1878 in the name of the concert of Europe. A first-class diplomatic crisis now occurred when Aerenthal suddenly annexed Bosnia, despite the fact that England and France were apparently unwilling to permit the opening of the straits. Neither France nor England was disposed to back Russia in this abrupt tearing up of the treaty of Berlin; the Young Turks had no intention of quietly permitting Russian warships to move back and forth in front of Constantinople; and the Serbs were enraged at not being consulted and considered that the annexation of Bosnia with its large Serbian population was a direct attack on their nationalistic aspirations. Why not then another international congress to review the work done in 1878? The English and the French were agreeable to that but not the Germans or the Austrians, who had no intention of attending another Algeciras. Germany and Austria would consent, they said, only if acknowledgment were given in advance that the Bosnian annexation was accepted. Russia now was in an uncomfortable dilemma; the Serbs were pressing hard for Russian help, and French and British aid was lacking. The Kaiser saw his opportunity and brought diplomatic pressure to bear on St. Petersburg to recognize the annexation. Russia was in no condition for war; she was too exhausted after her conflict with Japan. Therefore Russia yielded: she did not get the straits but Austria did obtain Bosnia. As a distinguished historian puts it: "The weakness of Russia was revealed to the world, the Straits remained closed, the minister's prestige at home and abroad was shattered, the central empires were triumphant, the Western powers dismayed."

The German victory in the Balkans was more than counterbalanced by renewed friction with England. In the background of Anglo-German relations there always lay the naval situation, a dangerous ground for disagreement after the Germans began building rapidly in the first decade of the twentieth century. A naval race between the two countries, however, could scarcely be said to have existed until the British virtually started one by laying down in 1905 the *Dreadnaught,* the first super-battle-ship. Whereupon the Germans followed suit. As both powers then began to construct this new type of huge battle-ship, Britain's superiority in naval vessels showed a relative decline since the pre-dreadnaught type, in which she possessed a tremendous preponderance, became less and less important.

In England the Liberals were in office pledged to expensive social reform. They had no zest for more battle-ships and they hoped to set an example by only authorizing two dreadnaughts for the year 1908. A new German navy law at this same date paid no attention to this British naval dove: the German law authorized four capital ships a year from 1908 to 1911 and not until after that was the rate of increase halved to two yearly. This resulted in a hasty conference in Berlin between British and German representatives which ended in recrimination. Thereupon a naval panic swept through England in 1909. "We want eight and we won't wait" was the popular slogan, as England insisted on maintaining the two-power standard, the English navy to be on a par with any two other navies in the world.

In Germany there was a hot dispute concerning this naval rivalry. Bülow, the chancellor, was for concessions and for slowing down the German rate of construction to three capital ships a year. All he wanted, he claimed, was a "risk navy," in other words, one sufficiently powerful to make it very dangerous to attack Germany. Von Tirpitz, however, head of the German admiralty, was in favor of pushing construction ahead at top speed. The Kaiser flitted from one side to the other but tended more frequently to rest on Tirpitz's perch than on that of Bülow. The British now went in for superdreadnaughts and six of their eight ships authorized in 1908 were of this variety. The result of this was to make the Germans change their plans and build superdreadnaughts also, a fact which delayed their program so that by 1912 instead of the thirteen great ships which the British had prophesied, the Germans had but nine whereas at the same date the British possessed eighteen.

This naval rivalry lay in the background of the next international crisis which arose in 1911. It came about as the result of the fast-moving Moroccan situation. Scarcely had the ink become dry on the agreement of Algeciras than the French began to strengthen their hold upon Morocco. In order to punish mutinous tribesmen near the Algerian frontier, they occupied villages in eastern Morocco; in order to quell anti-European riots at Casablanca on the Atlantic, they despatched thither an army of several thousand. Aggressive acts like the above brought about the downfall of Sultan Abdul-Aziz, a Francophil and the elevation of his brother Mulay Hafid, a Francophobe. But Mulay Hafid now leaned like his brother upon the French for support, for they had money. The bankers at Paris paid his debts in return for new concessions, and then fresh revolts broke out, this time directed against Mulay Hafid. The capital, Fez, was said to be endangered and to protect that city the French occupied it with an army early in 1911.

How long were the French to stay in Fez? The Quai d'Orsay really could not say; evacuation would take place when order was restored. The Germans grew uneasy as the weeks passed; they recalled the British occupation of Alexandria and Cairo and came to the conclusion that the end of Moroccan independence was not far away. Should that happen the Germans felt that some colonial pickings elsewhere might as well be gathered by the Fatherland. They began a number of conferences with the French ambassador at Berlin for a quid pro quo, but the French seemed unwilling to make definite offers. The Germans then tried to force the issue. They sent a small gunboat, the *Panther*, to the Atlantic coast of Morocco and stationed it off the seaport of Agadir to protect, they said, certain German merchants, who were in danger there.

Whether this was political blackmail or not it at least hastened the willingness of the French to negotiate. The German demand was for the French Congo in return for a free hand in Morocco. The French were horrified that Germany should expect so much and the latter country was said to have countered by offering to throw her colony of Togo into the bargain. Then came the intervention of England. That country, not having been consulted, was indignant and demanded an explanation of the *Panther's* spring. Before the German reply reached England Lloyd George, the radical chancellor of the exchequer, made an inflammatory speech in which, in indirect fashion, he hinted at war. His words were rather strong for pre-war diplomacy and Germany was deeply insulted when her own bad manners were imitated.

During August, 1911, peace hung in the balance. The English seemed quite willing to fight but nobody else was. The financial condition of Germany was none too pleasant; Russia warned France that she probably would not participate in a war unless France made concessions in Central Africa, and in France herself, the pacifist Caillaux was temporarily in power. In consequence France ceded Germany more than 100,000 square miles in the French Congo adjacent to the German colony of Kamerun and of very little value. Germany recognized France's right to a protectorate over Morocco. This ended the crisis of 1911, a very strange one, indeed, and only to be explained as far as England is concerned by her constant worry about Germany's fleet and her maritime ambitions. For Agadir, it must be remembered, was not inland but on the Atlantic.

One result of this crisis was a great speeding up of the German naval program. This disturbed the British, who sent their secretary of state for war, Lord Haldane, to see if something could not be done to stay the hand of the German admiralty. The Germans were not of one accord in regard to their shipbuilding program. Von Bethmann-Hollweg, the chancellor, thought it very undesirable to endanger Anglo-German relations further by still greater naval appropriations, and at times it seemed as though he had the ear of the Kaiser. But Admiral Tirpitz persuaded his Imperial Majesty that a further increase in the German fleet was imperative.

The German program primarily was directed at an enormous increase in personnel which called for four-fifths of the entire navy being permanently in commission. It meant also new battle-ships and new cruisers, a total by 1920 of 41 battle-ships, 20 battle cruisers, and 40 small cruisers. That program the Germans intimated they might modify or withdraw if a satisfactory political agreement could be had; which meant, from their point of view, an ironclad promise of neutrality on the part of England in case Germany became involved in a continental war. This Haldane could not offer, nor would the British cabinet hear of it. The British would promise not to join in any unprovoked attack on Germany, but that was as far as they were willing to commit themselves.

So the Haldane mission proved a fiasco with most serious results. Great Britain could and did build up her fleet against Germany's, but, expensive as that proved to be, it was not the gravest result of the Haldane failure. There was another card that Britain played at this time: she entered into a naval agreement with France. That country agreed to concentrate her fleet in the Mediterranean, there to guard British interests (by implication) while Britain moved her larger ships from the Mediterranean to the Channel and the North Sea to guard (by implication) French ports on the Channel and on the Atlantic. Accompanying this change in the location of their respective fighting craft there was an exchange of letters between Sir Edward Grey and

Cambon, French ambassador at London. The letters expressly stated that this agreement in the stationing of the warships was not to be interpreted as a restriction of the freedom of either government, that it was not to bind them to come to each other's military assistance. If, however, either government had reason to suspect an unprovoked attack by a third power, then consultation in common was to be taken by England and France for the purpose of preventing aggression and preserving peace.

This was the closest that England ever came to making an alliance with France. From the point of view of the French, these letters bound England to come to France's aid if attacked by Germany. Some Englishmen were to agree to this later, some to differ.

THREE LITTLE WARS

We turn now to the Mediterranean and to the Balkan Peninsula where three little wars, of 1911, 1912, and 1913, respectively, were destined to become three little curtain-raisers for the world tragedy of 1914-18.

The first of these wars was fought in 1911 by Italy against Turkey. The Italians saw their chance in 1911 and took it. In the midst of all the excitement of that year of Agadir, it seemed relatively unimportant that Italy should occupy Tripoli. There was nothing to prevent her doing so, since long ago she had secured France's blessing and that carried with it England's tacit consent. Germany and Austria were her allies and could not well object. There was, of course, Turkey, and Tripoli was a part of the Ottoman Empire. But that ancient vestige of an empire was in sorry plight with a recent revolution on its hands, and Italy therefore did not expect much if any resistance to her ultimatum that Tripoli be handed over to her.

The Turks, however, showed fight. Their scanty troops in Tripoli retreated to the interior oases from whence they could harass the invaders, and what was more important, Turkey refused to sue for peace. What were the Italians to do? They occupied the Turkish island of Rhodes and the Dodecanese archipelago; they bombarded the forts at the entrance of the Dardanelles: but the Turks did nothing except expel Italians from the Turkish empire and close the Dardanelles to the shipping of all nations. The mobilization of both fleet and army was proving very expensive to the Italians and the war might have dragged on indefinitely had not the whole Near Eastern Question been reopened by it. The Bulgars, the Greeks, the Serbs, and even the Montenegrins now saw their chance. Clever diplomacy, very largely Greek and Russian in its origin, healed for the time being ancient jealousies among these Balkan peoples and they prepared to take the warpath against the Ottomans.

Turkey, then, confronted with the likelihood of another war, and this time against the Balkan states, made peace with Italy. In the autumn of 1912 the treaty was signed. Tripoli was yielded informally to Italy, and the Italians agreed to withdraw from the islands which they had captured, once Tripoli was completely pacified. The Italians still occupied in 1943 those islands; their promise to withdraw was but a polite gesture, for they could always claim that any little riot anywhere in Tripoli was evidence that pacification had not been completed.

As the Italian-Turkish War drew to a close a new one commenced, this time between Turkey and the Balkan states. It was brief and decisive as far as its military features are concerned, and was followed in 1913 by a second war in the same area, also brief and decisive. These two Balkan wars form an integral part of the history of the Eastern Question; they also are intimately correlated with the diplomacy antecedent to the World War of 1914-18. Since their diplomatic aspects are of infinitely greater significance than their military details the latter are omitted here.

There were a number of factors which helped bring about the united front of the Balkan states against Turkey. Among them were: (a) the success of Austria in annexing Bosnia, which created fear in Bulgaria and Greece as well as in Serbia, lest it be but the forerunner of an Austrian thrust down into Macedonia, thus bringing an end to the territorial ambitions of all the Balkan states; (b) the recent success of the Albanians in resisting the Turks, which indicated that the strength of the Turkish army had been overestimated; (c) the encouragement of Russian diplomats who were striving hard to bring about Balkan unity; and (d) the Italian attack on Tripoli which not only gave renewed evidence of the weakness of Turkey but also demonstrated that the European concert was either unable or unwilling to prevent local wars. In consequence there followed a series of Balkan alliances and understandings binding Bulgaria, Montenegro, Serbia, and Greece together and a formal demand of these four allies upon Turkey for drastic reforms in Macedonia.

The concert of Europe now swung into action. The Austrian and Russian ambassadors (the latter presumably with tongue in cheek) handed in at each of the Balkan capitals a solemn warning that the six great powers would attend themselves to Macedonia reforms and if, despite their wishes, "war did break out they would not admit at the end of the conflict any modification of the territorial status quo of European Turkey."

One hour after the delivery of this note the Montenegrin representative at Constantinople asked for his passports and on his way home stated at Bucharest: "Montenegro wants territorial increase and will not give back whatever conquests she makes." Almost simultaneously the first Balkan war began—Serbia, Bulgaria, Montenegro, and Greece against Turkey.

These two wars in the Balkans, 1912-13, were to hasten and in part to cause the European holocaust of 1914-18. That, of course, had many roots—Alsace-Lorraine, Morocco, Anglo-German commercial and industrial and naval rivalry—but no single one was more important than the conflicting aims and ambitions of Austria and Russia in the Balkan Peninsula, the former country determined that come what might, Serbia should not succeed in becoming "the little Piedmont of the South Slavs," drawing into her fold the restive Slovenes and Croats of Austria and the rebellious Serbs of Bosnia, the latter country equally resolved that the Slavic folk of southeastern Europe should realize their nationalistic ambitions and that, too, with the aid and assistance of Russia. Since this was so, since Germany was tied to Austria, France to Russia, and England partially tied to France, it was evident that new and severe international crises were imminent if there should be any violent change in the territorial status quo in the Balkans.

Both Balkan wars were to result in such changes. In the first one the Bulgars, Serbs, and Greeks won amazing victories over Turkey. In fewer days than it took Moltke to burst the bubble of the Second Empire in 1870, the Balkan allies overwhelmed the Turks. Within one month the Bulgars routed the main Turkish armies twice and drove close to the defenses of Constantinople. Meanwhile, the S⸍bs struck south, forced the Turks out of Usküb, surrounded them at Monastir, and took 40,000 prisoners. And as they did so the triumphant Greeks not only pounced upon the Turkish islands in the Aegean, but pushing north and east captured Salonika at the mouth of the Vardar River. Turkey in Europe now practically had disappeared except for Constantinople and a few isolated fortresses, two of which in Albania were besieged by Montenegrins.

The Turk had been almost expelled from Europe. The four Balkan allies had won a smashing victory. If they avoided dissensions among themselves, and the Western Powers played them fair, their triumph meant nothing but good for the world. The Sick Man of Europe had been nearly relegated to Asia, where alone he belonged. The Macedonian problem seemed settled. Montenegro, Serbia, Bulgaria, and Greece had all received extensions of boundary which they sorely needed. The Balkan War had appeared to justify itself by promising blessings to mankind.

This happiness was not to be; the allies had been the victims of the very magnitude of their victory. They had hoped to win a few square miles apiece and to force a Christian governor on Macedonia, after a hard, wavering war. Instead they had almost exterminated Turkey in Europe! But they did not find themselves at liberty, after their victory, to distribute their spoils according to the division compacts which they had made before commencing the joint campaign. Now, one of the prime objects of the war had been to get some kind of a fair outlet for Serbia, preferably upon salt water. The Serbs, soon after their first successes, had struck into Albania, forced their way over the mountains, and for a few proud, hopeful days their flag had floated at Durazzo beside the blue Adriatic.

Both Austria and Italy were determined that it should be hauled down; they were prepared to act in defense of an Albanian nationalist movement which Serbia was anxious to crush in the bud; they objected to a clear belt of South Slav territory reaching from the Danube to the Adriatic, for both Italy and Austria were Adriatic powers and it was not to their interest to have a Slav state perched on the eastern shores of that sea. And as a corollary Montenegro should be forced to relinquish Scutari, the Albanian fortress, on which she had set her heart. Since the Turks were now gone, an independent "Principality of Albania," they argued, should be set up under the protection of the Powers, who were to provide it with a respectable sovereign.

The situation, therefore, was as follows. Bulgaria had seized most of Thrace, and by its location neither Greece nor Serbia could have that territory. But the Bulgars were also intensely interested in getting a great part of Macedonia. Here were the "unredeemed" lands of their people, and it was largely for them that King Ferdinand's armies had rushed to war. By the compacts made before the struggle began, Bulgaria was certainly to be given a great extension in Macedonia. Serbia and Greece could not deny this letter of the bond. But they could argue, with much moral emphasis, that conditions had utterly changed. *They* had expected (Greece indeed less than Serbia) to get their reward in Albania. From Albania they had been excluded by the fiat of the Great Powers. Was it just that, with Serbia denied nearly all her expected gains and Greece also part of them, Bulgaria should continue to exact her pound of flesh in Macedonia? The net result of that would have been to give Bulgaria the most of *both* Thrace and Macedonia and her allies very little new land anywhere. Obviously, here was a case which could be very dangerous if handled by the ungentle methods of Balkan diplomacy.

The European chancelleries were highly exercised over this situation and urged immediate termination of the war. The Turks were agreeable, and in May, 1913, the treaty of London ostensibly brought it to an end. Turkey ceded to the Balkan states not only all of her territory in Europe a short distance beyond Constantinople but also the island of Crete. But no proviso was drawn in this treaty as to how the spoils of war should be divided. Italy and Austria stood firm in regard to Albania, the Bulgars firm in regard to Macedonia, and none could foretell the outcome.

This situation led to the second Balkan war (June-July 1913) in which Bulgaria fought alone against her former allies, Greece and Serbia, and a new foe, Rumania.

That war came about as follows: It was very much to the interest of Russia that her Balkan protégés should not fall to fighting among each other, and the Czar offered to arbitrate the division of land won by the first Balkan war. It was very much to the interests of Austria (the constant enemy of Serbia) that the reverse should take place and it pleased Austria highly when the Bulgars proved very truculent, threatening to seize by force Macedonian land occupied by Serbs and Greeks. The latter formed a military alliance against Bulgarian attack and just in time. Without warning the Bulgars treacherously hurled themselves on the Serbs and Greeks, only to be badly beaten, the Greeks pursuing them over the mountains into their homeland. As this happened Rumania invaded Bulgaria from the north and Turkey struck at her erstwhile foe, now helpless. The Bulgars surrendered at discretion; there was nothing else for them to do.

There followed a peace treaty, that of Bucharest (1913). Bulgaria was all but expelled from Macedonia; she lost land to Rumania on the northeast, and even most of her gains in Thrace. Rumania gained at the expense of Bulgaria 2,687 square miles and 286,000 inhabitants. Serbs and Greeks had triumphed and they did so handsomely, Serbia nearly doubling her territory, annexing 15,000 square miles in Macedonia and about 1,500,000 people, Greece gaining 18,000 square miles and an added population of about 1,700,000.

The second Balkan war was now over. In a certain sense both conflicts might be regarded as frontier wars occurring in an out-of-the-way corner of Europe, and the fact that they were concluded without any of the six great powers taking up arms seemed to the optimistic a hopeful sign. Europe had passed through crisis after crisis in the twentieth century successfully, two in Morocco in 1905 and 1911, and two in the Balkans, in 1908, and again in 1912-13. Surely this must augur well for the future; surely those prophets of gloom who had shaken their heads at the very mention of the Balkans ever since 1878 and the Treaty of Berlin must acknowledge themselves mistaken. The errors of that treaty were now largely liquidated; the Turks had practically been expelled from Europe; Balkan nationalism had received due recognition; Bulgaria had been treated roughly, it is true, but so condign had been the punishment meted out to her that it might be many decades before she could dispute the mastery of Macedonia with Greece and Serbia.

On the other side of the ledger there were, of course, imponderables. How strong a force, for instance, was Pan-Germanism with its drive toward southeastern Europe; how strong Russian Pan-Slavism thrusting in that same direction; could a conflict between them be avoided? The defeat of Turkey was to some extent a blow at German prestige and the victory of Serbia an even greater one to Austria, Germany's ally. Austria, with Italy's help, had kept Serbia landlocked, away from the Adriatic; but she had been unable to prevent the aggrandizement of her troublesome neighbor, who had never become reconciled to the Austrian annexation of Bosnia in 1908. Now, even more than before, Serbia could be counted Austria's implacable foe.

One more year of peace remained to Europe and during it the powers which were the more conciliatory were England and Germany. Neither country wanted war, and both made gestures of peace toward one another while exercising a moderating influence on the two chief troublemakers, Russia and Austria. Anglo-German disputes of long standing concerning the building of the Berlin-Bagdad Railway were amicably settled, and finally so by a curious irony of fate in July, 1914. Russia was wildly indignant at the appointment of a German general to reorganize the Turkish army but found England unwilling to protest. The Austrians, their jails in Bosnia and Croatia overflowing with rebellious South Slavs, thought seriously of trying to annex Serbia outright but Germany restrained them.

The French, the Austrians, and the Russians, however, all vied with one another in heating troubled waters to the boiling point. France increased her loans to Russia for military service, elected Poincaré, an intense nationalist from Lorraine, to the presidency, and started to raise the term of service of the French conscripts to three years, thereby setting the pace for Germany to follow and that, too, rapidly, for the increase in the German army occurred as France debated the issue. Meanwhile Austria delivered a most provocative ultimatum to Serbia in 1913 to evacuate in eight days a part of Albania which that country had occupied in order "to preserve order." Sazonov, Russian foreign minister, journeyed among the small countries of southeastern Europe, holding forth promises of territorial enlargement at Austria's expense, and early in 1914 the Russian government held a Crown Council at which the forcing of the Straits by a military coup was seriously debated. "In the summer of 1914 peace was at the mercy of an accident."

SUMMER, 1914

Then, on June 28, 1914 came the assassination of the heir to the Austrian throne, the Archduke Francis Ferdinand, and within five weeks Europe was plunged into the maelstrom of World War.

The murder took place in Sarajevo, capital of Bosnia, the murderer a youth Bosnian student who was a member of the Black Hand, a secret society of Serbian terrorists. The deed aroused the horror of the whole civilized world, and sympathy for Austria was both deep and widespread in Entente countries as well as in those of the Triple Alliance.

Nearly a month passed before Austria took public action, time spent ostensibly in ferreting out the instigators of the crime, time more largely devoted in bringing about an agreement between Tisza, Prime Minister of Hungary, and Berchtold, Austrian foreign secretary, for the Magyar statesman was for caution, whereas the Austrian whose ideas prevailed was for condign punishment of Serbia and immediate aggression against that country.

On July 23, an Austrian ultimatum was delivered at Belgrade which, in addition to demanding apologies and pledges to refrain from anti-Austrian propaganda in the future, stipulated that Austrian representatives should participate in Serbian trials and that Serbia remove from her employ "all officers and functionaries guilty of propaganda against the Austro-Hungarian Monarchy whose names and deeds the Austro-Hungarian Monarchy reserve to themselves the right of communicating to the Royal Government." Forty-eight hours was given for the reply.

The Serbian reply was submissive in tone but in substance only partially so; to some of the Austrian demands it yielded and to none did it give a pointblank refusal. Nevertheless, within half an hour after the receipt of the Serbian reply the Austrian ambassador had left Belgrade, bag and baggage.

Austria and Russia now started to mobilize. On July 28, Austria declared war on Serbia; on August 1, Germany, realizing that Russia was mobilizing against her as well as Austria, declared war on the country of the Czar; on August 3, on the refusal of the French to give guarantees of neutrality, she declared war on France; on August 4, her troops invaded Belgium; and on August 4, England declared war on Germany.

How did it happen that Europe, having successfully weathered crisis after crisis in the twentieth century, succumbed to this one; what country, what government, or, indeed, what individual should be held the more largely accountable? The first question is difficult to answer, the second is impossible. Possibly in the last analysis the reason why this particular crisis became insurmountable was because it came so quickly, without premonition. That atonement must be made by Serbia for the Archduke's murder was generally agreed, but only the general tenor of the ultimatum delivered by Austria was known by Germany, and the text was not available until it was too late to make changes. Equally unpredictable was the immediate rush of Russia to Serbia's aid. In consequence there were only a few days granted to men of good will to fight for peace. Fear paralyzed action during this last week of July, and the militarists had their way.

Nor can any single power justly be accused of bringing on the World War, or any group of powers. Beyond doubt and beyond cavil it became clear afterwards that the Serbian government was guilty of knowing in advance that there was a plot against the Archduke which it made no effort to prevent; but Serbia was not one of the European Powers. How the latter reacted to the crisis we shall now describe, since the picture may be seen better if we paint it country by country rather than day by day.

The responsibility of Austria was heavy in that she used the death of Francis Ferdinand as an excuse for destroying Serbian independence. The Austrians neither expected nor wanted their ultimatum to be accepted and they drew it up with confident hope of its rejection. They were determined, *a priori*, to make war on Serbia. Furthermore, the Austrians, secure in their knowledge that they could depend on Germany, refused to listen to any warnings from Russia, from England, or even from their own ally. The Germans raised very pertinent objections to what the Austrians were doing, as we shall see later, but to them the Austrians apparently were completely deaf; to the many telegrams coming from Berlin they returned the vaguest replies, and even those that they did make were frequently so belated as to be worthless. Austria may justly be accused of dragging her own ally and all of Europe into the abyss.

So also, however, does Russia stand accused; the case against her is quite as black as that against Austria. In regard to Russia there are dark surmises; there are also demonstrated facts. As an illustration of the former, let us take the activities of the Russian ambassador at Belgrade who died as the war began. He was a notorious Austrophobe and on intimate terms with various Serbian officials who were privy to the plot which killed the Archduke. Was the ambassador conversant with it also? We can prove nothing. What we can prove is that Russia first began mobilization on a big scale and that the Russians lied about it to the Germans. Sazonov, the Russian foreign minister, first suggested that mobilization be partial only and directed simply against Austria-Hungary. He was persuaded by the military men that partial mobilization was impractical and the Czar signed an order for general mobilization on July 29. True, he shortly after cancelled this order but, owing to the pressure of the general staff, renewed it the following day. When the Bolshevists came to power in 1917 they placed on trial a number of high officials of the Czar's government, and the Russian chief of staff testified that the German ambassador at St. Petersburg protested to him against Russia adopting general mobilization in July, 1914, only to be told by the chief of staff on his honor as a gentleman that there was no truth in the rumor. "And all the time I had the order for general mobilization in my pocket," said the chief of staff.

Mobilization, it must be remembered, was considered generally by military men as tantamount to war. The Franco-Russian armies, as far as numbers went, were decidedly superior to those of the Triple Alliance. Once give Russia all the time she wanted to mobilize, and victory presumably should be hers.

Both Germany and France were decidedly less responsible for initiating the war in 1914. The old accusation against the Germans, the "Potsdam Plot," has been proved pure myth. In accordance with it the Kaiser is said to have summoned to Potsdam in July his principal military, naval, and civilian advisers together with certain key men in the world of business and finance and to have asked them if they were ready for war. They all reported that they were prepared except the financiers who asked for more time. This was given them and to allay suspicions the Kaiser went on a yachting trip to Norway. The only truth in the story is that the Kaiser took his cruise; most of the men named as participating in this plot were known to have been elsewhere. As a matter of fact it would have been decidedly better if there had been a crown council at Potsdam; in that case Germany would not have treated the entire crisis with such cavalier indifference as she did during its earlier stages. With almost criminal negligence the Germans told the Austrians to go ahead and that Germany would support them. This was the German "blank cheque" to Austria.

But on behalf of Germany it must be remembered that she tried during the last week of peace to prevent Austria from cashing that cheque. The Kaiser was pleased with the submissive character of the Serbs' reply to the Austrian ultimatum and considered it both unnecessary and unwise for Austria to proceed further. Even after Austria's declaration of war on Serbia the Kaiser urged his ally to be content with the occupation of the capital of Serbia across the Danube and to make no further conquests. "Halt in Belgrade" was the advice from Berlin.

The Austrians, however, paid no attention to these admonitions coming from Berlin, not even at the very end of July when it was almost inevitable that all Europe would be involved in disaster unless Austria was willing to delay. The German ambassador at London wired Berlin that England might become involved unless Austria's hand was stayed and Berlin relayed the warning to Vienna. And still later came these words: "We must earnestly and emphatically urge upon the consideration of the Vienna cabinet the adoption of mediation. . . ." The Germans now were seeking to undo the harm their careless promise of assistance had caused; but their Austrian allies refused to listen. An ultimatum from Berlin to Vienna, threatening non-support unless the Austrians did thus and so, was not sent. Such an ultimatum might have stopped the war; with what effect on German prestige later one can only sůmise.

What of France? Her responsibility for the war is less susceptible of proof than that of Germany, but possibly it may have been greater. Did the French give a blank cheque to Russia and, unlike their German neighbor, fail to protest its cashing? There is not a scintilla of documentary evidence to prove this, but there is circumstantial evidence to indicate its possibility, perhaps even probability. As far as we can judge France did very little to stop the war. A long telegram, somewhat ambiguously worded, was sent to Russia from Paris on July 30 which stated that it would be "opportune" for Russia not immediately to take steps which would give Germany a pretext for "a total or partial mobilization." In no sense of the word, however, could this message be considered a veto on Russian mobilization or even, for that matter, a solemn warning. Poincaré, the French president, does not seem to have been disturbed by the course of events and Isvolski, at that time Russian ambassador at Paris, even gloated over the situation, claiming afterward that he had brought on the war.

Isvolski's words, however, need to be discounted heavily; his previous career had not heightened his reputation for truthfulness. On the other hand, Poincaré was visiting St. Petersburg at the time of the assassination and the French President at that time had lauded the Franco-Russian alliance. Furthermore, the French ambassador at the Czar's court in his memoirs let slip a most interesting account of how the Russians informed him of their mobilization and how it made him *sursauter* (jump) with excitement since he knew this meant war. But the Frenchman warned his informant that he, Paléologue, was only the political representative of the French government and that any information concerning military matters should be reported not to himself but to the French military attaché.

To England a fairly clean bill of health may be given, up to at least Germany's declaration of war against Russia. Sir Edward Grey, foreign minister, did his best to preserve peace by suggesting first, direct mediation between Russia and Austria, and secondly, a conference of the ambassadors of Germany, Italy, France, with himself in London. The first of these proposals was unwelcome to the French, who were willing enough to have mediation between Serbia and Austria but not between Russia and Austria, since they were afraid that would weaken the Triple Entente; and the second was vetoed by Germany, who felt that a conference consisting of France, England, Italy, and Germany would result in a three-to-one adverse vote, since the Germans had no confidence in the good faith of the Italians. Beyond this Sir Edward Grey did little; but on the other hand, what could he have done? It has been suggested that he might have stopped the war by a direct threat to involve England in it on the side of France and Russia unless Germany bridled Austria; that he might have informed the French that England would not fight unless the Russians ceased to mobilize; that he might have made a direct appeal to Austria, based on England's ancient friendship with that country. Whether any of these three lines of action would have borne fruit it is impossible to say. Sir Edward was but one member of the British cabinet and the others were only partly informed on foreign affairs. The members of the cabinet were aware of the exchange of letters between Grey and the French ambassador which had taken place two years earlier (see p. 27) but this was not true of the House of Commons, ultimate source of authority in Great Britain in which were many pacifists. Sir Edward, therefore, was no free agent.

From the first of August, however, the date of the German declaration of war against Russia, the foreign policy of England was more open to question. Was that country in honor bound to France in case of war? The French were quite certain that she was and the French ambassador at London asked Grey if England was willing to erase the word "honor" from the dictionary when he refused to commit himself. Then, on August 2, the English recognized limited liability, at any rate, when they guaranteed the French coast against naval attack from Germany—the result of the exchange of letters. But beyond this was England obligated to stand by France? Nobody knew, least of all the Germans, who were very curious to discover and besought Sir Edward again and again for information but without result.

On August 4, British qualms were laid at rest by the invasion of Belgium. Here again Sir Edward refused to state in advance what England's position would be and the Germans had to guess at it. They took a chance and lost; but of course they might have gone through Belgium anyway in their desire quickly to dispose of the French.

England certainly was under treaty obligation (as was Germany) not herself to violate Belgian neutrality; but whether she was under obligation to fight other countries to prevent it is open to question. Such, presumably, had not been the belief of Gladstone when, during the Franco-Prussian War he had made supplementary treaties with France and Prussia agreeing to war against France should France violate Belgium and vice versa. England, it was noted, made no protest against the violation of Luxembourg's neutrality, yet her obligation to prevent such an act was similar to her obligation to Belgium. It is of course possible to argue that Britain interpreted her Belgian obligations purely in terms of self-interest. Belgium was on the seacoast and Luxembourg was not. In the days of Philip II of Spain, in those of Louis XIV of France, and in those of Napoleon Bonaparte she fought to prevent the Low Countries from falling completely into the maw of any great European power. Self-interest now indicated that she do likewise; that is evident. None the less, in so doing, England did support, and ultimately help to rescue, a small nation which, innocent of all war-mongering, was in no way responsible for the world conflict.

CHAPTER II

FIRST WORLD WAR (1914-16)

GERMANY was the foremost military power in Europe. In peacetime the Kaiser had in the neighborhood of 800,000 troops actually with the colors; but owing to her reserves Germany was able to put under arms nearly 5,000,000 men and still leave a sufficient number of civilians for necessary industries, transportation, and agriculture. Her ally, Austria, was more poorly organized. At the outset she was not able to mobilize more than 2,000,-000, although as time passed her large population enabled her to conscript larger numbers.

Russia, on paper, was the most important foe of the central empires. The Czar was reputed to have 1,500,000 Russians in barracks, even in days of peace. At mobilization this total was lifted to 5,000,000, and behind these were indefinite further millions if arms and officers could be found.

France, with a population two-thirds that of Germany, maintained a peace army approximately equal to that of her rival, and on paper slightly larger. Owing to rigorous conscription, trained reserves were large, and the Third Republic faced the crisis with rather more than 3,700,000 soldiers; but behind them was only two-thirds the manpower east of the Rhine.

As for the British Empire, its white population was approximately equal to that of Germany. If the continental system of conscription had held in the United Kingdom and her dominions, King George could have mobilized 4,000,000 or more troops. As it was, England, still clinging to her old professional army, had perhaps 250,000 regular troops when the crisis came, 160,000 of whom had been allocated for an expeditionary force.

Finally, Turkey and Italy had respectively 200,000 and 300,000 peacetime troops, and about 1,000,000 and 1,500,000 more subject to mobilization.

It thus became evident that battles in this war were apt to be unimportant unless hundreds of thousands were involved. Repeatedly in the first World War the fighting swayed continuously along enormous fronts with nearly 2,000,000 men at each other's throats. In the forty-seven days of the Argonne battle the Americans alone had over 1,000,-

ooo engaged. By the time the war ended the British Empire had over 5,000,000 men in her armies and the United States nearly 4,000,000. And as they did so the continental powers, except Russia, exhausted every resource to replace their war losses. The upkeep of all these soldiers required civilian armies as well as military. The railroad workers, the metal workers, the miners of coal and iron, the sailors on transports, the workers in factories were as essential as machine-gunners in the trenches. Food problems became as important as those of high strategy. Economic waste was incalculable. "War" had once involved at most the hiring a few thousand mercenaries and the devastation of a few counties. "War" now involved throwing to the winds the principles of sound finance, floating bond issue after bond issue, multiplying bank-notes, spending on every conceivable object from heavy artillery to foreign press propaganda.

Everywhere it was assumed that when the war was over the foe would do the paying; everywhere, also, the working class was kept from striking by constant increase in pay as well as by promises of "a new day" after victory. The war affected the home of nearly every man and woman and the diet of nearly every child. It was to cost over 7,000,000 lives and was to spread poverty, disease, and starvation throughout most of Europe.

No less noticeable were innovations in military method. Before the fighting it was understood that the new rapid-firing field pieces and the infantry magazine rifles had rendered old-style tactics almost impossible; but it required the test of experience to prove the utility of heavy artillery, the diabolical efficiency of machine-guns. Airplanes had been recognized as useful for scouting, but it took the war to prove their possibilities as bomb-throwers. In 1873 an American had invented a device for restraining cattle—barbed wire—that had proved valuable for military purposes in the Russo-Japanese and the Balkan wars. Now it was to assume enormous importance. Without the aid of barbed wire the four-year deadlock from the Channel to Switzerland might have proved impossible. As the war advanced certain other new factors came into play. In 1914 the submarine was an experiment, regarded by some as a dangerous toy, by others as an irresistible craft. In practice it proved neither. Once having learned to deal with it, warships were fairly safe from its attacks; but from 1915 on it became a matchless destroyer of commerce. The automobile and the auto truck now made their début in war, and after two years came the armored caterpillar car, the tank, a moving fort which crossed trenches, crushed barbed wire, and drove a highway for advancing infantry. And also there was poison gas, at first sent drifting upon the wind and then later flung at great range in artillery bombs.

THE SCHLIEFFEN PLAN AND THE FIRST MARNE

Their theory of warfare required the Germans to take the offensive immediately. They were outnumbered by Russia and at the onset had little or no advantage over France; but superior organization, equipment, and speed in mobilization could be relied on during the first few weeks to offset their foes' heavier numbers. The great General Staff at Berlin was under no illusion as to the fighting quality of its Austrian allies, but it had perhaps overestimated the ability of the Vienna generals to hold the defense against Russia. In their own abilities the Germans felt supreme confidence. The older Moltke had died in 1891, having devoted the last twenty years of his life to rendering his war-machine increasingly effective, and after him Count von Schlieffen, as chief of general staff, had continued the endless preparation for the next war. Under his direction a meticulously detailed plan had been made ready for the invasion of France by way of Belgium. Within forty days after the declaration of war the French armies were to be enveloped, then annihilated, and the German host was to pour into Paris. Meanwhile, the Germans would stand on the defensive in the east with about one-fourth of their troops, but the moment the French had been rendered impotent the superb German railroad system would shift most of the Kaiser's divisions to the Vistula. Deprived of her ally, feeble in her industrial development, demoralized by Czarist misrule, Russia would sue for peace. England was discounted. She might, possibly enter the war and land 100,000 troops in France; but it was thought they would arrive too late to save Paris. After France was done for, and with Russia crying for mercy, then Germany would negotiate with the mistress of the seas, or fight her, as the occasion might warrant.

The Germans, with this plan in effect, dashed to the war like salmon to the sea. For forty-three years their war-machine had been perfected for this vital moment; all was ready, not merely guns and ammunition but enough field-glasses for every officer, and any quantity of proclamations urging Poles to rise against their Russian oppressors, for use when the German armies turned against Warsaw. The troops left Berlin assured victors with "Pleasure trip to Paris" chalked upon their transport cars. Widely circulated was the alleged saying of the Kaiser, "By Christmas we will be home."

As soon as war was declared, German troops entered the neutral grand-duchy of Luxembourg despite the protests of its helpless government. Belgium's turn came quickly. On the morning of August 4 the Germans swarmed across the border by horse, automobile, bicycle, and on foot. All had their weapons ready, the chauffeurs driving with one hand, a cocked revolver in the other. By night the good folk of Liége were awakened by a cannonade, the German field batteries exchanging their first salvos with the forts around the city.

The violation of Belgian neutrality was no surprise, not even to the Belgians. The latter had long ago taken marked precautions to defend their own neutrality. Their engineers had built seemingly impregnable forts around Liége, Namur, and Antwerp. Liége would halt invaders from Germany, Namur those from France, and Antwerp would be a haven of refuge for the Belgian army if overwhelmed in the field. But the German experts remembered the dictum of Clausewitz, "the pit of the stomach of the French monarchy is between Paris and Brussels." The best available military road into France lay across Liége province—therefore they would take it.

The Germans came on with the speed of the wind. Liége withstood them a few days, but the mobile howitzers of the German army pounded the Belgian forts into powder, and by the 20th of August the invader was before Namur. Five days later this Belgian stronghold was in ruins and France lay open.

The French, meanwhile, acted unwisely. Instead of rushing to the aid of the Belgians, they attacked the Germans in Alsace, captured a few villages, and for a short time the city of Mulhouse. And now they were forced to confront the Teutonic tide at its crest, with only the help of some 70,000 British regulars thrown across the Channel. But the British "Tommies" and their French allies at least did not repeat the mistake of 1870; they were not surrounded. For ten sweating, bloody days they fought a rearguard action, frequently half-starved, and nearly dead with fatigue and loss of sleep. On came the Germans, too fast perhaps for their own good. By the 5th of September the First German Army under Kluck was at Meaux, fourteen miles from Paris. The French government was transferred to Bordeaux. Paris seemed doomed.

Then came the counterthrust, the first battle of the Marne. It began with a French attack on Kluck's right wing, so fierce that he was compelled to deplete his left wing to reinforce his right. By so doing, he left a gap between his left wing and the Second German Army, and into that gap drove the French and the well-nigh exhausted "old contemptibles" of England, as the British dubbed their own regulars. There was now a wedge between the First and Second German Armies, and both were forced to retreat. Such, in major outline, was the turning point in the first Marne, a sanguinary battle which really stretched almost all the way from Paris to the eastern frontier. For the Germans it must be said that the Schlieffen plan never was carried out, since Kluck's army had been short of several divisions withdrawn for the German armies facing Russia. For the Allies, for the first time since the war started, came a taste of victory. They now pursued the enemy but could not catch him. Safe behind the Aisne River, the Germans dug themselves in.

Before the end of September the main conflict shifted to the north— to French Flanders and to Picardy. Hither dashed the British army, and as many French divisions as well, in a race to the sea, striving to crowd around the German right flank and to squeeze the Germans out of western Belgium. In this the Allies failed, and again the German artillery and superior organization stemmed retreat. King Albert, with the Belgian field army, was holding out hopefully behind the forts of Antwerp; but when the Germans fell upon him there were no troops available to help except a few brigades of British marines, and Antwerp fell. The Belgian field army retreated to the mouth of the little River Yser, to a tiny strip of Belgian land which it was to hold as long as the war lasted. The French and British meanwhile came up in time to cover the Channel ports, and as they did so the Germans tried to blast their way across the northern seacoast of France. Ypres, an old Flemish city, stood in their way. Its defense fell mainly on the British. For days the situation remained indescribably dubious as thousands fought in a mud-sea. By bulldog courage the British held on until the exhausted Germans quit. Early in November the first battle of Ypres ("Wipers," the Tommies called it) came to an end and the great deadlock on the western front began.

The War in the East

Meanwhile, across all the seven thousand and more miles from Kurland to Kamchatka, millions leaped to arms at the behest of the great white Czar. His war-machine seemed operative; there were cannon and munitions in sufficiency for a short war; there were competent generals, and in the Grand Duke Nicholas there was a commander-in-chief of ability. Without German aid, Austria would have been helpless before the eastern blast, and within two months Cossacks would have galloped through Vienna.

Russia, however, had a weak frontier. The great Polish salient could be attacked simultaneously from north, west, and south. On the two Prussian sides the Germans had a network of strategic railroads, but there was nothing to equal them on the two Russian sides of that very artificial boundary. Despite this handicap the Muscovites mobilized with a rapidity that disconcerted Vienna and Berlin alike. The danger to France was recognized at Petrograd, and an instant effort was made to divert Germany's attention. By the middle of August a Russian army under Rennencampf forced the frontier and was in full advance on Königsberg. A second army under Samsonov struck northward from Russian Poland into East Prussia. At the very moment when the Germans rejoiced over their victories in Belgium there was a rush of terrified refugees into Berlin. The Cossacks were devastating East Prussia and alarmists were saying that the German soldiers must retreat to the line of the Vistula.

The Kaiser then summoned Hindenburg, a retired general, known to have made a close study of the system of marshes and barriers created by the Masurian lakes on the eastern frontier. While seated at a café in Hanover, he received a telegram appointing him commander-in-chief in East Prussia. His chief of staff was a younger general, Eric Ludendorff, who had already won fame before Liége. The two leaders had been placed in a partnership which was to influence the whole course of the war.

Hindenburg had inferior numbers, but he trusted to lakes and swamps to prevent Rennencampf and Samsonov from joining forces. Within a few days after his appointment he sprung his trap. Caught in the treacherous lake district, entangled in swamps and forests, the Russians were assailed furiously on their flanks. By the end of August Samsonov's army had been practically destroyed in the four-day battle of Tannenberg in which Hindenburg took 70,000 prisoners. Meanwhile, Rennencampf saved his own army only by precipitate retreat. Germany rang with the praises of Hindenburg and Ludendorff, who henceforth became the trusted heroes of the empire.

But if Prussia flung back the Muscovites, not so with Austria. The high generals of Francis Joseph, who had contributed so vigorously to forcing the war, were even below the modest standards set for Hapsburg efficiency. Late in August they undertook to invade Serbia and were repulsed ignominiously. And now, even as Hindenburg closed in on Samsonov, two of the Czar's best commanders, Ruzsky and Brusilov, entered Galicia. They met with feeble resistance; Lemberg and a great part of Austrian Poland passed under the Czar's power; and in Petrograd the Russian victories caused rejoicings that effaced the mourning over Tannenberg.

Thus began the long tragedy of the campaigns on the eastern front, costing more in human loss and agony than even the wars of gods and titans in Picardy and Champagne; for here there was no long deadlock along a stabilized war zone, and enormous armies, sweeping backward and forward over wide regions, carried all the work of the devil with them.

After Tannenberg the Germans did their best to relieve the pressure on Austria by a drive on Warsaw. The Russians put up a skilful and stubborn defensive. Twice the Germans penetrated deep into Poland, but twice Russian valor and winter mud forced them back. The year 1914 closed with the Germans holding about one-quarter of Russian Poland, but with the Russians themselves holding nearly all of Galicia. They were pressing through the passes in the Carpathian Mountains and threatening the plains of Hungary; they were dangerously close to Cracow, the stronghold and key position at the western end of Austrian Poland; and they were blockading and starving out a large Hapsburg army, in a great entrenched camp around Przemysl. Germany thus defeated Russia, and Russia, Austria.

Nevertheless, by December, 1914, Russia was in dangerous plight, despite the bravery of her soldiers. Nearly all the ammunition accumulated in the arsenals had been shot away, and the munition plants were inadequate for replacement. There was a growing shortage of all the tens of thousands of things which modern warfare requires and which only a great industrial country can provide. As early as October, 1914, the general at the head of the Czar's artillery is alleged to have gone weeping to the war minister: Russia, he said, would have to make peace owing to shortage of ammunition. Never before had the lack of sea-doors counted so terribly against what was apparently a mighty empire. The Baltic was closed by the German fleet. Only a trickle of supplies could come in via the White Sea, frozen half the year, or via Vladivostok and the Trans-Siberian. The Black Sea route was closed by the hostility of Turkey. If, however, the water-gates at Constantinople could only be opened, then Russia would be brought in contact with her allies once again; munitions would flow into Russia, and from that country would come surplus grain needed in the west. We turn now to efforts to open them.

GALLIPOLI

When the war-clouds broke there were two German warships in the Mediterranean. The Allies assumed that they would run for shelter into the Austrian Adriatic, but instead they made for the Dardanelles. Not by accident had they steamed toward Constantinople. The Young Turk rulers had already given secret pledges to Berlin, and late in October, without any declaration of war, a combined German-Turkish fleet bombarded Odessa. The Czar replied by declaring war on Turkey, an action followed by France and England. Vast prospects were thus opened, thanks to the supposed influence of the Sultan as Calif of the Moslem world, of an extension of the war to the east; and in Berlin there was now cheerful talk of the invasion of Egypt and confident prophesies that the invasion of India would follow.

Around Turkey soon raged unlimited warfare. During the winter of 1914-15 there was fierce fighting in the Armenian mountains along the Caucasus frontiers. A Turkish attack on the Suez Canal ignominiously failed, and the British declared a direct protectorate over Egypt; but the Straits of Constantinople were, of course, now sealed to Russo-British commerce. The munition situation in Russia was already giving great anxiety in London, while on the other hand the food situation in England was growing uncomfortable, and the release of the great South Russian crop would assist enormously. Would not the defeat of Germany be hastened if the Dardanelles and the Bosporus were in Allied hands?

The Turkish forts at the Dardanelles were considered fairly formidable, but Liége, Namur, and Antwerp had not proved too difficult for the new artillery. In London the civilian head of the British admiralty was Winston Churchill, full of driving energy and high imagination. The British war office was under Lord Kitchener, who had won a remarkable reputation in the Boer War. It was to Kitchener's great credit that from the outset he knew that his country must fight by land as well as by sea, and that the war would be long drawn out— "Three years," he predicted. But he was autocratic, self-centered, refused to accept colleagues except as lieutenants, concentrated too much business in his own hands. Kitchener was alive to the desirability of opening the Straits, but he already had promised the French heavy British reinforcements in Picardy, where there were great hopes of breaking the German front as soon as spring opened. He had no surplus troops available. Nevertheless, he let Churchill work out the problem of a British naval attack, although a land force would be needed in any case, if only to hold Constantinople after the navy had conquered it.

No enterprise that actually failed ever came nearer to justification. Its success would have convinced all the wavering Balkan kingdoms that the Allies were bound to triumph. The capture of Constantinople might have averted the surpassing agony of the Russian Revolution, might have rendered American intervention in the war unnecessary, and by mercifully ending the struggle two years earlier might have rendered a great service to Germany herself. All this hung on the razor-edge of fate during the spring and summer of 1915.

To reduce seacoast batteries by naval bombardment had hitherto been considered impractical, but the guns of the British battle-ships were very powerful. Churchill was overwhelmingly convinced of the desirability of forcing the Straits, and although his naval experts in London questioned, they did not veto the enterprise. The older battle-ships of the British navy could be used, and their loss would not weaken the dreadnaughts holding the North Sea against Germany. Turkish forces at the Straits were weak. As late as February, 1915, when the naval attack began, they numbered only 20,000, and were ill organized and widely scattered; and the forts were but poorly supplied with ammunition. There were 36,000 French and British troops available, and these once flung ashore, the defenders would have been demoralized and the fall of the forts well-nigh certain. But Kitchener neither sent his soldiers in time nor warned Churchill that if the British navy failed the British army could do nothing. There were orders and counter-orders to the forces on the transports. There were intrigues with Greece (then neutral) to get a Greek army corps to strike a blow at its old foe, the Turk. On February 19, the British ships, aided by a French squadron, attacked the outer forts of the Dardanelles and silenced them. Mine-sweepers penetrated far up the waterway. In Constantinople panic reigned, and the Sultan's harem packed for a hasty trip to Asia.

The first progress was not followed up promptly. Not until March 18 did the Franco-British fleet at length attack the inner forts, the key to Constantinople. The bombardment proved less successful than was hoped; the batteries were not permanently silenced. Late in the day, two British and one French battle-ship struck mines in an area supposed to have been swept clear, and were sunk. Nevertheless, it was assumed everywhere that the naval attack would be renewed, and there is now competent evidence that the Turks were nearly at the end of their heavy ammunition. Before the end of another bombardment their guns would have been silent, while the garrisons were fleeing for their lives.

But the British fleet had lost two battle-ships. It had been contrary to all naval axioms for ships to contend with forts. The technical heads of the admiralty had discovered that Kitchener was now willing to try to force the Dardanelles by a land attack, and were only too happy to pass the task on to the British army.

The Turkish forces were still few in number, and British troops had already been sent to the Dardanelles under Sir Ian Hamilton. But he found on arriving before the Straits that the transports had been so carelessly loaded that nearly everything needed for landing a great force and for fighting hard battles had been buried at the bottom of his transports. His ships therefore sailed away ingloriously to the nearest adequate harbor, Alexandria, to reorganize their cargoes; and the Turks had ample warning of what was coming.

A month earlier the Turks on the Gallipoli peninsula, covering the Dardanelles, could have been defeated by a swift attack; in March they were more numerous but still weak. If Hamilton had disregarded the advice of his routine-ridden quartermasters and had landed his men at that time, he might have entered Constantinople. But by April 25, when he made his actual attack with 60,000 men, his foes were ready. A capable German general, Liman von Sanders, had been put in command of the Turkish troops, and under him were many German technicians. Sanders had nearly as many men as Hamilton, and on the defensive the Turks were doughty fighters.

Despite underwater entanglements of barbed wire and shores lined with machine-guns, the British threw themselves ashore near the tip of the peninsula. Their losses were terrible (nearly 19,000 in the first two weeks' fighting), but they made good their landing. To penetrate inland to the heights of Krithia was another matter, and soon the British and the Turks were looking at each other across two lines of trenches in a deadlock as complete as that in France. Hamilton nevertheless clung on, waiting reinforcements without which nothing could be done.

Meanwhile, in London, owing to a cabinet crisis, Churchill ceased to be civilian head of the admiralty, and all projects for another naval attack lapsed. Kitchener ordered more troops to the Dardanelles, but they made haste slowly. The cabinet reorganization in Britain, it was alleged, caused three weeks' delay in sending reinforcements. At length, late in July, Hamilton had forces that three months earlier might have brushed the Turks aside like gossamer. But now, although he commanded 120,000, Sanders had approximately as many. The British, thanks to their command of the sea, were able to make a surprise landing at a new and unguarded point. A wholly new force was landed at Suvla Bay, up the peninsula to the north where (if success attended) the Turkish strongholds on the Straits could be overwhelmed from the rear. But it was now too late; the Turks were ready. Sanders had arrived at the scene of action, together with his able lieutenant, Kemal Bey (later dictator of the post-war Turkish republic). The magnificent valor of the English, Australian, and New Zealand troops wore itself out against the stubborn and skilful resistance of the reinforced enemy. By August the great attack had spent itself with none of the key positions taken. Hamilton had lost about 30,000 men in a single week and the entire campaign collapsed. Altogether the British lost at Gallipoli over 100,000 killed or wounded. The prestige of the great empire was shaken by this policy of "too little and too late." If the British admirals had heartily seconded Churchill; or if Kitchener had promptly sent a small army; or if the latter with less delay had sent a large army, Constantinople would have fallen, Russia would have been reached, and the duration of the war much curtailed.

Japan and Italy Enter the War

Meanwhile, two new allies joined the Belgians, the French and the British. They were Japan and Italy, the former declaring war on Germany in August, 1914, the latter declaring war on Austria in May, 1915.

Concerning the entrance of Japan, little need be said. The statement of Count Okuma, head of the Japanese government, may be discounted. According to him,

not only in the Far East, but everywhere else that may be necessary, Japan is ready to lay down her life for the principles that the foremost nations will die for. It is to be in line with these nations that she is at this time opposing and fighting what she believes to be opposed to these principles. Japan's relation to the present conflict is as a defender of the things which make for higher civilization and a more lasting peace.

The real reason was quite different. Japan saw a golden opportunity and took it, an opportunity to avenge herself on Germany for past hostility by promptly taking the German colony of Kiauchow. True, Japan was bound to England by treaty, but only in case of an unprovoked attack upon either England or Japan in India or eastern Asia. Germany was making no attack there, and as Winston Churchill afterwards acknowledged, "no clauses in the Anglo-Japanese treaty entitled us to invoke the aid of Japan."

The case with Italy was much more complicated. That country was a member of the Triple Alliance; she also, as we recall (see p. 20), had made agreements with both England and France, thus having a foot in both camps. That she was entitled to remain neutral was juristically clear, since Austria had not consulted Italy in the critical June and July of 1914 in regard to her Serbian policy, thus breaking the terms of the Austro-Italian alliance. This in itself, however, scarcely justified Italy in deserting her old allies and siding with their foes; for Italy in this war simply put herself up at auction and sold herself to the highest bidder.

It was a long-drawn-out auction, lasting for months. The Germans were willing to offer Italy a good deal of Austrian territory for Italy's neutrality, and the Austrians reluctantly agreed to the cession of the South Tyrol, occupied mainly by Italians. But the Allies offered far more for Italy's active participation on their side—not only the South Tyrol but the city of Trieste, a large part of the Istrian peninsula and of Dalmatia, Avlona in Albania, islands in the Aegean seized by Italy in her war with Turkey, and compensation in Africa if England and France annexed territory there after the war. This bargain was ratified by the treaty of London (April, 1915), and in view of its terms it is interesting to note what Woodrow Wilson told the Italian Chamber of Deputies on his visit to Rome in 1919. "Then back of it all, and through it all," said the President of the United States, "running like the golden thread that wove it together, was our knowledge that the people of Italy had gone into this war for the same exalted principle of right and justice that moved our own people."

Italy thus projected herself into the conflict, but a great disappointment awaited her optimists. For political and sentimental reasons her campaign was directed against Trieste. Therefore her general, Cadorna, was destined to throw away his men, ultimately by hundreds of thousands, on the Austrian positions along the Isonzo and in struggling to capture the Carso plateau which commanded Trieste. All through 1915 the Italians continued this warfare, spending themselves against rock and ice with but trifling advance.

RUSSIAN DEFEAT, BULGARIAN ENTRY, AND SERBIAN COLLAPSE (1915)

During the winter of 1914-15 the German military came to a new decision: they would stay on the defensive on the west and strike at the east on the blood-soaked plains of Poland. The German drive there in 1915 was under the command of one of William II's ablest field commanders, Mackensen, and it speaks well for the ability of the Russian generals that, despite a ruinous lack of ammunition, they were able to call back their troops involved in the Carpathian passes and to conduct an orderly and stubbornly contested retirement. No soldiers ever endured more ruthless punishment than did those of Nicholas II, last Czar of the Russias. During the first three months they fired more shells per day than their factories put out per month. They had plenty of men but no rifles to put into their hands, and only by the use of the bayonet could they halt the German advance. By September, 1915, the Russians had lost all they had gained and were driven back far beyond their own frontiers.

The Central Powers now turned their attention to the southeast. Throughout 1915 Bulgaria had been listening to offers from both sides, and had the Allies won instead of lost the Gallipoli campaign, Bulgaria would probably have yielded to their wooing. The Allies were hampered, however, by the auction held at Sophia; they had less to offer Bulgaria than the Central Powers. There was nothing, indeed, very tempting that they could offer, except Turkish territory which Bulgaria did not care for, and possibly a port on the Aegean, provided Greece might be willing to cede one in return for promises of Turkish land in Asia Minor.

What Bulgaria did want, and want very much, was Macedonian territory annexed by Serbia in 1913. Since Serbia was an ally of France and England, this land could not be decently ceded to Bulgaria without Serbian approval, and this the Serbs stanchly refused to give.

BALTIC SEA

WEST PRUSSIA
DANTZIG

GERMANY

POSEN

POSEN
(GERMAN POLAND)

SILESIA

BOHEMIA

KÖNIGSBERG
GUMBINNEN

EAST PRUSSIA

ALLENSTEIN

TANNENBERG

THORN

Masurian Lakes

VILNA

GRODNO

RUSSIA

Vistula River

WARSAW

LODZ

RUSSIAN POLAND

CRACOW

Dunajec

PRZEMYSL

GALICIA
(AUSTRIAN POLAND)

Carpathian Mts.

AUSTRIAN EMPIRE

HUNGARY

BREST-LITOVSK

PINSK

Pripet Marshes

KOVEL

VOLHYNIA

LEMBERG

BUKOVINA

RUMANIA

THE RUSSIAN FRONT
1914~15

+ + + + THE BATTLE LINES AFTER
THE RUSSIAN DEFEAT IN 1915

No such difficulty confronted the Germans. They were quite willing that Bulgaria should annex the Serbian conquests of 1913 in Macedonia. The Bulgars liked the German offer, and in the summer of 1915 it seemed as though Germany was winning the war. Therefore, they allied themselves with the Central Powers and agreed to hit at Serbia from the east as the Austro-Germans struck that unfortunate country from the north.

This meant the collapse of Serbia. The victorious Mackensen, in command of the Austro-German army, overran North Serbia in October, 1915, and the Bulgars almost simultaneously occupied their chosen districts in Macedonia. The Serbs, fighting bravely, retreated to Montenegro and northern Albania; but rapidly they were driven out

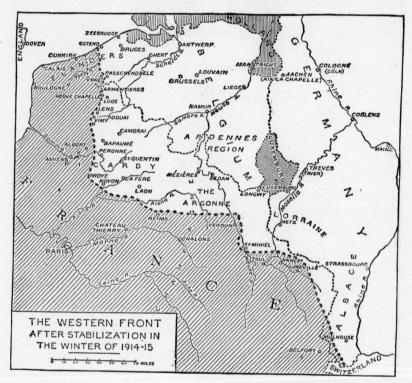

THE WESTERN FRONT
AFTER STABILIZATION IN
THE WINTER OF 1914-15

of these mountain fastnesses. By the end of February, 1916, all that was left of the Serbian army was encamped on the Greek island of Corfu, safe for the time being because the Allies controlled the seas.

The Western Front (1915-16): Verdun

Along the western front, meanwhile, approximately four million men were deadlocked. Thousands of cannon and tens of thousands of machine-guns sustained these hosts. Air combats were incessant. There were elaborate trench raids and reconnaissances, but so numerous were they that they seemed but a part of the day's work.

At long intervals would come battles, offensives designed to master large sections of the hostile lines. These contests were usually quite alike: intense artillery fire, the rush of infantry over earthworks and barbed-wire entanglements partly destroyed by the guns, the counter-fire of the enemy, trenches won, the rush of the enemies' reserves, counterattack, bombs, and bayonets. Then the offense would spend itself and the section of the front where it took place would settle down to standardized petty slaughter. Almost every such offense succeeded—that is, if pushed resolutely it could win a few lines of trench. Almost every such offense was defeated—never coming to a genuine break-through so that the enemy could be chased back into the open country. And all this went on continuously for nearly four years until new weapons and new warriors brought a return to something like a war of maneuver.

Both the French and the British tried their best in 1915 to break through, the former in the Artois district and in Champagne, the latter at Neuve Chapelle and at Loos. The results were disappointing. It proved possible to demolish the German front-line trenches with comparative ease, and even to capture parts of the second line. But behind this there was always a third, bristling and formidable. Before the artillery could be moved forward to destroy this barrier, the Germans were always able to hurry forward reserves and to concentrate their own batteries on the chief points of danger. These inner trench lines simply could not be stormed.

Then, as 1916 opened, the Germans in turn tried to recover the offensive on the western front. Germany had her own iron and coal; she was also managing by desperate economies to get along with her own cereals; nevertheless, the pressure of the British sea-blockade, like the finger on the wrestler's windpipe, was stifling the economic life of the Central Powers. Bread cards had been introduced long since, and many staple articles disappeared altogether from the German table. There was an especial absence of butter, lard, and all forms of fat. For innumerable things, like coffee, the German chemists provided ingenious *ersätze* (substitutes), but they were mostly sorry stuffs. Want of copper, rubber, cotton, and lubricating oils threatened. By the end of 1915 Germany was already undergoing privation. British sea power was throttling her; there must be a decisive counterstroke in the near future or the war would be lost.

A possible move might be more submarines at sea, and another was a telling blow by land. Russia had been driven back about as far as it was safe to drive her. She must be left for the time being to her own miseries. Troops could be released from the eastern front for another offense against France; and if France could possibly be driven out of the war a reckoning might then be had with England. The Germans did not, however, undertake a break-through on the main western front; they had learned the lesson of the Allies' failures of 1915. They resolved rather to win a startling success on a limited front; namely, by the capture of Verdun, the greatest of the barrier fortresses on the eastern frontier of the Third Republic. The moral shock to France, it was hoped, when she found herself unable to save this great *place d'armes*, hitherto also considered impregnable, would put her in a mood to negotiate.

Verdun had, indeed, been a pivotal position in the French military scheme since the beginning of the war. It was not an ordinary fortress but a vast entrenched camp, held by 175,000 men, and would never succumb to a mere park of siege-guns as did Liége and Namur. The Germans proposed to attack on a grand scale, using nineteen divisions. Preparations conducted with meticulous Prussian care were put through as secretly as possible and the French had only vague rumors of a coming German offensive. Where it was to strike none could tell.

The attack began with a bombardment, up to that time the most severe recorded in history. It was maintained incessantly for nine hours, during which time the French trench system seemed annihilated and "the craters made by the huge shells gave all the country-side an appearance like the surface of the moon." The German infantry then went forward. But there were still Frenchmen alive in the midst of the chaos and their artillery in the rear had not been silenced. The German advance at some points was halted and elsewhere stopped. Both sides fed into the furnace of this incessant battle men, guns, and ammunition without stint, and around Verdun raged the fiercest and most sanguinary struggle of the entire war.

The great General Staff could not now break off its undertaking if it would. To relinquish the attack on Verdun meant a confession to the world of a great defeat. Every trench-line, salient, and petty hillock along the front of twenty-two miles became the scene of titanic conflict. Certain forts and important positions were taken and retaken, until their soil was drenched with blood. The famous cry of the French privates as this contest blazed hotter, *"They shall not pass!"* was more than a battle-cry; it was the expression of an inflexible will. The spirit of the defense was summed up in a scribbling found upon a wooden casing of a bomb-proof shelter in the French firing-line, near the center of the battle:

Mon corps à la terre,
Mon âme à Dieu
Mon coeur à France.

Against this spirit, although the German Staff flung its armed men into the conflict as recklessly as it might fling coal into the furnace, victory was impossible. By sacrifices that threatened to cripple their war-machine, the Teutons, nevertheless, pressed the attack through April and May, for the prestige of Prussian militarism was at stake before its own people. By June the Germans were slowly working their way toward the inner defenses, but the French commanders were now simply sparring for time. They knew that Britain was about to make an unprecedented counterthrust. On July 1, 1916, began the battle of the Somme, and the German lines in Picardy were in deadly peril.

THE SOMME

The British Empire had roused itself slowly. As 1915 advanced the English realized that the war was not a grandiose sporting event on which they had placed unfortunately large stakes, and they buckled down to the task before them. A larger part of the front was taken over from the French, and behind that sector there was an accumulation of guns and ammunition calculated to outrival the German concentration at Verdun. The results were imposing; the country was ready for the major British offensive of 1916, the only one necessary, so the optimists thought, to win the war.

It began with the British raining shells, not on a narrow sector as at Verdun, but over a wide front, and it continued for six days. Then, on July 1, the British assaulted twenty miles of trenches just north of the Somme River while the French struck along the ten miles directly south. The artillery fire was withering, but the destruction wrought was incomplete. Much barbed wire was cut; but many machine-gun nests were still in action, and the German artillery in the rear had not been silenced. At the northern end of the battle line the British met with a stone-wall resistance and their assault there failed. On the south they made gains of one or two miles deep on a front of about seven miles. The French, under the skilful direction of Marshal Foch, met with somewhat greater success and with smaller losses—but nowhere was there a break-through in sight. So ended the first day of the Somme. But it was only the beginning. Haig and his men kept it up. The battle of the Somme was continued well into November, sometimes conducted fitfully, sometimes with rekindled fury. By the end of that time a wedge had been driven into the German lines along a front of over forty miles. The Allies had captured 350 guns and 65,000 prisoners, and the whole German loss was around 600,000. But the British losses had been about 450,000, the French 200,000. Technically, the Somme was an Allied victory, but it had brought no decision, and it was not able to avert one more great disaster to the Allies in the east—the overrunning of Rumania.

RUSSIA AND RUMANIA (1916)

Russia had been beaten in 1915, but not to her knees. In the winter of 1915-16 there was a revival of patriotic enthusiasm, particularly on the part of the bourgeoisie, who supplied the armies with fresh ammunition and supplies; the troops had kept their courage and morale, and the Czar had able generals. The result was that for the last time the war-machine which Peter the Great had originally fathered went forward to new campaigns with some enthusiasm.

The Central Empires had considered the Muscovites so completely defeated that in May and June, 1916, the Austrians started an offensive from the Trentino against the Italians. But no sooner had it got under way than the Russians struck once more and the danger to Italy was averted. The best troops of Francis Joseph had to be hurried back to Galicia, and even these would never have sufficed to prevent the undoing of Austria had not sixteen divisions of German veterans been withdrawn from the western front to hold back the Slavic deluge.

There was no such elaborate trench system in the east as in the west, and a war of maneuver, with rapid shifts of scene, was entirely possible. On June 4, 1916, all the replenished Russian cannon thundered and a few hours later their infantry charged. The brunt of the attack fell upon the Austrian armies commanded by the Archduke Joseph Ferdinand, and he, like so many Hapsburg commanders, let himself be caught unprepared. Many of his troops were Czechs with no zeal for the Vienna rulers, and they surrendered in droves. Within a few days the Russians had advanced fifty miles and had taken 70,-000 prisoners. Bukovina was again overrun and the Russians seemed on the point of taking Galicia. Then German help arrived, "like lime to strengthen wet sand," and Austria was saved.

It is difficult to visualize "these dim, weird battles of the east" when, with imperfect equipment and by sheer reckless energy and disregard of sacrifices, the Russians strove to force a decision by means of a million men at constant grips with nearly as many Germans and Magyars. By August this Russian attack had nearly spent itself; the ammunition accumulated during the winter was nearly exhausted; and within the czardom there were signs of demoralization. But the Russian successes were taken by the unfortunate Rumanians as merely an earnest of a still fiercer winter campaign, and late in August, 1916, the Rumanians forsook their neutrality and entered the war on the Allies' side.

The Rumanians, like the Bulgars and the Italians, sold themselves to the highest bidder. The Central Powers were quite willing to offer Bessarabia, Russian territory in which Rumanians were numerous; and the Allies were quite agreeable to giving away Transylvania, Hungarian territory in which Rumanians were in the majority. Of the two regions, Transylvania was by far the more valuable. But the Rumanians wanted more from the Allies; they sought the province of Bukovina, north of the Carpathians and a part of Austria; they demanded also the Banat of Temesvar, across the Danube from Belgrade in Hungary, occupied in part by Serbs as well as by Rumanians. Since the Serbs likewise desired the Banat, the Allies were unwilling to pledge it to Rumania, but they finally did so with certain qualifications—and Bukovina as well. Hungary, meanwhile, despite suggestions from Berlin, resolutely refused to cede any Hungarian land to the Rumanians, and the latter chose the side of the Allies, since their bid in the international auction was highest, and since Russian arms (temporarily) were victorious in the early part of 1916.

For a moment there was panic in Vienna and Budapest, and jumpy nerves in Berlin. For a fortnight the Rumanians advanced. Then the Germans struck hard. From the south, Mackensen, the conqueror of Serbia, drove into the delta lands of the Danube, the Dobruja, with a mixed host of Germans, Bulgars, and Turks, and the invasion of Transylvania was met by a German army after the Rumanians were fairly involved in the Carpathian passes. The invading columns were caught and routed. By gallant exertion most of the Rumanian units fought their way home again, but they were unable to save Bucharest and the national capital had to be shifted to Jassy in Moldavia. The northern third of Rumania was saved, temporarily, from the victors; but nothing could take away the effects of this new defeat of the Allies. The Central Powers, by this last success, reduced their eastern front enormously; they had access to the Black Sea; they had won in Rumania wide grain lands and great oil-wells which promised to ease their famine in food and fuel.

The War in Asia Minor and Mesopotamia: Kut-el-Amara and Bagdad (1916-17)

Only in one zone did the Allies make progress—the eastern frontier of Turkey. The Caucasus armies of Russia, substantially an independent force, routed a considerable Turkish army as early as January, 1915. A year later General Yudenich, leading 170,000 Russians on one of the most remarkable winter marches on record, forced his way through snow-blocked passes, fought a three-day battle with the Turks, and flung them back on Erzerum, key to Armenia. Within a month almost all of Armenia was in his hands. But here again advance was halted. The British attack on Gallipoli failed and Turkish reinforcements could now be hurried over from the west. The Muscovites were at the end of their lines of communication and were ill sustained from home; to penetrate farther into Kurdistan was impossible.

The British, however, were pushing the Turks hard from the south. The importance to King George's empire of the mouth of the Tigris-Euphrates rivers, the logical terminus for the Bagdad Railroad, was obvious. Almost immediately after Turkey thrust herself into the war, or was kicked in by the Germans (it was hard to say which), the British seized the delta-port of Basra and early in 1915 began pushing up the twin rivers. In September General Townshend captured Kut-el-Amara, the chief town along the river route to Bagdad. The capture of that old Saracenic capital was not essential to the safety of the empire, but the government of India, which had backed the expedition with men and money, urged Townshend to press forward. In November he was approaching the city of the Califs when, near the ruins of the capital of a yet older empire (Ctesiphon of the Persians), he collided with a superior Turkish army. Driven back on Kut, he was besieged by the Turks. An expedition was sent up the river to succor him, but it was held up by the winter rains and floods which turned the Tigris valley into swamps. Kut held out until April, 1916, when Townshend surrendered with 9,000 starving troops. It was now necessary for the British to take Bagdad or to lose face completely throughout all Asia. Heavy reinforcements, sorely needed in other fields, were therefore hurried to the miasmic, super-heated vallys of old Babylonia. The Bedouin desert tribes, who hated Turkish misrule, were carefully conciliated, and no mistake was made a second time in despising the foe. In February, 1917, Kut was retaken, and the next month a British cavalry column swung into Bagdad.

The capture of Bagdad restored throughout the East that British prestige which Kut and Gallipoli had shaken.

The War at Sea

Hardly had the first cannon thundered in Belgium before the influence of British sea power began to tell. Like a great bunker covering the German harbors, the physical length of Great Britain lay across the path of her foe to the outer ocean. German ships could find the Atlantic only through the vigilantly guarded Straits of Dover, or by a circuitous route to northward and westward, well through the North Sea. The British "Grand Fleet," the most powerful force of dreadnaughts in the world, mobilized far to the north at Scapa Flow, an island-locked area in the windy Orkneys. Here, for years, it maintained its chief base, unseen usually, but not unfelt.

The German battle-ships might, indeed, have crossed the North Sea and even possibly have thrown men ashore in the southern part of England, but (irrespective of their reception on land) the Grand Fleet would have been down upon their flanks at once. Never, in the whole war, did the Germans risk such an adventure. If they had tried to reach the Atlantic by way of Norway and the Shetlands, their foes would have been on them all the more quickly. As for the Channel passage, it was not held by a great force of battle-ships, but by sufficient lesser craft, sustained by mines, submarines, and coast batteries, so that any attempt to seize it would have been delayed until long after the arrival of the Grand Fleet. The result was that, most of the time, Tirpitz's costly creation, the German "High Seas Fleet" never saw the high seas at all, but lay in harbor watched by British spies.

So far as North Sea warfare went, excluding the ravages of mines and submarines, the German fleet had to confine itself to sudden raids on the east coast of Britain. A squadron of very swift cruisers would dash across the four hundred miles of gray water, drop shells on seaports, kill a number of civilians, and scurry back to safety. The British naval intelligence service, however, was efficient; and on January 24, 1915, when a raid of this sort was attempted by four German battle-cruisers, they found themselves suddenly in action with five more formidable British vessels, commanded by Sir David Beatty. The latter well sustained the traditions of Nelson, and the Germans fled incontinently toward Heligoland. Beatty pursued, and might have won a complete victory had not his flagship the *Lion* been partially disabled in her engines. As she dropped from the chase, his second in command failed to press the pursuit and the Germans got away, but with the loss of their slowest large unit, the battle-cruiser *Blücher*.

Meantime, on the distant oceans, the scattered cruisers that Germany had stationed in remote corners of the world had been chased down by their superior foes. For three months, the *Emden* ranged the Indian Ocean, an effective commerce ravager, until she was destroyed by the more powerful Australian cruiser *Sydney*. More dramatic was the career of the German squadron under Admiral von Spee, who found himself, with two good armored cruisers (the *Scharnhorst* and the *Gneisenau*), and several lighter vessels, on the coast of China. Japan had declared war, and was closing in upon Kiauchow; but Spee would not let himself be caught in a hopeless blockade. As became a courageous seaman, he struck out boldly across the Pacific, heading around Cape Horn; perhaps his intention was to slip back to Germany, per-

haps to give aid to the Kaiser's African colonies and to a party of South
African Boers who had blazed up in short-lived insurrection against
Britain. His voyage was a reckless, desperate venture, in any case, but
for a while it was crowned with success.

The British knew that he was approaching the coast of Chile, and
sent thither Sir Christopher Cradock, with a light squadron. Reinforcements were on their way to Cradock, but when he discovered the Germans off Coronel, south of Chile, he knew it was the part of English
seamen to fight, and he went down with his two largest ships. The third
escaped to tell the tale and London acted instantly—British prestige
on the seas was at stake. Two heavy battle-cruisers, and other formidable craft, were sent, full speed, to the South Atlantic.

Spee rounded Cape Horn, and endeavored to work his way north-
eastward. On December 8, 1914, he approached the Falkland Islands,
to raid what he imagined was an unprotected British colony, when,
above the headlands, he saw the tripod masts of the battle-cruisers.
The German admiral fled instantly toward the open sea, but his case
was hopeless. The battle-cruisers chased him with superior speed, then
sank his ships with superior gun power. One of his light cruisers (the
Dresden) got away but was later destroyed off Juan Fernandez in the
Pacific ("Robinson Crusoe's" island). Spee himself, refusing to strike
his flag, perished in the icy waters of the South Atlantic, as did nearly
all his crews. There were now practically no German warships at
large on the seas except one or two isolated commerce destroyers.

JUTLAND

On May 31, 1916, in the North Sea not far from the Danish coast
came the one great naval engagement of the war—the battle of Jutland.
Admiral Scheer, in command of the German "High Seas Fleet," tired
of inaction and tempted by the presence in home waters of large numbers of submarines, came out from behind his mine-fields, sending
ahead on scouting duty a squadron under Admiral Hipper, the nucleus
of which were five swift battle-cruisers. The British, aware that the
Germans were out, steamed forth to meet them. Their "Grand Fleet"
under Admiral Jellicoe was at Scapa Flow in the far north, but Admiral
Beatty, with a formidable squadron of battle-cruisers supported by
four modern battle-ships, was at Rosyth near Edinburgh. Both fleets
sailed to meet the Germans, but it was Beatty who first came in contact with them.

It was a haphazard meeting. The smoke from a Danish trader drew
Beatty eastward and Hipper to the west as their two fleets joined in
action early in the afternoon. In this first encounter the Germans were

victorious, two large British battle-cruisers being blown up and a third seriously crippled, while their foe suffered no major casualty. Nevertheless, Beatty presumably would have won the day as his heavier and relatively slower battle-ships swung into action, had he not suddenly found himself confronted with the main German fleet under Scheer toward which Hipper skilfully had maneuvered.

Thereupon Beatty fled north, notifying Jellicoe of his discovery. Jellicoe instantly steamed south to join Beatty, who was pursued by the Germans, and about six P.M. the two main fleets met. Scheer was ignorant of Jellicoe's presence and the superiority of the British metal and speed was assured. Almost before the German admiral realized it, the shells of his enemy began to drop around him. It was now the turn of the Germans to run for safety, one of their larger ships being wounded unto death and several others being thoroughly mauled. Jellicoe, however, was cautious in pursuit. He, unlike Beatty, would take no chance of losing his great ships to torpedo attack. Night was approaching and the setting sun gave the Germans an advantage, since it threw the British ships into sharp outline, while the gathering dusk partly concealed their own. When daylight came the Germans were no longer to be seen. Skilfully and incontinently, they had worked their way through the British fleet and had withdrawn to the safety of their mine-fields. Britain remained the mistress of the seas, albeit a somewhat shaky one.

In tonnage and men the British losses outnumbered the German two to one, but in the long run the British surely won that day. In order to defeat them Scheer would have had to destroy enough ships to render the British blockade ineffective and to give his own fleet free access to the Atlantic. This he failed to do. Jellicoe's task was far easier. He had only to preserve his own strength in order to maintain the status quo. Had he been able to destroy the German fleet, thus paving the way for raids along the German coast and for entrance to the Baltic he might have shortened the war. As things stood he could lose but not win the war in an afternoon. Cool-headed man that he was, he chose that course which preserved British naval supremacy at the least possible risk.

CHAPTER III

FIRST WORLD WAR (1917-18)

A FTER two and a half years there had been no decision. Except on the high seas, the Central Powers had been the more successful; but the Allies clung on doggedly and their superiority in man-power and matériel sooner or later presaged triumph unless events wrested victory from them. In 1917 unforeseen events did take place, but fortunately enough for the Allies they counterbalanced each other; one, the entry of the United States into the war, was a portent of disaster for the Germans; the other, the withdrawal of Russia from the conflict, a body blow to Allied hopes.

Public opinion in America, on the whole, sided with the Allies, a fact accounted for by sympathy for Belgium, historic friendship for France, "cultural ties" with England, and, as the war continued, by the fact that the Allies bought profusely in the United States. Certainly America did not want to see her best customers become bankrupt. On the other hand, German-Americans were numerous in the United States and so, too, Irish-Americans, traditional haters of England; those facts, together with the stretching of the laws of blockade in which England speedily engaged, tended to neutralize pro-Ally sentiment.

The United States, however, no sooner began vigorously to contest British interference with American commerce than she faced the submarine issue. On February 4, 1915, in retaliation, it was alleged, for the British blockade on foodstuffs, a "war zone" order appeared from Berlin: German submarines were ordered to sink enemy merchantmen, especially in the waters around the British Isles, even if their crews and passengers could not be rescued; furthermore if neutral ships entered the "blockade waters," they "could not always be prevented from suffering from attacks meant for enemy ships."

The destruction of unarmed ships without first rescuing crews and passengers was contrary to universally accepted doctrines of international law, and President Wilson protested formally against the German war-order zone, saying that the United States would hold Germany to "strict accountability" for harm done to American lives and property. During two months nothing serious happened. Then, in March, 1915, an American citizen perished when the British merchantman *Falaba* was torpedoed by a submarine, and on May 1 the American ship

Gulflight was torpedoed off the Scilly Isles with the loss of eleven lives. On the same day there was published in several American newspapers a formal notice warning United States citizens against traversing the war zone in ships of Britain or her allies. Within a week following came the submarining of the *Lusitania*, a British merchantman, unarmed but carrying ammunition. Upon this occasion 128 American citizens were drowned.

What would President Wilson do? He had urged his countrymen to be neutral "in both thought and deed"; he was a believer in international pacifism; and he was not particularly interested or conversant with foreign affairs. Some have thought that it was inevitable for the United States to favor the Allies because of the huge loans and credits obtained by the Allied governments in the United States with the tacit approval of the American government, and that the submarine issue raised by the sinking of the *Lusitania* was secondary in importance. This, however, remains a mere surmise. The fact remained that the Germans had violated important rights by sinking without warning an unarmed merchantship and that American lives had been lost. Clearly, action of some sort by the American President was in order.

Most German-Americans, Irish-Americans, and pacifist-Americans urged at this time, and continued to urge, that American citizens were not justified in running the risk of embroiling their country in war by insisting on their legal rights to travel on Allied merchantmen. They could either stay at home, or if business called them they could travel on such occasional liners as were entitled to fly the American flag or on ships of neutral nations—Dutch, Spanish, Danish. A compromise course of action, suggested but not followed, was for the United States to distinguish between Allied merchantmen carrying munitions and those that did not. On the former Americans should travel at their own risk; on the latter they would receive the full support of their government. The President, however, stiffly determined to stand by his original position. In his note to Germany he demanded disavowal and reparation for the sinking of the *Lusitania*; and he furthermore asserted that the United States "would omit neither word nor deed" in asserting her full rights under international law.

The Germans, on June 6, issued a formal order to U-boat commanders not to sink large passenger liners without warning; but nevertheless they had no mind to submit to Wilson's dictates and all through the summer of 1915 the sinkings by U-boats, with occasional peril to American lives, continued. As a climax, in August the British liner *Arabic* was torpedoed, and on board were Americans, of whom two perished. By this time, however, Bernstorff, German ambassador at Washington, convinced his home government that there might be limits to Wilson's patience. The submarine warfare, as then conducted, did not seem paying sufficient military dividends to be worth braving American belligerency. The German government, therefore, gave pledge not to sink passenger liners without warning, provided they did not try to escape or resist capture.

The situation thus drifted until the spring of 1916. There were various submarine sinkings, but none sufficiently serious to cause a break. An obscure negotiation was conducted by the President's confidential agent, Colonel House, endeavoring to get the Allies to enter into peace conversations with Germany; if Germany did not prove reasonable America (the suggestion ran) would "probably" enter the war on the Allies' side. Nothing came of this, perhaps due to the word "probably." House also tells us that he got the British reluctantly to agree to take wheat off the list of contraband, provided the Germans in turn would abstain both from gas attacks and submarining merchantmen. And nothing came of this either, perhaps because of intimations to Berlin from Washington, relayed by the Austrian ambassador to the United States, who had the impression from former Secretary of State Bryan that there was no likelihood of the United States fighting over the submarine issue.

On March 24, 1916, the unarmed passenger steamer *Sussex* was sunk by a U-boat in the British Channel. Twenty-five of her passengers were Americans. On April 18, the United States reminded Germany of the *Arabic* pledge, recited how it had been broken, and warned Germany that diplomatic relations would be severed if a change of policy did not take place immediately. Severing diplomatic relationship would inevitably ere long have led to war, and Germany was not ready for that. Her U-boats were still few, and she expected to win the European contest by land battles. If her military chiefs had profound contempt for America, Bethmann-Hollweg, still clinging to office as imperial chancellor, realized something of what might come to pass. He had still strength enough in the empire's counsels to force a change of policy. A promise was given that merchant vessels "were not to be sunk without warning and without saving human lives," although the clause was added that if Britain persisted in her blockade Germany reserved "complete liberty of decision." For the time being, the crisis was ended. The U-boats confined themselves largely to "cruiser-warfare," i.e., attacking Allied merchantmen from the surface and giving the crews a chance to escape in their boats.

During 1916, America went through the throes of a presidential election. Wilson's campaign managers capitalized the intense desire of a great part of the American people to keep if possible out of the European holocaust. *"He kept us out of war!"* was the campaign slogan with strong implications that if Wilson were reëlected he would continue the policy. In October, 1916, Bernstorff telegraphed to Berlin, begging that the U-boats conduct themselves moderately because "all Mr. Wilson's hopes of reëlection are based exclusively on the fact that, according to opinion over here, he has kept the United States out of the war."

In Germany, Wilson's reëlection was hailed as the triumph of the pacifist party in America. Meantime, the demand for "unlimited submarine warfare" against Britain was growing. Great numbers of U-boats had been built, and naval confidence in their efficacy was high. The food and fuel situation was causing intense hardship to German civilians. The peasants endured tolerably, but the thirty-five to forty million town dwellers had to go through the winter of 1916-17, "not on bread, meat and potatoes, but on fodder turnips." The army chiefs, the all-powerful circle around Ludendorff, accepted the assurance of the admirals that the U-boats, ruthlessly used, could speedily blockade England, create a worse food shortage than existed in Germany, and end the war abruptly in the Teutons' favor. Public sentiment strongly backed this opinion,—if this policy angered America so much the better; by a sham neutrality she had grown rich selling munitions to Britain—and now let her iniquitous profits cease! As Bethmann-Hollweg later testified, "the imagination of the people was fired . . . until [everywhere ruled] the honest conviction that the 'U-boat war' was the key to our salvation, and that he who opposed it was a traitor." The chancellor argued against this feeling, as he had argued against the military chiefs in 1914, but a second time, he was pathetically helpless.

WILSON'S PEACE PROPOSALS (DECEMBER, 1916): GERMANY RESOLVES ON "UNLIMITED SUBMARINE WARFARE" (JANUARY, 1917)

As 1916 approached its end, President Wilson, finding himself ever nearer the event he dreaded, sought peace by mediation. Germany forestalled him by capitalizing her Rumanian successes with a formal offer of peace to her enemies on December 12, but in very general terms. There was no renunciation of any claim upon Belgium; no repudiation of schemes of annexation clamored for by the Pan-German societies and the great Rhine industrialists. The Allied powers vehemently declared it was an insincere offer, intended to divide their counsels, and to entangle them in ruinous intrigues.

The President, however, persisted. On December 18, he issued a formal appeal to both coalitions to state their war objects in order to see if any reconciliation were possible. The answers from *all* official spokesmen were such that, from every belligerent capital, immediately came the protest that the attitude of the foe made agreement impossible. Nevertheless, behind the scenes the President's *alter ego* and "Père Joseph," Colonel House and Bernstorff, were striving desperately to secure some basis for possible mediation. The ambassador later made vehement claims that, if given a little more time and better support from Berlin, he could have induced America to put such pressure upon the Allies that they could not have refused to negotiate. On January 22, Wilson addressed the United States Senate in a somewhat mysterious speech on the necessary conditions of a "League for Peace," to be established when hostilities should cease. The war, he declared (to the anger of all Allied sympathizers), must first end in "peace without victory."

It was the last attempt to uphold his policy of neutrality which inexorable events were rendering impossible. Already in late December, 1916, the German admiralty had drawn up a report that if "ruthless submarine warfare" were permitted England would be starved out and forced to capitulate. Such warfare, it held, was "the proper means of winning the war; moreover it is the only means to this end." Bethmann-Hollweg, German chancellor, had grave misgivings, but his objections were overruled and the report was adopted at a conference at the German General Headquarters wherein the masters of the sword expressed bitter contempt for the civilian minister and his fears concerning the United States. "We are counting on the chances of war with the United States," cried Hindenburg, "and have made all preparations to meet it. Things can not be worse than they are. The war must be brought to an end by the use of all means as soon as possible." The actual rulers of Germany having thus spoken, a strictly secret order was issued in the Kaiser's name on January 9, 1917. "I order the unrestricted submarine warfare to be started with full energy on February 1."

On January 31, 1917, the German ambassador transmitted to the President of the United States the formal notice that, beginning the next day, in a wide ocean zone around Britain, France, and Italy, all navigation, that of neutrals included, would be "forcibly prevented." "All ships met within that zone will be sunk." A single American steamer a week was to be permitted to go to Falmouth, England, provided it was "painted with three vertical stripes, one meter wide, alternately white and red." Three days later Bernstorff received his passports and incontinently left Washington, while, simultaneously, Gerard was recalled from Berlin. In an address to Congress, Wilson, it is true, affected still to disbelieve that Germany would "pay no regard to the ancient friendship with America" and push matters to extremity, but this hope died a few weeks afterward. On February 28, the war feeling was blown still hotter by the publication of a note (actually intercepted and deciphered by the British intelligence service), sent in code on January 19, by Zimmermann, the imperial foreign minister, to the German minister to Mexico, proposing an alliance between that country and Germany, the latter country to finance Mexico and help her to "reconquer the lost territory in New Mexico, Texas, and Arizona, taken from her by the United States."

The last stand of the pacifists in the United States Senate was to hold up by a senatorial filibuster a bill authorizing the President to arm merchant vessels crossing the war zone; but the President, after denouncing "the little group of wilful men," armed the ships on his own authority. Followed then the Zimmermann note, seemingly a new evidence of German duplicity. On March 21 the President summoned Congress, and on April 2 he recommended they declare war. According to Wilson, Americans were to "fight for the ultimate peace of the world, and for the liberation of its peoples, the German peoples included. ... The world must be made safe for democracy." The congressional resolution, however, which declared war on April 6 spoke in somewhat less exalted language, reciting as grounds for action the wrongs committed on Americans by the German government.

The American entry came none too soon. On April 9, Rear-Admiral Sims of the American navy reached England to confer with Jellicoe, then first sea lord of the admiralty. The British admiral handed his American friend confidential tables showing that the U-boats had sunk of Allied and neutral shipping in February, 1917, 536,000 tons, in March 603,000 tons, and that the estimated figures for April would be in the neighborhood of 900,000 tons. Sims was astounded. "It looks," he said, "as though the Germans were winning the war." This also was Jellicoe's opinion, unless the losses could be stopped, and that, too, in the immediate future.

Germany thought so, too, and loud were the boasts rising in that country. "Today England sees herself in a situation unparalleled in her history," announced Helfferich, imperial secretary of the interior. "Her food supplies across the sea disappear as a result of the blockade which our submarines are daily making more effective. We have considered, we have dared. Certain of the result, we will not allow it to be taken from us by anybody or by anything." Ludendorff, meanwhile, told Bernstorff in May, "We are going to end the business by the U-boat war inside of three months." In actual fact, by April, 1917, Britain was within two months of the end of her food supplies.

Fortunately the American navy was in better shape than the army, and able to help immediately. On May 4, six slim, gray destroyers glided up the Irish coast and entered Queenstown harbor. It was "the return of the *Mayflower*"—the first token that the United States was really in the war. By July 5 there were thirty-five American destroyers off the coast of Ireland. The American flotilla in British and French waters grew all too slowly for the anxious observers; but it grew and was of decisive use.

Prior to May, 1917, the Allied navies had fought against the submarines by means of destroyers and light patrol boats cruising wide areas of sea, and by nets and mine-fields laid out across the British Channel and certain other important stretches of water. By such means it had been possible to give heavy naval craft fairly good protection. But the merchant vessels had had to shift for themselves. Now, however, the British admiralty determined to try sending large fleets of merchantmen through the war zone under naval convoy; and it was to large extent owing to the increasing numbers of American naval craft in European waters that the institution of the convoy system became possible. Thanks almost entirely to it and the devices which the naval escort could use (especially the "depth bomb") as soon as a U-boat periscope was sighted, the submarine campaign was first checked, then defeated. On the 20th of May, 1917, the first experimental convoy of merchantmen reached Britain from Gibraltar, safely defying the submarines, and apparently marking the relaxation of the sea-blockade of England.

The submarine danger was by no means ended; but it was held at bay. The first six destroyers at Queenstown multiplied presently into a great armada of American patrol boats; in 1918 an enormous barrier of mines, partly of American manufacture and laying, was stretched across nearly the entire upper entrance to the North Sea. Without serious hindrance, vast quantities of supplies, and over 2,000,000 United States soldiers were conveyed to Europe. Months before the German chiefs called for an armistice, they knew that the "ruthless U-boat campaign" had recoiled upon their own heads; it was a failure. America was entering the war effectively and the sole hope of German victory lay in exploiting Russia and breaking the western military front before the new ally from overseas arrived in force.

But if the American navy was thus able from the outset to contribute to the Allied cause, the army was not. Volunteers could have been had in droves, but the government decided upon conscription, and machinery to enforce it had to be created. Training camps had to be constructed and civilians sent to them could not be converted into soldiers overnight. A very small expeditionary force could have been despatched to Europe immediately, but such an act would draft officers and potential noncoms out of the country at a time when they were needed desper-

From LET THERE BE SCULPTURE *by Jacob Epstein (pub-lished by G. P. Putnam's Sons, New York, 1940).*

EPSTEIN'S BUST OF LORD JOHN FISHER. (See page xv *ante*.)

From Louis Raemaeker's A CARTOON HISTORY OF THE WAR

THE GRAVES OF ALL HIS HOPES

ately in the training camps. Therefore the American army did not contribute very much to the cause of the Allies in 1917.

THE FALL OF THE CZARDOM (MARCH, 1917)

Meanwhile, at Petrograd "dark influences" were at work. In 1916 the Czar removed his capable foreign minister, Sazonov, and in his place put the Czarina's protégé, Stürmer, an arch-reactionary, suspected of being pro-German. The atmosphere was charged with intrigue, and anything seemed possible. Rasputin, "religious impostor and libertine," continued to lord it over the Czarina, and therefore over the Czar, and his lodgings were popularly known as "staff headquarters." The Czarina wrote constantly to her husband of "our friend," and on one occasion urged the Czar to comb his hair with Rasputin's comb in order to get strength to resist the demands of his ministers.

It proved impossible to prevent the Duma from assembling and in November, 1916, Miliukov, the liberal leader, handled Stürmer so roughly that the latter slunk out of office. Everywhere, in the army, in the navy, in the industries, in the railways, in finance, and in the food supply there was mismanagement and corruption. Abuses barely endurable in peace became intolerable after two years of war. "If the German general staff," reported a commission to the Duma, "were allowed to direct our internal affairs and the conduct of the army it would do exactly what our government is doing."

But Stürmer had only been a figurehead for others more malevolent. There was Rasputin, whom the upper nobility hated, rightly fearing for the honor of their wives and daughters. They gave him a party, at which a group of princes too exalted even for the Czar to punish first gave him poison and then, when he failed to succumb, shot him dead. His body was flung under the ice of a canal and the slayers, not incorrectly, informed the police that they had killed a dog. But the Czarina mourned him passionately, and he had a saint's funeral.

Rasputin was a symbol, not a cause. Nicholas and his wife remained. The last Czarina had used all her influence from the commencement of the war to prevent her husband making liberal reforms. Her letters to Nicholas while he was pretending to command the army mingled personal pleadings with religious exhortations. "Don't laugh at silly old wifey; for she has trousers on unseen. Your faith has been tried and you remained firm as a rock. For that you will be blessed." She sent him holy images and ikons to strengthen his resistance to the liberals who were trying to reorganize Russia's broken war-machine. "We are living in the hardest times," she wrote late in 1916, "but God will help us through. Wifey is your staunch one, and stands as a rock.

behind you." And again, "Russia likes to feel the whip hand. How I wish I could pour my blood into your veins."

Thus Russia entered her year of crucifixion, 1917. The supporters of the government were growing fewer. The sacrifices of 1915-16 had shaken the loyalty of many of the higher officers. A number of nobles suggested a ministry which would enjoy public confidence, and there was talk of deposing Nicholas, even as the ill-starred Czars, Peter III and Paul I, had been deposed. As February advanced, the Speaker of the Duma waited on the Czar. It was time for plain speaking. Nicholas was informed that he could still save his throne if he would grant responsible ministerial government. If he did not do this, said the Speaker, there would be no further reports made by him to the Czar. But Nicholas dismissed the Speaker curtly without a word.

THE FIRST REVOLUTION (MARCH, 1917)

On Thursday, March 8, 1917, there was a gala performance in Petrograd at the Alexander Theater for the wealthy, while outside in the Russian cold long queues of women shivered before bakers' shops. In the Duma there was a perfunctory debate on the food supply and a few shops were looted. The next day the throngs in the streets were larger, angrier. Dense crowds seemed laughing, talking, always expectant. Cossacks patrolled the avenues but did not use their weapons. "You won't fire on us, brother," came from the crowds, "we want only bread." "No, we are hungry like yourselves," called back the soldiers. The city police, however, engaged in scuffles and arrested workingmen. On the tenth there were still greater crowds in the streets. Everybody was now asking, "What is about to happen?" The next day came street firing and some 200 were killed. A company of troops mutinied and refused to fire on the people. The Duma telegraphed a last appeal to the Czar at the front with the army. "Situation serious. Anarchy reigns in the capital. . . . It is absolutely necessary to invest someone who enjoys the confidence of the people with powers to form a new government. . . . Delay may be fatal." The Czar's ministers retaliated by ordering the Duma prorogued; but the deputies defied the order by refusing to disperse and by meeting elsewhere in the same building.

By dawn of March 12 the garrison of Petrograd had made up its collective mind; the troops would not obey the order to fire upon the city-folk. When certain regiments were ordered to send volleys into the crowd they shot their own officers. Presently, many soldiers headed an unorganized but very disorderly mob moving straight on the public buildings, and especially on the prisons where political prisoners were held. The only government now left in Petrograd was the Duma, and it threw itself between the city and anarchy. In great haste it chose an executive committee of twelve to act in its name until a provisional government could be set up.

Nicholas had been near the front when the tempest broke at Petrograd. Unnerved and away from his wife's influence, he at first hesitated. Then he started for the capital but revolting soldiers blocked the way. Two delegates from the Duma presently arrived and found the Emperor in his railroad carriage, "haggard, unwashed, and weary." The delegates informed him he must abdicate in favor of his son, with his brother Michael for regent. But Nicholas wept at the idea of "being separated from his boy." He demanded a sheet of paper, and drew up an abdication in favor of his brother the Grand Duke Michael. It was the last act of the czardom, for when the tidings reached Petrograd the city was in such a state that the Grand Duke, with obvious wisdom, declared that he could accept power only after it had been granted by a Constituent Assembly, elected by a plebiscite. So far as Russia had now any government at all, it was the provisional government headed by Prince Lvov, and composed of leaders among the liberal factions. The most advanced radical member was Kerensky, the new minister of justice—a "Social Revolutionary."

Simultaneous with this régime of moderates set up by the Duma, there was, however, another power, at first hard to estimate—the "Soviet (Council) of Workmen's and Soldiers' Deputies"—which desired passionately a republic, so far as it had any defined desires at all. For the moment, the "Soviet" (a roaring, gesticulating body) expressed faith in the provisional government. The armies and all the remote governments and provinces pledged allegiance. Nicholas II and his family faded out of view into captivity.

Russia seemed to have sloughed off the czardom without the miseries of the French Revolution and with relatively little bloodshed. The government seemed to be in the hands of moderate liberals, who would set up either a strictly limited monarchy, or, more probably, a democratic republic.

Spread of Anarchy (Summer, 1917)

The fall of the Czardom swept away those sanctions which hitherto had held together the empire. For the "Little Father," millions of peasants would fight and die; but for the provisional government there was no devotion—even though it did release political prisoners, restore autonomy to Finland, and introduce reforms. Prince Lvov and his colleagues who headed that government were convinced that a truly democratic régime could only be secured by first defeating the Prussian autocracy. But the nation had suffered terribly. The war had been the Czar's war. Now that the Czar was gone, let his war cease! The Russian people had no quarrel with the Germans. Constantinople, which had been pledged by the Allies, meant nothing to the Russian masses. Orders, issued by the Petrograd Soviet the moment the monarchy had fallen, destroyed discipline in the army, reduced officers to impotence, and practically placed the command with "Soldiers' Councils"—fantastic debating clubs. Soon two slogans began to be heard in the camp, in the village, and in city soviets (*a*) "self-determination," let every country decide its own future, and (*b*) "no annexations and no indemnities." By the middle of the summer the Russian war-machine was a wreck; in the farming districts the peasants thought about one thing only—how to seize the land of the proprietors; and in the cities the workmen, sullen and discontented, spent much more time in exciting talk than in working in the factories.

And now in all the villages and the little wooden *izbas* one potent idea came home to the *muzhiks*—the chance to complete the emancipation of 1861. The former serfs and their children had never forgiven the decision to leave to their former owners a large part of the farm lands. Now was the opportunity to seize them. "It was here that they sought their annexations and indemnities!" All the peasants knew of the war was that it had sent off their sons to fight with pitchforks against machine-guns and poison gas. The rural districts were soon everywhere in anarchy, the muzhiks seizing the estates of the helpless proprietors, and with all productive agriculture pershing amid rioting and confusion. From the demoralized army at the front, the soldiers (worried lest their neighbors at home take all the good land) deserted, literally, by hundreds of thousands.

In the cities, in the meantime, the workmen were for the most part socialists. They looked upon the revolution as their handiwork and they demanded drastic and immediate action toward the establishment of a socialist state. Particularly true was this of Lenin, leader of the more extreme socialists (the Bolsheviks), who had returned from exile in Switzerland in April through the kind assistance of the German authorities. Lenin was for immediate, instant peace. What he wanted was socialism in Russia, not victory over the enemy. He had but one enemy, anyway, and that was capitalism; he had no interest in the war, which he considered simply and solely as proof that international capitalism was in its death throes. The dawn of Messianic socialism had come and the end of the Russian bourgeois was at hand. Peace, bread, and land was his slogan, and this was the theme upon which he orated daily to the restless proletariat of Petrograd, spreading as he did so suspicion and hate of the provisional government.

As the army became more and more demoralized, and as discord grew at Petrograd, Miliukov, who had been provisional minister of foreign affairs, was forced to resign, since he had been committed to fight for Constantinople. The Duma had been elected by a very narrow franchise and carried no weight with the masses. Soon the virtual head of the government was Kerensky, hitherto counted a decided radical, but who, in any case, clearly realized the futility of trying to initiate a régime of democracy by opening the gates to the Hohenzollern.

Kerensky strove hard to combat the forces of disruption and anarchy; but he trusted too much to his eloquence and exerted no discipline over the army, where the soldiers were being taught by Bolshevik missionaries to distrust and hate their officers and to go back home and seize the old lords' acres. In July one Russian offense was staged against an unstable sector of the Austrian front. The first attacks were successful, but before a feeble counteroffensive the Russians simply ran away, trampling underfoot and killing the officers who tried to stay their headlong flight.

OVERTHROW OF KERENSKY: BOLSHEVISTS SEIZE POWER
(NOVEMBER 7, 1917)

While this went on at the front, at Petrograd the Soviet of Workers' and Soldiers' Deputies, among whom were a few peasants, was constantly arrogating to itself much more power and was falling ever more under the influence of Lenin with his gospel of "thorough." On July 14, the extremists tried to seize the government by force, but Kerensky had strength enough to stamp out the flames for an instant. Soon, however, the agitators were again at work; Russian industries became paralyzed; the peasants were not tilling the fields; and every wire and mail-bag brought to the distracted ministers new evidence of increasing demoralization.

In September, General Kornilov tried to force the provisional government to take round measures against the dissidents. A kind of military coup was projected, with Kerensky himself apparently supporting the scheme. But very many around him were fearful that a bold strike against the obstreperous Soviet would involve a return to the czardom. Kornilov was left unsupported and betrayed by men who had egged him forward. The coup failed and this was the beginning of the end.

Kerensky was detested by the Bolshevists, and as October advanced his position grew weaker and weaker. He frankly told the Western Powers that Russia was utterly weary and could play no active part in the war. The Bolshevists were now carrying on an active propa-

ganda everywhere, promising universal peace and utopia. Although
pledged to communism, their peace pledges pleased the peasants, who
looked only for a chance to enjoy the seized lands. The crash at last
came upon November 7, 1917, when the Petrograd garrison recognized
the authority of the "Revolutionary Committee" of the Soviets. Kerensky issued vigorous proclamations, but found himself almost without
armed supporters. Petrograd passed into the power of the Leninists
with very little fighting. Kerensky fled, tried to return with the aid of
a few Cossack squadrons too weak to recapture the city, and then disappeared completely. In Moscow the armed defenders of the provisional government were stronger; they yielded the Kremlin only after
severe fighting, whereupon the revolutionists proclaimed: "The provisional government has been deposed. The power of the state is now in
the hands of the Petrograd Soviet Workers' and Soldiers' Deputies."
And the Russian people were promised at once "the immediate offer of
a democratic peace, the abolition of rights of landlordship, the workers'
control of industry, and the establishment of a Soviet government."

Moves in Austria and Germany to Secure Peace (1917)

The war was now running into its third year, and another power
besides Russia was becoming weary. At Vienna, the new Hapsburg
emperor, the well-intentioned young Charles, was casting anxiously
about him. The fate of Nicholas II afforded little lasting encouragement, even if it eased the military situation. The Vienna ministers
knew that their ill-compacted government was cracking under the
strain and was likely to fly asunder. "It is no good telling me," reported Czernin, Charles's foreign minister, "that the monarchial principle is too firmly rooted in Berlin and Vienna for the monarchy to be
overthrown. This war has no precedent. If the monarchs do not make
peace in the next few months, then the people will make peace over
their heads; and then the waves of revolution will sweep away everything for which our sons are fighting today." Prophetic words, as were
others in a report which Charles caused Czernin to draw up and send
to William II himself. The Austrian case was stated plainly, "Our
military resources are coming to an end. We must begin negotiations
before our enemies are fully aware of our exhaustion. The burden on
our people is now intolerable. The bow is so taut that it may snap at
any moment."

Charles even went so far as to negotiate with France, telling Paris
that he would not sacrifice his country for the sake of a German
victory and that to get peace he would use his influence to support
"the just claim of France in relation to Alsace-Lorraine." But the

French promptly called attention to the claims of Italy; what concessions for her—not, of course, at Hohenzollern, but at Hapsburg expense? Charles could not bring himself to sign away Trieste and the Trentino. As for his pleadings with Germany, William II professed himself proud and confident—the U-boats were sure to win. The Russian news was increasingly favorable. The German people, tried and straitened as they were, had a loyalty to their government incomparably superior to that of Charles's Slavic subjects to the Hapsburg régime. In 1914 Austria had hustled Germany into the war; in 1917 Germany steadfastly refused to let Austria force a disadvantageous peace. So both monarchies together went down to ruin.

Meanwhile, in Germany Matthias Erzberger, leader of the powerful Catholic Center party in the Reichstag, hitherto an advocate of wholesale annexations and exploitations, astonished a group of colleagues by telling them that "the war could not be won." His reversal of attitude caused a sensation in inner political circles; and speedily his opinions leaked out when he introduced resolutions before the Reichstag. "The Reichstag strives for a peace of understanding and the permanent reconciliation of the peoples. With such a peace, forced requisitions of territory and political, [or] economic oppressions are inconsistent."

Such resolutions the great General Staff that now ruled Germany met with unconcealed anger and gnashing of teeth. Their particular rage was against Bethmann-Hollweg for having failed to maintain "the home front" against the enemy. The discredited chancellor now faded into private life. In his place the military autocrats set up a colorless Prussian official, Michaelis, who would at least do his masters' bidding. The Erzberger resolutions were passed by the Reichstag, but their effect was instantly destroyed by the announcement of the new chancellor that he accepted the proposition "as he understood it"—the time for shaking the hold of the war lords was not yet.

The French Offense of 1917 Fails: The Pope Proposes Peace

In France, also, there was, presently, great discouragement. The war had come home to the republic as it had not to Britain, nor even to Germany. Nearly all the fighting on the western front had been on French soil. Several of the richest and most populous departments were in the clutches of the enemy, and the youth of the country seemed bleeding away. The situation was so desperate that the French decided to make one grand, furious assault on the Germans, hoping, in conjunction with the British, to break the iron ring and to force the war into the open. There had been complete failure in 1915 and 1916 to accomplish this, both on the part of the Allies and on that of the Central Powers, but General Nivelle, successor of Joffre as commander-in-chief of the armies of France, was so buoyant and so optimistic that he persuaded not only his own government but that of Britain as well that it could be done.

Nivelle attacked in April on fifty miles of front between Soissons and the Suippe in Champagne. He was entirely confident that the first day of fighting would see his men in Laon. As a matter of fact, he flung his main strength upon the Chemin des Dames, along the Aisne, which the Germans had been laboriously fortifying for two and a half years. The first rush of the French attack enabled Nivelle to boast of taking 21,000 prisoners and 183 guns within four days; but his own losses had been appalling. Part of his battle orders had fallen into German hands, and Ludendorff and his lieutenants were completely ready. The French infantry found that their artillery had failed to clear the ground properly—they were mowed down by machine-guns, while they struggled with the unbroken barbed wire. Nivelle's casualties presently reached 107,000. The Germans were forced to cede valuable ground, but again no key positions were taken. There had been no break-through, and human energy could do no more. The Paris politicians were horrified at the profitless sacrifice; and on May 15, Nivelle was removed from command and replaced by the more steady Pétain. The new general had not merely to hold back the foe, but to restore the sorely shaken morale of the entire French army.

There had already been serious dissatisfaction among the French rank and file as to scanty leaves of absence, confusion in the medical service, and lack of many ordinary comforts, as well as reports from home of how munition workers, exempted from military duty, were getting fat wages, while the women and children struggled to wrest a living from the farms of the peasant conscripts. Now, in addition to great military discouragement, there were serious mutinies. Certain divisions near Paris almost broke out into a political revolution and "defeatism"—advocacy of giving up the fight and compounding with Germany—spread.

The secret of the mutinies was, in fact, so well kept that not merely did the Germans fail to learn thereof, but even the British and Americans. Nevertheless, the main situation could not be concealed. Russia was falling from the war. France was temporarily unable to push any offensive. Italy was very tired. American troops were coming slowly. On Britain had to fall the main burden of any real pressure upon Germany during 1917.

Under such conditions, in August, Pope Benedict XV tried to mediate. A gesture during the summer to bring the warring elements together by means of a conference of socialist leaders at Stockholm had failed, partly because of the suspicion that German forces were controlling the undertaking; partly because the Allies distrusted any movement under the auspices of socialists. The attempt of the Vatican met with greater respect but no better fortune. In substance, the Pope called on the warring nations to forget their losses and wrongs and to make peace on the status quo ante bellum. Something ought to be done, the pontiff suggested, as to Armenia, Poland, and the Balkans, and occupied territory should generally be evacuated. This would have released Belgium, but would have left Alsace-Lorraine to Germany. There was much well-intentioned wisdom behind the note, but the Allied Powers were angered at the calm method with which the Pope treated both coalitions as equally innocent or culpable; and the Vatican was charged with being extremely anxious about the fate of its old-time protectors, the Austrian and Bavarian monarchies. The result, therefore, was foreordained. Berlin answered with apparent cordiality: they would be happy to negotiate along the suggested lines. But President Wilson was selected by the Western Allies to be the chief spokesman. "The object of this war," he informed Pope Benedict, "was to deliver the free peoples of the world from the menace and actual power of a vast military establishment controlled by an irresponsible government which [had] secretly planned to dominate the world, and which was now waging war stopping at no barrier of law or mercy."

FLANDERS AND CAPORETTO

Despite the entrance of the United States into the war, the year 1917 was one of continued disaster for the Allies. The British were foiled in their offenses, as well as the French. Twice the former tried to break through and twice they failed. Their first offense came in Flanders, where, owing to unusual rain, the low terrain had been turned into a bog. A fair number of local successes were achieved, particularly at Paschendaele Heights, but that was all. The German grip on the Belgian coast and the coal-fields around Lille had not been broken. Then, later in the year, the British made a surprise attack near Cambrai, a surprise attack in more senses than one. This time there was no long artillery preparation: instead 400 tanks suddenly emerged from the haze of a November sunrise and went crashing through the German defenses, the infantry following. The use of tanks, begun at the Somme, was now vindicated; but unfortunately there were not nearly enough available, and a German counterattack won back most of the ground which the tanks had gained. Whereupon the western front settled down after this to another winter of local bombardments.

If the British were checked, the Italians were overwhelmed with disaster. During the summer of 1917 they had continued to beat on the Austrian defenses. Except for a short interval in 1916, they had always been on the offensive and they were so confident that this would continue to be the case that enormous quantities of supplies had been brought up to the head of the Adriatic between the Isonzo and Tagliamento rivers. No new bridges had been thrown across these rivers by which Cadorna's men must retreat, if defeated. The situation was dangerous unless dealing with an enemy who could safely be despised.

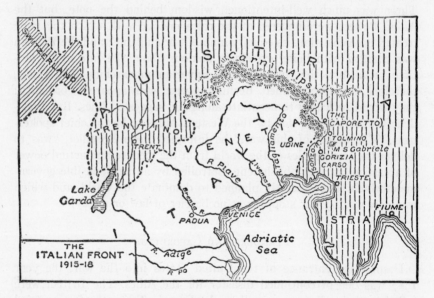

And there was another danger; the morale of the Italian army was running low. Few Italian peasants had any idea why they were at war; life in the Alpine trenches was very hard; comforts for the troops were even less in evidence than in France; and furloughs were difficult to obtain. From the outset Italian socialists had denounced the "capitalists' war," and now they redoubled their pacifistic propaganda. The peace proposals of Pope Benedict were taken more seriously in Italy than in most countries. When he described the war as "a useless slaughter," all the clericals in the kingdom seemed likely to agree with him, and their influence was widely extended.

Such was the situation when the Austrians commenced an offensive in the Isonzo Valley. From Tolmino northward that valley makes a sharp bend to the northwest, so that a passage of the river, in the neighborhood of Caporetto, brought the enemy directly upon what was the flank and rear of the Italian armies battling in the mountains east of Gorizia. From Caporetto, too, it was a relatively short and easy drive straight to Udine, the Italians' general headquarters. The line at this point was held by some of Cadorna's second-class divisions, in whom pacifist propaganda had been peculiarly active. It was at this point that the combined Austro-German army struck. The Italians went down almost by magic. Some held bravely; but they were simply overwhelmed as their fleeing comrades uncovered their flanks. At certain points the disaffected troops greeted the enemy with white flags, while reserve battalions in the rear refused to march forward. The result was that the whole Italian front near Caporetto was broken and the Teutons poured in as through a sluice.

Despite heroic struggles, it became evident that the Italians had sustained not a defeat but a national disaster. The gains of twenty-nine months of war were gone instantly. The southern armies along the Isonzo, near Gorizia, had to retire post-haste, or be cut off to a man. The roads and bridges for the retreat of three armies were not ready; and the great quantities of munitions near the front, of course, became spoils for the victor.

As it was, Victor Emmanuel's armies struggled back to the first protecting barrier, the line of the Tagliamento, with staggering losses, but found themselves too demoralized to hold the bridgeheads of that unimportant river; nor could the next stream from the Alps to the Adriatic, the Livenza, be defended more than a few days. The third river, before retreating clear to the great Adige, was the Piave. It was not a good military obstacle. In many places, the stream was not deep, and the line to be defended was very long; but the alternative to holding the Piave, was surrendering nearly all the magnificent province of Venetia, including Padua and Venice, to the invader. On the Piave, therefore, after a loss of nearly 250,000 prisoners, and of over 3,000 cannon, the retreating army turned at bay. If Cadorna had erred grievously in failing to provide for such an attack, he acquitted himself skilfully in the retreat, and salvaged more from the wreck than at one time seemed possible.

The crisis brought to the Italians aid which had been denied for their offensive. Six French and five British divisions were ordered entrained for cisalpine service. High French and British cabinet ministers and generals hastened to Italy, with moral support and counsel. For better or worse, Cadorna had forfeited the confidence of his troops; he was replaced on November 9, by General Armando Diaz. All this, however, would have availed nothing, had the German-led forces of the Central Powers been prepared to take full advantage of this sudden and unexpected success.

Fortunately for Italy, this was not the case. The Germans, under whom were Magyar and Slovak troops, were delayed by the very extent of their victories, and the need of mopping up the conquered territory. They were not prepared for a headlong pursuit. Thus, the Italians, many of whose surviving troops were "disorganized, worn-out, sullen, and bewildered," were given that short breathing time, during which a truly great people can pull itself together.

The knowledge that the country was in deadly peril, that preparations were being made to evacuate Venice, that if the Piave and Adige lines went, the Teutons might soon be in Milan, united the Italian nation. The clericals became patriotic; the pacifists and socialists became silent; a "spirit of desperate devotion ran from the Alps to Sicily." When the Austro-German attacks were renewed along the Piave and downward through the Alps, they were met with an iron determination. A little more ground, indeed, had to be ceded to the attackers, but the line of the Piave was not carried. The Teutons, for one moment, had seemed on the point of driving Italy out of the struggle with one great military thrust—but that moment had passed.

Nevertheless, the disaster at Caporetto seemed, for the moment, only to add one more misery to the Allies' winter. British and French troops, sorely needed on the western front, were in Venetia assisting Italy; Russian revolutionaries were negotiating a separate truce; and submarine warfare was constantly menacing England. In France the morale of the army had improved, but the privations of the long war were bearing hard upon the civilian population. There was, in fact, general discouragement among the Allies. Many were wondering whether the war was not likely to end with a general social revolution. The new Bolshevik dynasts in Russia were sending wholesale promises to the "have nots" throughout the world, and certain high financial groups were reported to have taken alarm. In November these forces were assisted by a letter in the London *Daily Telegraph* from no less a person than Lord Lansdowne, hinting that it might be best to stop talking about a knock-out blow and to see if agreement with Germany were possible. If the Germans were brought around a council table would not their demands be found reasonable, provided their foes were conciliatory?

This suggestion, however, ignored two factors which would have ruined any negotiation, or at least would have broken up the unity of the Allies, and delivered them singly to their enemies: (*a*) the consciousness of the Prussian military leaders that, if they consented to any peace which did not give the German people physical recompense for their sufferings, there would be a political upheaval in the Fatherland; (*b*) the passionate and ever-increasing determination of the

French people, as the price for their own sacrifice, to recover Alsace-Lorraine. The surrender of Alsace-Lorraine by Germany would, on the other hand, have been an intolerable humiliation for the Hohenzollerns; yet the announcement of any program by Britain or America which left the "lost provinces" to their Teuton possessors would probably have caused France in despair to negotiate for immediate peace with Germany, and to quit the war.

LLOYD GEORGE'S AND WILSON'S PEACE PROGRAMS: BREST LITOVSK

Early in January, 1918, largely to silence the report that Britain and America cherished vast selfish designs, Lloyd George and Wilson made clear their war aims. The British premier chose studiously moderate language: Britain was not fighting to destroy Germany, or Austria-Hungary, or those parts of Turkey which were genuinely Turkish, but Belgium and Serbia must be restored and, of course, the occupied parts of France, Italy, and Rumania. The "legitimate claims" of the Italians for union with people of their own race and tongue were to be satisfied, and "genuine self-government" must be given the Austro-Hungarian nationalities. In that event, the Hapsburgs might continue at Vienna, although no longer as the "instruments of the military autocracy of Prussia." An independent Poland was "an urgent necessity," and the Turks, although they might keep Constantinople, ought to let Armenia, Syria, Mesopotamia, and Palestine enjoy "separate national conditions." As for Alsace-Lorraine, there must be a "reconsideration of the great wrong of 1871" done to France; but concerning Russia, since her present rulers were negotiating separately with Germany, Britain could not be responsible for unhappy decisions.

These were carefully worded terms, skilfully calculated to drive a wedge between the allies of Germany and the Hohenzollerns, and to kindle all the dissident minorities, yet not to drive Germany to desperation. Wilson, a few days later, struck out somewhat more boldly. He practically repeated the British terms as to territorial settlements, but with slightly greater precision. In fourteen famous propositions (see p. 98), "the program for the world's peace," he laid down, for example, that there must be an "independent Polish State," to include "the territory inhabited by indisputably Polish populations" and assured of "free and secure access to the sea." As for France, "the wrong done in the matter of Alsace-Lorraine, which has unsettled the peace of the world for nearly fifty years, should be righted, in order that peace may once more be made secure in the interest of all." But concerning Russia, the President differed from the Premier; Russia was not to be abandoned to the spoilers, and the treatment afforded her by her sister nations was to be "the acid test of their good will."

In Austria the olive branch of the Allies was welcome, but not so in Germany. Count Hertling, the new chancellor (replacing, in October, 1917, the feckless Michaelis), repudiated the idea that Alsace-Lorraine could be possibly ceded back to France; and concerning every other point he was vague and defiant. Russia must be left to the "return of order, peace, and conditions of her welfare," which the Teutonic allies were then arranging for her. The fate of Belgium could only be settled after elaborate negotiation, and the occupied parts of France were "valuable pawns in our hands." Poland was to be reconstituted as Germany and Austria might agree among themselves—there was to be no outside interference—and so with nearly all the other points at issue.

At the dawn of 1918, it might have been possible for Germany to have driven a dangerous wedge between France and Britain and America by a conciliatory peace offer. The English-speaking powers, whatever their sympathies, would hardly have gone on making vast sacrifices solely to recover Strasbourg and Metz for a sister nation. But Hertling's speech cancelled any possible effect of Czernin's smoother platitudes, and almost convinced the most doubtful that Germany was playing for an absolute victory and a dictated peace. A few weeks earlier, William II, in an address to his armies, had promised that "we must bring peace to the world by battering in with the iron fist and shining sword the doors of those who will not have peace."

The confident tone of his imperial Majesty was due to the collapse of the eastern front, where the Germans had good reason to feel resistance had vanished. In December, 1917, the Bolsheviks sent their commissars to negotiate with the representatives of the Teutonic empires at Brest Litovsk in Poland, where a protracted conference took place, lasting to the March of the subsequent year, when a Russo-German treaty was finally struck. The Bolsheviks had overwhelmed Russia with surprisingly little fighting and they believed that a similar revolt of the proletariat in Germany was about to send not merely the Kaiser and Junkers, but the whole Teutonic burgher class the way of the Czar. After that, the capitalistic strongholds in France, Britain, and America must speedily crumble, and next would follow the obliteration of obsolete and oppressive nationalistic boundaries, when all peoples of the earth were fused together in the Marxian earthly paradise. The Bolsheviks were confident that their industrial "comrades" in Germany would prevent any advantage being taken of their own military helplessness. "We did not overthrow the Czar," declaimed Trotsky, "in order to fall on our knees before the Kaiser, and beg for peace." Marvelously were he and his associates to be undeceived.

The Germans knew exactly what they wanted and they intended to get it. Here was the first great dividend to be paid for the adventures of Pan-Germanism. The enormous empire of the Czars lay prostrate at their feet. The Russian delegates might talk lengthily of no annexations, no indemnities—the Germans had no objections to that, since they knew that ultimately they could compel the Russians to sign on the dotted line.

The victorious Germans were not moderate in their demands. They asked Russia to recognize the independence of all the Baltic provinces, of Poland, of the Ukraine, that vast southwestern section of Russia in Europe, occupied by the Little Russians, and stretching south and southeast of Poland to the Black Sea. Over these extensive regions, destined for the German orbit, puppet governments were to be set up by the conquerors. In addition, we must remember that important economic concessions were granted clear across Russia by the Rumanian treaty drawn up at Bucharest. The vista was now opened in Berlin of the control of the routes to the oil-wells of Baku, to the cotton lands of Ferghana, to the very mountain passes leading to British India. Austria received minor pickings and Turkey recovered territory on the Caucasus. Austro-German financial groups were to exploit the Rumanian oil-fields.

The Bolsheviks recoiled in disgust at the German proposals. Many favored rejection and the declaration of a revolutionary war. Lenin said Soviet Russia must accept or fight; to accept meant a chance to save the revolutionary régime; to fight meant defeat and conquest by the Central Powers. Trotsky favored refusing to make peace until compelled to do so by force. On February 9, the Central Powers signed at Brest a treaty with the Ukraine, and on the following day Trotsky made his famous "no peace, no war" declaration, to the effect that Soviet Russia would neither sign an annexationist peace nor go on with the war. The Germans therefore declared the armistice at an end and sent their troops forward toward Petrograd. Some of the Bolsheviks still wanted to fight; but Lenin, now supported by Trotsky, won a majority of the party leaders for peace. When the Bolsheviks agreed to sign, the Germans presented a revised text even more severe. There were more debates and Lenin said: "It is time to put an end to revolutionary phrases and get down to real work. If this is not done I resign from the government. . . . It is a question of signing the German terms now or signing the death warrant of the Soviet government three weeks later. . . ." Lenin carried the day and the Soviet delegates signed on March 3.

This Treaty of Brest Litovsk stripped Russia of approximately forty-four per cent of her population, twenty-seven per cent of her arable land, thirty-seven per cent of her average crops, twenty-six per cent of her railroads, thirty-three per cent of her manufactures, seventy-three per cent of her iron production, seventy-five per cent of her developed coal-mines.

The Western Front, March, 1918

Russia was helpless; Italy was reeling; France, despite American economic relief, was bleeding white and very tired; Britain was carrying on gallantly, but without that dauntless confidence that had inspired her sacrifices of 1915-16. America was still three thousand miles across the Atlantic.

The U-boat war had proved a disappointment to its promoters, but the surrender of Russia had restored the prestige of the great General Staff. If civilian Germany went through the winter of 1917-18 once more shivering with the cold, hungering on turnip-soup in lieu of meat and potatoes, with little children nursing on thin beer in lieu of milk, and with stripling youths and middle-aged men in broken health, drafted to the trenches by a pitiless conscription, it seemed, nevertheless, that the blessed end was in sight. Given time, the wheat-fields of Ukrainia and the oil-fields of Rumania would feed and warm the lands of the victors, and as for the military situation, conditions were still better.

It was known that the French army was dwindling in strength through the depletion of man-power. The British were paying the penalty for the awful losses on the Somme and in Flanders; and the U-boat warfare was diverting an enormous number of men into the Royal navy. Vast forces under the Union Jack had also to be maintained in Mesopotamia, Palestine (where Jerusalem had been taken from the Turks on December 10, 1917), and at Salonica. Besides all these, the danger of an invasion of England across the North Sea was reckoned with, 300,000 good troops being held in Britain to meet a very improbable catastrophe. As a result, Sir Douglas Haig commanded 180,000 less fighting men in March, 1918, than in March, 1917. The German high command knew all this. They knew that by March barely 250,000 Americans had reached France, and that the great bulk of these troops were too untrained to send to the trenches. It was time to stake everything on one great blow on the western front that could undo the work at the Marne.

In view of these facts, Ludendorff hoped to win the war by a grand final offensive on the western front. He aimed it at Amiens, since if he could take that old Picard city he would sever direct communications between the British and the French. The latter he could fling backward in demoralization upon Paris; the former he could hustle in ever-increasing rout to the Channel. Former offensives had failed because waged on too narrow a front; he would succeed now by breaking through on a wide one. He would use a method of offense tried out successfully against the Russians by which, instead of an intensive bombardment followed by a rush of infantry, the artillery hardly began its work before the infantry advanced in small detachments, infiltrating the enemy's positions, concealing their advance as much as possible, and using smoke-screens and mustard-gas to demoralize the foe. The German army on the western front was now trained for this kind of intensive warfare. For the time being Ludendorff could depend on a numerical preponderance, for the German veterans arriving from the now quiet eastern front outnumbered the available Americans. In fact it was now or never for the Germans; they must strike and they must win before there were too many Americans in France, and before the food shortage got too bad in Germany.

Upon the extreme south of the British line on the 21st of March, 1918, the storm broke, and before that day was spent the Germans had penetrated deep into the British positions. The British reserves were exhausted and the onslaught not stayed. The following day, as the British divisions lost contact with one another, came worse disaster and a frantic retirement to the Somme. On the 23rd the attackers swept across that stream; and as the gaps between the British units grew wider and wider, the chance of stabilizing the line grew more and more faint. Ludendorff seemingly had accomplished the impossible—a break-through.

Almost, but not quite. Never fought men in a manner more worthy of their inheritance than that unbowed remnant of the British army. From the south the French hurried up veteran divisions to fill the gap and to cover Amiens. The Germans still made headway but no longer rapidly, and in a few days they halted. Their communications lay across vast devastated areas; rain came to hinder their advance; and what was more, the hungry Germans stopped to fill their stomachs with the delightful and abundant food supplies left by the enemy. Nevertheless, on April 1, it was possible for Ludendorff to proclaim a magnificent success—90,000 prisoners and 1,300 guns.

Amiens was saved. But Ludendorff still had power for other blows. On April 9, the Germans struck again, this time further north. Portugal had entered the war as the special ally of Britain, and two divisions of Portuguese troops had been entrusted with holding part of the trenches. Again a dense fog aided the attack; again the first rush of the Germans was invincible. The Portuguese lines crumpled and the adjacent British divisions had just been withdrawn, sorely shaken, from the Amiens battle-zone and were not well reorganized. The English, therefore, retired sullenly across the old battle-fields, drenched now with the blood of three and a half years of war.

Once more the German offensive ebbed away. There had been great territorial gains for Ludendorff; he had won back from the British with one blow an area that his foes had painfully wrested from the Germans in many battles; but he had not forced Haig's line or put the British army out of action. By the end of April, this Battle of the Lys as it was called, was over. Ludendorff drew back to strike again, and once more respite had been given the Allies.

May, 1918, nearly passed before another great German offensive came. Meantime, the ocean was sprinkled with convoys of liners bearing the man-power of America. "The Allies are very weak," General Pershing had reported to Washington as early as December, 1917, "and we must come to their relief in this year, 1918. The year after may be too late." But during the winter the ocean convoys had been slow, and even the most hopeful of the commanders overestimated the period of training needful for the American troops before they could be sent to the battle-trenches. Nevertheless, in March, 84,900 were sent across and in April, 118,600. These numbers had seemed the reasonable limit, considering the shipping available; but with the whole war now on the razor-edge of fate, the British government drafted the liners from all its great trade routes, while the process of mobilizing and organizing in America was hastened to the uttermost. In May, 246,000 Americans were destined to cross the Atlantic, in June, 278,000, in July, 306,300. The government-controlled press of Germany denounced the figures published to hearten the Allies as gross fabrications and "Yankee bluff," but the General Staff, at least, began to realize that what it would do, it must do quickly.

Late in May, Ludendoff struck yet again, and a third time could boast of a triumph. He once again changed his objective. Abandoning the Channel ports and giving the British the time so ardently desired to recuperate, he aimed at Paris. His intelligence service told him that the line of the Chemin des Dames, along the Aisne, was held by only eight divisions, four French and four British, and that these were weary from fighting elsewhere and had been sent to this supposedly "quiet sector" to reorganize. Suddenly, on May 27, Ludendorff attacked with twenty-eight divisions on a thirty-five mile line. He had concealed his stroke excellently, and won immediate results. A deep zone of territory was lost to the Allies, and that, too, in the area directly covering Paris.

The Germans reported 45,000 prisoners and 400 captured guns. They were well down to the Marne, almost to the region fought over in September, 1914. Another such success, and they could talk of winning Paris. Foch seemed to have been caught napping. Three great attacks, and none of them halted without great Allied loss. There had been no time to organize any counteroffensive, for every interval had been consumed in reorganizing the shaken Franco-British armies. A few more such blows in the western battle-zone, and flesh and blood could endure no more; France would very possibly crumple, even if the last trench lines were not broken.

But Foch kept his head; he realized that his opponent had made two notable errors—he had given the British time to recover, and he had driven a pronounced but narrow salient into the Allied front up to the Marne. Unless that salient was widened, it was a dangerous base for further operations, and Ludendorff, understanding the case, struck again on June 9, this time near the western end of the great southern loop he had forced towards the Marne, in the sector just south of Amiens. Now, however, the defenders were not caught napping, nor were their reserves too far away. Some little territory was, indeed, gained by the Germans, but nothing of vital consequence. This "fourth drive" was practically over in three days, and the attackers had spent themselves so completely that it was impossible for them to do otherwise than halt and recuperate. Wellington at Waterloo had prayed for "the night or Blücher." Foch, accepting the respite, thankfully realized that Blücher, otherwise the Americans, was at length at hand. The Germans still heavily outnumbered the French and the English. It was known that the great General Staff was mobilizing all its resources for a fifth, a master effort; it would be the *Friedensturm* (the "Charge to win Peace"), the officers were telling their men in the German trenches. One more colossal effort—and France would be as Russia; then home to the Fatherland and glory.

THE SECOND MARNE

The *Friedensturm* was aimed to strike in two directions. Ludendorff knew that the deep salient or pocket he had created by his third offensive must either be enlarged or abandoned, for it was fed by but one railroad and it was open to attack from both flanks. In his fourth offensive he had tried to enlarge it on the northwest and had failed. This time he would strike to the east of Reims, to widen it on the northeast, while at the same time he would strike to the south and west of Reims toward the Marne. When the Germans rushed on this, their fifth and last offensive, they found the foe fully prepared. Their

blow struck to the east of Reims met with complete discomfiture.
Twenty-five picked German divisions were shattered by the French
artillery and no appreciable progress was made. Slightly better fortune
attended the German attack west of Reims in the Marne salient; some
ground was gained; the Marne was crossed near Château-Thierry;
progress on the military maps could be noted. But the salient in the
Allies' lines, though deepened, had not been widened.

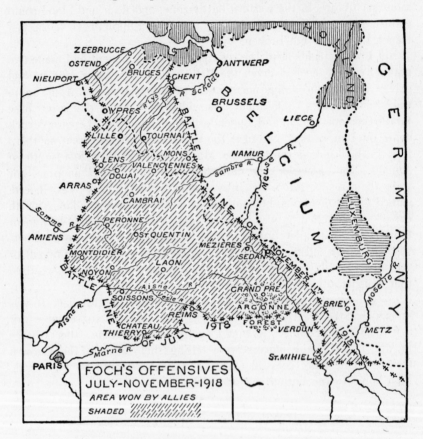

Foch's hour had come. Along the thirty-five mile western flank of
the great Marne salient, after a night of thunderstorms and high winds
which discouraged the German airmen, there emerged 321 Allied tanks
out of the shelter of the concealing woods. Behind them, striking all
the way from Château-Thierry to Soissons came Mangin's forces, thirty
per cent American. The advance swept through the first German defenses before the Teutons so much as realized what was happening.
When night fell the Allies had taken 16,000 prisoners and had gone
far beyond winning a local success. They were closing the end of the

German loop or pocket which had penetrated to the Marne. If they could only close it further, thirty German divisions would be trapped within. For the next few days the Germans struggled fiercely and at last escaped north to their old battle-grounds near the Aisne. They had lost the great gains of the first of June; they had lost something more precious, confidence in victory.

This Second Marne had been essentially a victory for the French, although British and American units had done their share. But Haig's army no longer stood with its back to the wall. In the respite it had been recruited, reorganized. Now it was the spear-head of the second Allied blow. Along a twenty-mile front in Picardy, Haig drove home with a force of French and British. A great zone of territory occupied by the Germans was recovered and 30,000 prisoners taken.

Three months and three days intervened between this British drive and the end of the war, an interval filled with incessant fighting. The initiative had completely passed into the hands of Foch, now generalissimo of all the Allied armies, and never once was Ludendorff able to make a serious counteroffensive. Foch struck now here, now there. The Belgians were again in action from that little strip of their fatherland near the Yser which they had held since 1914; the British were raining blows in Flanders and Picardy; the French were beating on the German lines along the Aisne and in Champagne; and the Americans, acting as a separate army, were putting through two major operations in the Meuse Valley.

The Final Franco-British-American Attacks

The German hosts on the western front had been fed by two trunk-lines of railroads—that through Liége and that through Sedan. The line through Liége was relatively safe, but by itself it was totally inadequate for maintaining the German army. The line through Sedan was within thirty miles of the Allied trenches near Verdun, but those miles included the Argonne Forest, a semi-wilderness of hills, woods, and ravines, ideal for defense, almost impossible for offense. Haig and Pétain (still in command of the French armies as coadjutor to Foch) undertook to force back the Germans across Flanders, Picardy, and Champagne by incessant attacks and pressure. They each had several American divisions in their armies, but the main American effort was elsewhere. Pershing undertook to cut through the Argonne to Sedan. When its trunk railroad was under the American guns, Ludendorff's armies must either flee in rout or capitulate.

Before cutting this railroad it was considered advisable that the Germans be driven out of the Saint-Mihiel salient near Verdun, and the task of doing so was assigned to the American army. Pershing fell upon this salient, using over half a million men. He won a relatively easy victory, since the Germans were preparing to abandon the salient anyway. Pershing then started forward on the main American offense, through the Argonne in the direction of Sedan.

The battle of the Argonne was the greatest battle in American history. It lasted forty-seven days, with only trifling intervals of inactivity. It was begun with 450,000 men, but as it raged other troops were thrown in until the whole number of Americans engaged was over 1,000,000. The American numerical preponderance was overwhelming and it must be remembered that the war-weary enemy was in retreat. Nevertheless, the German troops knew the terrain and the Americans did not. The forest country fought over had become an almost impenetrable tangle of fallen timber, an ideal place for nests of machine-guns and for labyrinths of barbed-wire. It was also cut by ravines so deep as to render tanks useless, and making it very hard for artillery to support the attackers. "It was a question of hard, slogging infantry fighting, and the American infantryman did slog hard," wrote a British general; by the middle of October "by continuous grim, dogged effort he won his way through."

As these events took place, the Belgians, the British, and the French had been equally, if not more, successful. The German armies in France were caught, as it were, between enormous pincers, the Belgians and the British on one side, the Americans on the other, and the French in the center shoving their foe forward. Everywhere came the rat-tat-tat of Foch on the retreating enemy, who retired in good order, putting up everywhere a stiff rear-guard action. "By October 5 the British had driven their way through the German defense system into the open country and had taken 36,000 prisoners." By the first of November the German forces were back where they had been in the summer of 1914.

GERMANY'S ALLIES SURRENDER

As far back as September, Bulgaria had given evidence of cracking. An Allied army which had occupied Salonica after the Dardanelles defeat, forced that entire nation to remain mobilized. The Germans had handed over to Bulgaria a goodly share of the conquered Serbian lands but had exploited the supply of food-stuffs. The Bulgarian army was illfed and lacked boots and clothing. At the very moment, furthermore, when German aid was needed most, German aid was withdrawn. Ludendorff required his men, his munitions, his money, elsewhere. Bulgaria, then, realizing that she had gambled unwisely, made peace quickly. There was little haggling over terms. The Bulgars agreed to demobilize their army, to evacuate all territory they had occupied, and to allow Allied armies free transit across Bulgaria to attack Turkey. The Serbs, now like raging lions, flung themselves on the small Austro-German detachments left in their country. They reëntered Nish, their ancient capital; and by the first of November they were again triumphantly in Belgrade, looking across the Danube where the first shots of the world contest had resounded fifty-one months earlier.

The collapse of Bulgaria was scarcely more rapid than that of Turkey. The Bedouin tribes of Arabia and Syria were now in full revolt against the Sultan. They had refused the summons to a Holy War against the English and were making active alliance with the latter, thanks largely to the extraordinary abilities of a young Oxford archeologist, T. E. Lawrence. The British and the Arabs together made Palestine too hot for the Turks. Jerusalem was occupied (Christmas, 1917), and during 1918 Allenby, the British commander, had pressed Liman Von Sanders, the German general in command of the Turkish army, north from Nazareth to Damascus. For that city there was a lively duel; but the British cavalry won the day and soon in Allenby's hands were 60,000 prisoners and 400 cannon; and what was left of the Turkish army was so dissipated that the rest of the campaign was merely one of marching. The Sultan had hardly a single organized force to put in the field, if Allenby elected to advance across Anatolia to Stamboul. On October 25, he moved north again and took Aleppo, the great Turkish base in North Syria.

The news of disaster came to Constantinople almost on the very wires that told of the surrender of Bulgaria. The "Young Turk" dynasts were sick of their German bargain. Now Syria was lost and Mesopotamia with it; Anatolia would soon be open, and the Allies, moving across Bulgaria, would soon be pounding on the Tchalja lines behind Stamboul. Allah manifestly had spoken, and it was useless to strive against destiny. Turkish envoys, therefore, negotiated peace with the British admiral in the Aegean. The Turkish army was to be demobilized, the Turkish waterways opened; alliance with Germany was repudiated, and the whole fate of the Ottoman Empire was to be left for the final peace conference. On October 31 hostilities in the Near East ceased.

This general collapse of the allies of Austria and Germany in southeastern Europe was almost instantly followed by that of Austria. It was high time.

Czechs, Poles, Ruthenians, Slovaks, Slovenes, Croats, whom the lordly Germans and Magyars had trampled upon and despised, were turning now against the oppressor. "Self-determination" and "a world safe for democracy," supplied oil for fires of discontent already smoldering. As early as January, 1918, a manifesto issued by the Czech deputies to the Austrian Reichsrat, demanded "full independence" for the Bohemian nation. In America and England an escaped Czech leader of singular ability, Dr. Thomas Masaryk, agitated with success for the official encouragement by the Allies of the separatist movement. "Czecho-Slovak" troops were allowed to fight on the French front, and by October, 1918, it was recognized by friend and foe alike that a Nationalist provisional government was ruling in Paris, and that the last ties of Hapsburg authority were on the point of dissolving in most of its old northern provinces.

It was not otherwise in the south. In the Slavic provinces, nearest Bosnia and Serbia, there had been a great running to and fro and girding against the Magyar oppressor. As early as April, 1918, there had been an imposing "Congress of Oppressed Nationalities" held at Rome. It was composed of exiles from nearly all the aggrieved Hapsburg subject races, but the Yugo-Slavs (South Slavs), had assumed a leading part. The "Pact of Rome" was then proclaimed, whereby (with the especial consent of Italy) the various South Slavic peoples—Serbians, Bosnians, Croats, Slovenes, and so forth—were to be united into a single state, "on the basis of nationality and self-determination." As the summer advanced, the control of the Hapsburg officials over the South Slavic provinces sank almost to its nadir. The Austrian army was still holding along the Piave, but behind it there was only rottenness and disaffection. The collapse of Bulgaria, allowing the Serbs to recover their homeland, came now as the signal for a collapse of about the last vestiges of Magyar authority in the southern provinces.

In Polish Galicia, matters were little different. After the defeat of Russia the Teutonic Powers had tried to set up a native Polish "Council of State" at Warsaw to consolidate their own military control of what had been czarist Poland; but the Austrians and Germans could come to no agreement as to how the Polish problem should be solved and the Poles resisted exploitation skilfully, using their new Council for a vigorous agitation for the union of *all* Poland under one government. In Galicia, even as in Prussian Posen, there existed intense yearnings for national reunion, and the simulacrum of a Polish government which German policy had established at Warsaw was ready to become a real government and sweep under its control all the Austro-German Polish lands, the moment the Teutonic empires seemed beaten. During the summer of 1918, tidings of woe thus came from every side to Vienna. The June offensive against Italy had failed; then in the fall the military situation became impossible.

Czernin had ceased to be the foreign minister of Emperor Charles, thanks to his anti-German attitude in 1917; but his successor, Baron von Burian, found the situation equally hopeless. In mid-September, he addressed a note to all the belligerents pleading for "non-binding, confidential discussions" of peace terms. It met with instant rejection from Britain and America, where the trend of events was well apprehended. After that, all that the Vienna cabinet could do was to make useless gestures to stave off the inevitable. On October 16, the Hapsburg Empire underwent its death-bed repentance. The unfortunate Charles proclaimed his monarchy a "Federal State" in which each people could form its own government. But the Allies and the United States were now warning Vienna that there could be no peace unless the Czechs, Poles, and Yugo-Slavs were to be allowed to quit the empire outright if they so desired; and Hungary was also preparing to cut the last tie to Vienna, and set up as a completely independent government.

Austria's plight was Italy's opportunity. The Italian army, assisted by French and British units, drove in a wedge between the Austrian troops. The Austrians and the Magyars surrendered wholesale and prisoners were reckoned at more than 300,000. On November 3 Austria quit the war and a week later the Emperor Charles abdicated. German Austria became a republic; there was another republic in Hungary, a third in Czechoslovakia; Galicia was joining a revived republic of Poland; the Croats and the Slovenes were federating with the Bosnians and Serbs in the new kingdom of Yugoslavia; and Rumania had repudiated the forced Treaty of Bucharest and was seizing Transylvania. The Austrian monarchy, founded in 1272 by Rudolf of Hapsburg, that artificial but convenient makeshift and fiction which had dominated Central Europe for 640 years, was dead.

These happenings progressively heightened Germany's gloom. There was now no hope anywhere on the horizon. The army on the western front was retiring in good order and was in no immediate danger of encirclement; but even if it reached the Rhine safely there was no chance of ultimate victory. Consequently, Germany sued for peace by way of Washington. She would be willing, so she said, to accept President Wilson's fourteen points and subsequent addresses as the basis of a permanent peace. The President replied that there could be no peace unless the Allies had a representative government with which to deal, and the German militarists temporarily thought of renewing the war. But it was now known that Austria was done for and other men than Ludendorff were in charge of Germany's destinies. Prince Max of Baden, now chancellor, was ill; but his subordinates baited the military chiefs boldly. "There is no hope," Ludendorff told his junior officers, "Germany is lost."

The army did not finally yield, however, until socialistic revolts in the Fatherland made it inevitable that it must. The German Socialists had been wholeheartedly for the war at its commencement, only one of them, Liebknecht, voting against the first war credits. Late in 1915, however, fifteen other Socialists joined with Liebknecht, seceded from the Social Democratic party, and formed that of the Independent Socialists. They were a very weak faction and not until the treaty of Brest Litovsk in 1918 was there really any considerable revolutionary propaganda in Germany.

But as the German people became more and more hungry, revolutionary sentiment spread, especially in the industrial centers and in the seaboard cities of the North. And now, with Germany's allies falling away, and with Foch's legions likely to pour over the frontier at any moment, a very small explosion could and did shatter the whole political structure. That explosion took place at Kiel, where the bluejackets, long disgruntled, hoisted the red flag of revolutionary socialism. This mutiny was no flash in the pan. By the 7th of November there were unkempt soviets claiming to be the government in Hamburg, Bremen, Hanover, Rostock, and lesser centers. The red flag was waving all over Germany; jails were broken open and hardened inmates released as an earnest of proletarian liberty.

Under such circumstances there was a revolution in Germany which complied completely with Wilson's demands that the Allies must deal with the representatives of the German people. The Germans not merely lost an emperor, they ceased to constitute a monarchy. On November 10 the Kaiser fled into Holland. On the same day Ebert, a journeyman saddler, accepted the chancellorship in the name of the Social Democrats, and straightway proclaimed the republic.

One day later came the armistice, the terms of which had been prepared at Paris by the Allied generals and admirals. The Germans were to surrender 5,000 cannon, 30,000 machine guns, 2,000 airplanes, and 5,000 locomotives. They were to evacuate immediately the "invaded countries" including Alsace-Lorraine, thereby automatically undoing the deed of 1871. They were to retire beyond the Rhine, and the Allied armies were to occupy not merely the western Rhinelands, but ample bridge-heads with wide radius opposite Mayence, Coblenz, and Cologne. All Allied prisoners were to be released immediately, all German mine-fields to be swept; six battle-cruisers, ten battle-ships, numerous smaller craft, and all submarines were to be interned in the ports of the victors; the remaining craft were to be disarmed and put under Allied supervision. In addition, the treaties of Brest Litovsk and Bucharest (with Rumania) were to be canceled.

At 5 A.M., at the first gray light of November 11, the German dele-

gates, meeting Foch in his salon car, put their hands to the great surrender. Through the cold, foggy morning sometimes a shell burst, sometimes a great gun bellowed. It was said that most of the combatants
were in a kind of stupor. They had fought so long, must they not fight
on forever? Foch had telegraphed to his generals, "Hostilities will
cease on the whole front on November 11, at eleven o'clock. The Allied
troops will not, until further orders, go beyond the line reached at that
hour." Suddenly, at one minute to eleven, the last "75" thundered on
its carriage. The ensuing silence was more startling than even the terrible chorus of a barrage.

Presently, against the skyline, lifting themselves above the trenches,
first cautiously, then bolder, were seen figures—staring, gesturing. They
were Germans, gazing curiously. Americans, Frenchmen, Britons grew
visible likewise. Machine-gunners unbuckled their belts, gave stiff
salutes toward the opposing barbed-wire, and next walked deliberately
toward the rear. And then a sound "like the noise of a light wind"
could be heard, whether the troops stood at Verdun or in Belgium.
Across four hundred miles, millions of men were cheering from the
Vosges to the sea.

CHAPTER IV

PEACE TREATIES AND THEIR AFTERMATH
(1919-23)

NOT until late in January, 1919, did the peace conference convene. The fact that it was called a conference instead of a congress is significant, for, unlike the Congress of Vienna in 1815, the representatives of the enemy's country were not invited to participate. Terms of peace were decided by the victorious Allies alone and the Central Powers, strangled economically by a rigorous blockade, were compelled to sign on the dotted line.

The long delay in opening the conference, which did not meet until nine weeks after the armistice, was due in part to England, in part to the United States. In the former country a Parliamentary election had been long overdue; one should have been held in 1917, but the exigencies of the war had led to its postponement. Lloyd George was earger to obtain a fresh mandate from his country, and what could be a more opportune time than now, when fresh from victory he could feel assured of a comfortable majority! In America two reasons led to delay. One was that Congress convened in December, and since President Wilson was determined to go to Paris, the conference could not well be held until after his annual message to Congress had been delivered. The other reason was the determination of the President to have nothing to do with proposals suggested by the French for determining peace terms.

Soon after the armistice the French ambassador at Washington delivered these proposals. In brief, they provided for an immediate meeting of the larger Allied states to dispose of Germany's colonies, to draw new European boundaries, to decide upon reparations. This once done, a general European congress would be invited to Paris to ratify (and perhaps modify) what the large states had done, and to concoct plans for a league of nations to settle future international disputes and to end war. If the President would accept this proposal, it was to be understood in advance that all secret treaties would be canceled.

But the President was unwilling. He thought it wrong to dictate the peace. The Germans had not made an unconditional surrender but had made a definite bargain based on his own fourteen points and subsequent addresses. Especially essential to him was a league of nations and *it,* according to the French program, was made subordinate to colonies and boundaries! Furthermore, the French had hinted that they might favor changes within Germany which went much further than simply democratizing that country. The President felt that he must be on guard against wily European diplomats and he was determined that the adoption of general principles (that is, the league of nations) must have priority over disputes concerning boundaries. Therefore he insisted that the conference should await his arrival.

The peace conference, once in session, worked hard. It was subdivided into no less than fifty-eight committees (that at Vienna in 1815 had only eight) which held 1,646 sessions, drew up reports, and submitted them to the statesmen responsible for the final treaty. In theory the latter represented all countries participating; in practice they were first the "big ten" and afterward the "big four." England, France, Italy, the United States, and Japan, with two delegates each, made up the council of ten. Japan dropped out and the council was reduced to the other four countries, represented by one man each—Lloyd George for England, Clemenceau for France, Wilson for America, and Orlando for Italy. Since the last-named statesman was away a great part of the time and but little interested in those matters which did not concern Italy, the final settlement in the last analysis depended on the other three men.

Of these, Lloyd George, clever, adroit, elastic in temperament if not in conscience, acted as intermediary between Wilson and Clemenceau. The President of the United States and the Premier of France did not love one another. Wilson, unfortunately, conceived the idea that America was the only country participating in the conference which had no selfish aim to serve. He was more prophet than statesman and envisaged a new moral order based upon certain idealistic though vague principles. Clemenceau, above all things, wanted security for France. The oldest of the three men, he was the most experienced. His memory went back to the Franco-Prussian War and he was determined above everything else that the Germans should not threaten France again. To him the President was a visionary fellow who must alternately be bamboozled and conciliated.

These three were to decide the fate of the world. The problem they confronted was complex. Three empires lay in ruin—the Russian, the Austro-Hungarian, and the German. The first was convulsed by a most genuine social revolution which had already begun to spread in the other two. In Austria-Hungary the various nationalities were at each other's throats, and in Germany a day-before-yesterday democratic republic, without prestige and without any real majority behind it, was struggling to restore order. Meanwhile, a resuscitated Poland was stirring with new life, a half-dismembered Turkey lay at their mercy, millions of weary soldiers clamored for demobilization, new boundaries had to be fixed somehow, damages assessed, and three strident democracies—France, England, and America—consumed by propagandized hate of Germany, must be watched and placated.

Nor was this all! The Germans had not surrendered unconditionally: They had been promised terms and the Allies were in honor bound to their adherence. The terms, both numerous and ambiguous, were the fourteen points of President Wilson, plus his public addresses made between their promulgation and the armistice. The terms conflicted flatly with certain secret treaties made during the war among the Allies; they conflicted flatly with sundry promises of a financial nature made by Lloyd George to the British electorate within a month after the armistice.

The fourteen points of the President in abbreviated form were as follows:

1. Open covenants of peace
2. Freedom of the seas
3. Removal as far as possible of economic barriers
4. Reduced armaments among all nations
5. An impartial treatment of colonial questions having in mind the best interests of native peoples
6. Evacuation of Russia, and an invitation to join the league
7. Restoration of Belgium
8. Restoration of Alsace-Lorraine to France
9. Italian frontiers to be drawn "along clearly recognizable lines of nationality"
10. The various nationalities of Austria-Hungary to have free development
11. The Allied Balkan states evacuated and access to sea for Serbia
12. The Turkish parts of the Ottoman Empire to be independent but with a chance for "autonomous development" for other nationalities other than Turkish
13. An independent Poland with access to the sea
14. "A general association of nations under specific covenants"

These points were to be supplemented by certain presidential addresses which stressed "self-determination" of peoples as a cornerstone of the peace and insisted that there be "no punitive indemnities." The Germans were to pay, not the cost of the war, but for damages inflicted upon invaded territory.

Two changes were made in these terms before the Germans laid down their arms, and both changes were the results of British insistence. Freedom of the seas was deleted altogether; the British would have nothing to do with so dangerous a principle. A gloss was also put upon the President's statement as to what the Germans were to pay, specifying that they were financially responsible for losses incurred by the civilian population of the Allies upon land, sea, and in the air. Had this not been done, no money at all would have come to England, since that country had not been invaded.

Here then was the bargain; let us see what happened to it. Just what point number one meant, nobody ever knew. Some of the Americans seem to have conceived of the peace conference as a kind of political convention open to the press, with all Allied countries having a vote and with America engineering a transatlantic bloc with the possible collaboration of Cuba, Brazil, and Panama. But the French and British had no intention whatever of giving such allies as Panama and Siam a vote equal to their own, and Wilson quickly gave way in this matter of open covenants, contenting himself with occasional full meetings of all Allied representatives wherein the decisions of the inner council might be ratified. From his point of view the league was what mattered. Provided that "open covenants" were arrived at therein, he would be content.

Point number two was, as we have seen, never a part of the final bargain. Point number three was ignored by the peace conference. It has been argued that the general economic confusion in which the world lay in 1919 made it impossible at that time to do anything about it. Point number four in regard to disarmament, as far as the treaty of Versailles was concerned, was enforced against the Germans alone, their navy being rendered a nullity and their army reduced to 100,000 men. Insofar as number four called for mutual disarmament it would seem as though it was violated. But again it has been argued, albeit with some casuistry, that the fight for disarmament continued, as we shall see, for many years, and might ultimately have been won, had it not been for the advent of Hitler and Germany's withdrawal from the league.

Point number five in part was fulfilled. No one, not even Wilson, had any idea of returning the German colonies to Germany, and from the beginning there was some kind of an idea of trusteeship for these colonies under the league. Australia, however, wanted to annex New Guinea outright, as New Zealand wanted to annex Samoa, and the Union of South Africa, the German Southwest Africa. France also sought annexations, and over the colonial question there was a real tussle. The idea of giving the various Allied countries "mandates" over alien territory was one originally fathered by the British Labor party, and it was accepted. Mandates were divided into three categories: (*a*) mandates were regions like Syria and Iraq, lands presumably fitted within a reasonable time for independence; (*b*) mandates were for Central African territory wherein closer supervision was to be given;

(*c*) mandates were to be certain German colonies like German South-west Africa, over which the laws of the mandatory power were to apply even more directly. Between *c* mandates and outright annexation, there could not well be in practice very much distinction. As a result of this threefold classification, the British dominions got essentially what they wanted. So, too, did the French, by slipping a little clause into the peace treaty (presumably unknown to Wilson), whereby it was made legal for France to insist on universal military service in those portions of German territory which fell to her share in Africa. That this could be to the best interests of the natives concerned would appear more than a bit dubious.

Point number six, in regard to Russia, fell by the wayside unless one is to consider Russia's ultimate entry into the League of Nations several years later as its fulfillment. Nothing is more difficult to unravel in regard to the conference than the treatment of Russia. The special envoy of the United States, Mr. Bullitt, returned to Paris believing that Lenin was quite tractable and willing to make such great concessions that further effort to defeat Bolshevism either by force of arms or diplomacy should cease. Wilson apparently refused to support his envoy and Bullitt resigned. French, British, and American aid to those armed forces in Russia opposed to the Bolsheviks, meanwhile continued.

Points number seven and eight may be considered carried out satisfactorily.

Point number nine, on the other hand, may justly be held violated, and that, too, almost completely. The Italian frontier was not drawn "along clearly recognizable lines of nationality," but the reverse. Somewhere between 200,000 and 250,000 Germans in the Upper Tyrol were included in Italy. About fifty-two per cent of the people in the Istrian Peninsula, now given to Italy, were of non-Italian nationality, and three-quarters, if not more, of the population of the annexed regions in Dalmatia on the east coast of the Adriatic were non-Italian.

The reason for this violation of Wilsonian principles is to be found in the "secret treaties" made between the Allies during the war; and the fact that they were not abrogated upon the acceptance of Wilson's fourteen points and subsequent addresses is (the one question of reparations aside) the strongest single argument against the treaty settlement as a whole.

For purely military reasons the Allies had, as we have seen (see p. 49), paid high for Italian support. The French and British now claimed that they were honor bound to keep their word to Italy. Wilson asserted that the acceptance of his principles canceled the secret treaties made earlier. There certainly was something to be said for this point of view. Early in the war, before American troops embarked for Europe, the Allies might logically have expected Wilson to inquire into these treaties, but apparently he did not care to know about them. Now that they were brought to light he was horrified.

The American delegates could find no argument at all in favor of taking Upper Tyrol away from Austria, but they did discover plausible reasons for the Italian annexation of the Istrian Peninsula. Population strains were so mixed in the peninsula, they said, that it was impossible to tell very much about census statistics, and after all the Austrian government before the war had iniquitously imported Slovene laborers just for the purpose of swelling the anti-Italian total. As for Dalmatia, it was argued, the cities on the coast had once been Venetian outposts and the Austrians for a long time had been playing dirty politics and oppressing those of Italian blood. Dalmatia, as a whole, was Italian in culture even if not in blood, and it was absurd to expect Italy to be content with a potential enemy directly opposite her on the eastern shores of the Adriatic.

Curiously enough, the President himself took no interest in the Tyrol question where his principles were so clearly defied. What enraged him was the Italian demand for Fiume on the eastern shores of the Adriatic, the former port of Hungary, a demand not based on the Treaty of London, which had left Fiume for the Yugoslavs, but founded on his own principle of self-determination. The Italians could not have it both ways, said President Wilson, gaining certain territory because of the secret treaty and yet other territory because they invoked his principles.

As a matter of fact, the Italians had no real claim of any sort to Fiume if the populous suburbs where the Slavs predominated were counted in the population. Consequently in this Fiume matter the President dug himself in and refused to budge. He even went to Rome to appeal to the Italian people over the heads of their representatives at Paris, but to no avail. The Italian poet-warrior, D'Annunzio, seized Fiume with an armed force and defied all comers, and the ultimate solution of the problem did not occur until after the peace treaties had been signed. A separate pact between Italy and Yugoslavia, signed in 1924, the Treaty of Rome, finally gave Fiume to Italy, in return for which the Italians surrendered to Yugoslavia a part of the Dalmatian coast assigned them by the Treaty of London.

Point number ten was violated in spirit if not in letter. The original idea had been to make the various nationalities in the Austro-Hungarian empire merely autonomous, to turn that great sprawling region into a highly decentralized state, possibly on the model of Switzerland. The Czechs of Bohemia, however, had fought so valiantly on the Allied side that it was felt that independence should be their reward. As for the Rumanians who inhabited Transylvania or eastern Hungary, a separate partition treaty had already guaranteed their return to the kingdom of Rumania. That treaty, to be sure, had been nullified by Rumania's separate peace treaty with the Germans. None the less it was felt that the Rumanians were as much entitled to self-determination as the Czechs.

THE BALKANS IN 1919

(Courtesy of the New York *Times*.)

Taking up one after another of the countries now carved wholly or in part out of the old Hapsburg lands, we come first to Czechoslovakia. An unfortunate name was given to it, one implying the union of Czechs and Slovaks. There was really no necessity of uniting them, except that the Slovaks, formerly under Hungarian rule, were scarcely strong enough to stand by themselves unless united with the Czechs, a much more numerous and advanced people formerly under Austrian rule. By placing both Czechs and Slovaks in one country, and by joining to them the old Hungarian province of Ruthenia, a queer-shaped state was evolved, looking somewhat like a tadpole with its head in Bohemia and its tail in Ruthenia.

Bohemia, if taken by itself, was an old country not manufactured out of whole cloth to please the Czechs. Its capital, Prague, had been a foyer of Christianity and culture at a time when the Teutonic tribes to the north were semi-nomadic barbarians, and at Prague had been established the first university in Central Europe. During the sixteenth century, however, Bohemia had fallen under Hapsburg sway, and in the seventeenth and eighteenth centuries it had become more and more Teutonized. During the last half of the nineteenth century, the submerged Czech nationality, perhaps always in the majority, had reasserted itself, but even as late as 1914 the predominant class in Bohemia, certainly in wealth and possibly in culture, had been South German, looking to Vienna.

The Czechs in Bohemia outnumbered the Germans by possibly three to one, and to a large extent it was impossible to give Bohemia or Czechoslovakia any reasonable boundaries at all without including in them a large part of the 3,000,000 Germans in Bohemia, for the country, topographically, was a flat pocket or plain surrounded by mountains, and the majority of the Germans lived on or near the border. Nevertheless, as the Americans on the Czechoslovak committee demonstrated, some 300,000 of these Germans in Egerland and in two other border districts might have been permitted to join the Reich without serious strategic injuries to the boundaries of the new country.

But it was not the Germans alone who were denied in this instance the right of self-determination. If the boundaries of Czechoslovakia had been drawn fairly on an ethnographical basis, instead of looking like a tadpole the country more nearly would have resembled an hourglass. Only by including thousands of Poles on the north and possibly 750,000 Magyars on the south was it possible to make Czechoslovakia bulge out in the middle. Furthermore, for economic reasons it was considered essential that Czechoslovakia include land where these Magyars lived, since the only railway connection between Prague and eastern Czechoslovakia went through the old city of Pressburg on the Danube in Hungary and through parts of Slovakia where there were more Magyars than Slovaks.

The Magyars suffered even greater losses elsewhere. Rumania had, as we have seen (p. 57), been bribed into the war by Allied promises of (*a*) Bukovina, north of the Carpathians and formerly a part of Austria—in Bukovina thirty-four per cent of the population was Magyar; (*b*) Transylvania, or eastern Hungary—with a population largely Rumanian, but with a large Magyar and a lesser German minority; (*c*) the Banat of Temesvar, across the Danube, north of Belgrade, where Serbs, Rumanians, and Magyars were hopelessly mixed. All three regions were lost to Hungary, the Rumanians receiving Bukovina and Transylvania and dividing the Banat with Yugoslavia.

To do justice to both the Magyars and the Rumanians on the basis of self-determination was impossible. A large part of the Magyar folk in Transylvania, for instance, were located well toward the Carpathian Mountains and between them and their fellow-Magyars was a solid section of Rumanians. Nevertheless, the peace conference might have been much more just in regard to Hungary's eastern and southern boundaries, for at least 500,000 Magyars on the western borders of Transylvania were included in the greater Rumania, while some 250,-000 odd, on the borders of the Banat, were included in Yugoslavia, the excuse in the former case being that it was essential for Rumania to have possession of the only railroad running north and south through West Transylvania.

Arguments raised at the peace conference in regard to strategic boundaries, railroads, and economic necessity were numerous, and always the French insisted that the new nations must be *viable:* these were one-way arguments, never made in behalf of Austria and Hungary, enemy states, but ever appropriate to Italy, Yugoslavia, Rumania, and Czechoslovakia. Both Austria and Hungary received harsher treatment in respect to boundaries than did Prussia after Jena. Vienna, a city of 2,000,000, former commercial and banking entrepôt of the Danube valley, now was left to starve in the center of a tiny country, largely mountainous, where almost every boundary was but an hour distant by train or automobile. Budapest at least had food supplies from the Hungarian plain, but the city itself was much too large for the purely agricultural population left within the truncated confines of the new Hungary.

Meanwhile, Germany was to recognize the independence of Austria, a neat way of preventing the Austrian Germans from pleading self-determination and joining forces with the Germans in the Fatherland.

Since both points nine and ten involve the question of the treaties of partition, it would perhaps be well to consider them both at greater length. They bedeviled any peace of justice, and possibly, if Wilson had not been so intent upon his League of Nations, he would have seen the futility of even attempting a peace based upon his principles unless the Allies had agreed to scrap these treaties altogether. Self-determination and secret treaties, such as those drawn up during the war, partitioning spoils, could not be reconciled.

Nor was it a question of Rumania and Italy alone. Other secret treaties kept bobbing up as the conference progressed. The French, British, and Russians had made one dividing up the Turkish empire.

Russia was now out of it, but in accordance with that treaty the French had been promised Syria in return for England's taking Palestine, Mosul, and the valley of the Tigris-Euphrates. During the war Colonel Lawrence had intimated (to put it mildly) to his ally, Emir Feisal, that Syria should go to the Arabs. The English, it was now claimed, would double-cross the Arabs if the French obtained Syria. Seemingly, if they kept faith with Wilsonian principles, they must be prepared now to double-cross both French and Feisal, in case the Syrians should, in accordance with self-determination, prefer independence.

During the course of the war England also made a treaty with Japan, whereby in return for Japanese naval assistance it was agreed that Japan should retain the concessions in Shantung which the Germans had wrested from the Chinese and also all German islands in the Pacific north of the Equator. Since the Americans had been largely instrumental in getting the Chinese into the war on the Allied side, it seemed quite unfair to them that Japan should engorge herself with Chinese territory. The Japanese, however, insisted that her treaty right must be carried out to the letter and that England should keep her word with Japan.

Why not rather keep her word with Wilson? It might be a matter of abstract ethics whether or not a later agreement (such as that to conclude peace on accepted Wilsonian formulas) wiped out earlier ones as Wilson argued; but it can not well be disputed that the partition treaties prevented any general application of self-determination on any universal scale.

They certainly made confusion worse confounded in the old Austro-Hungarian empire. If the Allies had stuck to their original purpose to decentralize and to make autonomous but not independent the various nationalities inhabiting the Danube valley, they presumably would have been more realistic and more intelligent in their work. Bad as the old empire had been, at least this could be said for it: It had a common currency, a common fiscal policy, a common army. Now, instead of one army, one fiscal policy, one currency, one tariff border, there were five: Austrian, Hungarian, Rumanian, Czechoslovakian, and Yugoslavian. This was obviously expensive and impractical.

Even if five independent nations inhabiting a region primarily designed by nature for one alone could have succeeded in ironing out their respective jealousies and particularisms, any likelihood of any such successful outcome went glimmering as a result of placing so many and so important minority groups in nations which they disliked. But, of course, from Wilson's point of view, there was at least the League of Nations as a solvent for future problems, to say nothing of minorities treaties in which the succession states as well as Bulgaria

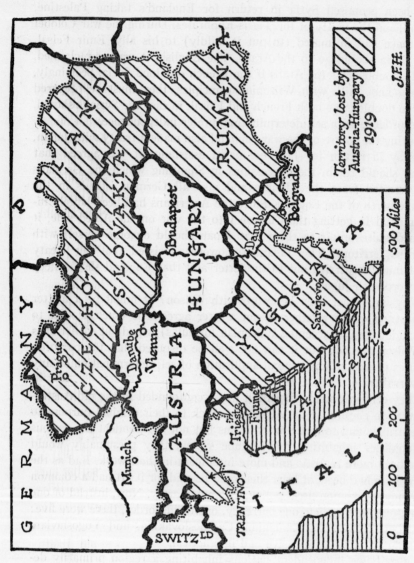

THE OLD AUSTRIA-HUNGARY IS BROKEN UP BY THE 1919 TREATIES

(Reprinted from J. F. Horrabin's *An Atlas of Current Affairs* by permission of, and special arrangement with, Alfred A. Knopf, Inc.)

and Turkey joined, treaties guaranteeing fair treatment of minority groups.

Returning to the fourteen points, numbers eleven and twelve may be said to have been part way successful. The Treaty of Sèvres with Turkey, which was to last but a few years (see p. 246), could not be said to have rendered impartial justice to the Turks; but it did provide for mandates, and the hope of autonomous development was held out to Syrians (under French guidance) and to Armenians, whose war-wrecked and poverty-stricken homeland it was hoped America would administer and succor.

Point number thirteen (Poland) was fulfilled—at considerable injustice to Germany. That Poland should be resurrected was fair enough, and that she should own a corridor to the Baltic was not without justification, even if such a corridor did separate East from West Prussia. Access to the sea had been pledged by the fourteen points, and while that did not necessarily involve the ownership of the corridor, it was true that, keeping rather strictly to the valley of the Vistula, Poles did outnumber Germans.

Where the principal violation of Wilsonian principles came in, as far as Poland was concerned, was in Silesia. That province had been either Austrian or Prussian for many hundred years. It was, with the Saar Valley, the principal source of Germany's coal, and its prosperity had been created by German enterprise. The Allies proposed giving all of Upper Silesia to the new Poland, and Wilson, particularly favorable to Poland, insisted thereon. The original treaty provided for so doing, but Lloyd George and the British were determined at the end to insist upon a plebiscite. After the treaty was signed, the vote was taken and Upper Silesia voted German. Whereupon a dirty trick was played upon the Germans. Instead of repatriating all of Silesia to Germany, the boundary line was drawn in such a zigzag fashion as to leave most of the coal-mines to the Poles. True, the population closely adjacent to the mines was Polish, since the mines were worked by Polish labor. True, also, the holding of the plebiscite for the entire region (not very large) carried the implication that the vote was for Upper Silesia as a whole. True, also, if Germany was to lose both the Saar (see p. 113) and Upper Silesia, it would be difficult to see how she could make sufficient money wherewith to restore invaded territory.

We come now to the last point, that which provided for a league of nations. Both Americans and Britons were entitled to credit for this innovation in international machinery. Before the conference there certainly had been greater interest shown in England in the potentialities of a league than in America. An important organization had existed for some time in the former country to secure a league of nations, and

THE BEACON LIGHT.

[Lord Robert Cecil is taking a leading part in the campaign for making the objects of the League of Nations better understood. The campaign opened on the anniversary of the Armistice.]

(*Punch*, Nov. 12, 1919. Reproduced by permission of the proprietors of *Punch*.)

under Lord Phillimore it had drawn up a constitution for such an organization which afterward, with certain modifications, became the framework of the Covenant as afterwards adopted. On the other hand, no plenipotentiary at Paris was as devoted to the league as President Wilson. He served as chairman of the peace conference committee on the league; he introduced certain important changes into its constitution, such as Article X, which guaranteed the territory of members against external aggression; and unquestionably for the sake of the league's adoption he consented to gloss over a number of specific injustices in the peace settlement as a whole.

How to bring about a league of nations was a thorny problem throughout a good part of the peace conference. The representatives of the smaller nations were jealous lest the larger powers control the league. The French rejoiced in the idea of a league, provided one was created with teeth—that is, with an international army to enforce the league's decisions, the commander of which presumably would be a Frenchman. The Japanese were willing to consent to a league; but they, too, had a price, namely, the official recognition of racial equality. It was comparatively simple to placate the smaller countries by providing for an assembly in which every country not represented on the council should have a vote. The French were brought in line by the promise of a treaty between England, the United States, and France which guaranteed the eastern boundary of France. The Japanese gave way and accepted the League without recognition of racial equality, but as they did so they were the more firmly determined to dig in on their rights to Chinese territory, as the President was to discover toward the close of the conference.

Meanwhile, difficulties loomed in the United States. The congressional elections of 1918 had gone against the Democratic party and interest in the League of Nations in America was lukewarm. Ex-President Taft, a firm friend of the league, warned Wilson that opposition to the League was growing daily in the United States, and that it could not possibly be overcome without definite amendments to the Covenant providing for recognition of the Monroe Doctrine and for free withdrawal at any time of any signatory. Wilson, therefore, made a hurried trip home in the midst of the conference, publicly to defend what was fast becoming with him the dearest goal of his life, a league of nations. Returning to Paris he fought hard for the two amendments which Taft had told him were essential, and these amendments he succeeded in imbedding in the Covenant.

The League of Nations, as finally drafted, provided for an assembly representing all countries with one vote each, and for a council of nine members, five permanent and four elected by the assembly to serve for one term each. Permanent seats were to be given to the United States, Great Britain, France, Italy, Japan. The headquarters of the League were to be at Geneva, where a secretariat or permanent board of officials was to be located. Attached to the League was to be a World Court for the settlement of international judicial disputes and an International Labor Office, which it was hoped might standardize conditions of labor throughout the world. The Assembly of the League was to meet in Geneva once a year, the Council four times a year, but not necessarily in Geneva. The latter body also could be summoned any time if danger threatened world peace. All members of the League were obligated to submit disputes between them to arbitration or to the Council for review. Decisions, to be effective, had to be unanimous, a qualification resting on both council and assembly.

So much for the fourteen points. To some extent they were, as we have seen, fulfilled, to some extent defeated.

THE FINANCIAL SETTLEMENT

What perhaps in the long run was more important than anything else relative to a peace of justice were the financial clauses of the projected treaty. Not only are the fourteen points directly involved here, since they called for the restoration as well as evacuation of the occupied lands, but also the President's public speeches between the publication of the fourteen points and the armistice, in which he affirmed that there should be "no contributions" and "no punitive damages" but that the invaded territories should be restored.

Just what did that mean? The British were worried; they had lost a good deal from air raids, but their territory had not been invaded. Their principal financial loss had come from the German submarine; but again there was no invasion of territory unless the High Seas be considered as belonging to Britannia. Therefore, in order to make certain that they would recover something from the Germans, the Allied governments gave an important gloss to Wilson's formulas in this important statement: "By it [that is, restoration of invaded territory] they understand that compensation will be made by Germany for all damages done to the civilian population of the Allies and to their property by the aggression of Germany by land, by sea, and from the air." In other words the Germans were obligated by the peace contract to pay for submarine and air-raid damage, as well as for destruction of property on land by marching armies.

So much and so much only were the Germans to pay. That is the clear meaning of the reservation or gloss given by the Allies to Wilson's general formula. But when they came to sign the treaty the Germans were confronted by quite different demands to explain which we must go back to Lloyd George. In the general election held in England directly after the armistice, there seemed to be a lack of enthusiasm on the part of the electorate. Lloyd George and his supporters found there was but one way to arouse it, namely, to excite the voters by promising to put the Kaiser on trial and to make the Germans pay the costs of war. The Prime Minister had already promised the Germans that they should pay certain specified sums which necessarily excluded the costs of the war. But that made no difference. Lloyd George was a mercurial man, an actor who reflected what his audience demanded. True, as he tells us in his book,[1] he qualified his promise by the words "Germany should pay to the utmost limit of her capacity." But even that qualification did not excuse him from promising one thing to the defeated enemy and quite another to the British electorate.

As a result of this double dealing, the British were in bad case when the conference met. Their bankers assured them that the Germans could pay $100,000,000,000, not the Allied cost of the war but an approximation to it. But actual damage done to Allied shipping, to the invaded territories in the way of destruction of houses, mines, and factories, plus fines levied on the civilian population of Belgium, amounted approximately to only some $10,600,000,000. This the Germans could have paid and presumably would have paid had this been the total of the bill. Because it, or some like sum, was not made the total assessment levied against the Germans, the treaty was dishonest.

To get the Americans to agree to exorbitant reparations was not easy. The French were just as willing as the British to squeeze the last penny out of Germany, since altogether aside from the popular hatred of Germany in France and the war psychosis and jangled nerves resulting from the strain of conflict, the French feared lest Germany get up on her feet again, and the best way to prevent that was to ruin her financially. But this was not true of the Americans. They, too, suffered from the waves of anti-German hate which suffused the whole Allied world; but they at least had no reason to fear a recuperated Germany, and after all the promise to the Germans came from Woodrow Wilson, and his name was at the bottom of the agreement in accordance with which Germany quit the fight.

Nevertheless, the British found a way to persuade Wilson. The able premier of South Africa, General Smuts, a delegate to the conference, invented a formula. War pensions, according to the general, were a legitimate charge against the Germans. The mighty host of soldiers in the Allied armies were not like ordinary soldiers. They had been drawn from civil life and to civil life they would return. Therefore, injuries

[1] Lloyd George, *The Truth about the Peace Treaty*, I, p. 463.

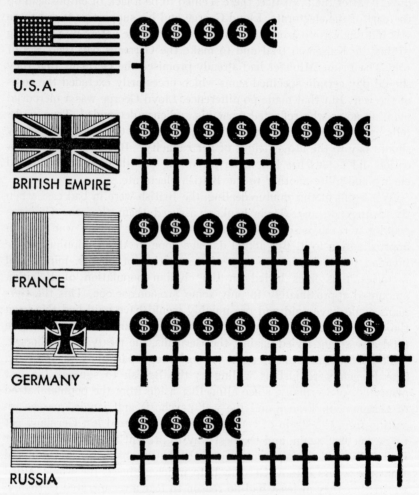

COST OF WORLD WAR

U.S.A.

BRITISH EMPIRE

FRANCE

GERMANY

RUSSIA

Each coin represents 5 billion dollars
Each cross represents 200,000 lives lost

(From Faulkner and Kepner, *America: Its History and People*, published by
Harper & Brothers. Courtesy of the Pictograph Corporation.)

they had received in the conflict were injuries sustained by the civilian population.

The lawyers on the American commission were quick to see the lack of logic in the general's argument. It really amounted to saying in another way that Germany should bear the cost of the war, for if injuries received by soldiers could be included in the bill because they were normally civilians, why not all war taxes, since they in turn had to be paid by civilians? Once admit pensions and separation allowances and the bill could be pushed almost as high as desired.

Wilson yielded to this argument of Smuts. The President was fatigued and weary, and he was no economist. "Logic be damned," he is reported as saying to his advisers, "I am going to sign for pensions." One wishes the President of the United States had not thus cavalierly dismissed logic!

What should be the total amount? Nobody could tell, and therefore it was decided that the treaty should assess no definite sum but should provide for an Allied commission to report within two years the amount due from the Germans and how it was to be met. In the meanwhile, the Germans were to lose the coal of the Saar Valley and of Upper Silesia, almost one-third of their total coal production, and were to deliver from their remaining supply to France, Italy, and Belgium 40,000,000 tons of coal a year for a period of ten years. All their larger merchant ships were to be given over to the Allies, half of their smaller ones, and one-quarter of their fishing fleet. Five thousand railway locomotives in good condition were to be surrendered and 150,000 railway carriages. These provisos virtually guaranteed the impossibility of Germany's paying the bill that yet was to be assessed, since her greater wealth came from her industries and commercial prosperity. But in order to make assurance doubly sure that the bill would be sufficiently high, the cost of all Allied commissions in Germany and the cost of the Allied army of occupation which was to be kept there fifteen years was added to whatever other sums might be due.

Wilson did want to be just to the Germans; but he wanted his League even more. It must be remembered that at this time many issues were pressing for settlement simultaneously, a very vexatious one being the boundary of France. That country would have liked to go all the way to the Rhine. Since this was impossible, owing to American and British objection, the French desired a thirty years' military occupancy of this region. The British and the Americans together persuaded the French to cut this period down to fifteen years, and the latter reluctantly agreed.

Then came the question of the Saar Valley, valuable for its coal. Louis XIV originally had conquered part of this German valley and the French had extended their conquest during the French Revolution. In 1814 the Saar had been restored to France, but after Waterloo in 1815 it had been taken away from that country and had been given to Prussia. Now France desired to reannex the Saar.

The valley was a small one, but valuable, thickly populated with German-speaking people. Wilson was determined that the French should not annex the valley, but he did yield to its occupancy by the League of Nations for a term of fifteen years, after which a vote was to be taken by the inhabitants as to whether they desired to become part of France, part of Germany, or to stay under the League. The French coal-mines had been flooded by the Germans during the war and this occupancy by the League was to insure to France the coal of the Saar. France was to own the mines, not the valley. After fifteen years, if the inhabitants voted to return to Germany, that country must buy the mines from France.

Herein have been described the main provisos of the so-called peace settlement. By the Treaty of Versailles, made with Germany, that country lost relatively little territory. Alsace-Lorraine, three tiny enclaves on the Belgian border, measured more readily in hundreds of yards than in miles, a part of northern Schleswig given to the Danes after a plebiscite, the city of Memel on the northeastern boundary with surrounding territory to the League of Nations (Memel's population was about 20,000, mostly Germans, but Memel and, the whole region, about half the size of Rhode Island, contained possibly as many Lithuanians as Germans); the city of Danzig to the League of Nations (some 300,000 Germans here); but Danzig was at the mouth of the Vistula and was regarded as an essential port for Poland; the district of Posen to Poland (the greater part of the population unquestionably Polish); the Polish Corridor, and a large part of Upper Silesia, also to Poland. For most of these losses of territory there was real justification; and as far as they are concerned, their cession could not be called a failure to live up to the bargain whereby Germany ceased fighting.

For the economic settlement there was no justification. The demand that the Kaiser and high German officials be tried by Allied law courts was a vindictive absurdity, and almost as absurd was the celebrated clause in the treaty, number 231, whereby Germany acknowledged on the part of herself and her allies entire responsibility for the losses suffered by the Allies during the war. Even worse was the fact that the economic blockade of Germany continued during the sessions of the peace conference. In this connection perhaps it would be well to keep in mind the words of the German representative when summoned to Versailles to receive the treaty. They are as follows:

I do not wish to answer reproaches with reproaches, but if it is from us that penance is demanded, then the Armistice must not be forgotten. Six weeks passed before we obtained it, and six months before we learnt your conditions of peace. Crimes in war may not be excusable, but they are committed in the struggle for victory, in anxiety to preserve national existence, in a heat of passion which blunts the conscience of nations. The hundreds of thousands of non-combatants who have perished since the 11th of November through the blockade were killed with cold deliberation, after victory had been won and assured to our adversaries. Think of that, when you speak of guilt and atonement.

Separate peace treaties also were signed with the other Central Powers, that of St. Germain with Austria, Trianon with Hungary, Neuilly with Bulgaria, Sèvres with Turkey. All of these four treaties violated the Wilsonian doctrine of self-determination to a greater or lesser degree, very decidedly so in the first two treaties, much less so in the last two. Much less important than the Treaty of Versailles, they none the less were a part of the settlement.

On the whole, the latter was a very unsatisfactory affair. No Talleyrand had represented Germany in Paris, and the Germans practically had been forced to sign on the dotted line. The American President, breathing forth idealism, had put his name to a treaty which in all that concerned economics was a breach of faith with the enemy, and toward the end Wilson had proved much more vindictive to the enemy than Lloyd George, whose conscience, or whatever passed for conscience, led him all too late to advocate more lenient treatment. The Prime Minister of England, on the other hand, had been responsible more than any one else for the reparations muddle, although it must be acknowledged that the French were his close seconds in so acting. The treaty was so bad that General Smuts thought seriously of not signing. About all that could be said in its favor is that it might have been worse; it might have annexed the Rhineland to France; it might have divided Germany again at the River Main, as she was divided in 1866; and the treaties of St. Germain and Trianon might have given the Czechs a corridor across the Hungarian plain which they asked for, thus separating Austria from Hungary and joining Czechoslovakia with Yugoslavia. These absurdities were at least avoided. It is a wild exaggeration to speak of the settlement as a Carthaginian peace, as many writers have done. Carthage was demolished and its site sown with salt. In the last analysis, the defeated Germans had received much fairer treatment than they themselves had meted out to the defeated Russians at Brest Litovsk. The men of Versailles not only did not demolish Germany but left open two ways of mitigating the harshness of their terms. There was the Reparation Commission which might show sense in tuning down the economic settlement, and there was, of course, the League of Nations, to which the idealists clung, in despair mingled with rapture.

From 1919 to the Ruhr

The four years which succeeded 1919 were full of disaster for Europe. The peace treaties seemingly settled nothing and confusion became worse confounded. Worse than that: the economic burdens borne by the European peoples became heavier and more intolerable than they had been during the war.

The first country to repudiate the Treaty of Versailles was the United States. The reasons which motivated the United States Senate were not as admirable as they might have been. The senators did not oppose the Treaty because it was unjust and a repudiation of Wilsonian promises; what they objected to was the League, the only ray of light, and a dim one at that, in a world black with angry hate. Even so, Wilson could have secured ratification had he been willing to accept drastic amendments to the League. Upon his refusal, the Treaty was rejected by the Senate and the presidential election of 1920 confirmed its rejection, the United States choosing to make its own separate treaty with Germany.

The effect of so doing was profound. It meant that the United States would not be represented either at Geneva (a term now constantly to be used as a synonym for the League of Nations), or on the Reparations Committee which was to assess the final bill against the Germans. It also served notice on the French that their concessions at Paris in return for American and British guarantees of their eastern boundary lines were useless. Even if the Senate had approved the Versailles Treaty, it is improbable that it would have accepted the additional triangular treaty between France, England, and the United States in regard to that guarantee. Now it was evident that the latter was a worthless bit of paper; for with America dropping out, England no longer was under unilateral obligation arising from that treaty to defend France.

France, indeed, in the hour of victory felt very uneasy. Three times within one hundred years her soil had been invaded by the Germans; suppose they should come again? For the time being the French had them in the gutter; Germany was convulsed with civil strife, without allies, and defended by an army reduced to 100,000. French troops, not German, kept the "Watch on Rhine." But suppose this situation changed? There were 20,000,000 Germans too many, so the French thought. France had wanted a league of nations equipped with an international army but had given in to the British and to the Ameri-

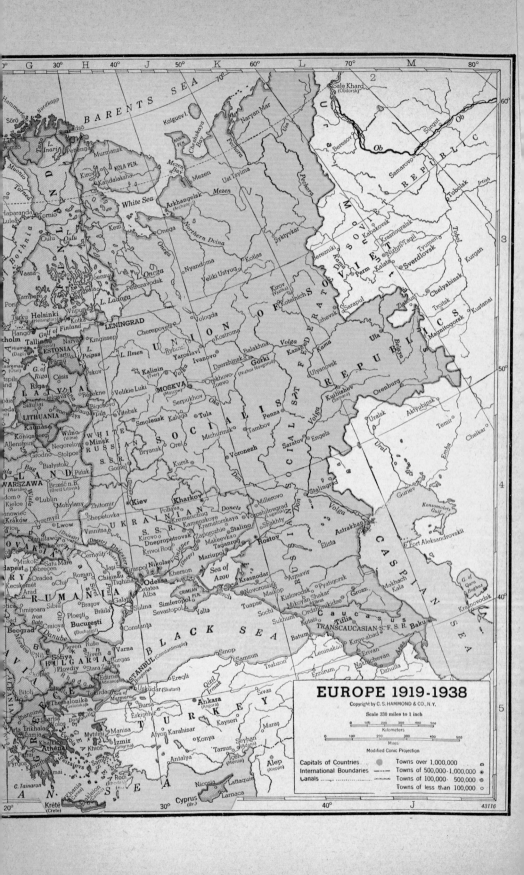

EUROPE 1919-1938

Copyright by C.S. HAMMOND & CO., N.Y.

Scale 330 miles to 1 inch

Kilometers

Miles

Modified Conic Projection

Capitals of Countries	Towns over 1,000,000
International Boundaries	Towns of 500,000–1,000,000
Canals	Towns of 100,000– 500,000
	Towns of less than 100,000

43116

cans; she had wanted to separate the Rhineland, which lay west of the river, from the Reich, or at least to occupy it for thirty years, and again she had yielded, cutting in half the period of occupancy; and now her third bulwark against a revived and powerful Germany—the Anglo-American guarantee—was down. Under such circumstances she not only determined to keep the German foe in economic vassalage but to surround him with a chain of states bound to herself in defensive alliance.

The French found it easy at first to secure allies. A close alliance with Belgium was consummated very soon after the Versailles Treaty, and shortly after, both Czechoslovakia and Poland joined France in a military alliance, thus surrounding Germany on three sides by prospective foes.

Czechoslovakia owed a great deal to France. That country had recognized and equipped the Czechoslovakian national army, had offered Paris as a temporary headquarters for the Czechoslovakian government, and had supported through thick and thin the claims of Czechoslovakia at the peace conference, ever insisting that the new nation be made *viable*, have economic resources and a creditable transportation system, whether self-determination was violated or not. In vain had the "Sudetendeutsch," as the Germans in the old Austrian province of Bohemia were known, begged for the recognition of that principle. They were told it was impossible to employ it, that they must rest content with the promise (never fulfilled) that the Republic of Czechoslovakia would be constituted on the Swiss model as a federative rather than as a unitary state.

Nationalistic minorities in this ward of France were clearly marked and from the beginning were troublesome. About two-thirds of the population were Czech or Slovak; but a great many Slovaks liked the Poles or the Magyars better than they did the Czechs. About one-quarter of the total population was German, bitterly opposed to Czechs and Slovaks alike. The remainder, approximately 1,500,000, consisted of Magyars, Jews, Poles, and Ukranians, not easy to handle. Nevertheless, Czechoslovakia lay like a great bastion in Central Europe, and the French were delighted at the thought of a powerful Czechoslovakia threatening Germany on the south. The definite Franco-Czechoslovak alliance was not formally completed, it is true, until 1924, but from the beginning French advice, French money, and French military aid were placed freely at the disposal of this new state, the most important of all the smaller satellite nations that France hoped to attach to herself.

To the east of Germany lay Poland, another potential French ally. The Poles had been divided among themselves during the war as to how Poland might be resurrected. Some of them, among whom was the conspirator and revolutionary patriot Pilsudski, were bitterly opposed to Russia and thought it might best be accomplished through the instrumentality of Austria. Others thought the best hope lay in supporting Russia against Germany. Consequently, Poles fought on both sides in the World War. But after the victorious Austro-Germans set up a puppet state of Poland in the midst of the conflict, Pilsudski was disillusioned. Unwilling to support the Central Powers, he was thrown in prison, not to escape until after the armistice, after which he placed himself at the head of a temporary Polish government at Warsaw.

Meanwhile, a Polish army had been organized in France in 1918 and the Poles in it had fought on the western front for France. Other Poles were on the Italian front, some on the Italian side, some on the Austrian, and still other Polish troops were deep in the Ukraine. It was Pilsudski's task to get them all home, to draw up a constitution, to establish boundaries, to resurrect a nation.

In all these endeavors he received the staunch backing of France. She sent the Polish troops from the west through Germany as early as April, 1919; she assisted Pilsudski with money and munitions; she supported his demands at the peace conference fully and effectively, and if the French had not been opposed there by Britain, Poland would have dipped into former German territory even more than she actually did.

The Versailles Treaty practically determined the western boundaries of Poland, but toward the east Pilsudski's ambitious imperialism was unchecked—except, that is, by British disapproval, which the Polish chieftain ignored. He occupied Kiev in the heart of the Ukraine; he pounced upon Vilna, capital of Lithuania, to the northeast; he pressed on against the Russian Communists. The latter fell upon Pilsudski hip and thigh, and only through the timely arrival of a French military commission was he rescued from disaster in a battle before Warsaw, which staved off communism from Poland and incidentally from Central Europe. The Treaty of Riga (1921) with Russia, which followed, extended the Polish boundaries well to the east, not so far as in 1772, the date of the first partition of Poland, but far enough to place some 4,000,000 Russians under Polish sovereignty.

Thanks also to French connivance, Pilsudski was able in 1923 to retain Vilna, in spite of the League of Nations. The French had been somewhat embarrassed when Poland and Czechoslovakia had almost come to blows over that small sector of Upper Silesia known as Teschen, for France wanted both Poles and Czechs as allies. That difficulty, however, was ironed out in 1920 by a division of Teschen between the two contestants, and now, thanks again to France, the Poles secured the better part of what was left of Upper Silesia.

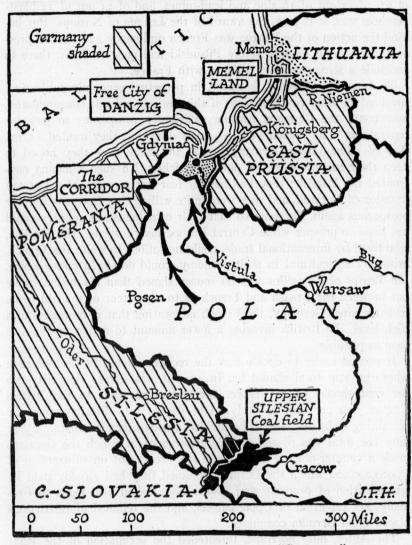

GERMANY'S EASTERN FRONTIER AND THE "CORRIDOR," 1921

(Reprinted from J. F. Horrabin's *An Atlas of Current Affairs* by permission of, and special arrangement with, Alfred A. Knopf, Inc.)

The hot-headed Poles had tried to seize that rich district by a military coup in 1919 but were headed off since the great powers at Paris had provided for a plebiscite in Upper Silesia. Despite the fact that the Germans won the vote for the district as a whole, France insisted that it be divided, and in the final settlement of 1921 French aid was again given Poland. The award to that country of 53 coal-mines out of 67, of 11 out of 16 zinc and lead-mines, and of 21 out of 37 blast-furnaces was, it is true, the award of the League of Nations. But behind the action of the League was French diplomacy and French pressure, for several months before Pilsudski had gone to Paris, there to conclude a strong military alliance with France.

To keep the Germans, however, in perpetual economic subjection, involved an inner contradiction; if this desired end was consummated, how could the Germans become sufficiently prosperous to pay for reparations? The French were in a nasty dilemma; they wanted a great deal of money from Germany but at the same time they hoped to keep their eastern neighbor poverty-stricken. No such dilemma confronted the English; they had neither fear nor memory of a German invasion of England, and they were quite willing that Germany become prosperous again, the more so that their own industrial country could not hope to prosper while Central Europe lay prostrate. The English, who lived by international trade, could not afford to wait; the French, primarily agricultural in their economy, could do so. In consequence, the Treaty of Versailles was no sooner signed than dissension broke out between the British and French as to the extent of the bill to be levied against Germany, the French advocating that it be raised to a high level, the British favoring a lower amount to revive business as soon as possible.

It proved easier to decide how the receipts should be divided than what the sum total should be. In 1920 it was agreed that fifty-two per cent should go to France, twenty-two per cent to the British Empire, ten per cent to Italy, eight per cent to Belgium, and the remaining eight per cent to be divided among other countries. A year later the total was placed at $56,000,000,000; at which the Germans made a counter-offer of $12,500,000,000, contingent on subtraction of $5,000,000,000 which the Germans claimed they had already paid by sequestration of property and goods. They asked also loans to Germany, her retention of Upper Silesia, and the removal of restrictions placed upon German commerce.

The Allies, duly horrified, threatened the occupation of the Ruhr Valley, the heart of industrial Germany, and the Germans made a new offer. Again it was for $12,500,000,000, but without hypothetical deduction of $5,000,000,000 and with the promise of rebuilding by German labor the destroyed villages and towns of France. This, in turn, the Reparations Committee rejected but lowered its own demands to $32,000,000,000, a figure the Germans, after vain protest, reluctantly accepted.

Did the payment of this sum lie within the bounds of possibility? It could be paid in only three ways: (*a*) by the transfer of actual gold from Germany to the Allies; (*b*) by services, the Germans repairing in person the damages they had done and delivering commodities like ships, coal, and so forth, to the Allies; or (*c*) a revival of international trade whereby the Germans could build up credits throughout the world which might be assigned to the Allies.

Method (*a*) was impossible. Thirty-two billion dollars was more than twice the actual amount of all known gold in the world and but a tiny fraction of the world's gold supply was in Germany. Method (*b*) was unacceptable. The French had no intention of permitting an invasion of German carpenters, masons, and plumbers for the rebuilding of French towns, thus throwing French artisans out of work. The British already had more ships than they could find cargoes for and their own shipyards were deserted. Their coal industry also was paralyzed, injuriously affected already by reparation payments of coal made to Italy and France. There remained then method (*c*). The success of this depended on the willingness of foreign countries to lower their tariff barriers against German goods. The United States was unwilling to do this, as was also France. To the east Poland was erecting, and not demolishing, tariff walls, and beyond Poland lay Russia in the throes of the Communist Revolution—an old German market now almost ruined.

It is conceivable that given a sufficient length of time the Germans might have paid by method (*c*). To do so, however, meant rigid economy and continuous sacrifice for many years, so many that babies born in the midst of the war would have become old folk before the yoke was lifted from their shoulders. The Germans were not willing to put such a yoke upon themselves. They had been forced to accept responsibility for the war and had so signed on paper; but this they had done because they were strangled by the Allies' economic blockade. In the name of victorious democracy, Woodrow Wilson had made them promises which had not been fulfilled. Why then submit to economic slavery? They had signed the peace treaty rather than starve and they would accept the reparation settlement rather than starve: but they felt no responsibility for either the one or the other.

In less than two years the reparation agreement bogged down. The Germans paid the $250,000,000 due in 1921; but so swift was the decline of their mark in the money markets of the world and so swift was the flight of capital from Germany that in 1922 they asked for and received a partial moratorium. Great Britain now took alarm and Lloyd George, still prime minister, summoned an international world economic conference at Genoa. Desperately he hoped that the United

States would participate, for if that happened the obtuse Yankees might realize that one reason for making the Germans pay was to obtain the wherewithal with which the Allies might pay their war debts to America. Desperately, also, did he hope that France might rescind her announced intention not to discuss reparations at this conference. Since both hopes were entirely imaginary there was no real reason for the conference at all. The Germans came and again offered to pay in kind but not in money. The Russians came and struck a treaty with the Germans. Since neither Soviet Russia nor the German Republic had funds, it was comparatively simple for them mutually to cancel each other's indebtedness. Other results Genoa had none.

On July 15, 1922, the Germans made their last cash payment; for the rest of that year they were granted a temporary moratorium. The latter was inevitable, since German currency was crashing to oblivion. Four German marks were almost equal to the American dollar in 1914; when the reparation agreement was signed the ratio was 56 to 1. But by November, 1922, it stood at 7,000 marks to the dollar, and was gone now beyond recovery.

The French were very angry. They had sunk huge sums in rebuilding their own devastated areas, and they believed that the Germans were wilfully issuing paper money to make reparations impossible. The inflation in Germany had artificially stimulated industry there and German factories were in full blast. Thereupon the French determined to seize their foes by the throat and by the hair, and, in January, 1923, the forces of France marched into the Ruhr.

The valley of the Ruhr, east of the Rhine, was neither very wide nor very long; but it was the heart of industrial Germany. Nine cities with over 2,000,000 inhabitants lay within its narrow confines, as also eighty per cent of the coal and eighty per cent of the blast-furnaces left to the Germans. Without the Ruhr, Germany could not exist as an industrial nation. Nevertheless the Germans decided to resist by the only means that lay within their power—the general strike. German miners refused to dig coal for the French masters, German puddlers refused to work the blast-furnaces, German engineers would not operate the valley's intricate transportation system. Nothing lay before Germany but helpless poverty; but since the mark had already sunk so far, why not print more and more until the cost of the paper exceeded the value of the numerical digits put upon it? By the end of 1923 this had happened; the mark was now worth two and a half trillion to the dollar and milk was priced at 250,000,000 marks per quart.

The Germans thereupon surrendered and agreed to renew reparation payments if some new basis could be found for so doing. Their middle class had been virtually wiped out. Houses, life-insurance policies, everything that formerly had possessed monetary value was lost to millions of Germans. Almost nobody was employed in industry; practically everyone had suffered except peasants and profiteers.

As for the French, their victory was tasteless. Even before the World War, their debt had been colossal and now they staggered under it. Their adventure in the Ruhr had been most costly and they had nothing in return. They in turn would soon have to devalue their own currency and in the meanwhile they had lost the sympathy of the British, and the Germans, putting into effect the Tolstoyan program of "non-resistance to evil by force" had not been unsuccessful in withstanding them.

All things considered, the dark clouds which hung over Europe in 1919 looked even darker in 1924. The Ruhr invasion of 1923 had seemingly crushed Germany, but without helping the French exchequer. The French still held the military hegemony of Europe, for what it was worth; they had the largest army and supporting it were the armies of Czechoslovakia and Poland, French-trained. But Russia was an imponderable factor; suppose Germany should go Communist and join with Russia? Mussolini meanwhile had risen to power in Italy and was challenging both the status quo and the League of Nations. France had a permanent seat on the council of that organization and since nothing could be done without the unanimous consent of that council (and perhaps not much even with it), France had nothing to fear from the League. On the other hand, could she depend upon it in time of need? Furthermore, a new dictator had risen in the Near East, as we shall note later, and in that quarter of the globe French influence had declined greatly. There seemed to the French but one clear line to pursue—by diplomacy and by money to secure as many allies as possible; to keep up the iron ring around Germany; to continue as she had done in the past to follow the traditional rules of power politics. How disastrous a policy this was to prove, we shall see later.

CHAPTER V

THE UNION OF SOVIET SOCIALIST REPUBLICS (U.S.S.R.)

PEACE of a kind dawned on Western Europe in November, 1918, but in Russia there was not even a semblance of peace. The Bolsheviks (the Reds) faced civil war in their own country, large sections of which were either indifferent to the Revolution or actually under control of anti-Bolshevik factions (the Whites), supported everywhere by Allied sympathy and in many cases by Allied money and Allied soldiers.

During the last stages of the war, English and American troops had occupied Murmansk, the Russian seaport on the Arctic Ocean—this to prevent the capture of war matériel by the Germans. The French, after the collapse of Germany, had landed detachments at Odessa on the Black Sea; and at Vladivostok on the Pacific both the Americans and the Japanese landed forces, ostensibly to protect supplies and to guard the Trans-Siberian and Chinese Eastern railways. These various Allied interventions greatly encouraged those former adherents of the Czar who were set on reëstablishing the old régime. To their side now hastened many of the Russian Cadets (the former Constitutional Democrats), some of the Mensheviki (minority socialists), and a few of the old Social Revolutionary party. The Reds found themselves hemmed in on all sides. Allied detachments had captured Archangel on the White Sea and threatened them on the north. On the west an ex-Czarist general, Yudenich, aided by White Russians and some Estonians, headed toward St. Petersburg (now Petrograd and soon to be called Leningrad). From the south a large White army under General Denikin, outfitted by Allied guns, airplanes, and tanks, was marching toward Moscow. Meanwhile, at Omsk in Siberia, an anti-Bolshevik directorate, with some claim to be the legal successor of Kerensky's deposed administration, seemed strongly entrenched. Backed by the warlike Czechoslovak troops, who had fought viciously with the Bolsheviks on their retreat toward the Pacific, and by numerous ex-Czarist officers, this directorate in western Siberia, soon to fall under the control of Admiral Kolchak, a White, apparently was quite as strong as that of the Reds centering in Moscow.

The Bolsheviks in 1919 confronted a situation somewhat parallel to that which the French Jacobins faced in 1793—disaffection from within and intervention from without. Like their radical French predecessors, they met the first with militant terrorism and the second with patriotic zeal. Trotsky, the Red commissar for war, created *de novo* a Red army which made up in morale for what it lacked in equipment. Soon it began to win victories. As in the case of the Austro-Prussian invasion of France in 1792, the Allied intervention was only half-hearted. On the former occasion the approach of the second partition of Poland in 1793 had diverted Allied interests elsewhere. Now, after the terrific strain of four years' fighting, the Allies had no stomach for adventures in Russia. The French, from a financial point of view, were likely to lose most from a Bolshevik victory, since the Russian Reds had repudiated the Czar's debts, and France had loaned more money to Russia than any other country; but on the other hand no troops in Europe were more war-weary than those of France, and mutinies among French soldiers and sailors at the Black Sea ports made Paris hesitant to support Denikin's advance. The British were in somewhat similar case. They had a huge surplus of unsalable war supplies, speedily depreciating in value, and these they placed readily enough at the disposal of the Whites; but the lives of British soldiers were another matter. A general strike of the British trade unions was imminent if British regiments were ordered to fight the Bolsheviks, and the Lloyd George cabinet shrank back from any such commitments. Both British and French had hoped that the Americans would do something to defeat the Reds, and there had been talk at Paris of General Pershing's leading his relatively fresh forces against Trotsky. But the Americans were not interested; they withdrew their meager detachments from Vladivostok and from Murmansk and declined to participate in the anti-Bolshevik front, except to support the barrier of smaller states backed by the Allies (from Finland to Rumania), that the Bolshevik infection might be kept out of Europe.

Partly owing to these facts, Trotsky's armies proved victorious. They were led in many cases by former officers of the Imperial Russian Army, who preferred to fight for their own Russia, even if revolutionary, rather than for the Whites with their foreign support. The Whites, moreover, had no uniform command. The more they advanced into the heart of Russia, the more they embittered the peasants. Had they been willing boldly to proclaim constitutional and economic reform and formally to recognize peasant ownership of the land, it is possible that the result might have been different. But even this partial acceptance of the revolution the Whites were unwilling to concede; they wanted their old rights and their former property restored. And so the peasants, at first more or less indifferent, ultimately sided with the Reds against the Whites; confronted with terrorism as practised by both factions, they decided that the Red was the lesser of two evils.

The civil war was over by the end of 1920. For a time it looked as though the Poles, acting on the advice of French officers and equipped with French guns, might overcome the Soviets. The Poles drove south and east from Warsaw, captured Kiev in the heart of the Ukraine; and as they did so Baron Wrangel, heading a new White army in the South, advanced north from the Crimea. Both Wrangel and the Poles, however, were routed. Wrangel followed Denikin into exile at Constantinople, and the hard-pressed Poles were in danger of losing Warsaw and would have done so, had it not been for French assistance (see p. 118). Peace followed. Russia was still an "outlaw" country in the eyes of Western Europe and none of the Allied powers recognized the Soviet government; but on the other hand they took no further steps to defeat the Russian revolution by force of arms.

Left to themselves, the Bolsheviks were free to put into operation their long-cherished dream of a socialist state. They were without funds; they were inexperienced in the practical details of both government and business; and they had on their hands a backward and poverty-stricken peasantry comprising ninety per cent of the population, quite content with the individual ownership of their land, and to all intents and purposes untouched with Marxian ideas of a state-controlled economic life. So exhausted, indeed, were the Reds at the end of the civil war, that the rest of Europe confidently prophesied that their régime could not last. Trains, it was said, did not run in Russia; telephones did not operate; grass grew in the streets; all business was at a standstill; and in Moscow and Petrograd even the houses were falling to pieces. So thought the enemies of Red Russia.

But one thing they forgot—the energy and enthusiasm engendered by a blind faith in a new ideology and in Nicolai Lenin, the embodiment of it. Lenin, a conspirator for decades, came from the lesser nobility. His brother had been put to death as a university student for conspiring against Alexander III, and Lenin himself had been expelled from a Russian university for political agitation. Watched by the police, he went to St. Petersburg, advocated Marxian doctrines, was arrested and exiled for three years to Siberia. He came back, plunged into socialistic propaganda, spent much time at London, Paris, and Geneva, and was the foremost Russian delegate at the Second Congress (1903) of the Second International at Brussels. Here he led the fight of "the hards," or the Bolsheviks, against the "softs," or the Mensheviki, in other words that of the uncompromising Marxians who opposed any coöperation with bourgeois parties against their more opportunist fellows. The Bolsheviki at first won the day, hence their name, which

POLAND (ARROWS SHOW AREAS TAKEN OVER AFTER RUSSO-POLISH
WAR OF 1920)

(Reprinted from J. F. Horrabin's *An Atlas of Current Affairs* by permission of,
and special arrangement with, Alfred A. Knopf, Inc.)

means majority. But the Mensheviki, meaning minority, turned the
tables at last, and Lenin's group met defeat.

When the abortive revolution of 1905 broke out in Russia, Lenin
slipped back to his own country. Here he again experienced defeat as

he had in 1903, for the revolutionary tempo shortly slowed down, as the Czar won back power and prestige and revolutionary socialism was at a discount. The Cadets (the liberals) held the spotlight, and Lenin hated all Cadets, holding that they were "vermin who take possession of the battlefield when the heroes have been defeated"—the heroes in this instance being the striking workmen of Moscow and St. Petersburg. Lenin's own liberty, if not his life, was in danger, for he was living obscurely on a false passport. There was nothing to do for the time being in Russia, and therefore he quit the country in 1907, not to return for ten years.

This second period of exile was spent for the most part in Switzerland and in secret propaganda work. Lenin remained at the head of the Bolsheviki, but the world knew nothing of them or him. In the first Russian Duma there was little talk of socialism, and what there was came from the handful of Mensheviki in it. The Bolsheviks were not even represented. Consequently, when Lenin, with the kind permission of the Germans, came back to Russia in 1917 in the midst of her new revolution, there were few to note that fact or to realize how shrewd the Germans were in importing this dynamic protagonist of proletariat revolt.

Yet this stocky, middle-aged man within three years was to become a dictator in Russia, the first of the series of twentieth century dictators to gain power in Europe. His success was not due to his being a brilliant thinker. His books, for the most part, are disappointing; they are replete with wild assertions unsubstantiated by fact; they parrot Marx and Engels, and, by boldly clapping down the word "scientific" on untested hypotheses, presents a façade of deep intelligence which is not warranted by their contents. How, then, account for the universal acclaim meted out to Lenin in Russia?

To some extent it may be credited to luck; to some extent to the complete optimism and self-confidence which made him proclaim the last battle as always the final victory. To some extent also it was due to his character. His revolutionary career had been a long one, and his reputation among revolutionaries for sincerity and determination was of the highest. He knew how to direct the energies and how to incite the loyalties of his fellows. The inflammatory but brilliant Trotsky, generally a lone hawk and a suspicious one, finally became his devoted disciple. The Georgian outlaw and ruffian, Stalin, an exile in Siberia as the revolution of 1917 broke, became another.

But in the last analysis, perhaps the major explanation of Lenin's power lay in the fact that he was the high priest of a new and virulent religious faith. Such a theory would have amused him greatly, if such a single-tracked mind could have been capable of amusement. How

could any one be said to be a religious prophet while proclaiming that
his followers must be active atheists, and that religion was "the opiate
of the people"? Closely examined, however, this statement is no para-
dox. Lenin, we must remember, had faith in one thing—the Revolution.
Capitalism (the world) was at an end; communism (heaven) was at
hand. It would come, to be sure, on this earth, but so rapid and so
lovely would be its advent that all need for government would disappear miraculously, and justice everywhere would reign triumphant,
as class ceased to struggle with class in a society in which class was
non-existent.

Lenin, like a good Communist, would object instantly to the word
"miraculously," holding that there was no nexus whatever between
such an objective and scientific idea as communism and the miraculous.
But the real scientist ever holds his hypothesis tentative, and is constantly retesting and reverifying not only his observed data but the
hypotheses from which they are derived. It was not thus with the
Marxians, to whom economic conclusions were axiomatic. As a matter
of fact, the theoretical foundations of their belief—and Lenin was a
convinced Marxian—rested on assumptions which were sufficiently
dogmatic and all-inclusive as to become essentially a religious creed.

That creed, in summary, consisted of the following tenets: (*a*) all
thought of a future life must be abandoned, or else it will be forever
impossible to organize society upon a just and satisfactory basis;
(*b*) the individual ownership of private property, the father of capitalism and imperialism, brought on the World War and the nemesis of
the old order; (*c*) the communal ownership of goods and the adoption
of the Marxian formula, "from each according to his capacity, to each
according to his needs," is a categorical imperative; (*d*) that ownership
can only be obtained by a dictatorship of the proletariat; (*e*) that in
the course of time dictatorship will no longer be needed, for a classless
society will not require any government; (*f*) the writings of Marx,
Engels, and Lenin prove the above propositions up to the hilt and
make it unnecessary and even heretical to seek elsewhere for any
elucidation of human problems. The Communist explanation is inclusive, complete, final. Nothing need be added; nothing must be sub-
tracted. All who oppose this creed, both within and without Russia,
are enemies who should receive no mercy, and their defeat may be
sought by utilizing any and every means available.

Such was the Communist creed, a religion held with fanatical zeal
by fanatical men.

The acceptance of it, however, was not at first wide-spread nor was
Lenin universally acclaimed as the Revolution started. It must be
remembered that when he arrived back in Russia he was the accepted

leader of only one of the three socialist parties and that the Mensheviki and the Social Revolutionists also were powerful, to say nothing of
the Cadets. Only little by little, from the summer of 1917 to the conclusion of the civil war, did Lenin and his gospel become the accepted
creed. Possibly, more than anything else, it was the man's cocksureness
that insured his victory. He, almost alone, among the leaders, was
always utterly and completely confident that he knew exactly what
should be done. At a time when the Cadets were still trying to keep
Russia in the war, it was Lenin who started the cry for "peace and
bread." He denounced the war as an imperialistic one in which Russia's
allies were as bad—though no worse than—the Germans. No annexations, no indemnities, Russia to quit the war and to fight one of her
own against the bourgeoisie within her borders. The Cadets were
traitors to the Revolution; it was not a *liberal* revolution; it was the
Communist Revolution, the greatest, and the best and the *final* revolution.

Such outspoken ideas, for the time being, meant trouble for Lenin,
who was accused of being a German agent conspiring against the provisional government, and it was necessary for him frequently to take to
cover. Even after the November Revolution, when the Bolsheviks
seized power, the leadership of Lenin was not a certainty. When the
elections for the Constituent Assembly which met in January, 1918,
were held, it was found that the Social Revolutionaries were in a
majority and that the Bolsheviks had only about twenty-five per cent
of the membership. That assembly was given short shrift by the
soviets; it held one session and then was ended by the fiat of the Petrograd soviet. Lenin's excuse was that of Robespierre or that of Cromwell—the assembly did not represent the will of the people.

What was that will? Patently it was above everything else to stop
fighting. The Russian soldiers were brave; but no soldier can endure
endless waiting for his comrade to be killed so that he may equip himself with that comrade's rifle. Peace and land, Lenin knew, were what
the Russians wanted, and he proposed giving them both, and if necessary, peace at any price. In view of the intentions of the Germans to
annex Russian provinces, it was not easy for the soviets to swallow his
formula altogether, and at first Lenin was in a minority in the Council
of People's Commissars, as the tentative revolutionary government was
called. Some of the commissars were for further resistance, and even
the realistic Trotsky preferred a Fabian plan by which there would be
neither peace nor war, the Russians simply retreating before the Germans. But finally Trotsky changed his vote to Lenin's side and the
latter won by a majority of one.

The peace with Germany proved popular, as did also the early legislation which the commissars favored. All non-peasant estates were immediately confiscated and placed in the hands of locally elected committees. So also was it with the homes of the wealthy nobles and bourgeois which were now open to residence for the proletariat of the cities. The banks were taken over and their funds appropriated. All debts of the former government, both national and international, were repudiated. All large factories became government property. And to suppress any objections to these stiff measures, the Cheka, or secret police, was organized and given plenary power. In the summer of 1918 the R.S.F.S.R., the Russian Socialist Federated Soviet Republic, was inaugurated and within two years, with the collapse of the Whites, it was omnipotent in Russia.

Lenin now had a few more years to live (he died in January, 1924), and during them he bent himself heroically to four major tasks: (*a*) the consolidation of power in the hands of the Communist party, the new name assumed by the Bolsheviks in 1918; (*b*) the spread of communism throughout the world by the establishment of the Third International; (*c*) the abolition of individualist business enterprise in Russia and the socialization in that country of all means of production; (*d*) the transformation of the entire folk psychology of the Russian people, whereby sanctions imposed by the old moralities and the old ethical conceptions shriveled up, to be supplanted by new concepts, strange and bizarre to both Asiatic and Western culture.

Ostensibly, Russia was now a republic, a word which ordinarily in the twentieth century had come to imply a certain quantum of belief in democratic or at least representative institutions. This was not true of the Russian republic; from its inception the R.S.F.S.R. was simply a mechanism through which the Communist party controlled Russia in the name of the proletariat. Therefore, it is far more important to analyze that party and its organization than the theoretical framework of the government. In theory, every Russian adult, except for certain specified social classes, like employers, men working for private gain, clergymen, former employees of the Czar's administration, and so forth, was qualified to take part in the government and to vote. In theory, also, those who voted elected freely, although indirectly through their local soviets or councils, an All-Russian Congress of Soviets, which elected an executive committee, which in turn chose the Council of People's Commissars—seventeen men at the head of the government.

But theory does not always coincide with practice, and since all voting had to be done by show of hands, and since the urban soviets, full of workmen, were heavily overweighted when it came to districting out Russia, it is easy to see how a highly disciplined group within the body of workmen, like the Communist party (it also had a number of peasant members) might readily remain master of the situation as it did.

So also was it when the government was again reorganized in 1923, as the R.S.F.S.R. gave place to the U.S.S.R. (Union of Socialist Soviet Republics). In theory again this step was intended to demonstrate how liberal the R.S.F.S.R. could be in dealing with the various nationalistic groups remaining in the Russian empire. The new constitution now recognized no less than nine different republics, bound together in one union, namely, the old R.S.F.S.R., the soviet republics of the Ukraine, the Transcaucasian republics (Azerbaijan, Armenia, Georgia), the White Russian republic, and three smaller ones in the eastern stretches of the empire in Asia. Each of these separate republics had a constitution like that of the original R.S.F.S.R.; each of them sent delegates to an All-Union Congress of Soviets, which again chose a central committee, as in the case of the original constitution described.

Now the idea behind this change from the R.S.F.S.R. to the U.S.S.R. was simple. Since the former constitution was socialistic, it must repudiate imperialism and all of its works. Therefore, the Russian soviet government must not tyrannize over the Ukranian, Turkoman, and all the other peoples, or other ethnic groups which happened to be within the geographical boundaries of Russia. These other peoples had the right to enjoy their own language, culture, indigenous institutions. Thus the theory ran, and consequently each one was set up as a separate republic. But we must not be deceived by these separate republics which, though republics in name, possessed much less autonomy than the states under the American system. For instance, to the union government fell not only those functions which almost always are attached to a federal government, such as war, peace, currency, and so forth, but also such matters as health, labor laws, and even, to some extent, education.

Constitutions, however, may be one thing and realities another, and especially true was this of both the R.S.F.S.R. and the U.S.S.R. In both of them Lenin took good care to preserve the iron grip of the Communist party It was the only party which had any legal existence. First through the Cheka and then through the G.P.U., names successively given to the secret police, the party controlled all elections, for it was very dangerous for any one to vote against the party nominee. There was no such thing under either of these two formal Russian constitutions, it must be remembered, as independent law courts. Judges might be removed at will, and the G.P.U. could arrest and execute at will any individual without his having any recourse to such law courts as were set up. In fact, the G.P.U. was more powerful than the famous Third Section of the Czars; it had more spies; it had more money; it even possessed a separate army to enforce its bidding. Quite similar to the dreaded Gestapo (secret police) of Hitler, the G.P.U. was both whip and scorpion in the hands of first Lenin and then Stalin.

The Communist party was composed of city workmen, ex-soldiers, a few poor peasants, and (afterward) of a few professional men. From its inception, all ex-nobles, priests, traders, bankers, and all the middle-class men of every description, together with their relatives, were in theory strictly excluded. One gained admittance only after a proba-tionary period and upon the recommendation of a number of members. Periodically, it was necessary to prove oneself worthy of membership, or else expulsion followed. Unless one was a confessed atheist, one could not join; unless one confessed the pure Marxian faith as laid down by Lenin, one could not join. From the beginning the membership was strictly limited, although of late years it has grown considerably. Periodic purgings of the lax and the Laodicean reduce its strength from time to time so that the number of Communists (party members, that is) is never fixed. Perhaps one may best think of it as having a membership fluctuating between 2,000,000 and 3,000,000, and closer to the former figure.

Of these the great majority continued to be urban workers and soldiers. Highly organized in little groups or cells in the Russian fac-tories, they watched and controlled local elections, reported men they disliked to the G.P.U., criticized or approved factory management, and sternly disciplined one another. Drunkenness, for instance, must never be indulged in by a Communist; he must not pay too much attention to women; he must be ever on the job as a good workman and as a good propagandist; he must not intermarry with the hated bourgeoisie (as much anathema to Communists as Jews to Nazis in Germany); he must bring up his children as good Communists; he must not let them be subject to religious instruction; he must see to it that they joined the "Young Pioneers," a youth organization attached to the Com-munist party; and above all things in heaven (denied existence) and on earth he must put loyalty to the party and to its principles as laid down by Lenin. For the party and the party alone was Russia's salvation.

Communism, to Lenin, was an international faith, and he set great store by the Third International, the instrumentality through which it was hoped that communism might spread throughout the world. The First International, as organized by Karl Marx, had petered out in the bloodshed at Paris in 1871, following the Franco-Prussian War, and the Second International, in existence at the outbreak of the war, and still more or less alive, was, in Lenin's opinion, hopelessly rightist in tendency, honeycombed with opportunist heresy, and impregnated with national patriotism. He would have none of this agency of Western social democracy, and therefore he promoted the Third International with headquarters at Moscow as a kind of clearing-house for revolutionary propaganda.

The actual relations of this Third International to the U.S.S.R. have always been a matter of hot dispute. According to official statements of the Soviet authorities, the Third International, or the Comintern, as they call it, is an independent body of world Communists who simply accept the hospitality of the U.S.S.R., hold their meetings or congresses in Moscow, maintain a permanent secretariat there, and function independently of the Soviet government. According, however, to the enemies of Soviet Russia, this explanation is a mere blind, and the Third International or Comintern is an agency of the U.S.S.R. which finds it convenient to disown the activities of the Comintern in public while supporting and directing them in private. The truth presumably lies between the two statements. There can be no question but that officials of the Comintern held important posts in the Soviet government and thus at least a kind of informal interlocking directorate existed. On the other hand the financing of the Comintern did come from dues collected from Europe, America, and Asia; and the opinions of German, American, and Chinese Communists were vented at the various congresses of the Third International and had influence in determining the policy of that organization.

The Third International was founded in 1919. Its announced aim was "to replace world Capitalism by world Communism, thus abolishing the private ownership of the means of production and with it the selfish lust for profits, exploitation of man by man, all inequalities based on sex, religion, and nationality; devastating crises and still more devastating wars." And this it hoped to do by establishing in every country a Communist party, disciplined, cohesive, and obedient to orders received from the Comintern, pledged to a revolutionary seizure of political power. At least this was true in Lenin's day. In later years the Third International became, until it was abolished in 1943, seemingly less revolutionary in act and willing, apparently, to work in harmony with "leftist" bourgeois interests.

For Lenin was a believer in the apocalyptic version of the Marxian faith. He thought the new heaven and the new earth just around the corner, that capitalism was (everywhere) on its death-bed, and that the universal revolution was imminent.

There was some excuse for this belief in 1919. In Hungary, in Germany, in Armenia, India, and China, Communist revolts either had broken out or were on the point of doing so. Particularly hopeful was Lenin of Germany. He was deceived by the semi-anarchy there into believing that Germany was on the point of going Communist, and he deserves no small amount of blame for the advent of Hitler, since his advice to the German Communists to have nothing to do with the Social Democrats, a policy followed even after his death, weakened the leftist front and made easier the advent of the Nazis (see p. 161).

Only as time passed did Lenin come to conceive of the world revolution as springing up first not in the highly organized capitalistic countries but rather in those regions where capitalism was weak and not yet firmly entrenched. Here, in what were called colonial or semi-colonial countries, it was held, lay the greatest hopes for immediate Communist success. If, indeed, there is any such thing as Leninism, as a philosophy amplifying and enlarging the doctrines of Marx and Engels, it may be found in Lenin's *Imperialism as the Latest Stage of Capitalism*, a book in which he developed that theme.

Largely on account of it, there was held in Baku in 1920 a congress of oppressed nationalities whom Russia and the Third International sought to rescue from their oppressors. Nearly 2,000 delegates from no less than 37 different nationalities attended the meetings. Prominent among them were the Turks, who, under Kemal Ataturk (see p. 248), appealed to Russia for help and got it. Lenin surrendered to Ataturk over 7,000 square miles, formerly part of the Czar's empire, and loaned him money and professional assistance in establishing the Turkish republic. Lenin likewise denounced the special privileges which the Czar's government had obtained at one time or another in Iran, Afghanistan, and China. He deeded land to Afghanistan, proposed that Moscow be linked to Kabul by air, offered to help the Amir in opposing Britain, "the most rapacious imperialistic government on earth." The close hookup of the Chinese Communists with Russia did not come, it is true, until after Lenin's death, but the idea of having one was his. To him Russia's influence in hastening the advent of the New Jerusalem could only come by shunning all contact with the League of Nations, a bourgeois institution controlled by capitalists, and by stirring up everywhere, but particularly in undeveloped and in semi-developed dependent countries, disorder, insurrection, and proletarian dictatorships.

THE NEW ECONOMIC POLICY

Meanwhile, neither industry nor agriculture was flourishing in Russia. The Communist leaders had no technical knowledge of business. They had been conspirators, publicists, politicians, or, if you will, statesmen. But they did not know how to manage factories, mines, banks. In consequence, production fell off so alarmingly that in 1920 it was less than forty per cent of what it had been in 1913 and in certain lines of skilled manufacture it was way below that low level.

Nor was this the worst. There was scarcity of food. The peasants who produced it knew nothing of Marx; they thought that the newly won land of the proprietor, the church, and the state belonged to them outright. They were willing to exchange their surplus wheat and meat for articles which they needed, like spades, and nails, and needles; but they had no intention of giving them away for paper money, rapidly depreciating in value as the articles they sought grew scarcer.

What was to be done? The dictatorship of the proletariat had seemed so simple. Its function was clear; to turn Russia into a socialist state, wherein none should work for their own gain but each for each and for his neighbor. Capitalism was the enemy; it was abolished by fiat. The bourgeoisie were the instruments of capitalism; they were abolished by fiat. "Let him not eat who does not work," was a good Marxian slogan —and also incidentally Christian, since St. Paul said it before Marx. But who was to direct how the work should be done; and how was production to be started again; and how were the people to eat? Lenin's first idea had been simply to appropriate the peasant's surplus; but the peasants saw no occasion for having any surplus. Then followed the creation of food armies, forcibly to collect food from the rural districts. The peasants hid their food, and the armed forces of the proletariat collected it with much bloodshed. Physical hardships, almost unendurable, were now met with in both town and country, and the wise shook their heads and said, "The revolution is over."

But Lenin would not have it so. Like a good soldier he decided on a strategic retreat. This was the *Nep* or new economic policy. In effect it was a partial return to capitalism. The state ownership of all the land of Russia was reaffirmed, but the peasants were no longer to have their surplus expropriated. Instead they were to pay a regular fixed tax and were free to do what they wanted with any surplus remaining. Since the land did not belong to them, they could not sell or mortgage it. But at any rate they had won a respite and were quiescent, particularly the wealthier and more ambitious ones, known as "kulaks," who received permission to rent land from their poorer neighbors.

Small industries, those employing under twenty men, were now, in accordance with the Nep, turned back to private enterprise, as was most retail trading and selling. Men thus engaged were known as "Nepmen" and were not highly regarded by the Communist party. But they were tolerated. The larger industries owned by the state were consolidated into great trusts, and foreign experts were hired at excellent salaries as advisors. These foreign experts and technicians were not desired as Russian citizens; they could not become members of the party, and had no political voice. Neither did the Russian Nepmen. One could not be a Communist and be a Nepman; one could not have the honor of voting and be a Nepman; but if one voluntarily chose to enter this humble class one could make money, always running the risk, of course, that high taxes might take it from you.

In addition to these changes, foreign corporations, as such, were invited to do business in Russia. The country stood in need of fluid capital and the best way to obtain it was to invite the foreigner in—under strict supervision. The proffered concessions promised goodly profits and many foreign capitalists took advantage of Lenin's offers. The economic tide began to turn and production reached its old level. Was this socialism or was it not? People rubbed their eyes; state socialism, or state capitalism, or call it what you will, seemingly existed side by side with individual enterprise. We keep the banks, the big industries, and the taxing power in our own hands, said the Communists, and as long as we do that we have not betrayed Marx. But seemingly they had postponed the millennium.

Yet not for long, in Lenin's opinion. All he had in mind was a brief postponement of that happy day. Very shortly it would dawn, and just as soon as the Russian proletariat could master the secrets of machinery. Motors, dynamos, tractors, electrification, power-dams, hydroelectric power, technology—in this direction lay salvation. Lenin particularly was captivated by electricity. His Marxian philosophy, basing all human happiness and well-being on materialistic accomplishment, led directly to the conviction that the machine, whether composed of flesh and blood or of copper and steel, was the only ultimate reality. He was also a Russian, as well as a Marxian, and he could not escape the tradition of Peter the Great. The great statue of that monarch in Petrograd had been hurled from its base amid the maledictions of the proletariat, for he had built his capital city by the forced labor of sweating peasants; but the tradition which he had set up of adopting Western ways of life still remained. Peter was cursed as the worst of despots, and the name of his city was changed to Leningrad; but he was none the less copied. To England, to America, to Germany, Lenin sent for chemists, agricultural experts, engineers, technicians. They would teach their secrets to his people. Then they could go back home and Russia would be a socialistic state, in fact as well as in theory. And it would not take long!

THE IDEOLOGICAL DRIVE

Meanwhile, there was to be no let-up in the ideological drive to use communism as the radical spearhead by which Russian life might become revolutionized. For the revolution was conceived of as something far more fundamental than a mere economic transformation of Russia. Certain ideas and predispositions had to be eradicated from the popular mind and certain others had to take their place. The family, for instance, as the unit of personal loyalty must go, and in place of it loyalty to class must come. Old ideas concerning sex, personal morality, and ethics needed uprooting; and above all it was held essential that man must believe in the ultimate validity and the ultimate victory of a materialistic conception of life.

The family in Russia, as elsewhere, had been based on differentiation of function, man the breadwinner and provider, woman the conserver and dispenser of what man provided. This conception seemed not only out-of-date but undesirable to the thoroughgoing Communist. Women should work as well as men in factory, field, and workshop. Children should be the wards of the state; in state nursery schools and state primary schools they must be taught that the idea of family loyalty was a selfish, restrictive influence which blinded man to the possibility of social brotherhood.

To break up the family, women were put to work. To break it up still further, free divorce was granted on the application merely of either husband or wife. This did not mean a bacchanalian orgy of sexual licentiousness. Good Communists were expected to refrain from overindulgence in sex in exactly the same way as they were to refrain from drunkenness, laziness, or anything else that might lessen their value as party members. From the point of view of the Communist, sex was comparatively an unimportant matter, a question of taste rather than of morality. The Communists did not advocate a community of women; they insisted on marriage laws and enforced them. But marriage became purely a secular affair. It was necessary to preserve it so that census statistics could be accurate, so that parents could be charged with the cost of supporting the young. If there were no children the state pretty much washed its hands of the whole affair. Even abortion in the early days was openly and legally practised. But afterward laws were passed forbidding it as a crime against society, since it tended to reduce the birth-rate.

Communism meant a complete break with the past in many other ways. Laws concerning murder, for instance, were revolutionized. In accordance with communistic philosophy it was not permitted to kill one's real or fancied enemy; but if such an act was committed as the result of sudden anger it took its place in the category of lesser crimes, as did theft when committed against the personal property of a Russian citizen. For such crimes there were jail sentences; but they were not inordinately long. What were infinitely worse in Communist eyes were offenses against the U.S.S.R. Let a man be proved guilty of petty graft and no mercy need be expected; line him up against a wall and shoot him! One real sin, as such, and one alone was recognized by Communists, the act of being "counterrevolutionary." All privileged persons under the old régime were suspected of this sin, and against them true Communists were expected to harbor bitter hate.

Favorite adjectives among Communist writers were "dialectic," "objective," "scientific," and "materialistic." Since the method of reasoning used by Marx was the dialectic, there would be no other good type of reasoning. Supposedly, Marx was also a great materialistic scientist and good Communists followed the master. Power machinery was materialistic and also something new to the Russians. From Lenin down to the humblest party member, they were fascinated by it. An early Communist poster of what a cathedral should look like represented a great dynamo in place of an altar, and above the altar, where perhaps in a Christian cathedral angels might be carved, the communist artist placed flywheels attached to the dynamo by moving belts. Chicago was hymned in Communist poetry because it was an "electromagnetic city," a true symbol of the Machine Age. All that was essential to the Communist view was to have more and more machinery, owned and operated by the people in common rather than by the individual.

It was difficult to implant such revolutionary ideals in the minds of the old; this was recognized. Consequently, it was all the more the duty of the state to capture the plastic minds of the young. As a result much emphasis was put on education. Young and old were both invited and urged to learn to read and write; but great care was taken with the texts used which centered on the teachings of Marx and explained history almost exclusively in terms of the Revolution of 1917. Competent teachers were lacking and the country was desperately poor, but none the less astonishing headway was made. Enthusiasm took the place of training, and if the pupils were shepherded rigidly into the Marxian fold, they at least learned how to read.

Since materialism and idealism are generally considered antithetical terms, it is always easy to underrate what the Communist party accomplished in the way of social amelioration. Machinery, for instance, devised to protect the workman's life and limb is materialistic, but the use thereof would seem to be idealistic, whether or not the person using it insisted that idealism was a played-out force. The Communists were keen about machinery of this description. They were prepared to do everything for labor, to take the homes of former noblemen and to turn them into sanitaria, to give vacations with pay to pregnant women for a considerable period both before and after childbirth, to provide free medical service, to lighten labor hours, to increase its rewards not merely by more pay but by encouraging cheap literature, cheap music, cheap movies, cheap education—and none of these cheap in the sense of being shoddy.

To be sure, this was all done with an eye toward propaganda, directly or indirectly. There was no freedom in Russia of any kind, except freedom to spread the new faith. The Communists pointed bravely at Pavlov and to his experiments in animal psychology to prove the contrary. But even here the reason they did not molest Pavlov is obvious: if dogs and mice are conditioned in all their acts by external influences, so also by analogy is man, and materialism scores another victory.

Therefore Pavlov the scientist they would leave alone; but not the Christian church. The latter underwent severe oppression in all of its branches, and although the Roman Catholic Church was a distinct minority in Russia, so successfully did the Roman pontiffs raise the hue and cry against the Communists that Rome seemingly became the principal enemy of the Communist creed.

There can be no doubt that communism was a denial of historic Christianity. For one thing, it insisted that there was neither a God nor a future life; for another it regarded sex as of trifling importance; and finally it denounced as undesirable and as counterrevolutionary all ideas commonly associated with the suffering servant of Jehovah, teaching instead that humility, patience, long-suffering were base and ignoble thoughts, not worthy ones. No doubt also that the Communists behaved very badly toward priests and monks, killing some, reducing those left alive to beggary, appropriating churches without remuneration for secular purposes, forbidding all charitable work done in the name of Christ, teaching atheism in schools, not permitting Christian schools even to be opened, turning children against their parents, and urging them as a patriotic duty to denounce their own fathers and mothers. Despite these obvious facts it is not without significance that in a curious kind of way there were points of similarity between Christianity and communism. Both religions sought the welfare of the poor. No matter how heartily the Communists might curse the otherworldliness of Christianity, it was evident that the Soviet zealots took a keen interest in social justice; no matter how heartily the Popes might berate the Communists for their materialism, it was evident that Pope Leo XIII himself had stated that the Church was concerned with the material welfare of the poor. That also was Lenin's business.

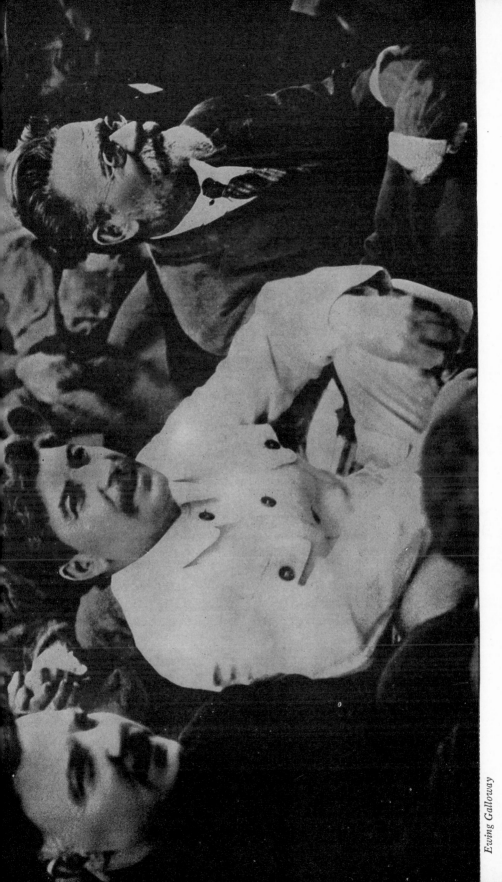

Ewing Galloway

LEFT TO RIGHT: VOROSHILOV, STALIN, KALININ, IN 1933. (See page xv *ante*.)

Inspecting the Cotton Crop of a Collective Farm in Soviet Russia (See page xv ante)

TROTSKY VS. STALIN

In 1924 Lenin died. He had been seriously ill for two years, the result of a lifetime of overwork and constant strain. All Russia paid him honor. His body, embalmed, placed under glass, and guarded day and night by soldiers of the Red Army, was placed in a red granite mausoleum, which became a holy place, a pilgrimage center for the Communist world. More honored than Karl Marx, whose obscure grave in a London cemetery few visit, Lenin and Leninism (as his doctrine came to be known) from now on, were regarded as the ark of the covenant, the foundation of the new moral order of humanity.

For Lenin's mantle there were ultimately two main contestants, Trotsky and Stalin. Of the two, the former was by far the better known outside Russia, and at the time of Lenin's death, within that country. Jewish by birth (Lev Bronstein was his real name), Trotsky had been an intimate collaborator of Lenin's. Twice he had been exiled to Siberia before the War, and in addition he had led a wandering life among the European capitals. Driven out of Paris in 1916, he had gone to New York, whence he came back to Russia and was made commissar for war in the new Bolshevik government. The success of the Red Army in 1919 and 1920 added laurels to his fame. He both wrote and spoke brilliantly and was keenly interested in spreading communism throughout all the world with the utmost speed.

Opposed to Trotsky was Stalin, who, unlike both Lenin and Trotsky, did not hail from the upper and middle classes but from peasant stock. Stalin was a Georgian from the Caucasus, a sturdy, taciturn, and rough apostle of violence. Destined for the priesthood and trained as a boy in a theological seminary, Stalin at eighteen forswore Christianity and accepted the Marxian gospel. He became a conspirator and leader of sanguinary strikes, and very soon was constantly in trouble with the police. Twice, also, he was sent to Siberia. Escaping from there, he was deported all the way to the Arctic Circle, where he was supporting himself by hunting and trapping when the Revolution broke out.

Throughout the summer of 1917, Stalin was one of the most efficient of the Bolshevik conspirators, and with the triumph of the Soviets he became not only commissar for nationalities but also commissar of workers' and peasants' inspection, and as such took a leading rôle in bringing about the ultimate Bolshevik victory. From the very beginning he was a member of the Polit Bureau, or inner steering committee of the party, and in 1922 he became its secretary, a post which he still holds, and one which has become under him the most important in all Russia. First and foremost, Stalin was a party man, and because of his long and intimate knowledge of the party's personnel, he had a certain advantage over the more versatile Trotsky, who, because of his very brilliance, was constantly making enemies.

The two men differed in policy. Trotsky was all for the world revolution, but Stalin considered that for the time being such a revolution was a dream. In his opinion communism should devote itself to perfecting the revolution within Russia. Trotsky had the greater support in the Third International, and the Chinese students at the University of Moscow paraded in his honor; but Stalin commanded the votes in the Congress of the Soviets and Trotsky was forced into exile. It was impossible, however, for Stalin to rid himself completely of Trotsky for several years or for him to entrench himself in power. According to tradition, Lenin himself had regarded Stalin as too brutal and too rough to head the party, and only slowly and by degrees was Stalin able to turn an acknowledged leadership into a dictatorship. It proved impossible permanently to expel Trotsky from the U.S.S.R. before 1929, and from Lenin's death until that year the leftist element of the party, of which Trotsky was the leading spirit, did its best to oust Stalin from the control lever. And even in that year, after Trotsky had set up his residence in Constantinople, Stalin's control was none too sure, for having defeated the left opposition, he was confronted by a new bloc on the right which thought he had gone too far in his ruthless determination to complete the work of socialism in Russia. Since that date, however, there have been few successfully to dispute in Russia with Joseph Stalin, and from 1930 to 1943 his will, to all intent and purpose, has been absolute.

THE FIVE-YEAR PLAN

Victory over Trotsky once secured, the Russian Revolution entered a new phase. Lenin had driven out the old ruling class and had thoroughly liquidated it; he had socialized big business completely, whether in land, commerce, or manufacturing; and on the ideological front his success in captivating the imagination of his followers both within and without Russia had been phenomenal. But two things he had not done: he had made comparatively little headway in changing the way of living of the Russian peasants, nearly eighty-five per cent of the population; and his dream of a technological revolution in Russia had not yet passed the blue-print stage. "Communism," he had said, "is soviet government plus the electrification of the country." Substitute the word *technology,* or the word *machine* for electrification and Lenin's meaning is clarified. He dreamed of a society in which manual labor would be at a minimum. That goal was far distant when he died. Stalin made it his business to introduce the technological revolution Lenin planned. He did it so thoroughly in the decade before the second World War that what he accomplished may justly be considered a second revolution.

In 1928 Stalin laid down a revolutionary program. It provided for the scrapping of the Nep and for a five-year plan or blueprint, whereby a tremendous speeding up in the production of capital goods was to go hand in hand with the complete socialization of the land and the substitution of farm coöperatives in place of individual enterprise. During this five years everyone in Russia was supposed to pull in his belt, to consume as little as possible, to work hard and long and scientifically in putting Russia in a place of leadership among the industrial countries of the world. Railroads, hydroelectric plants, steel-mills, tractor and automobile factories, more coal, more iron; a total increase of one hundred and thirty per cent was called for in industrial production. And as this was done, agriculture was to be modernized. The state proposed to establish and manage great model farms to serve as an example of what ultimately was to be expected of the peasants. The latter were encouraged to form coöperative groups (*kolkhozes*). If they objected, they were to be forced into these groups. After five years, private enterprise would no longer be found in Russia.

The difficulties which confronted Stalin were enormous. Russia was poor, desperately poor, yet he could not carry out the five-year program without hiring expensive scientists and engineering specialists from Germany, the United States, and elsewhere. At the same time it was necessary to import machinery and tools of precision. All this would take money, and the capitalistic world was chary of granting credit to Russia. It demanded ready money and this could only be had by Russian exports, either of merchandise or gold. Then, too, laborers had to be secured from somewhere and trained as skilled workmen, millions of them. They had to be drafted from the Russian peasantry (there was no other source of supply) and this at a time when the peasants were inevitably irritated by the revolution pending in agriculture whereby they were to be ordered to give up their individual land holdings and forced to join coöperative farm groups. Compulsion would be necessary; the peasants could not be enticed by high wages, for all available money would have to be spent for materials, tools, and foreign exports. Yet economy would be impossible. The expenses of the Red army were increasing, not diminishing. Between the threat of Japanese invasion in the Far East (see p. 273) and the enmity of the capitalistic West, Stalin did not dare diminish his army. In Lenin's day there was no danger threatening from Germany; but as Stalin came to power a wild-eyed agitator, Adolf Hitler, was inflaming his countrymen with bitter hate of Communists. Hitler might well become a serious menace. England, Italy, and the United States were hostile. There was need for haste as well as for money, so Stalin thought.

On the industrial front the principal center of activity was in the Ukraine, in the valley of the Don, in the Caucasus, the Urals, and in Western Siberia. In the Ukraine a great dam providing for the largest hydroelectric plant in Europe had already been projected. This, the Dneprostroi dam, was completed in 1932, making the Dneiper River navigable for 1,500 miles and providing 750,000 horse-power. At Kharkov, also in the Ukraine, a tractor plant was established which in short order was manufacturing 37,000 tractors a year, and near it was a plant for turbine generators and electrical equipment which by 1939 employed 40,000 men. At Rostov on the Don and at Stalingrad on the Volga mammoth steel plants, specializing in tractors and other agricultural machinery were erected, and so great was the industrial advance of this southeastern region that it, together with other sections of Russia, had topped by 1939 the entire agricultural machine production of the United States.

Still further to the east were the Ural mountains and Siberia. Here lay a land, the Soviet geologists soon proved, rich in minerals and far distant from any invasion, at least 1,500 miles from any European enemy and much further from Japan. On the eastern slopes of the Urals at Magnitogorsk were two mountains so rich in iron as to be one of the principal sources of that mineral in the entire world. Coal also was to be found in the Urals, and straight east from the two mountains some 1,400 miles from Magnitogorsk where the Altai mountains separate western China from Siberia were the Kuznetz coal reserves with over 400 million tons of accessible coal. Here lay the land of Stalin's imagination; here he determined, cost what it might, to develop an industrial region center to vie with Pittsburgh, Birmingham, or the Ruhr valley.

The far northern part of this region already was traversed by the Trans-Siberian railroad. Stalin proposed to double-track it, to drive a new railroad south to Magnitogorsk, to connect that city with the Kuznetz coal, to join these new railroads to the already existing Transcaucasian railroad which linked together the oases of Turkestan, and to make western Siberia a great inland empire.

Magnitogorsk was planned as the industrial center. To create a city, several hundred engineering experts were imported from abroad, some at a salary of $100 a day. Under them was an army of many thousand laborers, most of whom were dispossessed peasants or kulaks. The latter suffered much; food shortages were chronic and such food

COKE OVENS OF THE STALIN IRON AND STEEL WORKS AT MAGNITOGORSK

Women of Leningrad Form an Ambulance Squad

as could be had was mostly black bread, cabbages, and potatoes. The winters were bitterly cold, the summers unbearably hot and dry. Hastily constructed, ill-heated, and overcrowded barracks housed the men. Confusion reigned. Essential tools were missing, spare parts difficult to obtain, accidents numerous. From the scaffolding "inexperienced riggers fell and untrained bricklayers laid walls which did not stand." Skilled workmen were continually deserting. One locomotive working on the mine had thirty-four engineers in one year. Only one single-track railway led to the city and soon the workmen "were faced with the necessity of supplying themselves with hammers, saws, chisels, bits, small castings and other small tools which could be made in makeshift shops. Many materials, such as copper wire for rewinding motors, simply could not be had. The workers swore at the foremen, the foremen complained to the superintendent, the supply department telegraphed to Moscow. There was no copper wire." [1] But the city was built and in less than five years was swarming with over 200,000 inhabitants.

The story of Magnitogorsk is the story of a dozen manufacturing cities with mushroom growth in eastern Russia and in western Siberia during the nineteen-thirties. The coal deposits at Kuznetz, for instance, soon proved far in excess of the Magnitogorsk demand, and smelters at Stalinsk in the Kuznetz area became busily engaged in turning Magnitogorsk ore into finished steel. Stalinsk by 1939 was a city of 220,000, connected by rail with the Russian Transcaucasusian system on the south, with the Trans-Siberian system on the north and with Magnitogorsk to the west, and by 1939 the population of the surrounding district had risen to 800,000. Instead of having one Pittsburgh, Russia had two, both safe from European or Asiatic invader. There could be no doubt, on paper that is, that the first five-year drive was a success on the industrial front. No matter what the cost, both in human suffering and in money, the rails were laid, the factories built, the oil wells dug, the mines opened, the steel, the tractors (also the tanks) in operation. Officially the drive was declared closed after four and a half years—and in theory ninety-three per cent complete.

The above percentage was Stalin's estimate. It needs qualification. If measured in terms of rubles (money) the estimate is correct. But the ruble was a shifting standard, and since it had depreciated externally in value during the five years, the real increase in production was far below 93.7 per cent. Furthermore, the increase was one in industrial production only. It ignored the question of real wages, the amount of

[1] John Scott, *Behind the Urals* (Houghton Mifflin Company), p. 76. Reprinted by permission of the publishers.

goods that might be had in terms of rubles. The available food supplies did not increase; in fact they diminished. The great industrial undertakings were only accomplished by the semistarvation of many million workingmen, who lived on black bread and cabbage soup.

Difficult as it proved to be to introduce highly specialized industrial processes among a people who by tradition were primarily agricultural, it proved even more difficult to turn these same peasants into practising socialists, willing to give up their privately owned and privately tilled acres in order to share both work and gains with their neighbors. Nevertheless, Stalin determined to push the agricultural offense as hard as the industrial one. It would not do, in his opinion, to have Russia half capitalist and half socialist, and unless the reluctant peasants were driven into the practice of coöperative farming, such would be the case. The peasants were stupid and the patient state would show them the way by example, by state farms, by lectures on scientific agriculture, by attractive offers and bonuses to those peasants who pooled their resources, by harsh taxes levied on the recalcitrant.

It was soon discovered that there were a great many of the latter, well-to-do peasants, or kulaks, who had prospered, partly by working hard and intelligently, partly by hiring as farm laborers their more shiftless or less fortunate neighbors. These kulaks continued to exist somehow, even though taxed unmercifully, and the soviet authorities determined to "liquidate" them. They did so thoroughly. The kulaks were driven from their homes by the hundreds of thousands; they were forced to work in the lumber-mills of the North, in the gold-mines of Siberia, in the new factories. Soon there were hardly any kulaks left. By January, 1934, Stalin was able to announce that there were no less than 224,500 collective farms in Russia which, in the preceding year, sowed some 73.9 per cent of Russia's grain. Since an added ten per cent came from the state farms, the success on the agricultural front as well as on the industrial seemed assured.

Whether that success was worth the price paid for it is open to question. The forced industrial development of the country was put through to no inconsiderable degree by compulsory labor. The imagination of the Communists had been captivated by machinery and there can be no doubt that it was a part of their faith to work hard and long and with utmost enthusiasm. But while this was true of convinced Communists who organized shock brigades in the factories to hasten production, there were not enough of them for the task in hand. If it was to be accomplished within the time limits set, forced labor was essential and Stalin did not hesitate to use it. For this the kulaks were conveniently available, as well as thousands of political prisoners. Suffering greatly from lack of decent living quarters, and half-starved, these other groups provided much of the human raw material which poured into the industrial undertakings.

Furthermore, although factories were built and filled with machinery, although mines were opened, railroads constructed, iron dug from the hillsides and turned into steel, there were many bitter criticisms of the effectiveness of the result. It was claimed that the railroads broke down continuously, that the machines were so poor in quality as to be in many instances useless, that the tractors were too heavy and too clumsy to operate. To some extent it is necessary to discount these criticisms since most of them came from European and American technicians employed by the Soviet government, and it was only natural that they should compare unfavorably the efficiency and skill of the Russian workmen with that possessed by the highly trained industrial workers of the West to which they had been accustomed. But despite all this, the cumulative evidence would seem to indicate a very partial victory as yet for this industrial revolution in Russia, brought into existence by socialistic practice. Compared with American standards, Russian factories with ten times as many workmen turned out far less per capita. Machines always seemed to be breaking down, burning out, rusting, exploding. The new dynamos, locomotives, tractors, etc., were there, it is true, but they did not seem to be good tractors, locomotives, dynamos. Enthusiasm, it was found, could not take the place of mechanical skill; and the latter, it was demonstrated, could not be created overnight by fiat.

The results of the first Five-Year Plan in agriculture were more open to question. In the more advanced agricultural districts, such as the Ukraine and southern Russia, there was bitter opposition on the part of the peasants to Stalin's program. Throughout 1932 and 1933 famine raged in the Ukraine, due in part to unseasonable weather, in part to compulsory grain requisitions, in part to the unwillingness of the peasants to surrender their individual holdings. Some three or four million people lost their lives from starvation, and the country-side was well-nigh deserted. The Soviet authorities were not altogether displeased; the famine proved a convenient instrument for political policy, and after its ravages were over, there was less opposition to collective farming. Statistically, however, the official figures as released by Stalin in 1934 did not seem encouraging as far as the agricultural front went. From 1923 to 1934 the numbers of cattle, horses, sheep, and goats decreased alarmingly, and all that there were in their places were some 200,000 tractors! Theoretically, their presence on the Russian farms meant more acres cultivated and a greater consumption of cereals. Nevertheless, it is doubtful if the per capita consumption of grain at the conclusion of the Five-Year Plan was in excess of that under the Czars. The cost in terms of human suffering unquestionably was very high.

Stalin himself realized that, but like a good politician he did not acknowledge it. He made a statement called "Giddiness from Success," in which he announced certain qualifications in regard to rural coöperatives in which peasants might retain individual ownership of homes, gardens, live stock. Grain was still to be sowed and reaped by the kolkhozes, but a certain leeway was now granted to individual enterprise. Stalin likewise, and again merely by implication, toned down the harshness of the drive for industrialization by announcing a second Five-Year Plan, to be completed in 1937. Unlike the first plan, this one stressed consumers' goods. Factories were to be built for textiles, shoes, canning, candies, and no less than 350 of these factories were for food products. Prices of consumers' goods were to be lowered and the supply of them was to be augmented three hundred per cent.

It is too early as yet to know very much about the success of this second plan. The Communists, as might be expected, have hailed it as a grand triumph, and it is true that, as far as the Russian cities are concerned, certain improvements have been noticed in housing, food, and clothes. The long queues before food shops have shrunk and the people dress somewhat better than they did in 1934. Even the Communists, however, admitted that the tremendous dangers facing Russia on both west and east from Fascist Germany and near-Fascist Japan made it necessary to retard the advance hoped for in consumers' goods because so much money must be spent on armament.

Did Stalin Betray the Revolution?

Meanwhile, in certain respects, both in regard to external and internal policy, Soviet Russia became more and more conservative. As an instrument for stirring up world revolution, the Third International almost ceased to function. Lenin had hated the League of Nations but Stalin consented to enter it. The Communist parties outside of Russia were advised from the Kremlin that they should coöperate with liberal bourgeois groups against fascism, and in countries like the United States, China, France, and Spain the Communists either made common cause with such groups or tried to. Thus, in the United States, the Communists were friendly toward Roosevelt in 1936 and in instances actually supported him, adopting a stand in American politics more conservative than that of the old Social Democratic party hitherto regarded by all honest Reds as lukewarm and yellow. In China the Communists joined forces with their old enemy, Chiang Kai-shek, in opposing the Japanese (see p. 276), and in France and Spain Communists took a leading part in the organization of "popular fronts" to oppose reaction.

The same general trend to the right was noticeable also in internal affairs. In 1936 Soviet Russia adopted a new constitution which, on paper at least, seemed to denote that the U.S.S.R. was becoming both democratic and liberal. Freedom of speech and of religion was guaranteed (again on paper), and no longer was the scale weighted in favor of the more radical town and factory as against the more conservative country districts. All Russians were given the vote, even priests and kulaks, and voting was to be by ballot and not by show of hands.

Did Stalin have any real intention of going democratic? That may well be doubted. The control of the country still remained with the Communist party, the only one legally authorized, and that party remained in the hollow of his hands, as we shall note later. But perhaps Stalin did betray the Revolution, if not in whole at least in part, by drawing a line boldly between social classes in Russia, thus preventing instead of creating a classless society. Such was the argument of the exiled Trotsky who, driven out of his own country, out of Constantinople, and out of France, found a haven of refuge in Mexico. Trotsky insisted that the Russian Revolution was passing through its Thermidor, and that in the same way as the Directory, after the death of Robespierre, ended the real revolution in France so Stalin was doing the same for Russia.

The arguments adduced by the exiled leader to prove this point were various. He pointed out that Stalin, by approving a speeding-up process in Russian factories and mines, really was paying workmen by the piece instead of by the time, the more skilful workingmen getting higher pay and receiving favors from the authorities. He also asserted that the renting of land went merrily on in Russia, some kolkhozes renting land at a profit to others, some even renting land to individuals. Russia, said Trotsky, was now ruled by some 400,000 bureaucrats who feathered their own nests very nicely, drew more pay than workmen, had better housing, and rapidly were becoming class-conscious. In the army the old discipline and the old caste system was said to be cropping up again. The Third International, in the interim, had been stifled and a new revolution would be necessary if ever Marxian socialism was to win out. And to start this new revolution Trotsky sent out summons for a Fourth International.

THE PURGES

To what extent Trotsky continued from overseas to influence the course of events in Russia, it is impossible to state. Certainly many of the old Bolsheviks were discontented with Stalin's iron rule; some were of the right who disapproved of the abrupt ending of Lenin's N.E.P.; others were of the left, in sympathy with Trotsky. Both groups plotted against Stalin; both were ruthlessly liquidated by him in thorough-going purges.

In 1935-37 the world made note of many curious trials for high treason in Russia. They were not conducted by Western methods, for evidence was not introduced into the court proceedings, unless whole-sale confessions of willingness to sell out to the Germans and to be-tray the revolution be considered as evidence. Not only did almost every one put on trial freely admit guilt; the astonishing thing was that they tried to make this guilt appear as black as possible. The men placed on trial had been very high in governmental places, men like Kamenev, at one time a likely successor to Lenin; Zinoviev, for-mer head of the Third International; a considerable number of high-ranking officers in the Red Army, among then General Tukhatchev-sky, second in command; and finally numerous civil executives who were said to have wrecked railroads, trains, bridges, and to have re-tarded industrial production. Before he was through Stalin had gotten rid of almost every man of note who had participated in the Revolu-tion of 1917.

Was it possible that these men were guilty? The capitalistic West was sceptical; it suspected that secret torture before trial might have caused the confessions, or that by making them the poor wretches hoped to avert the wrath of Stalin from their families. Some even suggested that the confessions were made as absurd as possible in order that the outside world might read between the lines and realize that the trials were a farce and that Stalin's régime was one of stark tyranny.

On the other hand there was genuine evidence to show that there was a conspiracy among the accused to revolt against the Kremlin, to sabotage coal mines, war industries, transportation lines, even in fact to welcome German and Japanese invaders, to surrender the Ukraine to the first, the Maritime Provinces to the second in return for the support and assistance of these foreign powers in setting up a new and presumably Trotskyite régime. The generals who were executed certainly were hostile to the espionage practiced over them by the civil authorities and presumably were preparing a coup d'état. As the American ambassador at the time reported to Washington, "Stalin and the party leaders acted with great speed and ruthless severity. They hit first. Communism is their religion and in executing speedy justice for the violation of party principles they were in the strong position of 'serving the Lord.' It also served their interests well, for by such action they were entrenching themselves in power. By adding the charge of treason to the state, they became the bulwark of defense for that Russian nationalism that is being constantly stimulated by every form of propaganda possible."[2]

The total number of those executed by Stalin for treachery, treason, Trotskyism, and sabotage between 1935 and 1939 is difficult to estimate but presumably it was well over 10,000. Many were given no public trial at all, a simple announcement of their death alone being given. At the height of the executions there was a veritable reign of terror, when secret arrests were numerous and men simply disappeared. It was not healthy to inquire about their whereabouts and few did.

Nevertheless the great body of Stalin's countrymen were prepared, it seems, to accept his word without question, and even to worship at his shrine in a way quite similar to the contemporary attitude of Germans and Italians toward Hitler and Mussolini. Stalin, indeed, became so personally identified with communism that he equalled in stature both Lenin and Marx. And this was the more noticeable in that he remained essentially a silent man, neither given to oratory as was Trotsky nor to the written amplification of the Communist scriptures as was Lenin.

Russia's relations to foreign powers have been treated elsewhere in this book (Chapter XI), for they are part and parcel of the great international war-storm constantly growing more and more ominous in the period after 1933. As for the Russian experiment in communism in general, it is necessary to suspend judgment. The capitalistic West is perhaps no more able at the present time to strike a just balance between the good and evil in it than Edmund Burke was able to appraise the significance of the French Revolution. A rough approximation to the truth would be to assume that toward the end of the nineteen-twenties the average Russian was somewhat worse off than his grandfather (due to the pulling in of the belt and the determination at all hazards to industrialize his country overnight), that by the end of the next decade his lot had improved materially in respect to food and housing. He was now accustomed to electric light, his work was made easier by mechanical inventions, and his children were in school. The intentional and self-imposed deprivation of the preceding decade may or may not have been worth the price, but at least it was not ignoble in aim. The tyranny of the Czars, meanwhile, was succeeded by the tyranny of Stalin, and there was now less liberty for the individual than in the relatively easy-going Czarist days.

[2] J. E. Davies, *Mission to Moscow* (Simon and Schuster, Inc.), p. 202. Reprinted by permission of the publishers.

CHAPTER VI

ITALIAN AND GERMAN FASCISM

IT WAS just a bundle of sticks tied around an ax, but when borne by a lictor the mob gave way in ancient Rome. The Romans called that symbol of authority "fasces," and from it we derive our modern word "fascism," the contemporary answer of Italy and Germany to Russian communism, and to some extent that of other lands as well.

A strange doctrine is fascism, at once very old and very new. In so far as it concerns the dictatorship of an individual, of a Mussolini or a Hitler rising to well-nigh omnipotent power in times of anarchy, there is nothing new in Fascist doctrine, and one might as well use the term "Cæsarism" to describe it. In so far, on the other hand, as fascism is intimately correlated with capitalism, socialism, and twentieth century nationalism, it is new, strikingly new, unlike any hitherto existing dictatorship, whether that of Oliver Cromwell, Frederic the Great or Napoleon Bonaparte.

Fascism triumphed in Italy in 1922 with Mussolini's march on Rome, and in Germany in 1933 with Adolf Hitler's appointment as chancellor of the Reich. As might be expected, its character assumed different forms in the two countries in question, and German fascism, from its inception, has differed decidedly from the fascism of Italy. Nevertheless, the points of likeness far exceed those of dissimilarity. What, then, is fascism, and in what respects may it be said that it is alike in all Fascist countries?

Fascism is an all-embracing doctrine which demands a one hundred per cent surrender of the individual will in the name of mystical nationalism—with ends not clearly defined. This nationalism is beyond good and evil, and thus is deified. Therefore, fascism properly should be classed as a kind of religion like communism, the latter based on class-consciousness, the former on nationalism. As such, fascism is compounded of three elements—violence, state socialism, totalitarianism. Direct and clear is its repudiation of the Sermon on the Mount, for the Fascist insists that he only is blessed who smites and smites again. Emphatic is its assertion that the economic life of the people must be controlled by governmental agencies. And furthermore, since the be-all and the end-all of life is the exaltation of the state, all mem-

bers of it must act alike, think alike, obey alike. Such, in general outline, is the Spartan-like philosophy of twentieth century fascism.

How explain its origin? Such an extreme reversal of the main currents of European culture, especially since the Renaissance, could only
come about through revolutionary upheavals produced by disillusion-
ment, sharp suffering, social anarchy. This was the case in both Italy
and Germany. Both countries felt that they had been cheated by the
peace treaties; both suffered enormously from economic maladjustment; both were at the mercy of politicians unable to bring order
out of chaos; and, what is more important, in both there were large
numbers of ex-soldiers, young but toughened by war, unemployed, bitter, finding after four years in the trenches that back home there was
"greed in the saddle, disorder in the street, and poverty on the hearth."

RISE OF ITALIAN FASCISM

Since this greed, disorder, and poverty characterized Russia as well
as Italy and Germany, the question naturally arises why those two
countries did not turn toward communism. Several reasons explain
why. In the first place, both in Germany and in Italy the bourgeoisie
were too powerful, too numerous, too well led to be driven to the wall
by Communist uprisings. In both countries such revolts occurred; in
both they were snuffed out by the enraged bourgeoisie. Secondly, in
both countries, but especially in Germany, there was a tradition of
discipline and order and of national cohesiveness which militated
strongly against the Communist world revolution. And thirdly, one is
confronted with that insoluble equation, the personal factor, the adroit
cunning of Benito Mussolini in Italy, the mystical appeal to Germans
latent in the raucous vocal cords of Adolf Hitler.

Of these two fiery ex-corporals, the Italian is by far the easier to
understand. Benito Mussolini, ex-school-teacher, ex-journalist, ex-
laborer, and so forth, was an influential young Italian Socialist when
the first World War broke. In his father's smithy he had absorbed
The Prince of Machiavelli, with its cynical assertion that most men
are "ungrateful, fickle, false, cowardly, covetous ..." governed by fear
rather than by affection. Sorel, the French syndicalist, with his philosophy of strikes and violence, had been a favorite author of his youth,
and Gustave Le Bon's *Psychology of the Crowd,* with its teaching that
the mob is ever unreasoning, moved hither and yon by passionate exaggeration, had left its impression upon him. Indeed, Mussolini never
evinced any interest in the more scientific and theoretical aspects of
socialism. He was not that kind of socialist; rather, by nature, he was
inclined to masterful assertiveness, to stress will rather than reason, to

frighten rather than to conciliate, to bluff and to bluster, but always with shrewd finesse and instinctive feeling as to just how far it would be safe for him to do so.

Under ordinary circumstances Mussolini would not have risen to fame; but circumstances were not ordinary in post-War Italy. That country smarted from a sense of frustration; it had not really distinguished itself in the War; it had been saved from disaster only by Allied help and had won victory in the end only through French and British aid. Having sold herself to the highest bidder in 1915, Italy was now dissatisfied with her bargain. And she had not received all that she had bargained for! The Tyrol, Trieste, a part of the Dalmatian coast, and islands in the Adriatic and the Aegean she did obtain; but when France and England divided the German colonial empire between them, there was for Italy only the suggestion of a rectification of the boundaries of Tripoli (now Libya) and of Italian Somaliland. The Italians felt slighted. True, the German colonies were only being held in trust by France and Britain for civilization and the League of Nations. But why did Italy receive no mandates? Furthermore, in addition to the letter of the bond, the Italians had asked for Fiume at the peace conference; Fiume was not given them.

Then again, economic conditions in Italy were peculiarly distressing. Since Italy was a poor country, she had felt the strain of the war more than had France or England. Her finances after it were in terrible plight, and her currency had depreciated more than a third of its value. The well-intentioned but weak and purposeless men in charge of her government in 1919 had no plan, no program, by which the situation might be bettered. Brigandage broke out in the South, and the homes of landlords were burned; communism raised its head in the industrial North, and workingmen seized factories and announced they would operate them. Their experience was brief and unprofitable, and they gave back the factories to the former owners of their own free will. But anything might happen, apparently, in Italy, and if ever an affirmative voice was called for it was then.

Mussolini provided that voice. After the commencement of the war he had deserted his erstwhile friends, the Social Democrats, who opposed Italy's participation. Wounded, he was discharged from the army and founded in Milan a radical, pro-war newspaper. With the coming of peace he gathered around him a number of former soldiers and organized a small group, the *Fascio di combattimento*. Its program, like the original program of the Nazis, was a hybrid mixture of radical economic theory and extreme nationalism. No one thought it would amount to anything; it nominated two men for election to the Chamber of Deputies in 1919 and both were defeated. Nevertheless, when that neurotic man of letters, the poet D'Annunzio, pounced upon Fiume with a few adventurers in the name of Italy and was shortly forced to abandon it by the Italian government, Mussolini began to gather headway by denouncing the puerile and weak-kneed authorities who interfered with Italy's destinies. And later, when the government did nothing to prevent Communist seizures of the factories, his party grew. Under his leadership, antimonarchists, antisocialists, anticlericals and antipacifists gathered, all eager to attack some one. They found the Italian Communists, who were already surrendering the commandeered factories, an easy mark; and they launched their major offensive against them, thereby delighting the wealthy bourgeoisie. Organized into squads with semimilitary discipline, they began attacking all Communists, or men suspected of being Communists, administered castor-oil to their victims, and beat them up severely. Money, meanwhile, poured into the Fascist coffers and the ranks of the Black Shirts swelled with recruits.

By the spring of 1921 fascism was becoming popular in Italy with the middle and upper classes. Ostensibly, it stood for public order and the suppression of anarchy, and in the election to Parliament that year the Fascists won thirty-five seats. And along with this increase in popularity went a decrease in radicalism. Mussolini announced that he believed in monarchy, that he hated both communism and socialism, that his Black Shirts would prevent society from disintegrating as it promised to do with warring factions. In 1922 the Fascists held a grand congress in Naples which demanded either a new election or the inclusion of Fascists in the cabinet. Since the government would not listen to either alternative, a "march on Rome" began. The government offered no resistance; instead Mussolini was appointed prime minister by the King.

Parliament voted him dictatorial powers for one year and by its conclusion Mussolini was firmly seated in the saddle. To prevent ousting by subsequent Parliaments, he forced through the Chamber of Deputies a law which provided that in any election the party with the biggest vote automatically should receive two-thirds of the seats. The Fascists thereupon won a majority in the election of 1924, obtained their two-thirds of the seats; and from that date on, open and organized opposition to Mussolini's dictatorship withered away. The head of the Socialist party was kidnapped and murdered under suspicious circumstances; Socialists and Liberals fled from Italy; others voluntarily retired from public life; a few, ardent nationalists, entered the Fascist ranks. Mussolini, meanwhile, by law after law, made secure his own hold on Italy; he was made head of the state; he took over several cabinet posts in person; no law could be initiated except by him; and by 1928 all elections in Italy had become a mere farce, there being but one party recognized (the Fascist) and but one list of candidates for whom it was possible to vote (the Fascist list).

In Italy, as in Germany and Russia, the new-style dictators of the twentieth century operated through the instrumentality of a political party over which they held tight rein. Again, as in Germany and Russia, the victorious political party was limited as to membership, Mussolini much preferring a party of one million to one of ten; the one million could be better organized, disciplined, watched. Entrance to the Fascist party came under ordinary circumstances entirely from below, from auxiliary youth organizations. Almost at the cradle fascism began; when eight years old, a youngster might join one of these youth groups, graduate to another at fourteen, to another at eighteen, and finally present himself as a candidate for membership in the Fascist party at twenty-one. Ostensibly, it remained a political party, not the government of Italy. But only Fascists could be elected to Parliament and the law provided that the Grand Council of the Fascist Party (presided over by Mussolini) must be consulted by Parliament on important matters. Also, the Fascist Grand Council had at its disposal a private Fascist militia and there were even special Fascist magistrates appointed. The consequence was that within ten years after the march on Rome only the shell remained of a liberal constitutional monarchy.

Fascist domestic policy, both in Italy and Germany, followed parallel lines in one respect: within both countries it aimed at the complete subordination of the individual to the will of the state. Particularly true was this of all economic activity. In Italy the Fascists took control of economic enterprise by a peculiar invention of their own, the corporative state, which reflected both the origin of Italian fascism and the method by which it had won power. Most of the early Fascists had been socialists of a sort, at least to the extent of believing in state socialism or syndicalism but, we must recall, the Fascists had risen to power by rushing to the defense of private property. They were radicals and conservatives at the same time, pledged to obtain rights for workingmen, pledged to protect private property. The corporative state combined both of these ideas. Under it the economic life of Italy was divided into six main categories: manufacturing, commerce, maritime transportation, inland transportation, agriculture, and banking. In each group there was to be a syndicate of workmen and a syndicate of employers, thus making twelve legalized syndicates; and to them a thirteenth was added, a syndicate of the learned professions. In theory the thirteen syndicates were to be autonomous. All trade unions were forbidden, and employers and employees, as represented by their respective syndicates, were to work together and engage in collective bargaining in accordance with a "Charter of Labor" granted in 1927, whereby certain rules were laid down in respect to rates of pay, old-age insurance, holidays with pay, etc. All syndicate members had to be in good standing with the Fascist authorities and the autonomy granted was more superficial than real.

Two years later (1929) the syndicates were fused with parliamentary representation, and Parliament was now said to be functional, in other words to represent jobs and interests rather than districts or localities. In accordance with the new law, the thirteen syndicates selected 800 names and gave them to the Fascist Grand Council, which body also was presented with 200 additional names from other sources. Out of the 1,000 names the Council selected 400 as a Fascist list for parliament members. An election was now held, yes or no, to this official list. No other candidate could be voted for and the ayes naturally had it. Such Parliament as Italy now had represented banking, transportation and other interests, rather than electoral districts.

In this fashion the corporative state became identified with the national state. As an experiment in political theory it was interesting but not conclusive, for always behind the syndicates was the Fascist party and its Grand Council, the master and presiding genius of which was Mussolini. Nevertheless, for the corporative state this is to be said: The number of strikes diminished rapidly; the currency debacle was first halted, then checked, and a semblance of business recovery was noted, that is, if we judge simply from indexes of production. Excellent automobile roads were constructed by Mussolini's orders; large and spacious oceanliners owed their existence to his continued enthusiasm; and the "battle of wheat," namely, the effort to make Italy self-supporting in foodstuffs was waged strenuously and continuously by the energetic Duce, as Mussolini came to be called.

To all of this there was another side. Taxes of extreme severity were levied on the middle class, which groaned silently and paid. More serious was a decline in the standard of living of the poorer classes, already very low. There were no strikes; the workmen did not dare to strike. On the other hand they were conscious that others paid the costs as well as they. Mussolini could hardly be called a modern Robin Hood, robbing the rich to pay the poor. What he did was to exact a tremendous toll from all classes, partly to restore his country's credit, which did improve up to the great economic depression of the thirties; partly to pay for increases in armament made necessary by his determination to gain land by the sword or by threats.

The totalitarian doctrines of the Duce were less clearly defined than those of Hitler, nor did he crush out individual liberties quite as comprehensively as did his fellow-dictator in Germany. There was the same talk in both countries of the decadence of liberalism and democracy, the same boasting of national solidarity and racial prowess. But with this difference: the Italians seemed disinclined to carry out their slogans to their logical conclusions. The best illustration of this fact may be found in the field of religion. As a matter of logic, pure and simple, there is no room for any religion in a totalitarian state except the religion of the state. The Germans, being logical almost to the point of the irrational, proceeded, as we shall see (see p. 178), to persecute both Protestant and Catholic. In Italy this was not so. The tiny group of Italian Protestants were not molested by Mussolini and with the Roman Catholic Church he made friends.

The Lateran treaty of 1929 with the Holy See was proof that Mussolini, the Fascist, knew how to compromise. By it the long-standing political feud between the Roman Curia and the Italian monarchy was settled amicably. The Pope recognized for the first time the legality of the Kingdom of Italy and agreed to support it. Mussolini, on the other hand, paid a handsome price for this recognition. A diminutive state of a hundred or so acres which included St. Peter's and the Vatican was ceded to the Pope, completely independent of Italy from legal code to postage stamp. In this state the Roman Pontiff was to be sole ruler. Nearly $40,000,000 in specie and an even larger sum in Italian bonds was added. The Roman Catholic religion was recognized as the religion of the State, and the canon law of the Church added to the law of Italy, Mussolini thus granting the Church privileges which had long lapsed in regard to education and marriage. Compulsory education in the Catholic faith was now prescribed for all youthful Italians.

The victory of the Church seemed very great, but Mussolini, too, secured advantages. Ecclesiastics were now called upon to support his régime. Only one source of friction between Church and State remained, the possibility of papal interference with what Mussolini considered purely political issues. A society of Catholic laymen, the Catholic Action, caused the Duce some trouble; it criticized his labor policy and he promptly abolished it. The Pope at first stood by the society; but a compromise was effected. In the future the society was to be under the direction of bishops and not of laymen; and Mussolini, on his part, agreed that the incessant drilling of small Italian youngsters in the practice of arms should not interfere, as it had been doing, with religious instruction.

For the Duce's domestic policy there was perhaps this to be said: an Italy confused, baffled, discouraged, torn by factions, and ruled by weak politicians, gave way to an Italy united, ruled by a man who

IL DUCE, WITH HONOR GUARD OF HIS YOUNGEST WARRIORS. (See page xv *ante.*)

Top: GIRLS OF THE NAZI YOUTH PARTY
Below: HITLER YOUTHS OFF TO AID IN WARTIME HARVEST

knew what he wanted and knew how to obtain it. To be sure, there was a price, and a heavy one; liberties of the individual were snuffed out; newspapers printed simply what they were told; there was espionage, cruelty, and occasionally assassination of those Italians who opposed Mussolini. No mercy was shown the dissenters. Those who dared use pen or mouth in criticism either fled the country, going to France by thousands, or were rounded up and imprisoned, again by thousands. But the Duce's foreign policy was another matter. To it may be attributed the commencement of the second World War (unless that honor be granted Japan); for the Duce established the European precedent and set the pace for Hitler to copy. When Mussolini invaded Abyssinia in 1935, fascism showed its real hand and Europe has not been at peace since. So important, indeed, was that invasion and Fascist Italy's foreign policy that its significance is left to another chapter (see p. 280).

THE GERMAN SCENE: TROUBLES OF THE WEIMAR REPUBLIC

Far more complicated was the picture presented by Germany after the first World War. In the spring of 1918 German hopes were high; by autumn they were shattered. A year later came Versailles and renewed disaster. That treaty had been no Carthaginian peace; but it was obvious to all that the economic demands of the Allies could not be met without the virtual enslavement of German generations as yet unborn. The Fatherland in 1919 was in the abyss.

Under such circumstances, the constitution of the Weimar Republic was drawn up. It was a liberal, progressive, advanced constitution, and only slightly tinctured by the radicalism of the German Socialists who but one year earlier, as we have seen, administered the final blow to the Kaiser's régime. All Germans over twenty now had the ballot, and the new Reichstag which they were to elect was to govern the country through a chancellor representing a majority group or groups within it. The president of the new republic was supposedly a figurehead. The initiative, referendum, recall, proportional representation, and other up-to-date gadgets of the political scientists were included, and a gesture toward socialism was made by declarations concerning the unearned increment, condemnation of land (with indemnity), and an economic council.

This Weimar Republic was to last little more than a decade, and of its numerous elections and interminable party strife but trifling account shall be given. At no time in its history did any single party have a majority in the Reichstag. The Social Democrats, in the very first election held under the republic (1920), had by far the largest single repre-

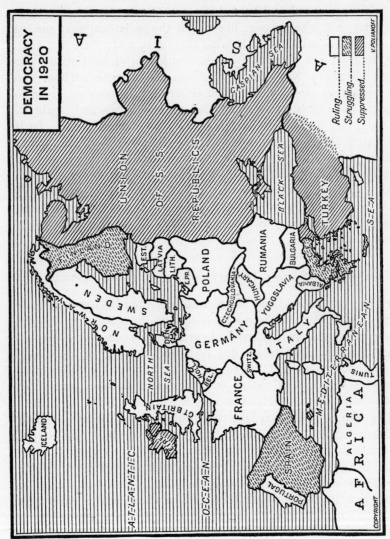

(From V. Poliakoff's *Europe in the Fourth Dimension*.)

sentation; but even at the beginning they were deserted by left-wing socialists who had formed their own parties. At the extreme left were the Communists, listening to the siren voice of Lenin, confident of a second revolution which would sweep away this bourgeois republic. Other socialists to the left were the Independent Socialists, who abhorred a bloody revolution which was the dream of the Communists, but who demanded the immediate expropriation of private property throughout Germany. Had these three groups of socialists stuck together, they might have had a majority over all and Germany might have been spared Hitler; but owing to the absurd overconfidence of the Soviet authorities, constantly meddling in German affairs, this chance was lost. Meanwhile, on the extreme right, were the Nationalists, the Prussian Junkers, ex-army officers, and other defenders of the old régime. Both Communists and Nationalists, when not at each other's throats, started little civil wars of their own. For several weeks the Communists were able to hold Munich; for a short time the Nationalists were in military possession of Berlin. Both revolts were crushed; but Nationalists and Communists remained in the Reichstag, prepared to knife the republic at the slightest opportunity. Other parties of importance in the early history of the republic were the Centrists (the old Centre party of the Catholic Church); the People's party (the old National Liberal party rechristened), the stronghold of the upper bourgeoisie; and the Democratic party, a renewal of the old Radical party under the empire, drawing its membership largely from the lower bourgeoisie. There were also a few other parties of less importance; that the National Socialists (the Nazis) did not come into prominence until 1923 and was of no special significance until late in the decade.

Who should control the destinies of the republic? For a long time the answer was an uneasy and constantly changing coalition of the more moderate groups. Sometimes a Social Democrat would be chancellor; sometimes a Centrist would be chancellor, supported in turn by Social Democrats and other factions; occasionally even a Nationalist would find his way into the cabinet. Election followed election for several highly unstable years, and the politically inexperienced Germans fought hard against terrific odds to bring some kind of order out of chaos. They were handicapped in many ways. If the Social Democrats had been somewhat more resolute, it is possible the skies might have cleared. But they had no Oliver Cromwell to lead them, nor any one else of ability, for that matter, who would dare to put through a genuine economic revolution by illegal means. The Social Democrats were democrats first and only secondarily socialists. They did not lift their little fingers against the property rights of the old nobility and the middle class; they did not even confiscate the wealth and the lands of the Hohenzollern family. The hands of the Social Democrats, and of all other parties, for that matter, were tied by proportional representation. Under it each party was represented in proportion to the number of votes which it received, and therefore the minor parties continued to live, although their existence was a continued threat against any consistent policy being carried out. Coalition government is generally weak government; and this was true of the different ministries of the Weimar Republic at the very time when Germany's principal need was for a strong government.

Then, too, from the Allies came no helping hand. They continued to treat Germany as a pariah country, whether republic or empire. She was excluded from the League of Nations; her natural resources were sadly diminished; and within four years of the signing of the peace treaty, the *poilus* were holding the Ruhr Valley by the throat. The utterly discredited Weimar Republic in 1923 suffered both from domestic malice and foreign levy.

HITLER

In that year of German crucifixion (1923) a wild-eyed, unkempt ex-corporal of the Kaiser's armies leaped on the table of the Reich commissar at Munich, fired his pistol in the air, and demanded a march on Berlin. There was no march on Berlin, but there was a parade in Munich which came to grief. Headed by General Ludendorff, men known as Nazis, carrying a strange banner, forced their way through the streets of this South Germany city until stopped by the soldiers of the republic. Ludendorff was permitted to pass, but no others. Shots were fired; some Nazis were killed; some saved themselves by quickly dropping to the ground. Among the latter was their leading spokesman and orator, Adolf Hitler, who promptly was thrust into prison.

Before this event he was an unknown man, and for several years afterward this absurd coup d'état which he tried to bring to pass was regarded simply as one of the almost innumerable street brawls which desperate men had been starting in Germany ever since the defeat of the Second Marne. That this uneducated and most unprepossessing Austrian nobody should become dictator of the Reich in less than ten years, and in seven years more raise Germany to heights unknown even to Bismarck, no one dreamed, presumably not even Hitler himself.

Napoleon's origin was most respectable compared to his; the Emperor of the French at least started his career as a well-trained army officer. But in the obscurity of Hitler's early days there seemed to be no gleam of promise. The boy Adolf had some slight, very slight, artistic talent which he hoped to develop in Vienna. Poverty-stricken, a physical weakling, he only kept body and soul together in that city by accepting the hospitality of charitable institutions and by standing in bread-lines. He was not strong enough for manual labor; he was not talented enough to win more than a few miserable schillings as a decorator of gift-cards. Living from hand to mouth among the lowest of the Vienna proletariat, lazy and shiftless, he spent much of his time in the casual reading of the obscure pamphlet literature of the Pan-German expansionists and in listening, whenever chance offered, to music. In Vienna Hitler developed a bitter dislike for his companions in misery; he detested workmen, socialists, and above all else, Jews. He hated Vienna, the Hapsburg monarchy, and everything around him; and in his queer, tortured mind he found vicarious satisfaction for his own unhappiness in dreaming of a Germany which knew of no existence outside the imagination, a Germany great and glorious whose men and women, in the grandeur of their bodies, in the nobility of their souls, in the might of their wills someday would dominate the world. He, Hitler, was a German!

In 1914 he enlisted in the German army and fought throughout the entire war. He was a brave soldier, a dispatch-bearer, who was wounded, gassed, and given the Iron Cross. When the armistice was signed he thought the end of all things had come. Germany, his one love, was broken; all that he hated was victorious—the Allies, international banking, international socialism, and the Jews.

The ex-corporal, wandering aimlessly in Munich, dropped into a beer cellar. He listened to talk of a German Labor party, no Marxian international, bloodless and colorless, but a *pure* German party which would repudiate such vague things as interest slavery and would fight to the death against such concrete actualities as the Treaty of Versailles and the payment of reparations. Four men around a beer-stained table—and Adolf Hitler! He joined the party as number seven and discovered that he had a wonderful talent—his voice. The party doubled and trebled its membership rapidly; men came to hear Hitler. Why?

The theme of his speeches was of the simplest: We did not lose the war; the German people always win! We were betrayed, stabbed in the back by Socialist and Jew. We have nothing to be ashamed of; we shall yet conquer. *"Deutschland Erwache,"* Germany, awake! Down with the international bankers, the international socialists, the evil Communists, the "November criminals," those who signed the Treaty of Versailles. We are not bound by that treaty; we will not be enslaved; down with Communist Russia; down with the Allies and their false promises! Throw off the shackles. *Deutschland Erwache!*

The German Labor party soon enlarged its scope. It became the N.S.D.A.P., the *National-sozialistische deutsche arbeiterpartei,* soon to be called Nazi, for brevity. The emphasis from the beginning was on the word *National,* and as the years sped on the labor aspect of the party's program grew less and less. The party was given a flag (Hitler was not an artist in vain), red because of its psychological stimulus, white circle on the red background that the flag might be distinguished from the Communist banner, and on the white circle a black, crooked cross—the swastika—symbol of human fertility in India, of anti-semitism in Russia.

Fortunately for the ultimate success of the Nazis, came the collapse of the 1923 *émeute.* That failure threw Hitler into jail, thus giving him time to formulate his dreams, and to bring to the boiling point the yeasty depths of his subconsciousness. And now, a captive, he wrote *Mein Kampf!*

This Bible of the Nazi faith, calmly and objectively considered, is a queer mélange of semi-truth and unadulterated nonsense, combined with an almost uncanny psychological insight into the mind of the mob. It is wordy, turbid, repetitious, ill written; but it does throw light on Hitler, his aims, methods, character. It is easier to tell big lies than little ones, the author tells us. The people are always gullible; they will believe anything if sufficiently repeated. Hitler is quite on a par with Mussolini in his contempt for democracy. The Jews brought about the ruin of Germany; they must be driven out of the country. France is pictured as the eternal enemy, but communism as Germany's more immediate foe. The Fatherland must arouse itself, must repudiate the Versailles *diktat,* must fight, must expand, must seize land in southern and eastern Europe. The Nazi party will do all this.

There is not much more in *Mein Kampf.* Hitler speaks at length of his early career in Vienna and how he came to detest the Jews; he exults in the way the Nazis were able to exploit mob psychology by the use of storm-troopers (hired roughnecks) instead of depending on police support in their early days. There is anticapitalistic talk of a kind; but Hitler really was not interested in economics. Where he lets himself go with feeling and abandon is when he talks about the *Volk* (people). But Volk means far more than "people" in the English sense; rather it implies an antecedent, primitive, racial throwback to a mythological German people invented during the days of the fight waged against Bonaparte by poets and philosophers and found useful by politicians. *"Blut und Boden,"* blood and soil—a sacred something in the German blood-stream, an equally sacred something in the earth on which Germans have lived. Here is nothing but a pouring forth of disjointed fragments from H. S. Chamberlain, Fichte, and Jahn, with stray bits of the Pan-German gospel picked up here and there by the casual reading of a tramp-artist in beer-cellar and public reading-room. We are also told why Germany lost the war, what kind of government befits the longed-for volk state and what ought to be the German foreign policy of the future. The policy of the Hohenzollern régime in international affairs is adversely criticized and Austria is assailed as partly responsible for the war; but what really lost the war, according to Hitler, was (*a*) the inefficient propaganda of Germany in comparison with England; (*b*) the traitorous character of German socialism; and (*c*) the poisonous infiltration of Jewish influence in the Fatherland. One thing Hitler instinctively grasped, the art of propaganda.

The great masses' receptive ability, [he tells us] is only very limited, their understanding is small, but their forgetfulness is great. As a consequence of these facts, all effective propaganda has to limit itself only to a very few points and to use them like slogans until even the very last man is able to imagine what is intended by such a word. . . . It was completely wrong to ridicule the adversary as was done in Austrian and German propaganda in comic papers. It was basically wrong for the reason that when a man meets the adversary in reality he was bound to receive an entirely different impression; something that took its most terrible revenge; for now the German soldier, under the direct impression of the resistance of the enemy, felt himself deceived by those who were responsible for his enlightenment, and instead of strengthening his fighting spirit or even his firmness, quite the contrary occurred. The man despaired. Compared with this, the war propaganda of the British and the Americans was psychologically right. By introducing the German as a barbarian and a Hun to its own people it thus prepared the individual soldier for the terrors of war and helped guard him against disappointment [1] . . .

On the other hand, concerning socialism and the Jews the future dictator of Germany was grossly partisan. There was, it is true, a socialistic revolution in the Fatherland as the war officially ended, and there was socialistic propaganda in favor of peace before that date; but the influence of the latter was very slight until late in 1918, not until after Ludendorff had admitted German defeat and Austria had betaken herself out of the conflict. As for the Jews, their history and their character, Hitler knew nothing. Page after page of *Mein Kampf* is devoted to their vilification. Those pages do not need examination if we remember that the ratio of casualties in the war for the German Jews was approximately the same as for the German Gentiles; that 35,000 Jews received war medals; that 23,000 Jewish soldiers were promoted to the rank of officer; that of less than 600,000 Jewish citizens of Germany, 100,000 bore arms.

[1] Hitler, *Mein Kampf*, p. 234, quoted by permission of the Houghton Mifflin Company, proprietors of the basic copyrights of all American editions.

The importance of *Mein Kampf* as a book is difficult to estimate. Certainly, it does not belong in the same category in the field of political science as Rousseau's *Social Contract* or the essays of John Stuart Mill. The voice, and not the pen, was the medium through which Hitler rose to power. On the other hand, it is foolish to dismiss *Mein Kampf* as simply the wild ravings of a paranoiac. After all, millions read this book, which possibly will rank in later years as the most famous or infamous production of the first quarter of the twentieth century.

Why National Socialism Continued to Grow

Hitler, once out of jail (1924), gave all his time to resuscitating the N.S.D.A.P. Only very slowly did it grow, for Locarno in 1925 (see p. 168) seemingly placed the Weimar Republic on a firmer basis, and not until as late as 1929 were Nazis much more than a joke among seriously minded Germans. Nevertheless, grow in numbers they did, and for a variety of reasons. Among them were: the peculiar appeal of the National Socialists to the lower half of the middle class, slowly slipping into the proletariat; the adroit use of propaganda; the financial assistance of wealthy Germans; and the absurd antics of the German Communists.

The middle class, particularly in the lower strata, felt the shock of Germany's financial disaster in 1923 more than any other. The peasants managed to live; they had their cattle and their gardens. The aristocrats had their rent rolls; and the wealthier bourgeoisie still owned factory and workshop which they operated as soon as the new currency, the rentenmark, was established. So also was it with the workmen who had no capital anyway to disappear with inflation and who could depend more or less on unemployment insurance. But there was no sun at all on the horizon of the little man of business, the people with money in savings-banks, those with insurance, the doctors, the dentists, the professional men, and the civil servants who had saved a little for retirement or for a rainy day. All they had was wiped out overnight. Vaguely, the N.S.D.A.P. was against big business, the little people liked that; it was against war profiteers (many of them Jewish), and the little people liked that. To all baffled and defeated and discouraged men it offered two scapegoats—the Versailles *diktat* and the Jews. Those who despaired the most and who thought the least were attracted as by a magnet.

The National Socialist propaganda was unique and telling. Hitler explained in his book how meetings held at night were always more effective than those held during the day in arousing the emotions, and most of the Nazi meetings were in the evening. Nothing was omitted that might arouse passion. The Nazis made great use of huge banners borne by their separate units. These flags were consecrated by the Fuehrer by touching them with that most sacred blood-stained banner borne in the tragi-comedy of 1923 in Munich. Singing and neon lights made their appeal. Hitler's advent was frequently delayed until excitement reached the fever pitch. As time wore on the Fuehrer traveled over large stretches of Germany by airplane. Search-lights would pierce the black night for his coming; bands would burst into martial music; and then the ex-corporal with magic voice would scream defiance at his various foes.

Where did the money come from to pay for uniforms, publicity, a Mercedes automobile and airplanes? In part it was derived from the sale of tickets; the Hitler shows were good ones; in part it came from the dues of party members, very considerable in the lump sum. But in addition there were contributions from the big industrialists, who contributed more or less impartially to all the anti-Marxian factions. These industrialists were not Nazis; but many of them thought the Nazis useful, since they beat up Communists in the street and demanded the rearmament of Germany, a pleasant note to the ear of the Ruhr steel men. Even the Nationalists, the Junker crowd, were sufficiently foolish to believe that Hitler, mountebank and charlatan though he might be, could be taken into camp and made a convenient tool for the reëstablishment of the monarchy. The Nationalists could not agree upon a candidate for the vacant imperial throne, some favoring Rupprecht of Bavaria, some the Hohenzollerns; but in the meanwhile a subsidy to the ex-corporal could do no harm.

Then, too, the Communist party in Germany continued through the nineteen-twenties to be a great help to Hitler. The Communists looked to Moscow for their orders and they received them. Nothing detracts more from Lenin's reputation as a statesman than his conviction that a Communist revolution was imminent in Germany, a Russian fantasy that lived long after Lenin died and still, perhaps, is cherished in Moscow. Lenin instructed his disciples in Germany to undermine the Weimar Republic; to hate and to abhor all Social Democrats, those traitors to the Marxian faith, instructions followed after Lenin's death. They fitted nicely into Hitler's hand; he denounced the Communists as base internationalists; he insisted that they went further, that they advocated loose sexual relations, free week-ends without matrimony, and so forth. The Nazis posed as the defenders of the German home. Purists of the pure (in theory), they harkened back to the folkways of the primitive Germans, their sexual cleanliness, their Spartan virtue. How these *Urdeutschers* would have revolted against the social decadence and flaunting vice of the contemporary republic in which the

Communists reveled! And there is a good deal of evidence to support the Nazi claim that such conditions existed in Germany after the war, as is true more or less in all countries after the strain of war, and particularly in those where the currency depreciates so rapidly that the wise thing seems to be to spend any money available while it still has purchasing power. But to the Nazi orator the purveyor of this vice was always the Jew and the Communist!

Under such circumstances, the Weimar Republic was fortunate to survive as long as it did. Assailed from both right and left, by Nationalists, Communists, and Nazis, it kept its head well above water until the world economic crisis of 1930-31. One reason why it did so was the tactful foreign policy of Gustav Stresemann, who was Germany's foreign minister in no less than ten different ministries between 1923 and 1929. During the war Stresemann had been a violent Nationalist, and after it he was the spokesman in the Reichstag for the German People's party, the right wing of the bourgeoisie. But these facts did not prevent him from realizing the immediate necessity of placating France and England if the republic was to get on a firm basis. Within one year after the evacuation of the Ruhr by the French, the Dawes Plan for lessening the strain of the reparation problem was accepted by Stresemann, and one year later he negotiated the Treaty of Locarno with the former enemies of Germany on the basis of perfect equality.

LOCARNO AND THE DAWES PLAN

That treaty guaranteed the western frontier of the Weimar Republic as drawn by the Treaty of Versailles, and the signatories—Belgium, Italy, France, England, and Germany—not only pledged themselves to respect it but also to enforce it. Thus the Germans of their own accord surrendered all claims to Alsace-Lorraine, and the French to further invasions of Germany to enforce treaty rights, such as the invasion of the Ruhr had been. The Germans likewise agreed to the demilitarization of Germany fifty kilometers east of the Rhine, as provided in the Versailles pact. Locarno was to go into effect with the entry of Germany into the League of Nations, which took place late in this same year, 1926.

Along with this partial settlement of political disputes and the recognition of Germany's political equality with her former enemies, came a very decided economic revival. The Reich after the war had no ruined cities to rebuild, and the very fact of inflation had enabled her to modernize her industrial machinery by borrowing huge sums which were repaid in marks which had no value. Furthermore, since the old mark now was worthless, her war loans, raised from her own citizens (domestic debt), were wiped out. There remained her debt to the Allies (reparations). This now, by the Dawes Plan, was placed upon a more intelligent basis than it had before. The latter plan was still a stop-gap; it was irritating insofar as it called for a certain amount of international control over German finance; it was annoying insofar as it made the amount of the annual total due from Germany depend on an index of prosperity which meant that the more prosperous the Germans became the more they had to pay; and it was discouraging, as it set no final total of indebtedness. On the other hand, it was an improvement which worked as long as foreign loans poured into Germany. The plan called for immediate loans which were granted, and these were followed by many private ones.

Stresemann, indeed, had accomplished much, but he was heavily attacked for not doing more. The fourteen points of Wilson had called for general disarmament; but all the Germans saw was unilateral disarmament as far as they were concerned and practically nothing accomplished by the other countries in this direction. The Dawes Plan, too, seemingly laid an almost perpetual burden on German backs, even if a slightly lighter one than that already carried. Stresemann realized this and worked hard to ease the burden still further. This he was able to accomplish by the Young Plan, 1929, which was adopted by general consent in place of the Dawes Plan. The new agreement provided a definite limit for German payment, lowering the total indebtedness. But unfortunately the agreement came too late. In this year (1929) Stresemann died and an economic blizzard began to sweep the world which transformed the situation and gave Hitler his great opportunity.

THE GREAT DEPRESSION AND THE NAZIS

The storm clouds burst on the New York stock exchange late in 1929 and a first-class panic followed in America. This meant not only no more loans to Germany but also the calling in of short-term credits to that country. Whereupon, in 1930, banks in Germany and Austria began to close their doors and German factories to dismiss their employees. In vain did the German chancellor appeal to the British and the French for help; the former, fearful of their own financial status, were afraid to aid; the latter were not only afraid but unwilling. A moratorium on reparation payments was, indeed, granted; but that came too late to be effective, and international trade was paralyzed.

Under such circumstances came the election of 1930. Both the German right and the German left strengthened their position against the moderate center; the Communists increased their representation at the expense of the Social Democrats, but that of the Nazis went skyrocketing upward. Before the election the Nazis, despite their clamor, had but twelve seats in the Reichstag; after it was over they numbered 107 and were the second largest party.

The chancellor was Brüning, a Centrist. For support at home he had to depend on a slight majority made up of many different party groups and on the backing of the President of the Republic, the octogenarian Hindenburg. Support outside his country he had none. A customs union with Austria which might have helped save the day had been vetoed by the French, a veto upheld on technical grounds by the World Court at the Hague. Neither politically nor financially was the republic to be aided in her death struggle. Meanwhile, unemployment rose by leaps and bounds, and starvation threatened. The very liberalism of the Weimar Republic was telling now against it. For years the Nationalists and the Nazis had been organizing and drilling informal private armies of their own, the former the Steel Helmets, the latter the *Sturmabteilung* (Brown Shirts). Even the peaceful Social Democrats had done likewise with the *Reichsbanner* corps. Germany was seething with violent disorder. Armed bands were attacking Jews and Communists, the former not retaliating, the latter fighting back.

Between the accession of Brüning in March, 1930, and the burning of the Reichstag building in February, 1933, which threw Germany into Hitler's power, the utmost confusion reigned. Plot and counterplot followed. There were two presidential and two Reichstag elections; there were innumerable street riots and many murders; and the political balance swayed backward and forward between the defenders of Weimar and the Nationalists, the Nazis, and the Communists who hated the republic. Much is still obscure concerning these three hectic years during which the Nazis and the Nationalists, wearing their private uniforms, marched out of the Reichstag and into it again, during which Brüning, a confirmed moderate and well-wisher of the republic, was compelled to rule largely by decree until he lost the support of the President, during which also the Junker aristocracy played constantly with fire (Adolf Hitler), only in the end to be badly scorched.

The three years were full of economic misery and semistarvation, since Brüning's answer to the world depression was economy. But they were also full of betrayals of one sort or another. Hindenburg, very old and perhaps not altogether in possession of his faculties, was reëlected by the Social Democrats, the Centrists, and other moderate groups. Yet within a few weeks after the election, he seemingly betrayed his constituents by dismissing Brüning, who had at the time a majority behind him. Von Papen, a Junker, was made chancellor by Hindenburg, but he in turn was betrayed by General Schleicher and other Nationalists who intrigued against von Papen. Schleicher, von Papen, and the Nationalists (Steel Helmets) were afterward betrayed by Hitler, who played cleverly for power and only obtained it by betraying also his own left-wing followers who took their socialism seriously. Possibly the "anti-capitalistic romanticism" which the coming Fuehrer had advocated hitherto, with its implied attack on land values and big business, had never been of any real significance to him; but it was imbedded in the platform of the Nazi party, and in order to obtain the support of the wealthy, Hitler threw most of it overboard, driving out of his own party many of his oldest and warmest friends.

Finally, in January, 1933, Hindenburg, field marshal, war hero, and president of the republic which he had sworn to defend, appointed ex-corporal Hitler as chancellor. This was done through the connivance of von Papen and other aristocrats, who thought Hitler would play their game. The Nazis, at the last election, had captured only thirty-two per cent of the votes and the Nationalist vote was less than one-third that of the Nazis. There was then no majority for the Nazi-Nationalist combination and another election was called, the third in one year. By the first and earlier election of 1932 the Nazis had captured thirty-seven per cent of the electorate and therefore they seem-ingly were declining in strength. The decline from thirty-seven to thirty-two per cent was serious; could they hope for a majority now? It looked as though they could not; but luck or treachery now stood them in good stead—the Reichstag fire!

Who destroyed the parliamentary building where the Reichstag met? "The slimy Communists did it!" shouted the Nazis, from a thousand platforms in Germany. "It was to be the signal for a Communist revolt; we and the Nationalists were in power; our General Goering nipped the plot in the bud or else there would have been a Red revolution." But that the Communists engaged in this act of arson there is no evidence, and everything points to the Nazis as having perpetrated this destruction. True, a half-witted young Dutchman, afterward executed, helped set the Reichstag on fire, and at one time he had been associated with Communists in Holland. But this fire was well planned, well executed, and required the help of several men. And there is some evidence, both direct and circumstantial, to indicate that it was done by a number of Brown Shirts, presumably under orders from that fire-eating Nazi, General Goering.

However that may be, it was the Nazis who profited. There were only three Nazis in the cabinet and they were supposedly kept well under control there by the numerical majority of Nationalists; but one of the three was Hitler, the chancellor, and they controlled the police. This latter fact really determined the result of the election in advance; Communist, Socialist, and even Centrist newspapers were suppressed and every possible hysteria was summoned to the Nazi support. And the increase in their vote which followed brought it to forty-three and nine-tenths per cent of the total. If we add to this, however, the eight per cent won by the Nationalists, it is evident that the coalition had fifty-two per cent, a narrow but clear majority.

The Reichstag met and the first thing done was to exclude from its meetings the 81 members elected by the Communists, an act which gave the Nazis, by themselves and for the first time, a majority over all. Followed then rapidly the abolition of the German trade unions, the abolition of the Social Democratic party, and that of all other political groups in the Reichstag except the Nazi. The Reichsbanner of the Socialists was dissolved without a fight and, unkindest cut of all, the Nationalists were forced out of the cabinet and their Stahlhelm abolished. The Centre party meanwhile voluntarily ended its own existence, and political parties, as such, were abolished in Germany with the exception of one, the N.S.D.A.P. All this took place rapidly during the year 1933 and, toward its end, Hitler, in a blaze of patriotic fervor, withdrew Germany from the League of Nations (see p. 282). As he did so, he asked for a vote of the German people in approval or disapproval of his various activities. A ballot was to be cast, a curious ballot. There were Nazi names printed on it and no others were permitted. One could simply vote *"Ja"* or *"Nein"*; there was no other choice. Before the election there was to be no propaganda of any kind except Nazi propaganda. To the Nazis belonged the exclusive rights to the press, to the radio, to illuminated night meetings, and brass bands. And the S.A., the storm troopers, Brown Shirts, guarded the polls and watched the voting. The result—ninety-five per cent voted *"Ja."*

Party government now was ended, liberty vanished, democracy dead; unless we credit to democracy this and similar plebiscites in what Hitler terms the Third Reich. Germany was on the verge of being a totalitarian state controlled completely by the will of one man, except in so far as he delegated that will to his leading subordinates like General Hermann Goering, a former aviator, now President of the Reichstag, and Joseph Paul Goebbels, the most learned of all the Nazis, a doctor of philosophy with a crippled body, whose venomous diatribes against the Jews had endeared him to Hitler. The Reichstag, it is true, continued to exist; but from now on it became merely a sounding board for Hitler's voice. Von Hindenburg still lived; but he was in his last illness and within a year was to die. Hitler did not choose to succeed him as president. That exalted title, he explained, belonged only to Hindenburg; he, Hitler, would be content to be simply *Der Fuehrer,* the man who founded the Third German Reich which would last 1,000 years.

Very thoroughly now did Hitler subordinate all things in Germany to the will of the Nazi party—his will. From 1934 to the outbreak of the second World War in 1939, the Nazis proceeded (*a*) to destroy root and branch all traces of a labor party in Germany; (*b*) insanely and abominably to persecute the Jews; (*c*) to attack the Christian Church, both Catholic and Protestant; (*d*) to revolutionize education; (*e*) to cast off one by one the last remnants of the Versailles pact; (*f*) to rearm to the teeth; and (*g*) finally, by an aggressive foreign policy, to plunge Europe into another war. The first four of these seven policies of Hitler will be discussed here; the remaining three belong to the field of international relations and will be taken up later.

The Nazis and Labor

Strangely enough, the German labor movement, apparently so strong on the eve of Hitler's advent to power, succumbed without a fight, whereas the churches, and the Lutheran Church in particular, seemingly weak and defenseless in the post-War period were able to withstand to some degree the will of the dictator. The German trade unions, which accepted disbandment without a murmur, were strong in numbers but weak in will. Their members were socialists who had looked forward for so long and so confidently to the time when Germany would *hinein-wachsen* (grow into socialism) that they were inhibited from realizing that their cause might be lost altogether unless they were willing to meet force with force. Many of their members were led by Nazi propaganda to believe that National Socialism, as advertised, was really socialistic. The Nazis, during their first year in power, certainly succeeded in reducing unemployment. They did so by extreme economic nationalism, by starting public works, by establishing labor camps, by ordaining export subsidies, by commencing (just how early it is impossible to tell) the rearmament of Germany. But nevertheless, for the time being, German labor was better off than it had been in several years, a fact which made the suppression of autonomous labor groups very easy.

Then, too, the Nazis announced a labor policy which in theory was favorable to labor. "Full authority downward, full responsibility upward," was their slogan, undemocratic, if you will, but not necessarily injurious to the material welfare of the workingman. If the latter lost his right to collective bargaining, that did not mean free competition in the labor market and the right of the employer to determine wages. Over both employer and employee now were placed fourteen labor trusts, who were to determine wages; and social honor courts with power to deal with labor disputes took the place of the old trade unions. Labor was forbidden to organize, but labor was not left completely helpless, for the Nazi party controlled the honor courts.

The historian, indeed, must walk warily for some time to come in generalizing about Nazi labor policy. In certain respects it was favorable to labor. A "Strength through Joy" movement was started, whereby free vacations at state expense were provided; six months' labor service (*arbeiterdienst*) was required of all Germans irrespective of social position and rank; German peasants were protected against usury and were assured title to their holdings in perpetuity; and great care was taken to prevent the price of foodstuffs customarily used by the poor, such as potatoes, margarine, and sausages, from rising.

The Nazis did not, to be sure, satisfy their own more radical members who hoped for a genuinely socialistic revolution and the ending of capitalism in Germany. But the latter were completely crushed by the bloody purge of 1934, and most of their spokesmen were killed. Just what happened behind the scenes is still obscure. There was talk of a second revolution, and Roehm, commander of the Brown Shirts, aroused the suspicions of Hitler. Just what Roehm was after it is difficult to tell; he wanted more power given the Brown Shirts and was jealous of the S.S. men, the Schutzstafel, or private police who guarded Hitler and who seemed to the storm-troopers a kind of aristocratic organization supplanting them. Roehm had been one of the more radical Nazis and he was thought to have been intriguing with von Schleicher, the ex-Nationalist chancellor and a general in the army, who might conceivably be stirring up a coup d'état against Hitler. It was also said that Roehm for a long time had been a notorious homosexual, a fact hitherto ignored by Hitler.

Suddenly now, in the summer of 1934, Hitler pounced upon Roehm and his more intimate friends and summarily put them to death. Simultaneously, Goering in Berlin slaughtered in cold blood many other Nazis, likewise General von Schleicher, his wife, and a number of other suspects. All told, upward of a thousand Germans were shot down in cold blood. "There was none of the courage of mercy. There was none of the coolness of wisdom." With berserker rage the Nazi chieftains acted, and bullets spat against cement walls as Nazi after Nazi with "Heil Hitler!" on his lips gave up his life. Hitler, in a long, rambling speech to the Reichstag, explained later that the victims of the purge were traitors, that they were dissipated, immoral, and deserved death. The world looked for some proof of the former statement; none was advanced. The immorality was nothing new, nothing hidden; it had not hitherto excited Hitler's rage. But even the sexual abnormality which characterized Roehm and certain other well-known Brown Shirts was not charged against all of those slain. A number of them, like von Schleicher, were not even Nazis. Could it be possible that von Schleicher had proof that Hitler had never received the Iron Cross for valor in the war; was he really intriguing with Roehm to overthrow the dictator; was there any significance in the fact that those Nazis employed in firing the Reichstag now were killed, thus ending any chance of their talking? Robespierre gave Danton a trial in the French Revolution; Hitler behaved otherwise to his old comrades.

THE NAZIS AND THE JEWS

Possibly the single most extraordinary fact about Hitler and the Nazi victory was the antisemitism which characterized it. Concerning the major facts there can be no dispute. After the Nazis come to power they excluded Jews from all learned professions in Germany, forbade them to practise law, removed their physicians from state hospitals, drove Jewish judges off the bench and Jewish professors out of the universities. Jews were excluded from all governmental posts, and one by one the various economic enterprises which Jews headed were "Aryanized," placed under non-Jewish management. Jews were compelled to dispose of their large business enterprises for nominal sums, Jewish-owned department stores, banks, printing-presses, manufacturing plants, were put under non-Jewish control. And finally Jews were subjected to an ever-increasing flood of humiliating insults, aimed apparently at driving all Jews and those of partial Jewish blood outside the country of their birth.

Hitler himself had written "the wretched Jew, enemy of the human race, the Jew, cause of all our miseries," and Goebbels, appointed minister of propaganda by Hitler, constantly referred to Jews as beneath the contempt of all decent men. But more important, perhaps, than the statements of these two Nazi chieftains were the fulminations of Streicher, a popular Nazi propagandist, whose foul sheet *Der Stürmer,* specifically blest by Hitler, was made compulsory reading in the German schools.

Der Stürmer, by cartoon and by story, stressed one major theme—the lascivious desire of the Jewish people to contaminate the German people by sexual intercourse with it. The Jewish religion, *Der Stürmer* said, called for the spreading of the seed of Israel among non-Jews; Jewish physicians could never be trusted because they gave anesthetics in order to rape German girls. Jews must not be spoken to on the street; they must have separate benches in the schools; no German girl was to be permitted to work as a servant in a Jewish home; she must never marry a Jew; the *Protocols of Zion* (an absurd forgery) was dug up to prove that Jews conspired to rule the world; rabbis were accused of drinking Christian blood in foul rituals; and by the Nuremberg laws none could claim to be a German citizen unless he could prove that all of his four grandparents were non-Jewish. Even the non-Aryan Christians, those contaminated by having one or more grandparents Jewish, were forbidden to give the Nazi salute. They were equally guilty of belonging to an inferior race. The Nazis wanted none of them; together with the Jews they were invited to emigrate, provided that most of their property was left behind.

The situation grew worse constantly, and when a young Jewish boy assassinated an official in the German embassy at Paris in 1938, it reached its height. Mobs roamed the streets of German cities, burning synagogues, smashing the windows of Jewish stores, stealing their contents, and beating all Jews they encountered. The authorities made no effort to stop them; instead they levied a huge fine on all German Jews, so huge as virtually to wipe out all remaining Jewish wealth. Some Jews escaped from Germany, penniless; but a majority, unable to obtain visas for countries beyond the seas or in Europe, sunk back into the depths of despair as the Nazis prepared to set apart ghettos for Jews, miserable districts in the more squalid parts of German cities in which Jews must live and out of which Jews would emerge at their peril.

Why this persecution of the Jews, the most vicious, the most barbaric in modern times? It was not just the dictatorship; Frederick the Great was a dictator, but he welcomed Jews in Prussia, and Napoleon was well disposed toward them. It has been urged that Germany was always an antisemitic country; but the facts do not bear out this interpretation. During the period of the Second German Empire, which lasted from 1871 to the Weimar Republic, there was far more active antisemitism in both France and Russia than in Germany. The Germans discriminated against the Jews even then, socially, and governmental and military rank was denied them; but Jewish students were not put on a narrow quota basis in the universities as in Russia, and the learned professions in Germany were full of Jews—Jewish doctors, Jewish lawyers, Jewish professors. Important newspapers, banks, business houses, were Jewish-owned, and mixed marriages were more common in Germany than anywhere else in Europe. The very presence of the numerous non-Aryan Christians refutes this argument. The latter were more than three times as numerous as the professing Jewish people, of whom there were only some 600,000 in the Reich.

It has likewise been suggested that economic competition brought about the Jewish persecution, the Jews being held up to scorn as battening on the ills of Germany, war profiteers, usurers, prosperous while others starved. The economic level of the German Jew was, it is true, relatively high; he did own most of the department stores which took away trade from the small shopkeepers, and there were Jewish usurers. But there was nothing new about this, and all the evidence at our command goes to show that the Jew did not benefit by the war. Like other Germans his income declined; and as a matter of cold statistics, the proportion of leading industrialists and bankers of Germany in the post-War period of non-Jewish blood was higher after the conflict than before.

Even less valid a reason is the assertion that the principles of National Socialism are so foreign to Jewish psychology as to make inevitable the exclusion of all Jews from a Nazi state. Jews, naturally, are opposed to antisemitism; but aside from that there was no proposal of the Nazis that Jews as such would automatically oppose. There are international Jews, socialist Jews, nationalist Jews, capitalistic Jews. In Italy Jews joined the Fascist ranks until driven out by Mussolini. In fact, there were certain tenets of Nazi philosophy which might be considered as rather attractive to Jews, particularly the idea of national unity transcending all religious barriers.

What then is the explanation? Possibly the best that can be given is the racial myth that Hitler expounded, the supremacy of Aryan and particularly Teutonic blood over all other racial strains. Some reason had to be given for this superior racial strain losing the war, and the inherent wickedness of Marxian philosophy was a partial one. But Marxism could not be dramatized quite so readily as that biological absurdity of the Nazis—the poisoning of racial purity by Jewish blood. The Jews were a convenient scapegoat. Communists as scapegoats had disadvantages; they were poor and there was no booty to be gleaned from them; they were Germans, and when they transferred themselves into good Nazis, or pretended to, they had no distinguishing marks. But the Jews had money, which might come in handy; they also had distinguishing marks; their names, their physical appearance—they were Jews. As such they offered a shining mark for the attack of the bigoted, and they became the principal scapegoat upon which was loaded all the unhappiness and misery of post-war Germany.

THE NAZIS AND THE CHRISTIAN CHURCHES

The Nazis' attack on Christianity is perhaps easier to understand than their animosity toward the Jews, but the evidence of it is slightly more confusing. Whether in the long run it was more serious than the open atheism of the Russian Communists it is difficult to say, for while the Communist attack was direct and open, that of the Nazis was indirect, insidious, and therefore possibly the more dangerous.

The Nazis never repudiated Christianity as a party; rather they tried to corrupt it from within, to twist and to distort its meaning.

Certain of the Nazis, to be sure, repudiated Christianity, lock, stock, and barrel. Seeking openly to reëstablish the pagan rites of their early ancestors, they resurrected Odin, Thor, and the old stone gods. By picturesque ritual and dramatic rites, they glorified bravery, loyalty, and physical force into a trinity of virtues. But these professed pagans were but a minority. What was far more characteristic of the Nazi attitude toward religion was the program of the German Christians. The latter threw out the Old Testament as a Jewish book, and many parts of the New Testament as well. They denied that Christ was Jewish and intepreted him as a kind of warrior who, by his death, had preserved the world from Jewish domination, an act of virtue duplicated by their Fuehrer, in turn a kind of second Christ. These so-called German Christians demanded that the swastika be introduced into the churches as a kind of sacred symbol, and that the church be regarded solely as a kind of adjunct to the government.

All Nazis did not go as far as these German Christians, and many of them were indifferent to the church, whether Catholic or Protestant, as was the case, apparently, with Hitler. Nevertheless, the latter was determined to put the Lutheran Church of the country under his direct control, and appointed as head of it a reichsbishop with German Christian tendencies. This met with such stiff opposition that Hitler withdrew his appointee and selected another. Many Lutheran pastors objected to taking an oath of loyalty to Hitler which would deprive them of freedom of conscience. In consequence, a number of them were put in concentration camps and others had their parsonages taken away from them.

Much to the surprise of the outside world, the Lutheran Church in Germany, hitherto considered more dead than alive as far as spiritual fervor was concerned, took on a new lease of life. Churches began to be filled, many coming, perhaps, not so much to worship the Lord as to show that they would like to voice disapproval of the Nazi tyranny in their own country. Going to church was about the only way they could show it.

The Roman Catholic Church also came in conflict with the government. It had consented to liquidate the Centre party and to retire from politics; but it would not consent to the untiring campaign of the Nazis in trying to break up all church youth organizations and compelling boys to join the Hitler *Jugend,* wherein they were taught that force alone ruled the world and that Christian ethics were better suited for a slave society than for a self-respecting Aryan nation like Germany.

Roman Catholic bishops in both Austria and Germany protested firmly in their pastoral letters against this almost complete assumption of authority by the State over the time and the activities of the young. Whereupon the Nazis fought back; they placed on trial many members of monastic orders on a variety of charges running from accusations of smuggling gold out of Germany to sexual malpractices; they banned the circulation of Catholic literature; they forbade Catholic processions; and they sternly insisted that the Church confine its activities to what the Nazis considered religious matters, education being distinctly not one.

Nazi threats on the one hand and the protest of the Pope and of Protestant pastors on the other, continued down to the commencement of the second World War in 1939, without any final solution or compromise being reached. To claim that in this general strife the Nazis met their match would be an exaggeration; nevertheless it is evident that the Nazis did not dare go too far in their opposition to the churches. They did not, for instance, close them; they did not forbid Mass being sung. In view of the necessity of unity in foreign affairs, even Hitler refrained from a completely totalitarian policy in church affairs, and the churches retained something more than the semblance of autonomy.

Possibly in this matter the Nazis felt that time was on their side. The older generation would die before long, and boys and girls who had experienced nothing outside the Nazi fold would take its place. The same thing would occur in Germany as was taking place (so they thought) in Italy—the coming to maturity of youngsters trained in a new faith.

Nazi Education

For the Nazis had a faith (of a kind) and they went about its indoctrination in a most thorough manner. Superficially, it copied the Italian model. Boys and girls were expected to join the various Nazi youth organizations appropriate for their age, there to drill, to march, to sing the praises of the new régime, to listen to its glories, to grow accustomed to warlike discipline, to learn in true Spartan fashion that luxury, comfort, individualism, were not for them. But in reality this Nazi faith was much more serious than its Italian counterpart. The Fascist teachings of Mussolini were never taken, one suspects, very seriously by him nor by the better informed Italians. The Duce found these very useful for a clever adventurer, but he never took pains to define them very closely. Not so with the Nazis. Their philosophy (if one can call it such) was much more definite. To the ardent Nazi the Fuehrer was a man sent by God, and in him were embodied all those racial characteristics which dated from Odin, Thor, Siegfried. The necessity of obedience, the hatred of Jews, the substitution of the state for the family as the social unit were encouraged and enforced. Studies in the schools which did not serve these ends were either curtailed or abolished. Pseudo-scientific racial nonsense was given a most prominent place; strength of body and steadiness of nerve, dangerous and arduous physical exercise were exalted over mental acumen and ability. The German universities, so famous in the Second Reich, and still important centers of learning under the Weimar Republic, now became the laughing-stock of the Western world. Famous teachers were driven from them for not hewing to the party line, standards were lowered, the course of study narrowed. Almost for the first time in German history, learning became unimportant; the duty of man was to obey, not to think.

That course of study may best be comprehended by an analysis of two books, *The Nazi Primer,* an official handbook for the young, as concise and dogmatic in its scientific absurdities as any book ever printed on this planet, and *The Myth of the Twentieth Century,* by Hitler's favorite philosopher, Dr. Alfred Rosenberg, a German Balt and Hitler's agent extraordinary for the promulgation of official Nazi philosophy, a kind of higher Dr. Goebbels, an alter ego and exalted press agent in one for a busy Fuehrer in the realm of thought and dogma.

In two words, *Blut* and *Boden,* blood and land, may be found the essence of Nazi educational theory. According to the primer about seventy per cent of the German people belong to the Nordic race which had the purest and finest blood in all the world. Most of the Nordics are in Germany. Their race, the primer assures us, "is uncommonly gifted mentally. It is outstanding for truthfulness and energy. Nordic men possess for the most part, even in regard to themselves, a great power of judgment. They incline to be taciturn and cautious. They feel instantly that too loud talking is undignified. They are persistent and stick to a purpose when once they have set themselves to it. Their energy is displayed not only in warfare but also in technology and in scientific research. They are predisposed to leadership by nature." About twenty per cent of the Germans belong to the Phalic race, second only in virtue to the Nordic. "Differences in the soul qualities of the two races are not very great. The Phalic man is less emotional than the Nordic man. He is said to be better suited for being the driving force under the leadership of Nordic men than for leadership itself. Great patience characterizes his pursuit of an aim. Never could he be as foolhardy, perhaps, as the Nordic man. He is governed by a strong feeling of loyalty toward other men. He is more good natured and more cordial than the Nordic man.

"The Nordic and the Phalic man seem, therefore, to be more nearly related to each other than to any other race."

Ten per cent of the Germans belong to the other four European races, the Dinaric, the Eastern, the East Baltic, and the Western. Fortunately only two per cent belong to the Western race, which has little steadiness and is not given to reason. "The difficult and the burdensome are repugnant to the man of the Western race. He is excitable, even passionate. The Western race with all its mental agility lacks creative power. This race has produced only a few outstanding men.

"All in all, the contrasts between the Nordic and the Phalic races and the Western race appear to be very great, but chiefly in the realm of mind and soul."

The primer describes the six European races in great detail in regard to physical appearance, shape of skull, color of hair, soul qualities, and the like. It laments the fact that great harm has come to the Fatherland by the adulteration of the pure Nordic blood-stream; but it is not too late to mend matters. The laws of heredity are then described in detail and the boys are instructed that the purification of German blood is their first duty.

Their second relates to the Boden, the German land. By this is not meant just the German Fatherland as entrusted to Adolf Hitler. "By German territory," the primer informs us, "we mean every region of central Europe which is inhabited by Germans in more or less permanent settlements and has received its cultural imprint from the German people." This region of German language and cultural influence is, indeed, spacious. In area it is about three times as large as the Third Reich and for the most part stretching to the south and east. Concerning it the primer narrates much dubious history. It seems that the Germans brought about the unity of Europe between 100 A.D. and 1000 A.D., and "The Reich of the Middle Ages," we are told, "was about six times as large as it is today." Since the Thirty Years War, it appears, the Germans have been ill-treated, that is before the advent of Hitler. Their land was taken from them. "We are," laments the primer, "volk without space."[2]

What the primer states in simple language Dr. Rosenberg elaborates in sonorous and mystical praise-paens. The lost continent of Atlantis sunk beneath the ocean the Doctor peoples with Nordic heroes. "These swarms of Atlantis men," he assures us, "went forth in their swan boats and their dragon boats" on conquest bent. They fought like heroes and they were very brave; but they were also very

[2] All quotations from the Nazi primer are taken from H. L. Childs' translation, courtesy of Harper & Brothers.

soulful. "Soul," the Doctor pontificates, "means race seen from within ...; race is the outer form of the soul." It appears that only races have souls; individuals do not. The race is immortal. A nation is simply the physical embodiment of a race.

First above all comes race! The race must be cherished, guarded, exalted, and also strengthened by the most up-to-date genetic methods, by breeding men like cattle or like plants, and especially by decontaminating the German blood-stream of Jewish blood. It also must find elbow room in crowded Europe.

In order to secure it the new German education aimed straight at preparation for inevitable war. The Nazi overlords did not intend to stop with the reëstablishment of the old frontiers of Germany, or even with inclusion within the new Germany of racial brothers excluded from the old Reich, in Austria, Hungary, or elsewhere. The intimation in *Mein Kampf* is quite clear. "The frontiers of the year 1914," wrote Hitler in that book, "signify nothing at all for the future of the German nation." His people were "penned into an impossible area." They had a right to more land and would take it.

Lebensraum, living space for eighty million cramped Germans, must be found, and preferably to the east and south where the rich soil of the Ukraine stretched down through southern Poland all the way to the Black Sea. Here was superb *Lebensraum,* closely adjacent to Germany, where also there were many settlers of Germanic blood, small islands in a sea of Slavic people. To annex it would be in line with the ancient tradition of civilized Germany on guard against irruptions of Asiatic barbarians. Furthermore, proposals for its annexation always could be coupled with denunciations of Communists, and so not be altogether displeasing to blind politicians in London and Paris who might congratulate themselves with the thought that they were using Hitler as their catspaw in attacking Russia, and her horde of hateful Communists.

The Fuehrer, to be sure, would be glad to extend his boundaries even beyond the Ukraine. "How Germany has to work," he said in 1936, "to wrest a few kilometers from the ocean and from the swamps while others are swimming in a superfluity of land! If I had the Ural Mountains with their incalculable store of treasures in raw materials, Siberia with its vast forests, and the Ukraine with its tremendous wheat fields, Germany and the National Socialist leadership would swim in plenty."[3]

In justice to Hitler it should be stated that the rest of this speech was devoted to the praise of the German worker. Nevertheless the quotation is illuminating, not only as showing the drift of the Fuehrer's

[3] Adolf Hitler, *My New Order,* p. 400.

mind, but also because it is in close harmony with what the Nazis liked to think was a new science, that of geopolitics.

The term *geopolitics* was invented by a Swedish professor of history and it dates back to 1916, when in the midst of the first World War he defined geopolitics as "the science which conceives the state as a geographical organism or as a phenomenon in space." The state, according to the professor, must either grow or wither, and that, too, in a geographic sense. Geographic space, and plenty of it, is politically essential. This was true, he wrote, of England and is today the position of Japan and Germany. It is clearly a case not of the lust of conquest but of "natural and necessary growth. ..."

The ideas of the Swedish savant received a setback after the war. When it was over, however, they caught the imagination of Major General Doktor Karl Haushofer, professor of geography and military science at Munich, an intimate friend of Rudolf Hess, in turn an intimate friend of Hitler and his most trusted confidant. After Hitler became chancellor he made Haushofer president of the German Academy and set his approval on the new science of space relationship.

What the latter really amounted to was a new rationalization of an old idea—imperial conquest. The Romans never heard of geopolitics, nor did anyone else, for that matter, before the twentieth century, but they did know what conquest meant. Economics, psychology, anthropology, politics, sociology, all were lumped together by Haushofer and fused in geopolitics as a justification for the seizure of land occupied by non-Germans. Certain new and poetic expressions were coined to give an emotional overtone to these ideas. Thus Europe and Asia became the "Island Continent," and the central plains of Eurasia, "The Heartland." It was the destiny of the Island Continent to be dominated by one integrated racial group, presumably the German *Volk*. Once under its control, global supremacy would be within its grasp because the Island Continent, owing to its space, resources, numerous inhabitants, would easily hold the world balance of power. Land power was held more important than sea power (thus reversing Mahan), provided there was sufficient land.

Hitler was determined that there would be sufficient for a thousand years of his Third Reich. His early speeches stressed the sacred character of German soil; his later fulminations tended more and more to emphasize the *Lebensraum* motif, space for cheated Germans, always at a grave disadvantage because room was lacking. Thus, Hitler reasoned, "Forty-six million Britishers dominate and govern approximately 16 million square miles of the surface of the earth. Thirty-seven million Frenchmen dominate and govern a combined area of 4 million square miles. Forty-five million Italians possess, taking into consideration only those territories in any way capable of being utilized, an area of scarcely 190,000 miles. That is to say: 85 millon Germans own only 232 000 square miles on which they must live their lives and 46 million B itishers possess 16 million square miles."[4]

Here was injustice which Hitler was determined to rectify. He brushed aside the fact that the greater part of Canada was frozen tundra, that the greater part of Australia was a waterless desert, that England was far more thickly populated than his own country, that Englishmen living in England had no control over the property of Englishmen living in New Zealand or South Africa. He did not stop to note that the phenomenal industrial development of the Reich necessitated the importation of Polish and Italian laborers, since there were not enough Germans available; he did not consider that the only way the land area of Germany could be increased would be by annexing lands already thickly occupied, primarily by Slavs whose increase in population per hundred thousand ran well ahead of that in Germany. The only indication of the Fuehrer's pondering upon his statistics is his obvious stacking of the cards in favor of Italy. Note the qualifying clause, "taking into consideration only those territories in any way capable of being utilized." As far as Italy was concerned Hitler was willing to subtract African deserts.

Potsdam had conquered Weimar; the Germany of Goethe and Thomas Mann was now under the heel of Prussian tradition. The Nazis brought Sparta back again; women were encouraged to become brood mares for the strengthening and augmenting of the race; and boys, trained in rough discipline, were to regard obedience to command and the fighting spirit as the culmination of German virtue. From these boys a future Nazi élite was to be selected which would take over in time the work of the founder. To train this élite, a number of castles were set apart in Germany where, in strict seclusion, the rulers of the future Reich were to undergo training. Entrance requirements were strength, bravery, unquestioned and unquestioning obedience to orders, and the course of study in these Nazi nurseries was of like ilk.

[4] Adolf Hitler, *My New Order* (Reynal & Hitchcock, Inc.), p. 874.

CHAPTER VII

FRANCE AND ENGLAND BETWEEN
TWO WARS

IN contradistinction to the three totalitarian powers—Russia, Italy, and Germany—both France and England remained loyal in the post-war period to the democratic, liberal tradition of the nineteenth century. In both countries there was Communist agitation, more noticeable in France than in England; in both there were signs of incipient Fascist revolution, much more noticeable in France than in England; but in neither country did communism or fascism become a really serious threat.

FRANCE

The aftermath of the war, in France as elsewhere, was unpleasant. Even before the advent of that struggle the finances of the Republic were in shaky condition; for light taxes, heavy expenditure for armaments, and an unbalanced budget had created a tremendous burden of debt. That situation had caused little worry in the pre-war days, for if the government was poor, the national wealth was astonishingly high; and for several decades France had become the leading banker of the continent. After four years of war, however, there was real cause for worry; France had borrowed to the limit everywhere, both within and without her borders; the huge sums loaned to Imperial Russia had been repudiated by the Soviets; and a tenth of battle-scarred France lay in ruins.

The Republic had pledged itself early in the war to make good all damage done by the Germans in the invaded departments, and this alone was a Herculean task. Northeastern France, occupied by German armies, had been industrial France. Here had been the great textile mills, their machinery now in ruins; here had been the coal-mines of France, now flooded by the Germans. Almost all of the small towns and villages in the battle-zone had been wiped out by shell-fire; thousands of orchards had been cut down, thousands of wells had been filled up or poisoned; the cattle and sheep had been killed or eaten, the houses destroyed.

The Germans, to be sure, in accordance with the Treaty of Versailles, were to pay for this damage; but how was France to extract money from Germany? And while the manner and method of doing it was debated, was rehabilitation to be delayed? The French said, "No!" And immediately they began, in somewhat reckless and extravagant fashion, to rebuild their factories and towns. In theory, the money thus expended was not part of the national budget but was kept in a separate account charged to the Germans. Upwards of $7,000,000,000 was thus spent; and of this sum but trifling part ever was collected from Germany.

Little wonder that the French franc could not withstand the strain. Despite the cleverest devices of clever bankers, the franc started to follow the German mark to the graveyard of repudiated currencies. And as this went on, larger and larger grew the issue of paper francs, thus hastening repudiation. The war alone had raised the national debt of France from 35,000,000,000 francs to 180,000,000,000 francs, and during the first five years of the peace that debt had nearly doubled. It was impossible even to pay interest upon it, and soon the debt was found to be maturing at the rate of 7,500,000,000 francs a month! The result was that the franc sank rapidly. In 1914 it had been quoted at slightly under twenty cents to the dollar but by 1926 forty-eight francs could be bought for that sum, and American tourists in Paris were goading the French to fury by pasting paper francs on their luggage together with hotel stickers.

There was trouble, too, in Alsace and Lorraine. Those two redeemed provinces promptly were incorporated into France proper and turned into three departments, for the Third Republic had a passion for uniformity, and all Frenchmen, it was held, should be subject to the same laws. But Alsace and Lorraine were overwhelmingly Roman Catholic. When they had been annexed by Germany in 1871 the Napoleonic Concordat with the Catholic Church still was the law of France, and the priests in Alsace and Lorraine had been supported by the state and the schools had been Catholic schools. The Germans had not changed the status of the Catholic Church in the two provinces, but when they were returned to France their inhabitants found that the Concordat had been repudiated, that the Republic no longer concerned itself with religion, that the schools were laicized. Furthermore, there was the ever important question of language bobbing up again. Most of the Alsatians used German as a primary language and the Republic changed overnight the primary instruction in the schools from German to French. No wonder, then, that protests were loud and numerous, and that agitation arose for autonomy under the Tricolor, similar to the agitation in the two provinces when ruled as a Reichsland in the Germany Empire.

And yet another never-ending source of worry to the French was the problem of security. The Germans still outnumbered them at the close of the war, three to two, and if Austria ever came to be included in the Reich, the disparity in numbers would be still more pronounced. The French had surrendered at the Versailles Congress their desire for the Rhine frontier in return for guarantees from England and America, as well as from the League of Nations, guarantees which they soon discovered worthless or of slight value. The problem of French security more properly belongs to the discussion of international politics in the post-War world (Chapter XI). But it never ceased to cause friction within France herself; it was intimately correlated to the financial problem, since it involved the construction of the expensive Maginot Line to the east, and since it further involved large loans to potential allies, such as Poland, Czechoslovakia, Yugoslavia, and so on; and it also played an important part in the constant swinging back and forth of the political pendulum between the different party groupings or blocs which controlled the government.

PARTY POLITICS IN POST-WAR FRANCE

The Third Republic never had been blessed or cursed with the two-party system. Instead, a dozen political parties were to be met with, and the art of government, both pre-war and post-war, consisted in bringing together a number of these into an alliance or bloc, whereby a majority could be secured in the Chamber of Deputies. In the period between the two World Wars, three different blocs contested political power in France, the *"bloc national,"* the *"bloc des gauches,"* and the *"front populaire."*

The first of these was generally conservative, consisting of right-wing politicians, middle-of-the-roaders, and a sufficient sprinkling of near-radicals to secure a majority. The leader of this *bloc national,* in the heyday of its triumph, was Poincaré, the hard-bitten French patriot from Lorraine who had been president during the war. The *bloc des gauches,* as its name implies, was more radical than the *bloc national.* It might properly be described as a working alliance of the center with the left-center, or the more conservative radicals. The United Socialists (orthodox Marxians) were wary of this *bloc des gauches,* and its real nucleus was the Radical-Socialist party, which, as far as tradition went, was more radical than socialistic. Its leading representatives were Herriot, popular mayor of Lyon, and Briand, now an aged radical and a broad-minded statesman who was willing to let bygones be bygones and to come to an amicable understanding with the Germans. The *front populaire,* on the other hand, was a genuine combination of left-wing groups under the leadership of

a cultured and wealthy Jewish citizen of the Republic, Léon Blum.
The creation of this bloc was something new in French politics. It did
not come into existence until 1936, and it brought together for the
first time the Radical-Socialists, the United Socialists, of whom Blum
was the titular head, and the Communists, hitherto strictly shunned as
ultra-revolutionary.

The *bloc national* should be given credit for doing two things—appeasing Alsace-Lorraine and saving the franc. The Roman Catholic
control of education was not restored in the two provinces, but provision was made for Catholic instruction, and great care was taken to
smooth over the injured feelings of the Alsatians so that their demand
for autonomy lessened.

More important was the salvaging of the franc. The *bloc national*
had been responsible for the invasion of the Ruhr, and after that fiasco
it was driven from power, the *bloc des gauches* taking over the government. But the latter did nothing to save the franc, and it was not until
Poincaré returned to power in 1926 that financial recovery really set in.
Poincaré, following a conservative course, cut expenditures to a minimum, reduced salaries and pensions, heaped on new taxes, and then
stabilized the rising franc at about four cents. The instant effect of
doing so was to cut down the national debt some eighty per cent in
terms of the old franc. Bondholders and all others living on a fixed income suffered heavily, and the creditor classes in general had to bear
the burden; but they did not object too loudly, for the franc no longer
depreciated, and it was recognized that it was better to lose four-fifths
of one's capital than to lose all, as would have happened if the franc
had followed the mark. For the first time in many years it was now
possible to balance the budget and there was an actual surplus!
Promptly, Poincaré took advantage of improved credit to retire bonds
paying a high rate of interest by issuing new ones at a low rate, to
reduce the floating debt and to restore France's credit throughout the
world. Something akin to the old pre-war prosperity of the country
was noted; the iron of Lorraine, the textile mills of Alsace added to
it; and, had it not been for the world economic depression of 1929-33,
all might have been well.

That depression, however, raised havoc in France as elsewhere.
Poincaré, old and feeble, retired from politics in 1929 and with his
going, French politics became very confused. Trade fell off rapidly,
tourists to France were few, there was much unemployment, and the
franc started to depreciate again. Royalists, Fascists, and Communists
paraded in Paris; pictures of Robespierre began to appear, and there
were a number of street fights. Premier followed premier in rapid succession, those between 1932 and 1934 all members of the Radical

Socialist party, and all speedily thrown out of office by adverse majorities in the Deputies.

FRANCE IS CUT IN TWO

In 1934 a Fascist revolution threatened. Its immediate pretext were unsavory revelations linking sundry conspicuous French politicians to what had come to be called "the Stavisky scandals." Stavisky, naturalized son of a Russian dentist and socially charming, had for a long time been mysteriously protected. Moving in high circles he floated worthless securities, forged checks, gambled with marked cards, and entertained lavishly. After he stole some 200,000,000 francs from the municipal pawnshops of Bayonne, legal proceedings were taken against him. He fled to the French Alps and was found dying in a hut. Rumor had it that he was murdered by the police to prevent his talking, a rumor which met with wide credence because of his intimacy with many cabinet members, the Minister for the Colonies having recommended his worthless securities to French savings banks, the Minister of Justice having postponed his trial, and the Premier himself having served at one time as legal adviser for one of Stavisky's accomplices.

"Democracy is another name for political corruption," screamed Léon Daudet, the royalist, and the ministry, under fire from deputies of both right and left, resigned. Daladier, the new premier, was unable to maintain order. The Croix de Feu, a veteran and Fascist organization, marched on the chamber, its partisans smashing windows, overturning buses and beating up a countermob of Communists. In expectation of trouble, Daladier had stationed troops at the Palais Bourbon. Troops and police opened fire, killing seventeen and wounding several hundred. Daladier then resigned and Colonel La Roque, head of the Croix de Feu, announced, "Our first objective is accomplished. Remain on duty and await further instructions."

Paris was in an uproar. The Fascist demonstration of the extreme right was followed at once by a drive toward the left, radicals, Socialists and Communists flocking to the "Popular Front" for safety from fascism. As a well-known French woman wrote in her diary, "One feels that France is cut in two."

This was indeed the case. Ever since the great French Revolution a unique schism had divided France, the people never wholeheartedly accepting that revolution as a permanent achievement. They were loyal to France, yes; but loyalty to the government (the régime), that was another matter.

For a time it had seemed as though that schism might heal, but the economic distress of the 1930's led both the wealthy and the poor to distrust political democracy and to lose faith in a régime rooted in the bourgeois ideologies of 1789. The Third Republic had survived serious difficulties in the past, but attacks then had come mainly from per- fervid Catholics and royalists, for the most part members of the privileged classes. Now the attack was a cross-fire from two direc- tions, from property-owners and men of wealth who found their eco- nomic status lowered by drastic depreciation of the franc, and from the workers suffering grievously beneath unemployment. French pros- perity depended on luxury trade, and economic shadow over Germany, Britain, and the United States ruined that prosperity, for the export of fine wines and wedding garments became negligible. Discontent grew rife, the gulf between classes opened wider, and from 1934 to the outbreak of the second World War German Nazis and Russian Com- munists were only too successful in keeping it open.

The part played therein by the Nazis was the more obvious if not the more fundamental. Their instrument was a young school teacher from Karlsruhe, Otto Abetz, afterwards chosen by Hitler as his am- bassador to what was left of the French Republic in 1940. Abetz residing in France became very popular there, posing as a devoted and non-partisan friend of all young Frenchmen and all young Ger- mans. He got them to meet together in a camp in the Black Forest and taught them to forget their differences. He became the paid agent of Von Ribbentrop, Hitler's choice to head Nazi propaganda and diplomacy outside of Germany, a man whose past career as a sales- man of champagne had given him a special entrée among the wealthy and special skill in handling them. Von Ribbentrop kept in the back- ground and entrusted Abetz with what he called "psychological sound- ings." Abetz had plenty of money and spent freely; he entertained French war veterans sumptuously in Berlin; he flattered French lit- erary men by insisting that there was a large demand for German translations of their works, which he subsidized; he financed French lectures, and he never ceased to proclaim that the Fuehrer had abso- lutely no demands to make on France. Sensible Frenchmen, he intim- ated, should be suspicious of England and should hate the Soviets. Ger- many was their friend; political democracy was dead; Communism threatened a world upheaval which only could be averted by over- throwing corrupt and degenerate republics. The French royalists and the right in general heartily approved the two-timing Abetz, who also won many friends on the left by constantly stressing pacifism. Few suspected that he was a slick wolf in sheep's clothing.

Abetz' adroit campaign was to some degree offset by Communist borings from within; but the Communists were neither so well financed nor so clever, and for two years France drowsed toward fascism.

Four premiers in these two years added to general confusion. Of the four, three were nonentities, and the fourth, Pierre Laval, since infamous at Vichy, was so underhanded and so tricky as to arouse the suspicion of all non-Fascists. Laval, posing as a pacifist in the first World War, had unquestionably aided Germany then by defeatist propaganda. Now his continuous postponement of a mutual aid treaty with Stalin, coupled with his comradely admiration for Mussolini, contributed not a little to French ills: internal strife at home and loss of influence and prestige abroad. Meanwhile, Léon Blum, leader of the popular front and of the French Socialist party, was murderously assaulted in public by members of the Action Française, a monarchist and Fascist organization, barely escaping with his life. And as this happened the government was vainly trying to curb semi-military organizations which were springing up, armed, on every hand.

BLUM AND THE POPULAR FRONT

Finally came the national election of 1936. Thoroughly frightened by the rampant onsurge of fascism, Radicals, Socialists, and Communists buried their disagreement for once and worked together. This Popular Front was politically successful since the Socialists for the first time in French history won a plurality of seats, and, when combined with the Radicals and Communists, had a slight majority over all. It was not only slight but extraordinarily shaky, since it rested on the support of seventy-one Communists who were too suspicious to enter the cabinet, and on that of so-called radicals, wedded by tradition to property rights. Nevertheless, for the time being the advent of fascism was stayed.

Léon Blum, the new premier, was a highly cultivated and wealthy Frenchman, more at home in art and literature than in the hurly-burly of bloc politics into which he had plunged more from duty than inclination. He was too soft by nature for the crisis which confronted France.

France was economically in the doldrums, and politically torn wide open by contending factions. Blum tried to save her by inaugurating certain reforms parallel in many ways to the American "New Deal" of 1933. He started in bravely enough by establishing a forty-hour week, holidays with pay, and government ownership of munition plants. He followed the precedent of America and of England in depreciating the currency; he even tried to wrest control of the Bank of France from the exclusive group of seventy families which had long controlled it. A wave of sit-down strikes then spread through France and these Blum seemed unable to control. He was a pacifist by conviction and that made it difficult for him to deal effectively with his enemies, whether domestic or foreign. Perhaps this was his blind spot. "We do not believe," he wrote, as did our forefathers in 1792 and 1848, "that there can be any good in war, nor that war can be an instrument for liberty. . . ." The sentiment was nicely phrased but scarcely revealed a man capable of dealing with the venomous Cagoulards, a secret Fascist society engaged in hoarding machine-guns and ammunition for the coming revolution of the right.

As the Spanish Republic slowly bled to death at the hands of German and Italian Fascists, and of foreign non-interventionists, Blum hesitated, and then lost prestige both within and without France. Whether England was responsible or not for the supine foreign policy of the Popular Front (see p. 306) is difficult to fathom; but even if England had supported a firmer French attitude toward the Spanish war, it is difficult to conceive a man with Blum's pacifist psychology standing up against the fire-snorting bullies of Italy and Germany. In little over a year he resigned in disgust owing to a quarrel with the French Senate over a money bill. The Popular Front lingered on six months and then faded out. To some extent it may justly be blamed for the consequent defeat of France, soon to follow, not for its ineptitude in foreign policy alone but because it fatally slackened the production of military matériel. But on the other hand, it may have saved France from a revolution in 1936, and its leaders, though blind to fascism's menace, were less deserving of censure than those Frenchmen who preferred Hitler and his gangsters to their own radical countrymen.

France now swung to the right again; sit-down strikes and the forty-hour week led to renewed financial trouble, and the gathering of war-clouds in 1938-39 made for conservatism, the majority being of the opinion that this was no time for further social reform. When Hitler occupied Prague in March, 1939, the Chamber of Deputies did not hesitate to endow Daladier, a Radical-Socialist premier, with power to rule by decree. The city of Marseilles was deprived of its autonomy and placed directly under the national government; unemployed workers on relief could now be sent anywhere in France the government chose to send them; the forty-hour week was abandoned, and the sixty-hour week became permissible. Something approaching a government of national defense was formed under Daladier—no new election was held, but the seventy-two Communists were regarded with suspicion, as Blum and his Socialists listened to the call of patriotism and joined Daladier and the more conservative deputies of the right and center in a different kind of a united front, this time against Germany. Unfortunately the unity thus achieved was merely superficial. In 1914 the French stood united against the invaders; in 1939 they did not. During the first World War France had been bled white, losing far more lives in proportion to her population than any other country involved. Frenchmen in 1939 had no stomach for fighting; they felt they could not go through with it again. That fact alone goes far to explain the débâcle that was to come in 1940. But it is not the only reason. Abetz had done his work far too well. Large numbers of Frenchmen had lost all faith in Liberty, Equality, and Fraternity, and tended to regard fascism, if not as desirable, then at least as more desirable, more unifying than communism. As for the Communists, they followed the party line laid down in Moscow. Since Russia was not in the war they considered themselves out of it. France was half conquered before a shot was fired.

BRITAIN

The end of the war found Britain unprepared for peace. A million soldiers came back home to wives and sweethearts, but in all too many cases there were neither homes in which to live nor jobs to work at. No new houses had been built for years and old jobs had been discontinued or were held by women. Many discharged soldiers were shell-shocked or otherwise impaired, unfit for jobs even if these had been available. To the conservatively minded all Britain seemed shell-shocked. The psychological rebound from the hardship of war, both civilian and military, led to a mania for dancing, jazz music, and American cocktails. The motor-scooter, pogo-stick and mah-jong, a complicated Chinese game, became the craze one after another. Journalism went "yellow" and university undergraduates went Bohemian; young women took to lip-sticks, stimulants, and to companionate marriage; the divorce rate doubled; and learned exponents of Freudian philosophy put all the blame for human unhappiness on "inhibitions."

The economic situation was both ominous and dolorous. England's foreign trade had fallen badly during the war and there seemed little likelihood of its recovery, not as long as Germany and Russia, two of her best customers, were too poor to buy. The British coal trade, overexpanded by the war, now came in competition with cheap German coal, turned over to the French and Italians as part payment on reparations. British shipping was surfeited with extra cargo space provided by the surrendered merchant ships of Germany just at a time when exports were falling off. British shipyards consequently became as idle as British coal mines. For a time it looked as though Britain would have to fight a war within after the war without, this time against unemployment. Her finances were in better shape than were those of her sister democracy across the Channel; but whereas

France at a pinch could live largely on her agriculture, to Britain foreign trade was a necessity of life.

This explains why the British speedily sought to change those economic clauses of the peace treaty which led to Germany's default on reparation payments and to the French occupation of the Ruhr. Lloyd George, who had been more responsible than any other man for imposing the economic penalties of the peace, promptly tried to reverse himself, and at an interlational conference at Genoa (see p. 122) had hoped that his magnetic eloquence might win the French over to his point of view. Lloyd George failed. His successor in office, Bonar Law, tried to prevent the French from entering the Ruhr. He failed. Bonar Law even offered to remit the French debt to England if the French would cut down correspondingly on Germany's debt to France. Again he failed.

The British were in favor of letting bygones be bygones and of starting up business again. They suggested to the United States that if the latter would cancel the British debt to America of some $4,000,000,000, the British would cancel continental debts due them far greater in amount. But the Americans had the idea that the British could and would pay, and so were adamant ("They hired the money, didn't they?"—Coolidge.) Thereupon the British signed a debt agreement with the Americans whereby they agreed to pay the debt in full over a period of sixty-two years but with reduced interest.

Lloyd George, meanwhile, lost his wartime popularity; he had promised to make England a land fit for heroes, and four years after the war that promise remained unfulfilled; with his usual buoyancy he had tackled the Irish problem, only to be rebuffed by Sinn Fein (see p. 217); the French refused to take him seriously in the matter of reparations; the Turks made mincemeat of his Near Eastern policy (see p. 210); and the enemies within his own Liberal party, numerous and influential, awaited impatiently his downfall. He was prime minister of a national coalition the mainstay of which was the Tory party which detested him. His prestige once gone, the Tories inevitably would drive him out. They did so in 1923 and took over the government on a one-party basis, first under Bonar Law, the Canadian-born British statesman who died within the year, and then under Stanley Baldwin.

First Ministries of Baldwin and MacDonald

The honor of serving first as His Majesty's peacetime prime minister belonged to Baldwin. Behind him was a large stolid, conservative majority which melted away in less than a year. Economic maladjustment, sometimes acute distress, blighted Britain during the earlier years between the two World Wars, and not until the middle 'thirties did the country begin to emerge from the shadows. Baldwin determined to achieve prosperity at once by a remedy more or less successfully applied some years later, namely, a protective tariff, rather on the American model. He advocated laws which would keep food and raw materials on the free list but protect manufacturing. His argument was intelligent, for why should England try to continue on a free trade basis when all the world was defending itself by tariff walls? But he was ahead of his time; England had become great, it was argued, in the past because of free trade, therefore she must continue on the old path!

In the ensuing election Baldwin won a plurality of seats but was without a majority. To the surprise of almost everyone the historic Liberal party, torn between the followers of Lloyd George and those of H. H. Asquith, came out third in the race, second place falling to MacDonald and his Laborites.

The Labor party in theory was socialistic. During the election it had advocated the nationalization of railways and mines, and a capital levy on large fortunes. To put it in control of Britain's fortunes seemed a most dangerous procedure. Yet that is what the British Liberals did. The alternative was to support Baldwin, and they considered Mac-Donald the lesser of two evils; after all, they would hold the whiphand over the Socialists and forestall any danger by voting with the Conservatives! As a matter of fact, there was no trouble. The Labor party had long been committed to the truly British policy of "gradualness." The idea of revolution was repudiated and the Laborites regarded Moscow with almost as much abhorrence as did the Tories themselves.

Once in office Labor took no steps toward a capital levy; instead it contented itself with various odds and ends of amelioration, the building of inexpensive homes on a moderate scale by government subsidies, the removal of taxes on cheap movie tickets and their reduction on sugar and chocolate. The Cabinet seemed quite bent on proving itself British first and Socialist second. MacDonald was an effective worker for international peace; he aided the inauguration of the Dawes' plans (see p. 169); he tried to gain the good will of the Japanese by suspending work on the great Singapore naval depot; and he even made certain friendly gestures toward Soviet Russia.

The latter brought about his downfall. Lloyd George somewhat earlier had renewed commercial relations with Russia and these Mac-Donald sought to implement by an Anglo-Russian treaty, a commercial, not a military or political understanding. But Russia to good Britons was still a most dangerous country, and when British Communists, supposedly under orders from the Third International in

Moscow, tried to sow discontent among British workers the British Liberals joined with the Tories and voted MacDonald out. A dramatic election followed. MacDonald might have been returned to triumph had it not been for a mysterious letter (presumably forged) purporting to have been written by Zinoviev, head of the Third International, urging the revolt of British workers. Middle-class Britain saw red in reverse and middle-class Britain had belonged for the most part to the Liberal party. In fear and anger lest MacDonald win, it surged to the polls and gave Baldwin a majority over all. The Labor party lost only a few seats; but the Liberal party was reduced to a mere thirty-six and no longer held even the balance of power. From this date on it was hardly more than a cypher in British politics.

The Second Baldwin Ministry

Baldwin returned to power in 1924 to be confronted by one of the most serious crises in British history. The British coal miner during the World War had won a decent working day of seven hours and had been granted minimum wages. The wage was not high but it soon proved impossible to pay it and at the same time operate the mines at a profit. The coal trade was in the doldrums everywhere in the world in the 1920's, owing to the increased use of gasoline, oil, and hydro-electric power, and the coal trade of Britain was in even a more precarious plight than elsewhere, owing to the great depth of the mines, which made their operation expensive, and to substantial royalties paid to ground landlords like the Duke of Northumberland, who held title and merely rented coal lands to operating companies and assuming no responsibility for management.

What should be done? The miners, highly organized, adopted a slogan and clung to it desperately: "Not an hour on the day, not a penny off the pay." The operators said there was nothing to do but close the mines. The government, in desperation, subsidized miners' wages and this kept the mines in operation. They could not do this indefinitely at the expense of the nation and therefore a commission was appointed to report in 1926 that the only salvation for the coal mining industry lay in closing certain uneconomic mines and in increasing the hours of labor in others.

Baldwin supported his commission, withdrew the subsidy, and the Trade Union Congress voted a general strike throughout Britain, all good union men, whatever their jobs, to lay down tools, certain exceptions being made for lighting, sanitary, and health services.

This was bringing revolutionary pressure to bear on Parliament, since if the Trade Union Congress could compel government to bow to its will in this matter it could do so in others and thus would become the real source of authority in the state.

The strike was badly managed. MacDonald and other leaders of the Labor party supported the miners in theory but had no stomach for a real fight on this issue; nor for that matter did the Trade Union Congress. Not so the British middle class. A vast number of amateur middle-class volunteers hastened to run the railways, to unload cargoes, to deliver food. There was little violence and the Trade Union Congress after only a few days rescinded the general strike orders. The miners, considering themselves betrayed, fought on for several months but ultimately succumbed. Parliament overwhelmingly supported Baldwin, and in 1927 passed an act curbing trade-union activities and making all general strikes illegal.

Aside from this, Baldwin resisted successfully the drive within his own party for a more authoritarian government. If he would not yield to the left, he would not give way to the right, which saw its opportunity at this time to strengthen the powers of the House of Lords. The Prime Minister, indeed, was not ill disposed toward labor; he brought about pensions for widows and he did lower the price of tea. Hopefully, he looked forward to an increase in international trade, of which there was some indication. "Safety First" was his motto; unemployment is bad, but not so bad as it was; all we need is to wait for clearer skies! This philosophy did not appeal to the impoverished electorate, and in 1929 it voted Baldwin out and MacDonald in once more.

The National Government

Again MacDonald had a plurality in the Commons, but again his total Labor strength was less than that of the Conservatives and Liberals combined. In foreign affairs this ministry was a creditable one, particularly in regard to disarmament, but at home his best efforts proved unavailing. His political dependence on the ever-diminishing Liberals continued to irk him, and furthermore there was revolt within his own party. The "wild men of the Clyde," as the leftist Laborites were called, demanded a capital levy and other impossible laws, and party discipline disintegrated. Before, however, an open rupture broke out, the coming of the international trade depression of 1930-33 brought about a financial crisis in England such as that country had not experienced since the black year of 1797, when she faced Revolutionary France without allies and the Bank of England suspended specie payment.

The storm broke in 1931. Unless drastic reductions were made in relief costs, the bankers held, it would be impossible to make the necessary loans to save the pound sterling and the Bank of England. MacDonald reluctantly consented to the economies demanded, but he found it impossible to carry his party with him. Thereupon he resigned and formed a "National Government" supported by Conservatives, Liberals, and those Laborites who stayed loyal to him. Instantly, a ten per cent cut was made in all forms of individual remuneration, from the unemployed on the dole to police, admirals, generals, and cabinet ministers. The government went off the gold standard, thus depreciating the pound; the budget was balanced, the necessary loans made, and financial England weathered the worst storm encountered in over a century.

The price was heavy. MacDonald was still prime minister, at the head of a coalition. But his own Labor party, which had been steadily growing in numbers and experience ever since its creation, received as deadly a blow as the Liberal party in 1886, and in the Parliamentary election of 1931 it sank to 52 members. The Conservatives rose to 470, a signal triumph; and the Liberals, divided into warring factions (one supporting the National Government, the other opposing it), netted 70 seats.

From 1931 to 1935 MacDonald headed this National Government. It was such in name only, since the Tories had such a large majority over all, MacDonald having behind him only a small rump of his old Labor party. The Tories now pressed for protective tariffs and this time they got them. A ten per cent levy was made on imports and some success attended the government's efforts to make reciprocal trade agreements with the Dominions. Thus unmourned and almost overnight died the free-trade dream of Cobden and of Bright. And it was not only free trade that perished. The National Government repudiated in fact, if not in theory, many other chosen tenets of laissez-faire; it compelled agreements to fix prices in many industries; it granted financial aid to agriculture; it guaranteed loans to railways and built motor highways; and it heavily subsidized the building of new homes for the poor.

During this third ministry of the Scottish socialist (really but a continuation of his second), the Liberal party disintegrated rapidly. There were Liberals who supported both the National Government and the tariff; other Liberals supported the government except on the tariff issue; other Liberals kept warm the dying embers of an independent Liberal party; and a tiny group of still other Liberals held aloof under the now scarred banner of that drummer boy of the World War, David Lloyd George. The Labor party was also torn asunder; the rank and file, bitter foes of MacDonald, were bereft now, not only of his leadership, but of any leadership worth the name. MacDonald himself was saddened by the hatred of the many common people who once had trusted him and who now assailed him as a traitor to labor. A sick and disillusioned man, he gladly surrendered the reins of office in 1935 to his erstwhile political enemy, Mr. Baldwin.

The latter still kept up the pretense of a National Government. He took advantage of a critical turn in international relations (see p. 304) to hold a new parliamentary election, and the country again underwrote the Conservative control of Britain, although with a reduced majority. This third ministry of Baldwin, like the third one of MacDonald, was of the stop-gap variety. Baldwin, like his predecessor, was old, tired, discouraged. He saw the country through a temporary flurry created in 1936 by the death of George V and the unwillingness of Edward VIII to be crowned without his right to marry an American divorcée being recognized. With the coronation of Edward's younger brother as George VI in 1937, Baldwin resigned.

He was succeeded by Neville Chamberlain, second son of Joseph Chamberlain. The new prime minister was considered not as brilliant as his older half-brother Austen, but as one nevertheless well suited to carry on the middle-of-the-road policy of the amiable Baldwin. The Chamberlain ministry was given over largely to foreign affairs, and we shall note later in another chapter how the constant surrender of the Prime Minister to the incessant clamors of Mussolini and Hitler tended to make him unpopular, not only with the Labor opposition but with many of the abler Conservatives.

Economic Recovery

Between 1932 and the outbreak of war in 1939 there was a slow but steady economic recovery in Britain. The proud commercial hegemony of the world which was Britain's in 1914 did not come back; certain of her former leading industries, such as coal mining, shipbuilding and cotton manufacturing, remained in the doldrums; and the bourgeoisie had more cause for rejoicing than the laboring poor; but the country as a whole did become more prosperous than at the height of the depression; unemployment was reduced and the budget was balanced.

The "New Deal" in America somewhat erroneously has been held to have copied British precedents. It did so in part; both countries went off the gold standard and depreciated their currencies; both countries developed social security programs, the British implementing what they had inaugurated before the first World War, the Americans copying British precedents; and both countries adopted complicated controls over industry. But here the general parallel comes to an end. In America the major answer to the economic black-out in the early 'thirties was found in public works. In Britain, as to some extent in the United States, it took the form of financial coöperation with business, provided management agreed to accept certain directions and controls.

Thus in Britain in 1932 a "Wheat Act" set standard prices for wheat and when the market price fell below that set, a subsidy was paid the wheat grower. In 1933 a "Potato Marketing Scheme" was devised whereby the acreage devoted to potatoes was first determined and then machines were provided for grading potatoes according to size, the sale of small potatoes being forbidden or permitted in accordance with the market prices as fixed. The national government established a "Milk Marketing Board" and all Britons who sold milk had to contribute to regional pools with provision made for a minimum price. Subsidies were granted for the beet sugar industry, for cattle raising; and by an intricate system of quotas what actually amounted to a protective tariff on agricultural products was enforced under another name.

Planned economy in manufacturing received a great impetus. Financial assistance was given manufacturers who would rationalize their plants, that is, buy up and destroy obsolete machinery, and consolidate, modernize their methods, reducing costs and also output. This method was adopted in certain sick industries such as textiles, coal, and shipbuilding. Thousands of old spindles were scrapped in cotton manufacturing; by a "Coal Mine Act" of 1938 the amalgamation of coal companies was enforced; in shipbuilding a subsidy was granted for new construction "if for each ton of new shipping two tons of old shipping were destroyed." And in addition the combination of the White Star Line with the Cunard Company was officially blessed with a subsidy granted in 1934 for the construction of the two gigantic liners, *Queen Mary* and *Queen Elizabeth*.

To encourage new industries a great deal of emphasis was placed upon electric power. A Central Electricity Board known as "The National Grid" was set up which subsidized one hundred and thirty-five generating stations, and as a result power became cheaper and very many new industries were developed, particularly in the neighborhood of London.

The problem of housing was also stressed. Subsidies paid builders and home owners for new houses began as early as 1923, and the duty of the government decently to house those on the lower income level has been constantly emphasized since that date. Altogether between the two World Wars over one and a quarter million new homes were constructed in Britain by governmental aid.

It cannot be said that the problem of poverty was solved; in fact, in certain areas, particularly in South Wales, and in sections of Northern England, it continued to be very acute. In 1933 the national government flatly refused to spend money on any larger scale in public works; that method of relieving poverty it considered extravagant and wasteful. In 1934 it did appropriate some £2,000,000 for the "depressed areas," a beggarly sum in view of the distress there. But it followed this in 1935 by a so-called "Means Test," whereby the dole given to unemployed men and women for their support and that of their families was reduced to the lowest possible minimum consistent with bare existence, a direct blow at the physical well-being of the nation.

"It was all very puzzling," wrote the English novelist Priestley in his *English Journey,* published in 1934.

Was Jarrow still in England or not? Had we exiled Lancashire and the North-east coast? Were we no longer on speaking terms with cotton weavers and miners and platers and riveters? Why had nothing been done about these decaying towns and their workless people? Was everybody waiting for a miracle to happen? I knew that doles had been given out, Means Tests applied, training places opened, socks and shirts and old books distributed by the Personal Service League and the like; but I was not thinking of feeble gestures of that kind, of the sort of charity you might extend to a drunken old ruffian begging at the back door. I meant something constructive and creative. If Germans had been threatening these towns instead of Want, Disease, Hopelessness, Misery, something would have been done quickly enough.[1]

What was the answer? The Labor party, of course, thought it knew. It wanted nationalization of railways, mines, and banking. But the Labor party was powerless, partly because a three-cornered fight in labor circles almost paralyzed that political party. The machinery of the Labor party was in the hands of conservative trade unionists who would have nothing to do with the Independent Labor party, strong in ability but weak in numbers. And neither the I.L.P. (Independent Labor Party) nor the official Labor party would have anything to do with the British Communists. In vain did Sir Stafford Cripps with his Socialist League endeavor to bring these warring elements together. Cripps, a brilliant and wealthy lawyer, was regarded with suspicion by orthodox labor and was expelled from the party. British workmen would not work together in politics. And even if they had been willing to do so, they might not have been able to carry the Parliamentary election of 1935, for the economic skies were brightening somewhat by that date and to the British poor, desiring employment above all else, half a loaf was an encouraging sign.

---

[1] J. B. Priestley, *English Journey* (Harper and Brothers), p. 327. Reprinted by permission of the publishers.

PACIFISM VS. PREPAREDNESS

More serious in the long run for Britain was the failure of her statesmen and of her people to realize the peril which confronted her abroad. The former, perhaps, may have been blamed too much for their folly in appeasing the Axis, since for the most part they did but follow the public opinion they should have led. The average Briton was most pacifically inclined; he was fed up with war and war talk; he placed a most curious and blind trust in the League of Nations even after the impotencies of that organization were manifest to all the world; and while he was opposed to Nazi terrorism he refused to consider seriously the Nazi threat to European peace. In all this the worker believed as many of his betters did.

Pacifistic propaganda made headway everywhere. The British masses were only mildly interested in the death struggle of the Spanish Republic; only a tiny minority was willing to risk war on its behalf. The appeasement of Hitler and Mussolini which is dealt with elsewhere in this book was not cheered, but the government which indulged in it was never in danger of an adverse majority in the House. One of the most popular books of the decade was *Cry Havoc,* published in 1933. It was made compulsory reading in hundreds of schools, and overseas the Department of Education in Toronto, Canada, alone bought 7,000 copies. Pacifists in the pulpit and in the press pledged themselves to participate in no more wars, and over one thousand enthusiastic British men and women agreed to march unarmed between the ranks of future opposing armies, there to die for peace. Even at Oxford the undergraduates voted that never again would they fight for king and country.

There were, of course, countercurrents, one stirred up primarily by Winston Churchill over air power, the other by British sea dogs concerning the American navy and Singapore. But these countercurrents carried little weight against the tide of "peace in our time."

THE SINGAPORE NAVAL BASE

The friction between British and American admirals in regard to the size and number of cruisers made good newspaper copy, but in reality it was of no great import. Far more significant was the long drawn-out debate over the creation of a great naval base at Singapore. The Washington Conference of 1922 (see p. 210) focussed attention on the Far East; it also brought an end to the Anglo-Japanese Alliance and thereby isolated the Anzac Dominions. Whereupon the British admiralty saw its chance to realize Sir Stamford Raffles' dream of the early nineteenth century—Singapore not only an entrepôt of Asiatic trade but also a naval bastion of empire. The Tory government of Baldwin backed the admiralty and in 1923 preliminary surveys were made.

Since £20,000,000 was about to be spent, an uproar arose in Labor and Liberal circles, where it was pointed out that the money might better be used to clear slums and to educate the young. Furthermore, they said, the fortification of Singapore although not technically a violation of the Washington treaty did violate its spirit and indicated a lack of faith in the League of Nations.

At this juncture MacDonald became prime minister and immediately work on the new base was suspended. And now a new uproar arose, this time in Conservative circles and in the Anzac Dominions, who felt that they were left undefended in case of future trouble with Japan.

MacDonald, as we have seen, was shortly shooed out of office and Baldwin promptly renewed the Singapore project. One main feature of it, the towing of a huge 50,000-ton drydock all the way from Britain to Singapore, was completed in 1928, much to the satisfaction of imperially minded Britons everywhere, and much to the dissatisfaction of Japanese public opinion, highly inflamed by the jingo press of Nippon.

The British Labor Party upon its return to office in 1929 was not pleased with the fortification of Singapore, but since so much money had already been spent on the enterprise they did not propose its abandonment. Work, however, on the base was retarded, so much so that the completion of what was popularly hailed as an impregnable Gibraltar of the Pacific was not attained until 1938. Nor was it then fortified against attack by land.

CHURCHILL SOUNDS THE ALARM

Far more significant than Singapore were the Cassandra prophecies of Winston Churchill, who, like his father before him, ever was a thorn in the side of Tory complacency. Outspoken and bulldoggish, the future war premier had no confidence whatever in disarmament proposals adumbrated in many conferences in the 'twenties and 'thirties. What dominated his imagination was the potential strength of the Third Reich and the rapid growth of the Nazi Party. He did *not* believe that *all* the Nazis wanted was equality of status, and he warned the Commons as early as 1932 that "all these bands of sturdy Teutonic youth, marching through the streets and roads of Germany, with the light of desire in their eyes to suffer for their Fatherland, are not looking for status. They are looking for weapons, and when they have weapons, believe me, they will then ask for the return of lost territories and lost colonies."

This speech was delivered in November, 1932, less than three months before Hitler was appointed Chancellor by Hindenburg. But Churchill was regarded as a firebrand who only caused trouble and MacDonald wished to make a pacifistic gesture at the coming Disarmament Conference at Geneva. Therefore, instead of increasing the appropriation for the Royal Air Force (R.A.F.) he diminished it.

Look out, cried Churchill, we are only fifth in potential air power (France, Italy, Japan and the United States all were rated above Britain); Germany is our nearest neighbor and Germany is rearming. But Churchill, according to Sir Herbert Samuel, Liberal leader in the Commons, used "the language of a Malay running amok," and few heeded his warning.

The skies now darkened rapidly; Germany left the League; Germany announced conscription; Germany rearmed fast. As she did so, Churchill did his best to arouse his lethargic countrymen. "It would be folly," he said in May, 1935, "for us to act as if we were swimming in a halcyon sea, as if nothing but balmy breezes and calm weather were to be expected." The British were increasing their air force at last, but the Nazis were increasing theirs at a faster tempo. Already they had surpassed Britain.

Came 1936, the abandonment of Haille Selassie in Ethiopia, the abandonment of sanctions, and Britain continued to fall farther behind. Midsummer holidays were due, but to Churchill rest and peace were illusions. "Do not forget," said he, "that all the time those remorseless hammers of which General Goering spoke are descending night and day in Germany, and that the most warlike ... people in Europe are becoming welded into a tremendous fighting machine. . . ."

"The army," he said in 1936, "lacks every weapon which is required for the latest form of modern war. Where are anti-tank guns, where are the short distance wireless sets, where are the field anti-aircraft guns. . . . .? Nothing has been done in the years the locust hath eaten, to equip the tank corps with new machines." In quality, British tanks were inferior to those of Germany, Russia, Italy, and the United States. The R.A.F., Churchill estimated, had 960 first-class planes, the Germans 1,500. "Owing to our past neglect," he affirmed, "in the face of the plainest warnings, we have now entered upon a period of danger greater than has befallen Britain since the U-boat campaign was crushed."

Baldwin's Parliamentary apology for this state of affairs aroused some criticism but few listened to Churchill. Not even in the year of Munich (1938) would they listen to him. "For five years," he said,

I have talked to the House on these matters—not with very great success. I have watched this famous island descending incontinently, fecklessly, the stairway which leads to a dark gulf. It is a fine broad stairway at the beginning, but after a bit the carpet ends. A little farther on there are only flagstones, and a little farther on still these break beneath your feet. Look back over the last five years. It is true that great mistakes were made in the years immediately after the War. But at Locarno we laid the foundation from which a great forward movement could have been made. Look back upon the last five years—since, that is to say, Germany began to rearm in earnest and openly to seek revenge. If we study the history of Rome and Carthage, we can understand what happened and why. It is not difficult to form an intelligent view about the three Punic Wars; but if mortal catastrophe should overtake the British Nation and the British Empire, historians a thousand years hence will still be baffled by the mystery of our affairs. They will never understand how it was that a victorious nation, with everything in hand, suffered themselves to be brought low, and to cast away all that they had gained by measureless sacrifice and absolute victory —gone with the wind!

Now the victors are the vanquished, and those who threw down their arms in the field and sued for an armistice are striding on to world mastery.

CHAPTER VIII

THE BRITISH COMMONWEALTH
AND EMPIRE

THE GREATER Britain overseas is neither commonwealth nor empire; it is both. The four Dominions, Canada, Australia, New Zealand, and the Union of South Africa, comprise the commonwealth; all other lands over which his Majesty's government holds sway, are the empire.

THE DOMINIONS

The first World War wrought great changes in the constitutional status of the Dominions. Not only had they raised armies and fought battles; they had been consulted openly, confidently, by Great Britain. Lloyd George's Imperial War Cabinet had been a true Commonwealth Cabinet, the premiers of the Dominions sharing in decisions of moment to the Empire, their influence and position well above that of many members of the ministry who debated on the floor of the House. The peace conference brought the premiers still greater prominence. The Dominions had separate representation, five British premiers, representing five different electorates, participating in the settlement of the war. Even if the Dominion premiers were subordinate in fact as well as in theory to their colleagues from England, their influence was felt in many ways. On the commission which dealt with Greece was Canada's representative; on that which decided Poland's boundary was Smuts of South Africa. Hughes, the Australian, was consulted about Czechoslovakia and reparations. Furthermore, in the projected League of Nations seats were duly provided for each Dominion; and at the grand conclusion of the Congress of the Nations in the Hall of Mirrors, their premiers signed the peace treaty separately on behalf of their own nations.

The Versailles treaty was ratified by all four Dominions, but not without considerable grumbling in three. In Australia Mr. Hughes announced that his government had not been sufficiently consulted; the Americans had interfered, and German New Guinea, which otherwise would have been annexed by Australia, was now only a mandate. Besides, as a result of the treaty the Japanese were now two thousand miles nearer Australia. In Canada there was criticism of Article X of the League of Nations covenant guaranteeing each signatory its territorial integrity.

Opposition in South Africa was stronger. There were three major political groupings: the South African Party, a union of British immigrants and Dutch farmers (Boers), pledged to reduce friction between the two nationalities; the Nationalist Party, a purely Boer organization bitter against British annexation of the two Dutch republics; and the Unionist Party, purely British in membership and spirit, intent upon opposing Boer or Afrikander nationalism, as it came to be called. The Nationalists desired to repudiate the treaty, since its authors had ignored their claims. At the conclusion of the War they had betaken themselves to Paris to urge before the peace conference the cause of the Boers. This they were not permitted to do, although an audience was granted them by Lloyd George. It was easy for him to argue that, since the Nationalists were in a minority in the Union, they could not well contend that they were deprived of self-determination. He had been their friend during the South African War; but the Union constitution of 1909 had met with their approval; they could not now reverse their position. The Nationalists returned home, angry. They found nothing to praise in the work of the peace conference. "The League of Nations," said one of them in the Union legislature, "was built on a foundation of pillage and hypocrisy." "The treaty," exclaimed another, "breathes the spirit of domination, jealousy and revenge." But they were helpless to prevent its ratification. The South African Party had a plurality of votes in Parliament; when assisted by the Unionists, pro-British to a man, a safe majority was assured. The S.A.P., as it was called, found a clever leader in General Smuts. The latter had no difficulty in maintaining his liaison with the Unionists, and the treaty therefore received the imprimatur of the Union government.

THE DOMINIONS AND BRITISH FOREIGN POLICY

For decades before the War the Dominions had been self-governing except as to foreign policy, which by general consent, although not by statute, had been left to the mother country. In 1919 it became a question whether they were even thus bound. The covenant of the League gave them seats in the Assembly; were their votes there to be considered British votes as such or were the Dominions virtually independent nations, free to determine their own foreign policy? Just what was their status? The situation was anomalous, even to British statesmen not customarily troubled by want of logic in constitutional practice.

Before the war many Britons, both at home and abroad, had argued in favor of imperial federation, closer unity; but after the war there were fewer to favor it. Hughes of Australia was violently opposed. "I think," he said, "the surest way of destroying this mighty empire is to tamper with its constitution. Complete autonomy of the parts is the foundation upon which it rests." In Canada, as though it was the most casual thing in the world, the government announced that a Dominion embassy would be established at Washington. As for South Africa, General Smuts announced in Parliament that the peace conference had been a "formal recognition of the new position of the Dominions, and that in foreign relations they were to take part and speak for themselves, and that they no longer would be bound by the voice and signature of the British Parliament."

General Smuts' political position was delicate. The South African Party which he headed was composed principally of Boers, and a continuous flow of deserters constantly made its way toward Hertzog and the Nationalist tent. The very brilliance of Smuts' speeches and his unrivalled mental acumen brought him under suspicion. This philosopher-statesman, so idealized in Britain, was he true to the Afrikander? The Nationalists intimated that he was not, and as a result turned the election of 1920 against him.

The political divisions in the Assembly, after the election, show some striking changes:

	Number of seats in 1920	After 1920
South African Party	53	41
(mainly Afrikander, but friendly toward the Commonwealth)		
Unionists	38	25
(solidly British)		
Nationalists	27	44
(Boer irreconcilables)		
Labor	6	21
(Socialistic and, for the most part, indifferent toward the Commonwealth)		
Independents	6	3

For the first time in the history of the Union the extreme party of independence had a plurality of votes in the Assembly; and in order to carry on the King's government through the agency of the South African Party, Smuts had to form some kind of coalition. To do this he turned first to the Nationalists, attempting to bring the two Boer factions together. The Nationalists, however, insisted on a republic; the S.A.P. stood staunchly for Dominion nationality within the Empire. On this point there could be no compromise. The general turned now to the Unionists. The latter were willing to do anything to defeat Hertzog, even to the extent of committing political suicide. This, in effect, they did since they agreed to destroy their own political organization and to merge themselves completely in the South African Party. The political atmosphere being thus cleared, Smuts struck home and appealed to the electorate, this time winning the election for the S.A.P.

DOMINION REPRESENTATION

In 1921 an imperial conference between the Dominion premiers and the British ministry convened in London. Winston Churchill, the ubiquitous, was colonial secretary then and the conference was ambitiously baptized by him, "Imperial Cabinet." The delegates from overseas, however, did not take to this innovation. Cabinet was synonymous with authority, and they feared centralized authority in London; that word and the word *imperial* was dropped, this meeting of British statesmen preferring the title of "Conference of the Prime Ministers of the Empire."

The program was extensive but the results meagre. The conference supposedly discussed the Pacific problem of the Anglo-Japanese treaty of 1902 and its possible renewal, the division of reparation receipts from Germany, the possibility of placating Indian opinion by alleviating the conditions under which Indians lived in the Dominions, and the possibilities of empire-settlement and migration. But the gravest question of all, that of Dominion partnership in British foreign policy, was left untouched.

Yet the problem of Dominion representation at the forthcoming disarmament conference at Washington showed the need for some common understanding in regard to that partnership. No individual invitation to attend had been given to the Dominions, since the American government thought it discourteous to the British government to issue one; whereupon the Dominions took offense. General Smuts intimated that if not invited in their own right they should ignore the proceedings; Hughes spoke of the American invitation to Great Britain alone as "slamming the door." Here was protocol with a vengeance, and Dominion sensitivity was only partially allayed by drafting an Australian, a New Zealander, and a Canadian on the British Empire delegation, Mr. Balfour signing the Washington treaty twice, once for the Empire and once for South Africa.

The ostensible object of the Washington Conference was the cutting down of naval expenditure; but this could only be obtained by abrogating or fundamentally altering the Anglo-Japanese Alliance. The treaty which inaugurated this pact, as renewed in 1905, guaranteed military aid in case "either contracting power should be involved in war in defense of its territorial rights or interests." That treaty threatened to involve Britain in war with America should the latter country come to blows with Japan. To make this impossible Britain and America had entered into special treaty obligations which provided for mutual arbitration of all difficulties. But the Senate of the United States amended this treaty in certain vital particulars and President Taft refused to accept the amendment. Thereupon the United States and Britain agreed, in 1914, to a treaty which provided for a peace commission to investigate all causes of difference between the two countries. This was not a treaty of arbitration, technically speaking; but Downing Street gave notice to Tokyo, although not to Washington, that it should so consider it, and would regard it as coming under the special clause in the second renewal of the Anglo-Japanese treaty in 1911 which excluded from the pact any country with which either signatory had a treaty of arbitration.

The Americans did not hear of this qualification until 1921, and in the meantime the race for naval supremacy in Pacific waters continued apace. British statesmen saw nightmares; they did not want to break with Japan; they did not want to antagonize America; and they must not antagonize their own Dominions. The Japanese, on the other hand, disliked the qualifications read into the treaty by the British in regard to America; the United States was ill disposed toward any Anglo-Japanese alliance; and the British Dominions, like the mother country, desired to avoid friction with America. The result was highly satisfactory to the Dominions, even if not to other participants; they at least obtained what they wanted, the abrogation of the Anglo-Japanese treaty and recognition for themselves as co-partners in the British Commonwealth.

The year of the Washington Conference was also the year of the Chanak incident, which demonstrated an unsatisfactory state of affairs as far as the relations of the Dominions to British foreign policy went. Mustapha Kemal, at the head of the Turkish Nationalists, having driven the Greeks into the sea, turned his forces against Constantinople. The porcelain treaty of Sèvres was threatened with destruction; and of the European signatories Great Britain alone gave proof of a willingness to defend it. Under Lloyd George's direction a small British force was landed at Chanak, on the Asiatic side of the Dardanelles, and an ultimatum delivered to Mustapha Kemal. The British pickets again faced those of Turkey as in 1915; war seemed imminent and the Prime Minister of England appealed by cable to the Dominions for support.

Except for New Zealand they were not as ready to give it as in 1914. The Prime Minister of the smallest Dominion cabled instantly: "Government of New Zealand desires to associate themselves with action being taken and will send contingent." Australia was less eager to offer aid. Hughes' cabinet was prepared "to associate itself with the British government," and was ready, "if circumstances required," to send an Australian contingent. Canada was even more reluctant, the Prime Minister stating, "It is for Parliament (the Canadian Parliament) to decide whether we should participate in wars in different parts of the world." South Africa aligned herself with Canada. "When the crisis in the Near East was raised," said General Smuts, "and this Government was addressed by the British government on the question of sending some contingents to take part in the operations that might take place in the Near East the Government replied that in a matter ... of such far-reaching issues they would not commit themselves unless they consulted Parliament."

The reaction of the Dominions to the Chanak affair was disconcerting; supposing a new and more serious crisis should arise, then what? The Dominions and India had participated in the treaty of Sèvres, which broke up the old Turkey; that of Lausanne, which patched certain portions of it together again, had been negotiated and signed solely by Great Britain. Did or did not Lord Curzon's signature involve the Dominions, logically, legally, or morally, in the support of it?

The answer of the Canadian Prime Minister was an emphatic, "No!" "We take the position," he said, "that not having been invited to the Lausanne Conference, not having been represented there, not having, for the reasons which I have mentioned, signed the treaty, the treaty does not impose obligations on Canada, and those parts of the Empire on which it does impose obligations are the only parts that should be expected to sign and ratify."

Shortly after, came Locarno (see p. 284) and when Britain signed that pact she did so with the express provision that the treaty did not apply to India or to the Dominions, unless they chose to sign. From now on it was evident that a distinction must be made in the future between the foreign policy of Britain and that of the Dominions. To quote article nine of the pact: "... the present treaty shall impose no obligation upon any of the British Dominions or upon India, until the Government of such Dominion or of India signifies its acceptance thereof."

This was a distinct constitutional departure. At Paris and at Washington the Dominions and Great Britain had stood together. At Lausanne the Dominions were not represented and Canada had therefore insisted that she was under no obligation to enforce that treaty. At

Locarno the objections of Canada were formally recognized as valid, and upon Great Britain and Northern Ireland alone fell the onus of supporting the treaty in the name of the Empire.

In accordance with international law, when Britain was at war so also were the Dominions. But in accordance with this treaty it was evident that they might claim not to be. Suppose any Dominion should issue a declaration of neutrality in a war in which Britain was engaged in defense of this treaty of Locarno. What then would be the status of enemy aliens in Bombay, what that of a British warship at Auckland? On the other hand, why should India and the Dominions pledge themselves to Locarno and an agreement purely European in its guarantees? Were the men of West Australia concerned with the delimitation of the Rhine frontier; could one ask them to fight for it?

Immediately there was talk of yet another conference. But could it accomplish anything? Too often, it was felt, had the Dominion premiers been summoned from their own preserves for a friendly chat with the Prime Minister of Britain. Why bring men from half way round the earth for an exchange of social amenities? All vestiges of British control in Commonwealth and Empire foreign policy had now disappeared. Such traces of subordination to Great Britain as might still be discovered were purely incidental in character, the British flag, the traditional right of veto of the Crown (as dead in the Dominions as in Britain), and the appeal to the Privy Council. Was it worth while to hold parleys over matters such as these?

Many thought that it was. In Australia and in Canada there had been agitation in favor of the appointment of native-born Australians and Canadians as governors-general. In Queensland the appointment of British-born governors had been resented. The Irish Free State had appointed a minister to Washington; why should there not be a representative of South Africa at the Hague, an Australian emissary at Tokyo? The Empire was confronted with a number of minor issues of this description which made for friction between the Dominions and the Motherland. Perhaps it would be just as well to have the Dominions understand, once and for all, that they were free in every respect to follow their own bent.

Baldwin's government wanted to make this quite clear and so it summoned still another imperial conference to meet in London in 1926.

THE IMPERIAL CONFERENCE OF 1926

For the first time in history the relations of the Dominions to the mother country were now defined. The Dominions are, the conference asserted, "*autonomous Communities within the British Empire, equal*

*in status, in no way subordinate one to another in any aspect of their
domestic or external affairs, though united by a common allegiance to
the Crown, and freely associated as members of the British Commonwealth of Nations."*

There was nothing new in this pronunciamento; everybody understood before this that the Dominions were free. None the less this
formal acknowledgment of equality cleared the air of any possible
suspicion of imperialistic rule, and also paved the way for the construction of a true system of coördination. The committee on inter-
imperial relations which drew up the above statement indicated in
outline how this might be done. Treaties in the future could be signed
by all the Dominions, by a number of them or even by one. All treaties
were to be in the name of the King, but none were to be negotiated
except by the governments concerned. In the Dominions the governors
were no longer to be considered the representatives of the British
government. Official communications in the future, therefore, would
pass not through the governors, as representatives of the British
Crown, but direct, government to government. Between the Dominions and Great Britain there was to be absolute equality.

From now on the only direct connection between Britain and the
Dominions lay through the Crown. The governor-general in each dominion represented the Crown and had the same function in his Dominion as the King possessed in London. Since the King of England
was constitutionally bound to accept the advice of his ministers it
followed that the King in Canada (the governor-general) was obligated
to do likewise. Theoretically, of course, this meant that the King
might approve one course of action in England and a diametrically
different one in Canada, where the governor-general, the King's alter
ego, was equally bound to accept the opinion of the majority in the
Canadian Parliament as expressed through the Canadian cabinet. It
might seem illogical that the Crown could be thus split, that the King
could have five different personalities, one for each dominion (governor-general) and another as King of England. Nevertheless such was
the British system as defined and practiced since 1926. The colonial
office had already ceased to exist as far as the Dominions were concerned and a new cabinet officer, secretary of state for the Dominions,
was one of his Majesty's ministers. But this official had no powers
except to convey information from one government to another. Even
the various governors-general were now selected by the Crown on the
nomination of the Dominion Prime Ministers.

This curious system meant that the fiction of the Crown was maintained while the authority of the British Parliament was liquidated.
There still remained even after 1926 a few who insisted that since Par-

liament was the source of all authority the decision of a mere imperial conference could not supersede it. To satisfy those critics Parliament passed in 1931 the Statute of Westminster which stated that no law passed by Parliament in the future had any validity in any Dominion without its express agreement. Thus a formal seal of approval was placed upon what already had become an accepted practice.

DOMINION LOYALTY TO THE COMMONWEALTH

First and foremost in devotion to the Commonwealth stood New Zealand. Of all the Dominions it was the smallest,[1] the most isolated, the most purely British in blood, and the most closely linked of all to the mother country by commercial ties. Ninety per cent of New Zealand's exports went to Britain in the nineteen-thirties, and despite the efforts of her Labor Party to build up home industries the one and a half million inhabitants of that country continued to rely on Britain for manufactured goods. And what was true of manufacturing remained equally true of banking.

With Australia and Canada it was otherwise. The five million Australians and the fifteen million Canadians were more independent; their respective countries dwarfed Britain in area; their populations were more heterogeneous in blood, and in both instances they were more economically independent, establishing their own industries and protecting them behind tariff walls.

Of the total exports of Australia, Britain took only half in 1935-36, most of the remainder going to the Dutch colonies or Japan. Australia had her own tariffs, her own army, her own navy. Between the two World Wars her attention was focussed on her own domestic problems, the building of a new capital in the wilderness, the financing of new railroads, the opening of her northern territory, and currency troubles resulting from overexpansion and the world depression of the early 'thirties.

Canada was somewhat similarly situated. The population of that Dominion was even more heterogeneous than that of Australia. The French Canadians kept aloof; the western provinces were full of immigrants from eastern Europe and from the United States. The descendants of the old Empire Loyalists who had fled the United States after the American Revolution were more British than most Britons; but they were in a minority. Commercially and financially Canada was closely tied to Britain, but even more closely tied to the United States,

---

[1] Newfoundland, Britain's oldest colony, had Dominion status in 1834. Being bankrupt, she asked to be relieved of the expense of self-government. Newfoundland is now (1943) governed by commission.

the latter taking a greater volume of her exports than the mother country.

Centrifugal forces in Canada and Australia were powerful but none-theless the attachment of those two Dominions to the British connec-tion was beyond cavil. Neither of them, for instance, hesitated to declare war against Germany in 1939. But the same was not true of the Union of South Africa. A change of thirteen votes in the South African legislature and the Union would have declared neutrality in the second World War. What was the reason? The Boer War had ended 'way back in 1902 and the British had done their best to make amends for harsh treatment of the two Boer republics during that conflict by turning over the destinies of all South Africa to their keeping, for those of Boer (Afrikander) blood were in the majority in the Union. Neverthe-less, memories of the old conflict stayed green and were the constant talk of the veldt. Smuts' popularity with his own people was great, but so, too, was that of General Hertzog, leader of the bitterenders, the more intransigeant Boers who composed the Nationalist Party. General Smuts had put down a strike among the gold miners and therefore was unpopular with the Labor Party. Here was Hertzog's opportunity. To maintain himself in power Smuts had brought into the fold of the South African Party the British voters. Hertzog now sought by the magic power of old association to draw out from it the Boers. "Come out of the House of the stranger," he said to them. The Boers are one in language, blood, and religion. South Africa is their first concern. The Labor and Nationalist Parties should stand as one against Smuts and his adherents, imperialists and agents of foreign capitalism that they were.

Socialism, to the land-owning Boers, was anathema; and the Labor Party was socialistic. To the miners, on the other hand, largely of British origin, secession from the flag of their youth seemed hateful. Was it possible to make a coalition here?

Hertzog cleverly constructed it, and with Labor the South African Nationalists signed a formal pact. By it the Nationalists pledged them-selves, if victorious, not to insist on secession from the Empire; by it, Labor pledged itself not to demand confiscatory legislation.

The alliance once struck moved forward to a victorious outcome. Again an election was held in South Africa and this time, to the dismay of the friends of the Commonwealth, Smuts went down to defeat. The seats held by the South African Party decreased from 72 to 53. Those in the possession of the Nationalists increased from 47 to 63. Labor enlarged its membership from 13 to 18. The alliance was victorious and the implacable Hertzog became Prime Minister.

This was in 1924, and from that date to the opening of the second

World War racial and economic strife was the norm in South Africa. Both Smuts and Hertzog were conservative at heart; both were intent upon suppressing socialist agitation among the miners and any agitation among the Negroes heavily in the majority in South Africa; both were Afrikander generals who at one time had fought against British armies; and both were Afrikander nationalists. The only real difference between them was that Smuts believed heartily in the British Commonwealth and desired his country to remain an integral part of it, whereas Hertzog, though seemingly appeased by the declaration of the conference of 1926, was innately suspicious of British influence and perhaps secretly hopeful that even the British Commonwealth would disintegrate. In 1932 the discreet and conciliatory Smuts went more than half way and patched up an uneasy truce with Hertzog whereby a new political party emerged, the United Party, avoiding the extremists on both sides, and this party with Hertzog as premier and with Smuts as deputy premier controlled South Africa to 1939. When war broke out then Hertzog resigned in a huff because he could not carry a neutrality resolution and Smuts became premier, supported by a very narrow majority, and then only with a promise that South African troops would not be ordered to serve beyond the confines of Africa.

IRELAND OR EIRE

Whether Ireland or Eire should be included in a discussion of the Commonwealth is a moot question. Disaffection in South Africa was rife but it was nothing compared with that in Ireland. During the first World War there was a rebellion in South Africa, but the rebels once conquered were treated with leniency; after the 1916 Easter revolt in Dublin of Sinn Fein (the Irish Republican Party) there was bloody repression, and death by court martial.

The Irish Republicans then adopted new tactics. They boycotted the Royal Irish Constabulary, and they inaugurated Sinn Fein courts of law. Since the members of the constabulary were Irishmen, the refusal of the community round about them to engage in any form of intercourse was an effective weapon. Farmers refused to sell to the constabulary; women would not sit by the members of it in church; no good Irishman, so said Sinn Fein, should even speak to these upholders of an alien rule. Meanwhile, British judges traveled about on empty circuits and held vacant courts. From fear or preference, or both, the people made use only of the irregular and illegal tribunals set up by Sinn Fein. Within a year these were the only courts functioning over a large part of Ireland.

Came then 1920, a year so black in Irish annals that to find its counterpart one must look to the seventeenth century. And now between Irish and British an actual war arose, none the less war although there were no battles, but only raid and counter-raid, murder and counter-murder. For a year and a half blood was to flow freely in Ireland. The sworn servants of the Crown vied with the members of the Irish Republican army in a saturnalia of crime and cruelty. The British, to assist the fast thinning ranks of the constabulary, introduced into Ireland an auxiliary police force, clad in the old army khaki, but with black glengarry hats. To wear their uniform anywhere in Ireland soon became foolhardy; to wear it after dark or without friends at hand was to invite death. To belong to Sinn Fein, on the other hand, or to be related by marriage to Sinn Fein politician or soldier was all too often held sufficient warranty for prompt execution. Throughout all Ireland the country districts were dangerous and even in large cities the sound of the curfew bell gave warning to beware of assassins.

Between the responsibility of Sinn Fein on the one hand and Dublin Castle on the other the historian can draw no fine distinction. In the words of Mr. Griffith, Sinn Fein's founder: "The military mind is the same in every country. Our military men are as bad as the British."[2] They were. The Sinn Fein army, commanded by Michael Collins, a youthful agitator, was ill disciplined, widely scattered, and composed largely of young boys. By it many acts of vicious cruelty were perpetrated, such as dragging unarmed British officers from their beds and slaying them in cold blood. The "Black and Tans," on the other hand, well paid, seasoned veterans in many instances of the Great War and hardened to suffering and misery, did not hesitate to burn and destroy the homes of those held suspect, and to shoot in the back prisoners whom they told to run for safety.

Lloyd George, Prime Minister, denounced the Sinn Feiners to high heaven; but after a year he changed his mind, suggested a conference, offered concessions. For weeks the delegates of Sinn Fein wrangled with the British in London. Dominion status was offered with safeguards, mainly in regard to military and financial matters. One by one, the safeguards were surrendered by the British. The question of allegiance proved a stumbling-block: The Irish would accept no allegiance to the King, but a majority of the delegates agreed "to be faithful to the King by virtue of their common citizenship" in the British Commonwealth. Even this, however, would not satisfy De Valera, the Sinn Fein president, and when he was voted down by a pro-treaty majority in the Irish Parliament, he started civil war. This came to an end by 1924, and the Irish Free State accepted dominion status.

In 1932 De Valera and his extremists carried the elections and swept

[2] P. S. O'Hegarty, *The Victory of Sinn Fein*, p. 47.

into power on an anti-British platform. Promptly, De Valera began cutting such slender links as still joined Ireland to Britain; he got rid of the British governor-general; he repudiated the financial agreement whereby, in return for the cession of two strongly Roman Catholic counties in Ulster to the Free State, the latter assumed responsibility for repaying to the British treasury money advanced in the past for the purchase of Irish homesteads; and what is even more significant, the Irish Parliament passed an act defining Irish citizenship as distinct from British citizenship. Eire, or Ireland, was now regarded by De Valera as a distinct and separate country, and when England declared war on Germany in 1939, Ireland, as every one expected her to do, proclaimed her neutrality, presumably thereby voiding her Dominion status and withdrawing from the Commonwealth.

Ulster, the northeastern province, remained aloof. The majority there so desired it, since it was Protestant in faith, largely industrial by vocation, and still in good measure descended from Cromwellian soldiers and Scottish business men. On the other hand, a very large minority in Ulster wanted union with Eire and still does. That it may some day become a majority is the lively hope of the rest of Ireland.

THE DEPENDENT EMPIRE

"George VI, by the Grace of God, of Great Britain, Ireland, and the British Dominions beyond the Seas, King, Defender of the Faith, Emperor of India."

Thus is written the title of the King of England. The numerous Crown colonies, protectorates and mandates of the Empire find no mention in the King's title. The presumption is that they belong to Great Britain, and in an old imperial sense. It is difficult to conceive of Zanzibar and Nyasaland as being of the Commonwealth. The inhabitants thereof share doubtless in the commonweal; but they do not participate in any common effort to direct or determine it. They are a part of the dependent Empire.

The colonial dependencies of the British Crown defy scientific classification. That happy disregard of formal logic which has contributed so much to Britain's greatness may be seen in the organization of her Colonial Office as well as in her constitutional history. A few men at Whitehall, at a minimum of red tape and expense, control through their agents the destinies of millions of people. And there is no general way, plan, or method for so doing. The Empire has grown at odd and casual moments, and no one in authority has ever been sufficiently doctrinaire to apply standard measurements to this living and still growing organism.

None the less one may classify the units in the dependent Empire roughly by types, and by describing certain given examples in each type some light may be thrown on the evolution of the whole. Open as such a method is to the charge of incompleteness it seems preferable to cataloguing paragraph by paragraph, with a brief description of each, the long list of Crown colonies, protectorates, and mandates which are included in the British system.

THE CHARTERED COMPANY

The oldest form of colonial control in the Empire is the chartered company, and the history of the Empire in its earlier years must take note of many such. One by one, however, they have disappeared. Gone are the East Indian, Royal Niger, and East African. In the twentieth century but two examples of this archaic structure, providing for the governance of alien peoples by a business organization, still survived— the British South African and the British North Borneo Companies.

The charter of the former, given by her Majesty's Government in 1889 for a period of twenty-five years, presented to the company extensive rights over an enormous stretch of territory in south central Africa. Rhodesia, as it was called, was larger in area than Germany and France combined. It offered good possibilities for European settlement, particularly that third of it which was located south of the Zambesi River. The South African Company was authorized to administer justice and preserve peace, as well as to build railways, open mines, attract immigrants. The British government, however, reserved the right to abrogate its charter whenever such an act might be deemed desirable, and to the Secretary of State for the Colonies were granted large powers of intervention.

The British South African Company was to rule in Rhodesia until 1922. During that time, although highly abused as a wicked instrument of the ruthless imperialists, it never paid a penny in dividends. And by its balance sheet in 1922 it is evident that while the company raised and spent £13,000,000 it had as assured assets only £8,000,000.

None the less the venture was successful. It had accomplished what Rhodes hoped it would; the land was cleared, towns built, railways constructed, mines put in operation, settlers introduced—by 1920 some 33,000 in number. And all this was the work of private enterprise which cost the British government practically nothing. The latter assisted in quelling a native revolt; it also acted as intermediary between the company and the Portuguese, the Germans and the indigenous tribes. But it was the enthusiasm of the directors, long sustained, that made this seemingly unprofitable enterprise both popular and possible. Although there were no dividends the initial capital was doubled and shares still sold at a premium. Many persons bought them, it was said, simply for the purpose of attending the annual meeting and coöperating in the imperial labors of this unique corporation.

The more dramatic incidents in the company's history, the trek of Selous with the pioneers past the hostile tribesmen of Lobengula, the occupation of Mashonaland, the search for gold, the founding of Salisbury, the Matabele rebellion, took place in the last decade of the nineteenth century. Cecil Rhodes may have been a failure in South Africa, but in Rhodesia he was a godsend. With the cattle nearly gone, the mining machinery wrecked, and heavy casualties in the Matabele conflict, the plight of both company and settlers was serious. By skillful palavers with the native warriors, by importing cattle and supplies, Rhodes saved the day. In feverish activity he sought, perhaps, to forget his evil connection with the Jameson Raid. Rhodesia began again to thrive and prosper.

The London directors, business men as well as patriots, now thought the time had come for dividends. On the other hand, the settlers, as they increased in numbers and learned to shift for themselves, became restless under the control of the company. By a partial reorganization of the administration they had been granted representation in the Legislative Council; but it was a minority representation, and at this they chafed. Between settler and company there were disputes, some concerning administrative expense. The charter was renewed in 1914, but constant bickering did not end until the company surrendered its prerogatives—at a price. The British government in 1923 paid the company £3,750,000 and the immigrants agreed to reimburse the government £2,000,000. The company became a mere business concern, owning a railway and certain mineral rights. As such it continues to this day.

Rhodesia was divided. Northern Rhodesia with scarcely any white inhabitants became an imperial charge as a native protectorate. In Southern Rhodesia the immigrants were placed entirely in charge of their own affairs. Indeed, to all intent and purpose Southern Rhodesia might be listed with the Dominions were it not for the fact that the 770,000 Negroes within its borders remained under the Colonial office in London.

The inauguration of responsible government in Southern Rhodesia left but one solitary example extant of the chartered companies of the old colonial days. The British North Borneo Company, with a charter dating from 1881, continued in control of the northern tip of Borneo, a district as large as Scotland. The Japanese conquest of Borneo has made the future of that company problematical.

THE CROWN COLONY

In the Colonial Office lists Crown colonies are now placed in the same category with protectorates as "colonies not possessing responsible government, in which the administration is carried on by public officers under the control of the Secretary of State for the Colonies." But when we come to analyze further the form of government found in these two score and more British possessions we find it widely variant.

There are certain points of similarity: a governor sent from England, and other officials, such as the commander of the troops, medical officer, judge or judges, bishop or clergymen; and in all the Crown colonies the more important of these gentlemen form the governor's council. But here the similarity ends. A number of colonies, such as St. Helena and Gibraltar, are without further governmental machinery. On the other hand a majority are equipped with a Legislative Council. In certain of these the members are exclusively nominated by the Crown; in others, as is the case in Fiji and Kenya, they are in part elected, with a provision that a majority of the Council be nominated. In yet others this proviso does not exist and a majority of the Legislative Council may be elected. Of this number Cyprus and Ceylon are typical. Three Crown colonies out of the total number approach to modern democratic ideas and possess a legislature of two houses with the lower one comprised entirely of elected members. Barbados, the Bahamas, Bermuda comprise the three. And to their number in all likelihood Jamaica will be added.

AFRICAN CROWN COLONIES: PROTECTORATES

Between the government of a Crown colony and that of a protectorate the line of demarcation is today somewhat shadowy. In the nineteenth century a protectorate was represented primarily by a large block of land under the protection of the British government, on which a British resident, appointed by and responsible to the British Foreign Office, exercised a more or less general and indirect rule through advice given to the native ruler. The inhabitants of a protectorate were indeed protected—but largely against annexation by German, French, or Portuguese. To some extent, in certain quarters, the British resident did protect them not only against the rapaciousness of their rulers but also against tribal customs. But as a rule, aside from driving out slavery and the slave trade, it was not expected that he would interfere with the organization of native life, either political or social.

At the present this definition of a protectorate needs decided modification. The majority of the protectorates have been given up by the Foreign Office and have been taken over by the Colonial; the central African Crown colonies have extended their control inland and have assumed new responsibilities for the guidance of native races; and at the same time the administrative authorities in the protectorates have extended their control and have interfered more and more in the economic and social life of the people subject to them. Crown colony government, therefore, and protectorate government tend to blend, and it frequently is difficult to differentiate between them. For instance, there is the British Crown colony of Sierra Leone and the British protectorate of that name. There is now in theory but one Nigeria; yet to all practical purposes the protectorate of Northern Nigeria still remains, a confusion in terminology thereby resulting which to any except the British might seem undesirable. The Governor of Sierra Leone is, for instance, the British resident for Sierra Leone. For the seaport and the territory immediately adjacent to it, the old colony of Sierra Leone, there is a Legislative Council on the familiar West Indian model, with a nominated majority. In the interior, in the protectorate, the decrees of this council are not binding; but the ordinances of the Governor, as British resident, are. In practice this frequently amounts to the same thing, since the friends of the Governor control the council. The protectorate, however, in both theory and practice, is less closely administered, more liberty being left to the tribal chieftains, sometimes the entire work of local administration being intrusted to their care.

This change has come about mainly as a result of the economic exploitation of the Dark Continent. The division of African territory among the European powers was largely complete by 1890; but boundaries in the hinterland were as yet very shadowy. To secure them, expeditions were sent out by the various European governments. The first aim of their statesmen was, as in 1890, to stake down claims rather than to develop wealth. The surveyor preceded the trader or planter; there was necessity for haste lest aliens preëmpt savannahs, streams, and forests that might prove useful in the future. And with the surveyors went the proclamation of a protectorate.

By 1904, however, with the Franco-British entente of that year, even the boundaries in the remote hinterland had, in most cases, been determined. And as this process drew to a conclusion a new one began, namely, the building of railways, the development of sugar, coffee, and cacao plantations, the exploitation of palm oil and rubber resources, the pushing on into the interior of the white trader and all that it implied. From Sierra Leone in the west to Nairobi in the east, from Khartoum to the Zambesi; in Northern Nigeria, Nyasaland, Uganda, and the Gold Coast one found the white man now appearing. And missionary, trader, native chief, and government official were obliged to re-adjust their mutual relations. The British had really entered tropical Africa; had they come as associates, partners, neighbors, or governors, and to what extent or degree?

This question was variously answered in different parts of the Dark Continent. Of course, in every section which they entered the British, like the other Europeans, came as overlords. Since they knew more than the Negroes, an acknowledged fact, they assumed they knew best how the natives should be governed, an inference which was not inevitable. But in determining the form of this governance the new-comer followed either one of two methods, the west African or the east African. In the former, reliance was placed primarily on indirect rule. According to its principles the British resident endeavored to make himself as inconspicuous as possible while exalting the power and prestige of the native chief; in the latter or east African method the rule was direct. In accordance with the west African system private ownership of land on the part of the whites was forbidden and tribal ownership on the part of the Negroes encouraged. In the east African system the land policy was reversed. The natives were segregated on reserves set apart for them. White immigrants, on the other hand, bought or leased land from the Crown and remained apart from the Negro.

Indirect rule has thus far had decidedly the better record. Where it has been practiced in Nigeria and elsewhere in West Africa there has been less friction than in Kenya Colony in East Africa where settlers own land in freehold. In Kenya there has been continuous controversy between the white immigrants and the indigenous people, accompanied by loud complaints, both from the Negro and from missionaries speaking on his behalf, of the treatment of workers on the great plantations. Compulsory labor may be forbidden; but how else can a poor black secure money to pay taxes except by working on a white plantation? Theoretically he might gain it by selling the surplus produced on his reservation: but suppose the latter is too circumscribed and too infertile to produce a surplus? And such, unfortunately, in all too many instances, was the rule.

One result of the first World War was, as we have noted, the mandates, trusteeships created by the peace treaty under the League of Nations. Britain held a number of these mandates and their history very properly belongs to imperial rather than to Commonwealth history. But the most important of all the mandates, Palestine, is treated elsewhere. India likewise, still far in 1943 from Dominion status, is reserved for separate treatment, for Indian history in modern times is too closely linked to the nationalistic awakening of Asiatic peoples to be separated from it. There remains, then, Egypt, a country which, like Ireland up to the recent years, might properly be included in any summary of the Empire-Commonwealth.

EGYPT AND THE SUDAN IN 1938

(Reprinted from J. F. Horrabin's *An Atlas of Current Affairs*, by permission of, and special arrangement with, Alfred A. Knopf, Inc., publishers.)

The story of England's relation to Egypt during the interval between the world wars parallels in some ways her relation to Ireland. In the land of the Pharaohs there was seething discontent; and the rising tide of nationalism noticeable everywhere in the post-War world led to nasty riots in Cairo and other Egyptian cities, directed against the protectorate which England had proclaimed over Egypt during the war. These demonstrations Britain alternately met by stiff opposition and conciliatory concession; with the emphasis on the latter word, for military occupation of the Nile Valley was expensive and the British lion was in a generally pacifistic mood.

Three times did Britain yield to Egyptian pressure. In 1922 she announced that Egypt was "an independent national state," but coupled this declaration with the acceptance by Egypt of reservations in regard to the stationing of British troops there and the acknowledgment that foreign interests in that land were under British protection. The Egyptians, greatly irked by these "safeguards," refused to ratify the treaty which embodied them. Followed then more riots and the assassination of the British governor-general of the Sudan. Thereupon the British levied heavy fines and seized customs houses. Then, when Mac-Donald became prime minister again in 1929, the British held out the olive branch; they offered a treaty whereby their troops would be withdrawn to the canal zone, Egypt to be completely independent but joined in military alliance with Britain. Once again the Egyptian Parliament refused ratification, and a final settlement was not made until 1936. The agreement reached on that date was on the model of the British proposals of 1929. It called for a military alliance, but the Egyptians were under no obligation to fight unless Egypt was invaded. The British agreed to limit their peacetime forces to 10,000 soldiers and to station them only in the canal zone. Naval bases at Alexandria and Port Said were granted to Britain, likewise the right to move troops over Egypt in time of war. The Sudan was to remain under British control, with special rights there reserved for Egypt. In accordance with this treaty Egypt broke off relations with Germany in 1939 but did not declare war on that country.

CHAPTER IX

THE LESSER STATES BETWEEN TWO WARS
(1919-39)

THE growth of communism in Russia and of its totalitarian counterpart, fascism, in other countries was symptomatic of a general reaction throughout all Europe to the liberal ideology of the nineteenth century. Only a small part of the continent seemed immune to this general wave of discontent, namely, the four Scandinavian nations—Denmark, Norway, Sweden, and Finland, and the small democratic states of Switzerland, Holland, Belgium, and Czechoslovakia.

From 1815 to 1905 Norway had been linked to Sweden under the House of Bernadotte. For all that time there was a Norwegian Parliament, but foreign affairs were conducted under Swedish auspices. The Norwegians in their unfertile valleys would have been desperately poor, indeed, had it not been for the sea. As it was, they not only became noted fishermen but built up an excellent mercantile marine, having in the early twentieth century the largest in the world in proportion to population. Naturally, therefore, they desired their own consular service, and because King Oscar II tried to keep it in Swedish hands, the Norwegian Parliament voted to separate from Sweden and to have a King of Norway.

A prince of Denmark was selected for this honor and under him Norway became more and more democratic; the Norwegians already had universal manhood suffrage, but in 1913 they extended it to include women, and such slight power as had remained to the King in the way of vetoing legislation was abolished.

Swedish democracy, likewise, grew rapidly in strength in the years before the first World War. Until 1863 Sweden had been ranked as one of the more conservative countries in Europe, retaining a strong monarchy and being governed by a kind of medieval estates-general of four houses—nobility, clergy, burghers, and peasants. From that date onward, however, a steady and constant change in the direction of democracy took place, the result of the impact of the Industrial Revolution, for Sweden was not only rich in timber but in iron ore. Woman suffrage, old-age pensions, progressive legislation gave Sweden the reputation of being one of the most advanced democracies in

Europe; and the World War seemed to strengthen rather than to weaken Sweden's devotion to democratic ways, that country becoming noted as one which kept to the "middle way," whereby capitalism was so checked and guarded by consumer coöperatives and state intervention on behalf of the poor that the latter remained content with the security which they had gained. Disparity between rich and poor was reduced to a minimum and Sweden seemingly became a kind of middle-class paradise.

It was not otherwise in Denmark. During the long reign of Christian IX (1863-1906) there was sturdy resistance on the part of the King to democratic innovation, but toward the end of his reign, and during that of his successor, particularly in 1914-15, Denmark went decidedly democratic, both houses of the legislature being elected by universal suffrage, and the powers of the king becoming nominal. Even before that time, however, the growth of coöperative agencies for the standardizing of Danish agricultural products had given the Danes good training in democratic practices. About one quarter of all the Danes lived in Copenhagen, one of Europe's most charming capitals, where the extremely modest royal castle of a democratic king is quite obscured by a magnificent city hall redolent with the pride of equalitarian burghers.

The fourth Scandinavian country, Finland, had lain under the heavy yoke of Russian imperialism from 1809 to the Revolution of 1917. Finland, soon after, jumped into popular notice as a thriving progressive democracy. The Finns paid their debts, experimented democratically with prohibition only to end it, encouraged modern architecture, turned their capital, Helsinki, into a model city, and desperately prepared to defend their hard-earned freedom from renewed Russian aggression in 1939. True, as far as blood and language are concerned, Finland belongs in a separate category from the other three Scandinavian states; but institutionally, as well as geographically, she justly may be considered as linked to Denmark, Norway, and Sweden.

All four of these northern countries were members of the League of Nations, and the Danes in particular took a lively interest in its work, a Dane serving on the commission on the Saar Valley, another on the high court, and Denmark herself being elected to serve a term on the council of the League. All four of these countries also have consulted together from time to time during the intervals between the two world wars. They organized a Scandinavian bloc; they invited coöperation from other small countries, such as Holland; and within them neither fascism nor communism seemed to have gained a foothold.

Switzerland is another democratic country, fortunate in that her annals have been so quiet. The twenty-two states or cantons which compose Switzerland were bound together by a federation in 1815 and by a somewhat stronger one in 1847 after a brief civil war of three weeks. In almost all matters apart from national defense the twenty-two cantons preserved their autonomy, and six of these semi-independent cantons in this miniature country are so small that pure, unadulterated democracy is possible, voting being conducted on cantonal business directly in huge mass meetings out of doors. Universal military service holds in Switzerland, but the soldier owns his own rifle and takes it home with him. As a result of Nazi pressure, some slight curtailment of free speech was in evidence in Switzerland in the years just before the outbreak of the second World War; but this was precautionary merely. The Swiss, like the Finns, were ever careful to preserve their liberty and their democracy if they had to fight for it.

In the Netherlands and in Belgium the picture was not radically different. In both of these lands there was much greater concentration of wealth, in the former in commerce, in the latter in manufacturing and mining. Partly because of this, partly because of surviving religious disputes, the Netherlands and Belgium can hardly be considered fully as democratic in their constitutional practice as the other democracies we have taken up, for the former country did not adopt universal suffrage until 1917, and the latter not until after the war. Nevertheless, fascism and communism made relatively little headway in either land. The daughter of the Queen of Holland married a German prince, but the Queen and her country both seemed more concerned in regard to the Prince's personal behavior than for fear lest he import German ideas; a curious form of Roman Catholic fascism developed in Belgium —the Rexist movement—only to be routed at the polls. The Social Democrats still remained a powerful faction in the Belgian Parliament, but by definition they were stanch defenders of democracy; and the same also may be said for the Belgian Catholic party.

There remains the republic of Czechoslovakia. Within the borders of this new, or resurrected, country (depending on the point of view) there seemed to lie great promises for the future of democracy. The Czechs, indeed, appeared not only capable of solving those problems which confronted the other small democracies but able also to settle minority problems by democratic means. Surrounded by Fascist and semi-Fascist states, the Czechs were a beacon of light and reason until overwhelmed by the German inundation of 1938-39.

The Czechoslovak state, as set up by the Allied powers in 1919, was both republican and democratic. The legislature, elected by universal, secret, and compulsory voting, was empowered to choose a president to serve seven years. The Czechs themselves were socially democratic; there was little difference in wealth among them; until only recently the great estates and more important industries had been in German hands; the majority of the Czechs had been workmen or peasants.

There was bound to be some trouble, since one-third of the population was non-Czech. The Slovaks caused friction and so did the minority Poles and Magyars. But most troublesome of all was the German minority that lived, for the most part, toward the German border. These Sudeten Germans (a name derived from the Sudeten Mountains) had just cause for complaint. There were discriminations made against the German language; there were other grievances, mainly economic, and, above all, the sense of injustice at being included in the Czechoslovak nation against their will. But it could not be justly said that these Germans were downtrodden; politically they were on a basis of complete equality with the Czechs; they could and did have their own parties in the parliament at Prague; and, up to 1935 when the crisis came about, there were no less than three German parties—the German Agrarian, the Christian Socialist, and the Social Democratic, the three together polling sixty-five per cent of the German vote.

The Czechoslovak Republic justly can be criticized for overcentralization, and some considered that it would have been wise from the beginning to have federalized the country on the Swiss model. The Czechs were afraid to do this. Not having enjoyed freedom for centuries (it was in 1526 that the Austrian Hapsburgs absorbed the Bohemian Crown), they dared not risk the adoption of Swiss federalism. Meanwhile, secure in their military alliance with France, protected, supposedly, by a friendly Russia, the Czechs occupied what seemed to be a strongly defended bastion in Central Europe, an outpost of democracy between Nazi Germany on the north and semi-fascist Austria on the south.

POLAND

Among those countries which were neither totalitarian nor democratic, Poland was the most important. That nation, resurrected from the dead by the World War, insisted, as we have seen (see p. 118), on continuing the war after the war by an aggressive anti-Russian campaign not concluded until the treaty of Riga in 1921. By that date Pilsudski had carried the frontiers of his country eastward beyond those of 1793. Shortly afterward came the Polish occupation of Vilna, forcibly torn from Lithuania, and by 1923 Poland had become a country of 150,000 square miles, with a population of 28,000,000. In area larger than Italy, in population larger than Spain, Poland could now claim to be the sixth most important European state.

But it was a very weak state. Only on the south might it claim to have any natural boundary, the Carpathian Mountains. To the east, the north, and the west, purely artificial boundary lines were drawn, and as one approached those lines the population was of mixed nationality—Polish-German, Polish-Lithuanian, and Polish-Russian. No country in Europe had so many large minority groups within its borders. There were approximately 5,000,000 Ukranians (Little Russians), 1,500,000 White Russians, 750,000 to 1,000,000 Germans, an indeterminate number of Lithuanians, and some 3,300,000 Jews within Poland. The country was very, very poor. During the World War, Russian, German, and Austrian armies fiercely had swept back and forth across the Polish plain, and the subsequent two-year war against Russia had added to the devastation. Live stock had been killed, forests destroyed, towns, villages, railways, and bridges ruined. Furthermore, the Poles were without experience in self-rule. Throughout the nineteenth century they had kept alive their longing for nationality, but actual practice in free government had been denied them. To organize a government based on free discussion rather than on force was well-nigh beyond their power.

Nevertheless, in the halcyon days of 1919, with sweet freedom in the air, they did their best. The *Sejm,* or Polish Parliament, which assembled in that year was elected not only by universal suffrage but also in accordance with the principles of proportional representation. It drew up a constitution (1921), and a very liberal one, somewhat on the model of that of the Third Republic, the president possessing very limited power.

Pilsudski, Poland's strong man, considered that feature a direct slap at himself, which it was, and so he declined to accept the presidency. With Achilles sulking in his tent, Polish politics degenerated speedily into a series of factional fights which only came to an end with a coup d'état on the part of Pilsudski, who marched on Warsaw in 1926 and overthrew the government. Pilsudski, however, did not make himself dictator or establish a totalitarian régime—at least not at first. Instead, he again refused the presidency, although consenting to act as premier. From 1926 to 1935 Pilsudski's rôle in Polish history is difficult to disentangle. The General certainly played strong-arm politics, even at times imprisoning hostile deputies of the Sejm. Twice he resigned the premiership, only to continue to manipulate elections and parliamentary blocs; and to all intent and purpose he was about to become dictator at the time of his death in 1935, when a new constitution was adopted, one described as an "authoritarian democracy," whatever that is.

That constitution had one very unusual feature. It made an emphatic

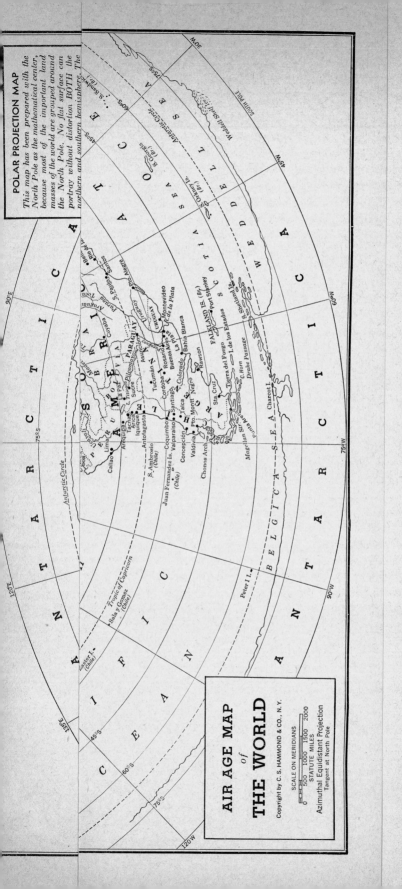

POLAR PROJECTION MAP

This map has been prepared with the North Pole as the mathematical center, because most of the important land masses of the world are grouped around the North Pole. No flat surface can portray without distortion BOTH the northern and southern hemisphere. The

AIR AGE MAP
of
THE WORLD

Copyright by C. S. HAMMOND & CO., N. Y.

SCALE ON MERIDIANS

STATUTE MILES
0 500 1000 1500 2000

Azimuthal Equidistant Projection
Tangent at North Pole

denial that a totalitarian government was desirable—did not Article 5 state: "The creative action of the individual is the lever of collective life."? On the other hand, the peculiar method adopted for selecting the president of the Polish Republic pointed in the opposite direction. He was to be chosen by a college of electors composed of high officials and members of the Sejm. If the incumbent in the presidential office approved, no further steps were necessary. If, however, he chose to nominate a candidate not approved by the electoral college then a popular vote should decide between the two nominees. Extensive additional powers were also granted the president. He was authorized to issue ordinances having the authority of law during such times as the Sejm was not in session. His authority in this respect was limited by certain exceptions, and he could not interfere with the budget nor levy taxes, but nevertheless his constitutional powers greatly exceeded those granted to the president of the United States.

In the few years remaining to the Polish Republic before its annihilation at the hands of Germany and Russia in 1939, the political pendulum swung back and forth, not between right and left but between right and center. The Communist party was forbidden and the only question was: would Poland swing into the fascist column or continue halfway democratic? Army officers took an active part in this struggle. In the cabinets were a number of generals and colonels, and General Smigley-Rydz, commander-in-chief of the Polish army in the one-month war of 1939, was made a marshal and then officially declared "first person in Poland after the President." The marshal, in the eyes of liberals and socialists, was a suspect; he was said to be committed to a fascist program. But this could not be proved.

Poland, as the year of her doom drew near, was most dangerously balanced between democracy and totalitarianism. Superficially the country seemed strong. A Polish port, Gdynia, was constructed on the sandy wastes of the Baltic and through it flowed considerable commerce; a Polish mercantile marine was in the making; and there were even demands for Polish colonies. Seemingly, the government was in good position financially, with monopolies of alcohol, salt, matches, tobacco, and lotteries to buttress up its treasury. But this was on the surface only; below was a poverty-stricken peasantry, so poor that in eastern Poland matches were divided four ways before being struck. The "colonels," now sitting in the political saddle as well as in the military, did not know how to deal with poverty, were not interested in poverty, nor were they more enlightened in regard to the minorities.

The Germans, the Ukranians, and the Jews in Poland continued an outcry about the discrimination levied against them. Scattered throughout western Poland, German landlords complained that their leases were illegally defined by Polish law courts, and that, contrary to the Treaty of Versailles, the use of German in schools was frowned upon. The Ukranians asserted that they were deprived of the cultural autonomy promised them, and that even Ukranian Boy Scouts were disbanded by Polish orders. The Jews, who comprised some twenty-seven per cent of the city population, were humiliated by "ghetto benches," separate seats assigned to Jews in university lecture halls, a practice encouraged by the government, although not ordered by it. The Jews also were subjected to boycotts, again indirectly approved by the government, and when various antisemitic riots took place, the authorities apparently encouraged rather than discouraged them. The treatment given the minorities in Poland was far less fair and just than that guaranteed by her sister republic, Czechoslovakia. In fact, nowhere else in Europe were minorities more at a disadvantage than in Poland. That country, indeed, was in sorry plight as the German hordes drove over the western borders in September, 1939.

SPAIN

The only large European state spared the horrors of the first World War was Spain. The King, the court, the army, rumor had it, favored the Germans; but British commercial interests were dominant and, isolated as Spain was from the Central Powers, neutrality had been a necessity. Spain therefore had escaped much; and a lucky thing this had been for her, since long years of anarchy and turmoil lay ahead, only to end in one of the most sanguine and desperate civil wars waged in all history.

After the War Spain swung violently to the right under a military dictatorship (1923-30), then violently to the left under a radical republican government, greatly influenced by communistic ideas (1930-36), then violently to the right again (1936—?) under a military dictatorship established through the active support of the Italian and German dictators, while anticommunist France and England stood idle, partly in the vain hope that the Fascist tide would not rise farther, partly because they could not agree on joint action, partly through actual timidity caused by their own unpreparedness, and partly through cold indifference to the veritable crucifixion of the Spanish people.

Spain in 1919 was a constitutional monarchy, but not a well-governed one. Most of the Spanish people, however, were so long accustomed to misrule that opposition to King Alfonso and to the junta of corrupt politicians who controlled the country was not highly developed. There were, however, danger signals flying in two places—in Catalonia, the northeastern province of Spain, and in Morocco.

Catalonia was at once the most prosperous and the most radical section of the Iberian peninsula. It contained the large manufacturing city of Barcelona; it possessed a language and a literature peculiarly its own—the Catalan—for not until the nineteenth century did Catalonia cease to be at least partially autonomous. During the World War the deputies from Catalonia in the Spanish *Cortes* (parliament) had protested as a body against the weight of taxation borne by their constituents, and at the conclusion of that conflict, Catalonia demanded a revision of the Spanish constitution whereby Spain should become a federated rather than a unitary state, the various provinces having parliaments of their own.

In Spanish Morocco, meanwhile, there was active rebellion. Spanish troops sent to defeat it were badly mauled by the Moors, and King Alfonso lost such little prestige as he had managed to retain by issuing orders which resulted in further defeats, one of which resulted in the death of over 10,000 Spaniards. An investigation of these disasters was promptly suppressed (1922), and loud were the complaints in press and Parliament. Alfonso decided to abdicate not his throne but his constitutional authority. Having made arrangements with General Primo de Rivera for a coup d'état, he left for France.

The General established himself (1923) as military dictator, brought civil liberties to an end, ruled by court martial. For a while it seemed as though Rivera might be as successful as Mussolini, since in many ways he resembled that condottieri chief. Seemingly, the general was a kind of human dynamo, very conceited, and not without ability. He ended successfully the revolt in Africa; he organized a political party, the Patriotic Union, standing ostensibly for country, religion, and monarchy; and he shared political power with it. Unlike Mussolini, however, he grew less popular with the passing years rather than more so. The Spaniards proved more fractious than the Italians; there were mutinies in the army; there were anti-Rivera demonstrations in the universities; and Rivera himself did not enjoy robust health. Suddenly in 1930 he resigned, and Alfonso immediately restored the constitution suspended in 1923 and announced the election of a new Cortes.

But it was too late to save the monarchy. Most Spaniards considered Alfonso responsible for the late dictatorship and they did not hesitate to demand his abdication. The monarch refused to abdicate, but once again fled the country; and as he did so in 1931 the republic was proclaimed in Madrid.

The foundations upon which it rested were shaky from the beginning. Few Spaniards had any use for a King who never did anything but run away from trouble; but aside from that one slender thread of unity, there was no common agreement as to the kind of government best suited to the country. On the right were those who favored a political revolution, but who looked askance upon any social revolution which might undertake a redistribution of land, and an educational program which would take away from the Catholic Church its traditional monopoly of Spanish education. On the left were innumerable grades of revolutionary sentiment, running from that professed by Social Democrats (gradualists in temperament, hoping for the piecemeal establishment of socialism) all the way to the more extreme dogmas of the Communists (some favoring Stalin, some Trotsky, but all for the red flag and immediate revolt), and to the Anarchist-Syndicalists (very strong in Barcelona), believing in no government at all and defiantly hoisting the black flag of anarchy.

Delegates drawn from these divergent groups drew up a constitution calling for a "republic of the workers of all classes," a title indicative of a certain leftist tendency in the constitution which was reflected by provisions that made for exclusively lay education and for the confiscation of large landed estates. The more conservative members of the constitutional assembly were not pleased. The more extreme right, namely, the few followers of the exiled Alfonso and those known as Carlists, who favored the pretender to the Spanish throne, began once more to plot against the republican régime, and the moderate right (much larger in numbers) became disaffected.

Shortly it became more so, as the constituent Cortes drove the Jesuits out of Spain and tried to put through an educational program without religious instruction. Under the circumstances it was perhaps foolish to act thus, for the country was over forty per cent illiterate, and to set up a sufficient number of schools to provide overnight for the 250,-000 children educated by the monastic orders was impossible for such a poor country as Spain.

The Spanish republicans, indeed, fell into the same error as did the revolutionary leaders in the French Revolution: Being more or less contemptuous of religion and thinking it moribund, they awoke the Catholic Church out of its lethargy. They sequestrated immediately all property of the Church not directly used for religious purposes; religious orders were forbidden to teach (except instruction to their own members); the crucifix was removed from all class rooms; divorce was freely granted; and complete separation between Church and State guaranteed.

The Pope immediately protested against these anticlerical clauses in the constitution, and many Spaniards promptly renewed their interest in a religion which lay dormant but never dead. They found themselves annoyed by the republic in many other ways; they were angered by the success of the Catalan radicals, who were soon able to obtain a high degree of autonomy for their own province; they were worried by the confiscation (with little or no compensation) of the great estates, estimated at 50,000,000 acres, which were to be given to the peasants. These factors converging together brought about an uprising in Madrid and Seville in the name of a conservative republican dictatorship.

This revolt of the right was quickly squelched, but no sooner was that done than a rising of the left occurred, this time on the part of Anarchists who wanted no government at all and who fomented strikes to do away with it. Confronted, therefore, with revolt and counter-revolt, the constituent assembly felt far from secure as Spaniards voted in 1933 for their first national Parliament under the new constitution.

The popular vote went to the right, although the center parties in the Cortes, together with the left, could have had a small majority. The center, however, preferred the right to the left, and combining with it made possible a rightist ministry. It proved a weak one. Violence broke out on every hand. In Asturias, a mining district in northern Spain, Communists and Socialists forgot their differences and descended on the town of Oviedo. For nine days they held it, sacking banks and churches, and putting many priests to death. In Catalonia Premier Companys proclaimed Catalonia independent of Madrid. And elsewhere in Spain an organization began to be heard from known as the *Falange Española,* started ostensibly for the purpose of protecting nuns from molestation but soon to become famous as a Spanish Fascist party, bent upon the destruction of radicalism by force. The government did, indeed, succeed in crushing out the revolt in Asturias and in Catalonia, but against the incipient anarchy breaking out, now here now there, it seemed powerless, and in a new election to the Cortes in 1936 it met with repudiation at the hands of the electorate.

This time Spain swung to the left, as the various radical groups, so frequently at each other's throats, combined in what was known as the *frente popular.* Out of 473 members chosen, the leftists now had 266, the center parties 65, and the right only 142. This was the last general election held in Spain. Civil disorder and mob violence prevailed well-nigh everywhere. The various Marxist and anarchist groups claimed that they simply countered violence by justifiable reprisals. The Falangists (Spanish Fascists), on the other hand, reversed that argument. Where the truth lay, none can tell. The facts are that nerves were frayed and patience exhausted on both sides. The conservatives claimed that the government permitted radical mobs to fire churches and to kill priests and nuns, and only intervened when conservatives tried to prevent such acts. The republican government, not communist nor socialist nor anarchist, but influenced none the less by these three groups, asserted that it had a preponderant voice in the Cortes and represented the will of the Spanish people, that the Falangists violated that will, that they took the law into their own hands, that they compelled magistrates "to sentence their opponents and acquit their members." One thing and only one is demonstrable: "the left did not know how to win, the right did not know how to lose. . . . Blue shirts and red shirts covered breasts in which hatred was hatching the most terrible revenge. The shadow of murder was spreading over Spain."[1] For many a year it was to remain there.

Murder is not too strong a word to use for the civil war which raged through Spain from 1936 to 1939, a vicious, cruel and bloodthirsty war in which not Spaniards alone but many other Europeans, as well as Americans and also Moors, took active part. It began with a revolt in the army, many officers of which were enemies of the republic. Under the command of General Franco, who had been exiled to the Canaries by the republican government, a part of the army stationed in Morocco revolted and invaded Spain, accompanied by the Moors.

The revolt spread, particularly in western Spain, where a Falangist capital was set up at Burgos. Slowly the rebels in the South and West gathered strength, joined forces, and were at the very gates of Madrid. Associated with the Falangists were the Traditionalists (Carlists), and both groups from the beginning had the active sympathy and coöperation of Hitler and Mussolini. It seemed as though only a miracle could prevent the Fascist occupation of the Spanish capital.

That miracle almost occurred; the republicans matched zeal with zeal, and if they lacked military training they had numbers on their side, and also help from without. Airplanes from Russia speedily engaged in duels with Italian planes over Spain, and volunteers dashed to their assistance—exiled Germans, Italians, and radical youth from a dozen countries.

The war soon took on the aspect of a fight between international communism and international fascism. Hitler and Mussolini sent armed help to Franco, the former planes and many technicians, the latter doing likewise, and supplying artillery and infantry as well. The Russians soon withdrew their active support, but from England, France, and the United States several thousand individual Communists and left-wing sympathizers dashed to the rescue, forming an international brigade for the defense of the Spanish Republic. The president of the Spanish Republic was no Communist and his premier, Caballero, was only a Social Democrat; but so loudly did Hitler and Mussolini proclaim the Holy War, and so strongly did the Holy See proclaim the conflict a crusade of Christianity against communism that a large part

[1] A. Mendizabel, *The Martyrdom of Spain*, pp. 264-265.

THE VICTIM

Spain. "Whichever Wins, My Agony Endures!"

(*Punch*, Aug. 12, 1936. Reprinted by permission of the proprietors of *Punch*.)

of the world somewhat wrongly regarded the war as purely a Communist-Fascist duel.

The Spanish Loyalists, as the republicans were called, managed to stave off the inevitable for over two years. They hung on tenaciously to Madrid, even though the Fascist forces were entrenched in the suburbs; they administered one smashing defeat to the confident Italians advancing from the north on that city; but the war in the air they could not fight. Relentlessly, the Fascists with the help of German and Italian planes swept north and west, conquering the poor Basques, who were at once both good Catholics and stanch republicans. With uncalled-for cruelty, low-flying planes carried death and destruction to innumerable small towns. The Loyalists were compelled to abandon Madrid as a capital, though they still kept military control of that city, and they moved their headquarters to Valencia. Then came Franco's drive to separate Valencia from Catalonia. It succeeded, and the Loyalists moved their capital to Barcelona, prepared to put up their last fight in the radical northeast. Soon all of Spain was lost except Madrid and Catalonia; Barcelona fell to the enemy, and the Loyalists, driven up close to the French border, crossed into France. The war was over, Madrid surrendering shortly after.

It had been fought with the utmost ferocity on both sides. The Moors in Franco's employ had been guilty of particularly abominable practices, but for that matter no mercy had been shown by either faction. Meanwhile, the conflict had important repercussions elsewhere in Europe, hastening the military advance of fascism in Italy and Germany, slowly awakening England and France to the dangers which confronted them. But these international aspects of the Spanish Civil War must be left to another chapter.

AUSTRIA

Now let us follow the fortunes of the Austrian Republic. It was proclaimed in Vienna on November 12, 1918, one day after the armistice, and in the beginning it was quite democratic, with a constitution resembling that of the Weimar Republic. Slowly but surely, however, the democratic features gave way under the force of circumstances to a full-fledged dictatorship in 1933 under Engelbert Dollfuss, a dictatorship resembling that of Mussolini in certain respects and strikingly different in others.

From the very day of its birth the Austrian Republic was afflicted by two well-nigh incurable diseases—lack of economic self-sufficiency on the one hand and deep-rooted ideological antagonisms on the other. Austria had a large population within a very small area; worse than that, it contained within its borders a large city which once had been the commercial and banking capital of the Danube valley, and which now, having lost its economic hinterland, was in danger of starvation. The plight of Vienna, terrible beyond belief, was alleviated by the League of Nations. In 1922 Britain, France, Italy, and Czechoslovakia backed an international loan through the League for $135,000,000 and Austria struggled to her economic feet, reorganizing her currency and preserving her economic life, albeit with much difficulty, until the international financial crisis of 1929-30.

There were, however, other troubles. The majority of Austrians called themselves socialists; but between the Social Democrats of Vienna, moderate Marxists, and the Christian Socialists of the rural districts there was profound disagreement. The new constitution was federal in character, and since half the money raised by taxation had to be handed over to the particular province in which it was raised, the Social Democrats of Vienna found that they had more money to spend than had the Christian Socialists of the country districts. Vienna spent this money freely in building very decent homes for the working classes and raised increased sums for other social purposes by virtually confiscating the property of the wealthy by high taxes.

The Christian Socialists, much more conservative, disapproved of this radical procedure; they were also attached to the Roman Catholic Church and they hated the agnosticism of the city socialists. They were somewhat akin to the Centre party in Germany, although more powerful, and like that Centre party were really between two extremes, that of the Social Democrats on the left, and that of the Nationalists on the right.

The Austrian Nationalists were divided into two groups; one, under Prince von Starhemberg, was aristocratic, agrarian, Catholic, and, after the advent of Hitler to power, opposed to the submergence of Austria in Germany; the other group consisted of Pan-Germans, clamoring loudly for *"anschluss,"* or union with Germany, before long virtually becoming an Austrian Nazi party taking orders from Berlin. Both sections of the Austrian Nationalists added together were in a minority in Austria; but for that matter, neither the Christian Democrats nor the Social Democrats had a majority, and since these two groups would not work in harmony, a democratic government soon became almost an impossibility. The aristocratic Nationalists founded a private army of their own, the Heimwehr, commanded by von Starhemberg; the Social Democrats countered by another private army, the Schutzbund. That of the Nationalists was not opposed to a monarchial restoration; it numbered some 60,000 and was better drilled. In the Schutzbund, on the other hand, there were some 100,000 men devoted to the republic;

they knew less about fighting, but they did have arms and they were opposed to reaction.

For several years a rather confused political fight followed, mainly along the lines of city against country. During most of that time the Christian Socialists nominally held the reins of government; but they had little jurisdiction over Vienna; their common ground with Starhemberg was slight, and with the Austrian Nazis they had no common ground whatever.

Soon, as the Nazi propaganda spread in Austria, the Christian Socialists under Dollfuss were confronted with a grave decision. Their control of the country was extremely precarious. Dollfuss, an ardent Roman Catholic, was chancellor, and he kept his post by a temporary and tentative alliance with the Social Democrats. The Chancellor sought and obtained the warm friendship of Mussolini as insurance against Hitler and the Nazis, but for it he had to pay a heavy price. The Duce did not like Social Democrats and, to keep the Duce on his side, Dollfuss broke off his alliance with them, and with the help of von Starhemberg established a Christian Socialist dictatorship.

It was not done without severe fighting. The Social Democrats, warned by the example of what had taken place in Germany one year earlier, in 1933, went on general strike. As they did so, Dollfuss sought to disarm them. The Social Democrats thereupon barricaded themselves in the new apartment houses which they had built for the workmen of Vienna and for several days defended them against machine-gun fire. Forced to capitulate, they were disarmed and disbanded and Dollfuss ruled, a Fascist dictator.

It was a "Christian Corporate State" which Dollfuss set up in this year of 1934 with the cordial approval of Mussolini. The republic vanished and democracy vanished with it. A number of corporations with hand-picked members were organized, and these were to elect a president and to rule the country. A parliament was provided with power of veto over the acts of the corporations but with no power of initiating legislation. The real government was Dollfuss, assisted by Starhemberg.

The new Christian Corporate State, having repulsed an attack from the left (the strike of the Social Democrats), was immediately threatened from the right by the Austrian Nazis. With the backing apparently of Hitler, the Austrian Nazis now tried to destroy the Dollfuss régime. Their coup d'état almost succeeded; desperate Austrian Nazis invaded the chancellory and brutally murdered Dollfuss; the radio was about to announce the new revolution, and Austrian refugees on the border in Bavaria were ready to rush across into Austria.

But the plot failed; Mussolini was furious at the murder of his

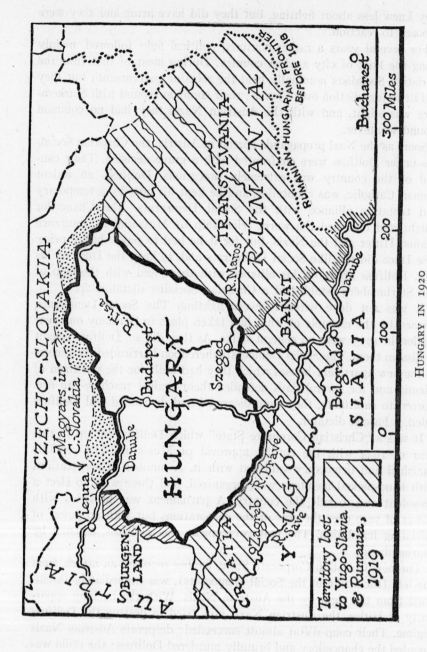

HUNGARY IN 1920

(Reprinted from J. F. Horrabin's *An Atlas of Current Affairs*, by permission of, and special arrangement with, Alfred A. Knopf, Inc., publishers.)

friend Dollfuss, and Hitler at this time was in no condition to oppose the Duce. Starhemberg remained loyal to his late leader and acted promptly. The ringleaders were executed and this curious Christian Fascist state survived the storm. The new chancellor of Austria was Kurt Schuschnigg, and Starhemberg became vice-chancellor.

The dictatorship continued, but it was very weak. The Social Democrats, who might have defended the country against Nazi aggression from Germany, now were no more, and their leaders were in prison or in exile. The Austrian Nazis for the time being had been dispersed or were in jail. But Schuschnigg himself was in the minority and did not dare hold an election; there had not been one since 1930; and Dollfuss, with all his personal charm, had become chancellor with a majority of only one. Schuschnigg had neither charm nor, as events were to prove, the backing of Mussolini. He might have gone ahead without the former but the latter was essential if this tiny Austria was to survive as an independent state. As soon as it suited the Duce to act in conjunction with Hitler, Austria was lost, as we shall note later.

EAST OF AUSTRIA

East of Austria, in Hungary and the Balkan states, the general drift of political life went in the direction of totalitarianism. In Hungary, Yugoslavia, and Greece dictatorship rose in the post-War era, and in Bulgaria and Rumania representative government rested on a very shaky foundation. The discussion of Turkey will be left for the succeeding chapter.

The recent history of Hungary may be briefly noted. Here, as in Austria, a republic was proclaimed at the close of the war. Quickly it was snuffed out by a Communist dictatorship and for nearly six months the red flag flew in Budapest. Then came a counterrevolution, this time to the right, as Admiral Horthy of the old Hapsburg navy set up a restored monarchy. Ever since then (1920) Hungary has been a monarchy of a sort; a monarchy without a king, for Horthy ruled simply as regent; a monarchy limited by a parliament of restricted powers, chosen by a narrow suffrage by voters deprived of the protection of the secret ballot.

Hungary was and is a country of large estates, great landlords, illiterate peasants. The Magyar nobility, retaining its economic and social privileges, was not discontent with the new status quo, that is, within the country. It would not and could not forget the Treaty of Trianon, whereby Hungary had been so tremendously reduced in area, and irredentist ambitions to recover the lost lands showed no signs of abatement with the passing of the years. On the other hand, the government of Hungary was stable as well as arbitrary. Twice did the Magyars' former king, Charles of Hapsburg, lead an expedition to recover his lost throne; twice was he driven back, and even for a while imprisoned. Some day, the Magyars said, they would choose a king; but they were in no hurry to do so, nor were many of them enthusiastic about the House of Hapsburg.

Economically, Hungary was in sounder case than Austria, for whereas both countries contained a large city cut off by tariff boundaries from the outside world, Budapest was not nearly as large as Vienna, and the former city, in addition, was in the midst of a large and fertile agricultural plain. Then, too, the League of Nations was kind to Hungary, and through its agency large sums were granted to rehabilitate the country. Had it not been for two things—the economic depression of the 'thirties and the Nazi régime set up in Germany—domestic politics in Hungary might have remained tranquil. But like all other agricultural lands, Hungary was hard hit by the decline of grain prices which was incidental to the depression; and German Nazis, flushed with victory, lost no time in trying to stir up internal discord in Hungary as they did in Austria.

The Hungarian National Socialists (Nazis) used three arguments to good effect—antisemitism, revenge for Magyar territory seized by Yugoslavia, Czechoslovakia, and Rumania, and the semisocialistic plea that the big estates should be subdivided among the peasantry. Needless to say, the third of these arguments had little weight with the Magyar nobles; and furthermore, since most Magyars, poor and rich, were ardent Catholics, the attitude of German Nazis toward the Church of Rome acted as a brake on the growth of an indigenous Nazi party in Hungary. Nevertheless, the Magyar Nazis increased rapidly in number, particularly in 1938 and 1939, as Germany swallowed up Czechoslovakia, offering as she did so tidbits of that former republic's territory to Hungary.

"The Kingdom of the Serbs, Croats, and Slovenes," or Yugoslavia, was torn by internal dissensions from the very beginning. Serbs and Croats soon found that they could not agree; and the Slovenes, by far the weakest element in this triangular grouping, took sides with the Croats. The Serbs, in the majority, were not content with having their capital, Belgrade, the capital of the new kingdom, and with the acceptance of the Serbian dynasty; they also wanted a unified rather than a federalized constitution. The Croats, proud of their culture and tradition, their use of the Latin rather than Cyrillic alphabet, their religion which was Catholic, not Orthodox, looked down upon the more numerous Serbs and were determined to preserve their own particularism.

What almost at times might be described as undeclared war was waged between Serbs and Croats from 1920 to 1939. In the course of it, King Alexander, taking advantage of the perpetual strife in the Yugoslav Parliament, took the reins in his own hands and ruled for a few years as a despot, pure and undefiled. Finally he relinquished part of his authority to a parliament organized on the model of that of Fascist Italy, in so far that whatever political party won a plurality of seats at an election was guaranteed two-thirds of the final membership. Two political assassinations bespoke the low tone of political life in this Yugoslav kingdom. One was that of the leader of the Croatian Peasant party, the spokesman of regionalism and federation; the other that of Alexander, murdered while visiting France by a member of a secret Croatian society. The Serbs thus had a taste of their own medicine, since a secret pan-Serbian society had been responsible for the murder of the Austrian Archduke in 1914. Alexander's oldest son, eleven years of age, was now proclaimed as Peter II of Yugoslavia, and the government, in the hands of a regency, nominally returned to constitutional methods. The Croats, however, were not content; and as the war-clouds gathered once more over Europe in 1939, they were actively engaged in plots to disrupt by internal revolt this South Slav kingdom, so large in area, so desperately poor, so torn by internal strife.

Rumania, as far as statistics went, emerged from the World War a European state of importance, her area doubled by the annexation of Transylvania, Bukovina, Bessarabia, and a large part of the Banat of Temesvar. She was even larger in size than Italy! But beneath the surface there was discord. Minorities were more troublesome in Rumania than in Czechoslovakia and Yugoslavia; Magyars, Jews, Germans, Ukranians, Russians, and Bulgarians comprised a good quarter of the population; the peasantry, close to Russia and subjected to Communist propaganda, demanded the splitting up of the great landed estates; and as a further source of constant discord there were scandals in the royal family, well aired and well ventilated. When the old King Ferdinand died in 1927 his son and heir, Carol, was living in Paris with a mistress for whom he had sacrificed the throne. The latter's young son Michael was proclaimed king, but before long Carol returned to Bucharest to assume the throne for himself. Unsavory quarrels between the Queen Mother, Marie of Rumania, a granddaughter of Victoria of England; Helen, the queen, daughter of the King of Italy; Magda Lupescu, the mistress; and Carol II of Rumania, crowned in 1930 and a most temperamental sovereign, filled the European press and unsettled Rumania still further. As for the King, he ruled sometimes in accordance with constitutional principles and sometimes not. Between fascism, antisemitism (the Jews were very numerous in Rumania), communism, the "Green International," a term very loosely applied to the spasmodic efforts of landless peasants in southeastern Europe to obtain land, and the endless friction of the divergent minorities, the position of Carol was far from pleasant. That he showed considerable ability in suppressing the "Iron Guards," as the Rumanian Fascists are called, and in keeping an uneasy equilibrium in his distracted country, none could deny.

MINORITIES MAP OF THE BALKANS IN 1938
(Courtesy of the New York *Times*.)

In Bulgaria the forms of constitutional government were preserved for the most part in the intervals between the two World Wars. But the reality was somewhat different from the theory: toward the Yugoslav and Greek frontier there were frequent uprisings of the Bulgarian irredentists who had crossed the frontier in Bulgaria after 1919-20; throughout the rest of Bulgaria Communists were actively at work, and so also the Green International. There were assassinations, bombs were thrown, army officers cashiered, and King Boris was now about to become a dictator and now about to refrain from assuming that dangerous rôle. What might be called a kind of authoritarian democracy characterized the Bulgarian scene, for there continued to be a parliament and within it there were political parties. The only real authority, however, was a group of army officers who pulled the wires in the parliament, their puppet politicians voting in accordance with suggestions, gentle or forceful as the occasion dictated.

Throughout this period Greece swung backward and forward between monarchy and a reputed republicanism, ending up in 1936 under a military dictatorship with General Metaxas at the helm. King Constantine, driven out by the Allies in 1917, came back in triumph to Athens in 1920, only to lose the throne again in 1922 as the result of a disastrous campaign against the Turks (see p. 248). His son, George, succeeded him, only to be deposed in turn, as a republic was proclaimed in 1923. For the next twelve years there was nothing but confusion and disorder, the venerable and now aged Venizelos trying in vain to bring back some semblance of stability. Premier followed premier during this black period, when Venizelos generally was in eclipse and when it seemed at times as though he was the only patriotic Greek. Suddenly in 1935 the country swung to monarchy once more, the exiled King George returning. As far, however, as one may peer beneath the cloudy uncertainties of Greek politics, the King was but a figurehead for the very capable and conservative Metaxas, who ruled with an iron hand until his death in January, 1941.

Throughout all the Balkans there was little evidence of any progress, and none at all of stability during the post-War period. Everywhere there seemed to be a regression to some form of despotism and arbitrary rule. So was it also with various other small countries in Europe, too unimportant for detailed analysis, such as Albania, Portugal, and the tiny independent states south of the Baltic—Estonia, Latvia, and Lithuania. Dictatorships, veiled, open, semi-veiled, were the lot of all of them. Indeed, of the new countries brought into being by the peace treaties of 1919, Finland and Czechoslovakia alone showed signs of progress during these distressing times.

CHAPTER X

ASIA DURING TWENTY YEARS OF ARMISTICE (1919-39)

RAPID change, seething unrest, revolts, revolutions, and a tremendous war (China vs. Japan) were to be the lot of Asia during this interval of twenty years between wars in Europe. Yet the Asiatic picture is more pleasing than the European one, for in Turkey, Persia, Afghanistan, India, and China there seemed always hope of a better day about to dawn as the cry of "Asia for the Asiatics," only raised intermittently before 1914, resounded loud and clear in the two decades after Versailles.

TURKEY, 1919-39

In no country was it raised more successfully than in Turkey. In 1919 the fortunes of the Ottoman Empire seemingly had reached their nadir. Continuously at war since 1911, except for a few months between the second Balkan and the first World War, Turkey seemed done for. The victorious Allies were in possession of Constantinople, of the Tigris-Euphrates Valley, of Palestine and Syria. It never occurred to them that they would have trouble in partitioning the Sultan's realm as they saw fit. They determined that the Turks should be excluded entirely from the Arabian peninsula, the French and the British sharing that enormous area, for the most part divided into various mandates under the League of Nations. Then, by the Treaty of Sèvres (1920) which three Turks were dragooned into signing, Greece was extended eastward to include Thrace and Adrianople so that only a tiny strip of Europe was left to the Turks behind Constantinople. Even that ancient capital of the Ottomans was not given to the Turks in full sovereignty, since a wide zone on either side of the Sea of Marmora was to be controlled by an international commission. Greece was also accorded the choicest part of the western littoral of Asia Minor around Smyrna, where there were many Greeks. Meanwhile, by an Anglo-Franco-Italian agreement, the choicest section of the southern coast (Adalia) was to fall to Italy, and the French were to preëmpt for themselves Cilicia, directly north of Syria. The Turks were to be pushed inland to the upland plateaus and highlands, and not even all of these inferior dis-

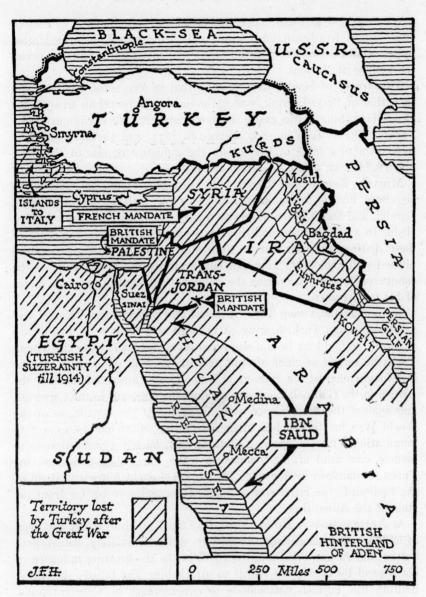

TURKEY'S WAR LOSSES, 1919

(Reprinted from J. F. Horrabin's *An Atlas of Current Affairs*, by permission of, and
special arrangement with, Alfred A. Knopf, Inc., publishers.)

tricts remained to them, since two republics were planned in eastern Asia Minor, Kurdistan, and Armenia, it being hoped that the United States would assume responsibility for the latter as a mandate under the League of Nations.

This treaty of Sèvres, harsher than that of Versailles, harsher even than that of Brest-Litovsk, was well-named "the porcelain treaty," for like Sèvres china it was easily shattered, and that almost immediately. Turkey, like Prussia in 1807, France in 1871, and Germany in 1919, took on a new lease of life, under the guidance of one of the most remarkable men of the twentieth century.

Mustafa Kemal, the "Ghazi," the Victorious One, or Ataturk, as he chose finally to be known, takes rank with Hitler, Mussolini, Gandhi, and Sun Yat-sen in any summary of twentieth century nationalism. In a way his accomplishments were more notable than those of these distinguished gentlemen, since starting with nothing he accomplished well-nigh everything, not simply throwing off the yoke of the conqueror but revolutionizing the religion, the language, the very mores of his countrymen.

In 1908, as the Young Turks marched on Constantinople, Kemal was a colonel in the Turkish army. A brusque and silent man, but highly patriotic, he had long been a suspected revolutionary. Under the Young Turks he served as chief of staff against the Bulgars; before that he had fought against the Italians in Tripoli; and after that against the British in the Gallipoli campaign, against the Russians in the Caucasus, and against the British once more in Syria. At the conclusion of the World War he did his best to persuade the Sultan not to submit to humiliating terms of peace. Failing in this, he left Constantinople to assume command of the gendarmes which the Allies permitted the Turks to maintain in Anatolia. The Sultan thought himself well rid of the firebrand; the latter saw a chance to organize revolt far from the guns of the Allied fleet.

At Angora in Asia Minor, Mustafa Kemal put himself at the head of a Turkish nationalistic movement which ultimately defied both Sultan and Allies. The Sultan tried to break the growing influence of his general by urging the Kurds to attack him, and failed; the Allies, inviting the Turkish nationalists to a conference at Constantinople, arrested and deported many; but they also failed, since the suspicious Kemal refused to attend. Instead, he raised an army of some 25,000 ill-paid and ragged troops and defied all comers.

Whereupon the Allies bethought themselves of the Greeks, and the latter, encouraged by a British loan, drove inland at Kemal from Smyrna with 80,000 soldiers. In 1921, at the Sakkaria River in central Asia Minor, they were met by Kemal, and a fourteen-day battle ended such rosy dreams as King Constantine of Greece might have harbored of a restored Magna Græcia. Almost instantly the wily French saw the writing on the wall and withdrew from Cilicia, and soon afterward the Italians gave up their claims to Adalia.

The Greeks, however, still thought they had the backing of England and continued the fight. Kemal forced them back to the sea. Their retreat became a rout, and early in 1922 they evacuated Smyrna as the Turks swept into that city. England was very angry at both the French and the Turks: at the former because they had given up Cilicia without conferring with the English and because, it was rumored, the thrifty French had sold old uniforms and rifles to Kemal; at the latter because they had humiliated England's friend, Venizelos. England still held the Dardanelles and actually landed troops on the Asiatic side to bar the way to Kemal so that he might have no chance of pursuing the Greeks into Thrace. But Lloyd George thought better of it; the beating of the war drum in 1922 sounded but dimly in the Dominions, and England refused to enforce the Treaty of Sèvres by unilateral action. She tried to settle the Turkish problem by negotiating with the Turkish Sultan, ignoring the Turkish Nationalists led by Kemal; but the latter deposed the Sultan, who fled Constantinople on a British warship. Then England consented to confer with Kemal and his National Parliament. At Lausanne in 1923 a treaty was struck whereby all Anatolia, as well as Constantinople, Adrianople, and eastern Thrace were recognized as integral parts of an independent Turkey, and whereby, in a separate Græco-Turkish convention, all those Greeks within its borders were to be deported to Greece, in exchange for Kemal's promise to accept in Turkey all Turks still remaining in Greece. This same year Turkey became a republic. Its president was Mustafa Kemal, commander of the Turkish army, creator and master of the one political party recognized by Parliament, to all intent and purpose a complete dictator. Thus, within five years after the World War forced a negotiated peace, he drove out the conqueror and restored the independence of his country. A military dictatorship could have been his for the asking but he preferred one of a different sort. In the very year of Lausaunne (1923) a Turkish republic was proclaimed and a constitution adopted. Under it the Ghazi was a man of unique power. He became president of the republic, president of the council of ministers, president of the assembly, and president of the people's party— the only one which the law recognized. Like Mussolini he did not hesitate to fill many offices at the same time, and like Mussolini again he took great delight in introducing startling innovations.

Only in the case of the Ghazi they were more numerous and more fundamental than those introduced in any post-War country with the possible exception of Russia. For the Ghazi was determined to "Westernize" Turkey from the very roots, not simply in laws, religion, and economics but in language, culture, and even clothes.

The sultanate had already been abolished, but the califate remained, and a relative of the ex-Sultan was Calif, still holding, as representative of the Osmanli line, this ecclesiastical primacy honored by a large part of the Moslem world. Mustafa Kemàl determined to divorce his country entirely from any theocratic traditions, and therefore he abolished the califate and drove into exile all remaining members of the Osmanli family. The legal code of Turkey was then transformed. All legal sanctions derived from the Koran and Moslem jurisprudence were ended, and the new Turkey took over the Swiss code as the basis of its civil law, its criminal being based on legal prescripts drawn from the Italian and German codes, and its commercial law based on the German. At this wholesale destruction of the religious foundations of Turkey, the principal Moslem state, there were loud outcries, and in the east the Kurds rose in rebellion. Speedily they were crushed by an army of 80,000 and the leader of the rebellion executed in the public square of Angora. Turkey was to be a secular state!

Its capital was placed not at Constantinople, henceforth known as Istanbul, but at Angora, renamed, Ankara. This desolate, windswept town in central Asia Minor forthwith became the center from which the ever-restless and ceaselessly active Kemal spread reform after reform among his thirteen million fellow-Turks.

Among these the most striking was the persistent and successful effort to change the costume of the Turks. The red fez, customary head-gear, was abolished, and Turks were compelled to wear hats. First the Ghazi shocked every one by appearing in a Panama; then he introduced the képi, or brimmed cap of the soldier, into the army; then all civil servants were ordered to wear European hats with brims; and finally, all who did not voluntarily adopt the new head-gear were imprisoned. By the same method the salaam or oriental greeting was made illegal, and so also the wearing of veils by women. The personal appearance of the Turks was thus Westernized.

Turkey went Western all the way in regard to women; they were given the franchise; they were elected to Parliament; they were encouraged to enter business; they were forced out of their Eastern seclusion. And all this was done partly by example, partly by statute. The Ghazi was neither anchorite nor puritan, and was much given to cocktail parties and to dances, always, however, with women present. Those who sought his favor copied his manner. Women found it worthwhile to dress according to the latest Parisian fashion and men found that it helped advance their interests to swing their partners. "Oriental music no longer satisfies the Turkish soul," so said the Ghazi, and promptly Oriental music ceased. Soon in this land, where from time immemorial man and woman never walked together in public but always the man in advance, the woman humbly following, mixed classes of boys and girls were studying the nude of both sexes in art schools.

We must change our language, said the Ghazi, as he set the example by taking the name Kemal Ataturk. Arabic words, Greek words, French words must be exorcised from speech and pen. Turkish must be pure; Turkish must no longer be written from right to left but in the reverse or Western fashion; nor were the old characters to be used, for in the West Latin characters were customary. There were not many printing-presses in the country, and such as Turkey did possess had no Latin type; that made no difference; it must be bought. Not many Turks could read and write, and those who could found it irksome to learn the trick all over again. Nevertheless, it had to be done. First, on the postage stamps appeared the new letters; then they blossomed forth again on the paper currency; then it was announced that beginning in 1929 no printed matter might legally appear in Arabic type. Indefatigable in this reform was Ataturk; he gave lessons in the new script to all and sundry; he would stop in the middle of a state ball and with chalk in hand would explain on a blackboard how good Turks must in the future write their letters. His enthusiasm was contagious; all Turkey went to school; and soon books began to appear in purified Turkish, written with Latin characters.

Ataturk was also interested in everything that concerned economics and the physical well-being of his people. He found a country which still plowed with wooden sticks shod with iron, and harrowed with logs weighed down with stones; a country without banking facilities, or railroads worthy the name; disease-ridden, unsanitary, without irrigation, and without manufacturers. Problems like these were grist to Ataturk's mill. Olives and figs, cotton and tobacco were developed by him as staple crops; medical inspections were held; the ravages of syphilis were reduced; agricultural experts were hired; prize cattle were bought; railroads were laid; and the village of Angora grew into the avenue-lined city of Ankara. Nor was defense neglected; the straits were fortified; armaments were bought in both Germany and England with fine impartiality; and a merchant marine was started.

Ataturk planned wisely but he forgot one thing—nature. He lived not only vividly but too richly. Tobacco, wine, women, endless labor, and endless dissipation took heavy toll, and in 1938 he died in his fifty-eighth year.

PALESTINE

Stretching south from Turkey for thousands of miles lay Arabia, for the most part a tremendous desert, with oases here and there and certain fertile strips of land, particularly on the Mediterranean littoral and in the east where the Tigris-Euphrates Valley joined Arabia to the Asiatic mainland. Lost to the Ottoman Empire by the World War, Arabia was in a ferment after it, the scattered nomadic tribesmen who comprised most of its population having in many instances drunk the heady wine of nationalistic aspiration and being quite uncertain what to do next.

Arabian post-War history can scarcely be taken up with the peninsula as a unit, for such a history must inevitably stress growing nationalism; and since there never was an Arabia in the national sense, it is necessary that we turn to certain sections such as Palestine, Syria, and Iraq, and from them perhaps draw some conclusions as to the drift of affairs in the Arab world.

The history of Palestine during the twenty years' armistice between two European wars was confused, hectic, contradictory. In 1917 it was the happy thought of the British government that this ancient foyer of Jewry might become again a Jewish national home, and to make it such the British government publicly pledged itself. In doing so it forgot two important facts: first, that the Arabs in Palestine outnumbered the Jews eight or nine to one; and second, that those Arabs who had enlisted to help the British drive the Turks and Germans back through Palestine and Syria into Asia Minor during the last half of the war considered, rightly or wrongly, that Britain had promised an independent Arab state which would include Palestine. Britain, however, stuck by her word to the Jews. There had been no such formal pledge to the Arabs as there had been to the Jews; and furthermore such assurances as had been given the former were not to be interpreted, so said the British, as including Palestine. There was plenty of room in the peninsula for an independent Arab state without including Palestine, the British asserted; so they went ahead with their plans for a Jewish national home protected by Britain as a mandate under the League of Nations—Britain thus to be trustee for civilization, and incidentally for Jewish Zionists.

When the plans for this new state were published in 1922, both Jews and Arabs were dissatisfied, the former discovering that Britain, with the necessity of mollifying many million Moslems within her empire, had no intention of creating a purely Jewish state; that latter displeased that there was even the rough semblance of one and angry that Sir Herbert Samuel, an English Jew, should be the first governor of what appeared on the surface a British Crown Colony, neither Jewish nor Arab.

In organizing the administration of the mandate, Samuel tried to hold the balance even between Arab and Jew; to his advisory council he named four Moslems, three Christians and three Jews, a fact which pleased neither Jew nor Arab; he limited to a certain degree Jewish immigration, a fact which angered the Jews but did not satisfy the Arabs, who did not want any immigration at all. Before long the British were at their wits' end. It was not that Palestine was unprosperous. London made no charge for the imperial troops which garrisoned the mandate and defense therefore cost nothing. Meanwhile, into the country poured much Jewish money which went for power plants on the Jordan River, for building a new university at Jerusalem, for the construction of a Jewish city at Tel-Aviv on the sea coast, for the purchase of land from Arabs for Jewish agricultural colonies. What caused increased unhappiness and riots, ultimately bordering on civil war, was the conflict between Jewish and Arab nationalisms. The Jewish Zionists, numerous, enthusiastic, and exceedingly well financed, looked forward to the resurrection of a Jewish state; the Arabs, both within Palestine and without, awakening, perhaps, for the first time in their history to a sense of national consciousness, considered Palestine theirs, resented the presence of the Jewish interloper, and opposed all British schemes for the division of power between Jew and Arab.

Manwhile, the immigrants, mainly from Poland and Rumania, increased rapidly, doubling the Jewish population by 1929. The Arabs began to fear for their land, not the wealthy Arabs who sold it to the incomer, but the Arab peasants who found themselves dispossessed by the new owners. These peasants attacked the immigrants and killed many; but the British sent reinforcements to Palestine and preserved order; and as they did so world Jewry continued to pour money into Palestine. That country scarcely felt the depression of the early 'thirties, so great was the influx of new capital; Haifa was made a modern port, and from it, all the way across the desert a pipe-line was laid to Mosul, thus tapping the oil-fields of the upper Euphrates Valley. There was even talk of a railroad to Bagdad.

And still the Jews flocked into Palestine. The advent of Hitler in Germany stimulated their advent greatly, so much so that in 1935 no less than sixty thousand reached the land of promise, and the Jews by that date had increased to almost one-third of the entire population. Thereupon, the next year the Arabs declared a general strike in which a thousand lives were lost.

This resulted in the British sending a Royal Commission to Palestine in 1937 to investigate and to recommend. It produced a voluminous report which angered both Jew and Arab. The Commission proposed that Palestine be divided into two independent countries, one Jewish, one Arab. The mandate of the League of Nations, which Britain held, was to be ended, but the cities of Jerusalem and Bethlehem, sacred to both Jew and Arab as well as to Christian, were to continue under British protection and were to belong to neither of the two new countries.

The report was a counsel of despair. The two new states would be too small to be self-sufficient units, for the total area of even the undivided Palestine was only approximately that of Wales or Vermont. The proposed Jewish state, the smaller in area but with the best land, contained some 300,000 Arabs who would have to be uprooted somehow and placed elsewhere. And even into this Jewish state, immigration on any considerable scale was to be forbidden for a number of years, just at a time when Jews throughout all Central and Eastern Europe were desperately seeking a harbor of refuge. The Arab state suggested would be larger and was promised access to the sea; but that was small comfort to Arab nationalists, who pointed to the original promises made to them by the British high commissioner to Egypt as early as 1915, when they plotted in connivance with him to revolt against Turkey. The report of the Commission glossed over these promises and did not even mention certain British guarantees to prominent Arabs in 1918, assuring them that their political and economic rights would be safeguarded in the new Palestine.

The Arabs now rose in arms and the British found it necessary to dispatch several thousand troops to Palestine. Concentration camps were established, Arabs were deported, sporadic attacks on Jews sternly punished. The partition commission, sent out in 1938 to draw up the boundaries of the two new states (for Britain still clung to the new proposal), gave up its task as hopeless, and a conference of Zionists and Arabs in London in 1939 accomplished just nothing at all. In view of the fast approach of world war in that year, it seemed best to the British to postpone further action, but in the meantime to close all immigration to the land of Canaan for the time being to many thousand Jews who clamored for entrance.

LEBANON AND SYRIA

In 1916 the Russians, French, and British made, as we have seen (p. 105), a secret agreement dividing the Turkish Empire between them. The share allotted to France was generous; it included Lebanon and Syria to the north and east of Palestine, reached deep into Asia Minor still further north, and toward the east even beyond the headwaters of the Tigris. After the war the claims of the French were drastically cut, but they did receive, in the final settlement, Lebanon and Syria as a Class *a* mandate under the League.

For a time it appeared as though France would prove herself even more unsatisfactory as a mandate power in Lebanon and Syria than England in Palestine. There was no Jewish problem to perplex the French, but the Arab nationalism with which they had to deal was at once more vociferous and better organized than Arab nationalism in Palestine, and the French had the added necessity of stepping warily between a great variety of religious faiths, for there were numerous sects of Christians, like the Maronites, and divergent brands of Mohammedanism, such as that professed by the Druses, a warlike, schismatic Moslem tribe, in Lebanon and Syria.

For a good sixteen years after the establishment of the French mandate in 1920 there was serious trouble. Part of it may be traced to the French demand that the mandate should be in the name of two different countries rather than one, for from the beginning the French favored Lebanon, a narrow stretch of territory facing the Mediterranean, over Syria which lay behind it, although neither geographically nor racially was there good reason for so doing.

But there was a reason of another sort. Lebanon, with its capital at Beirut was for the most part Christian, and French influence there had been strong since time immemorial; Syria, on the other hand, was almost entirely Moslem. Therefore the French favored the former land at the expense of the latter, a policy which was shortsighted in the long run, for by enlarging Lebanon as they did, they brought within its boundaries a large group of hostile Moslems, while at the same time, by shutting off Syria from the sea, they antagonized the Moslems residing there and increased the xenophobia already prevalent among them.

Then, too, the French were too eager to gallicize both Lebanon and Syria. They did not realize that paternal methods which succeeded with the barbaric tribes of Northwest Africa were inapplicable to this more settled and more highly developed corner of the Arabian peninsula. The French, for instance, were eager to spread their language through the schools, to teach Arab children to sing the "Marseillaise"; and the more they insisted on planting their own culture down upon the Syrians, the more restless the latter became.

Finally, by 1926, there was open rebellion. It began among the Druses in the hill country and then spread widely. There was fierce fighting in Damascus, the capital of Syria. The French behaved with unpardonable cruelty in that city, bombarding its most crowded quarters both from the air and from the citadel. Thereupon the civilized world was shocked and the French high commissioner was withdrawn. From Paris came orders for a change in policy.

For the next ten years there was constant pressure put upon the French by Arab nationalities to withdraw altogether from Syria, and constant yielding of small points at issue by France. There were arrests, there were strikes, but there was no more open rebellion. Finally, in 1936, the French gave way almost entirely and signed treaties with Lebanon and Syria. In effect these recognized Syria and Lebanon as independent states which were to be admitted to the League of Nations, thus bringing the mandate to an end. The treaties were made for a duration of twenty-five years, and while they were in force France was to be permitted two airplane bases in Syria and the right to station troops in two specified areas; in Lebanon, she retained the right to station troops wherever she saw fit. The final solution, on the whole, was an Arab victory.

IRAQ AND SAUD ARABIA

In 1920, when France received Syria as a mandate, the British obtained another on similar terms—the Tigris-Euphrates Valley with its three important cities, Mosul on the upper Tigris, Bagdad on the middle Tigris, and Basrah sixty miles above the Persian Gulf, at the confluence of the two rivers of ancient Mesopotamia. All indications pointed to a difficult and not too lucrative future for the British in this new outpost of empire. Even as they secured their mandate, a revolt of the native tribesmen kept these trustees of civilization cooped up in the cities. The Arabs had no chance of winning; the British airplanes were a guarantee against that. On the other hand, the pacification of this region, known as Iraq, was very expensive, and the British in 1920 were seeking no further expansion by land or sea. Consequently, a policy of non-intervention with strict economy was adopted.

The boundary of Iraq joined on the west that of the British mandate for Palestine and that of the French for Syria. The eastern part of their Palestine mandate the British early cut off from Palestine proper, renaming it Transjordania. No Jewish immigration was allowed there; some day the British thought it might prove a useful bait to satisfy Arab nationalism, and in the meanwhile it afforded a good stepping-stone of empire, an airplane base on the way to India. Iraq's other western neighbor, Syria, was in the midst of turmoil, for the French were driving out of Damascus, Feisal, a former ally of Britain in the World War who had been chosen King of Syria by local Arabs. Why not then transfer Feisal from Damascus to Bagdad and set up a new kingdom there of Iraq? To do so would relieve the French of further trouble with Feisal, would placate the latter by giving him another throne, would put England in the good graces of the Arab world, and would bring to an end the beastly expense of governing Iraq, for the rebellion there in 1920 had cost Britain £40,000,000.

Feisal, it seemed, was willing to accept an election to the new throne, and was proclaimed king in 1921. His reign lasted twelve years, and fruitful years they turned out to be. It was a desolate region over which he governed and the three million inhabitants of his new kingdom, brutalized by Turkish misrule, occupied a region half desert, half swamp. To imbue them with patriotic spirit for an invented country called for skill, patience, and perseverance. Feisal possessed all three qualities.

Troublesome was the situation in the North, in the neighborhood of Mosul. The population here consisted largely of Kurds, a non-Arab Moslem folk whom Turkey desired to join to their fellow-Kurds in Kurdistan. But it would never do to let go the oil of Mosul, so argued the British admiralty, and Mosul was made an integral part of the new Iraq. But the British had pacified this country very largely by employing as soldiers the Assyrians, supposedly a Christian folk of Nestorian antecedents, and Feisal had both Kurds and Assyrians, unhappy and dissatisfied, to deal with.

He also had to come to terms with the wild tribesmen on his western frontier and particularly with Ibn Saud of the near-by Nedj, a blood enemy of his own father, former ruler of Mecca, and therefore his personal enemy as well. Then, too, there were the British who, though perfectly willing and anxious to surrender their mandate, demanded always a quid pro quo in the way of safeguarding British interests, political, economic, military.

Four different treaties were struck with Britain during Feisal's reign, all of them marking successive stages of devolution on Britain's part, until finally, in 1930, one was drawn up whereby Iraq and Britain became allies in case of future war, the former granting certain facilities in respect to air bases, the latter agreeing to provide officers to train Iraq's army. In 1933 the treaty went into effect, the mandate ended, Iraq became a member of the League of Nations, and Feisal died.

His death was a signal for renewed troubles. The poor Assyrians, having lost their protector, England, crossed the border into Syria looking for new homes. Not finding them, they tried to get back into Iraq and were massacred by the Iraqui. Feisal's young son proved less able than his father, and before long (1936) a military dictator threatened to bring an end to such trifling constitutional guarantees of liberty as Iraq had achieved. He was careful, however, not to interfere with the oil route (Mosul to Haifa via pipe-line), or with the imperial British air route, which went via Jerusalem to Transjordania, through Iraq to India, Singapore, and Australia.

The greater part of Arabia lay far to the south of Palestine, Syria, and Iraq. Here stretched the inhospitable desert over which roamed bands of nomadic Bedouins, loosely—very loosely—belonging to five separate Arab kingdoms, with boundaries ill defined and political authority shifting back and forth like the sands of the desert.

Of the five kingdoms, three were particularly important—the Hedjas to the east of the Red Sea, Nejd in the interior of the peninsula, and Yemen in the southwest corner, bordered by the Red Sea on one side, the Indian Ocean on the other.

Again, of the three kingdoms, that of the Hedjaz seemed the more likely to gain the permanent hegemony over the peninsula; within its borders were the holy places, Mecca and Medina, and over it ruled Husein, father of Feisal of Iraq, and at the time of the World War a firm friend and ally of Britain.

Husein, however, ran into difficulties; he has assumed the califate over the Moslem world without due thought to the susceptibilities of other Arabs to say nothing of Indian Moslems; he was blamed (for no fault of his own) for French activities in Syria and for Jewish activities in Palestine; and ultimately he refused to sign a treaty with Britain because that country demanded that he formally acknowledge the British mandate for Palestine. Therefore, when he lost British support, he could not withstand the energetic Ibn Saud, ruler of Nejd and regions adjacent thereto.

The followers of the latter were puritanical as well as fanatical Arabs; they were Wahabis, Moslem fundamentalists who harked back to the primitive rigors of the Moslem code, and they had no use for the winebibbers of the Hedjaz. Under Ibn Saud they attacked Husein, captured Mecca, and annexed the entire kingdom of the Hedjaz (1926). Shortly after, Ibn Saud led his Wahabis against the Yemen. That kingdom he did not annex, although he absorbed oases adjacent to it. By 1934 the Arab kingdoms had been reduced to two, that of the Hedjaz and Nedj, ruled over by Ibn Saud, and the less important kingdom of the Yemen.

Ibn Saud proved himself a decidedly efficient administrator; he obtained from England recognition of his independence; he entered into treaty relations with other states; he established permanent colonies for wandering tribesmen, trying to teach them to live in houses rather than in tents; and best of all he brought law and order to the caravan routes which traversed the desert, ending brigandage, introducing motor-cars and the wireless.

IRAN

During these troubled years the ancient and sadly harassed Persia blossomed forth as Iran, a proud and at last completely independent country, strongly nationalistic, very wealthy in oil, and under the iron rule of another dictator, Rheza Khan Pahlavi.

Persia suffered severely during the World War. The nationalists, annoyed for many years by Anglo-Russian control of their country, favored the Central Powers. Upon receiving encouragement from the Turks to wage a Holy War on behalf of Islam and aided by German gold, they revolted against the puppet government of Teheran and twice defeated the Russians and the British in the field. Later in the war their cause looked even brighter, when the Bolshevik Revolution of 1917 led to the withdrawal of Russian troops. But the British had their eyes not only on Iraq to the west, but on Afghanistan and Baluchistan to the east. They could not suffer a loss of prestige at this critical moment, and also they had in mind Persian oil. Troops were needed, and troops were sent, and the British were able by 1918 to sweep through Persia, all the way to the Caspian.

In 1919 Persia tried to gain admission to the Versailles Congress, but a British veto barred the way, as in the case of Egypt and Ireland. England was "top dog" and was determined to remain so, for both political and economic reasons. This same year she concluded a treaty with the de facto Persian government, whereby in return for a loan of £2,000,000 she gained the power of dictating the economic and political policies of that country to whatever extent she deemed necessary. The idea that Persia should be given to Britain as a mandate under the League was rejected; the Anglo-Persian treaty was a much simpler method of control.

This treaty was highly unpopular in Persia and almost immediately there was civil war. The Nationalists declared a provisional republic, hoping with Communist aid to drive the British out of the country. They made good headway, but their Russian allies demanded that the red flag be hoisted and the Persians refused. Russia withdrew and the revolt collapsed.

Scarcely, however, had it died down before it was renewed, this time by a nationalist coup d'état which captured Teheran and overthrew the government. The rebels lost no time; they instantly repudiated the British treaty (England this time making no effort to enforce it); they struck a new treaty with Russia, that country voluntarily surrendering all rights obtained in Persia by the Czar; and they drew up a long list of social and political reforms.

Prominent among the rebels was Rheza Kahn Pahlavi, commander of the Persian army and soon the most influential man in the country. As minister of war he worked in close harmony with Dr. Millspaugh, recommended by the American State Department as economic adviser. The two men achieved wonders; they unified the country, balanced the budget, opened schools, built roads. Pahlavi acted as a kind of advanced agent for Millspaugh, conquering and subduing restless tribesmen, the American following after with plans of economic rehabilitation.

Meanwhile, Pahlavi grew more and more popular; in 1923 he became prime minister while still keeping command of the army; in 1926 he deposed the weak and useless Shah and proclaimed himself Shah-in-Shah. Ever since that date the tempo of life in Persia has been speeded up. Pahlavi's career runs parallel in many ways to that of Ataturk: he abolished the old; he introduced the new. He changed the name of Persia to Iran; modern hats had to be worn; women were sent to schools, and coeducational ones, at that; railroads were ordered and a huge railroad station built in the capital (this before the railroads); the Persian language was purified; the priests were held in check (not to the extent that they were in Turkey, for the Persians were more religiously inclined than the Turks); the capitulations were abolished; foreigners lost all power.

Yet between the dictator of the new Iran and his Turkish counterpart one striking difference was to be noted—Pahlavi was the more Asiatic in temper; he insisted on surrounding himself with a good deal of pomp; he was difficult to meet; he always traveled in style, the roads being kept clear of all traffic when he and his retinue made royal progress in their motor cavalcade. Justice was more Oriental in Iran than in Turkey, and men critical of the Shah-in-Shah simply disappeared. Pahlavi was very sensitive to criticism; his private life was hidden; how many children he had was a matter of guesswork.

But he made Iran independent, very much so. He refused to build railroads where the British wanted them; he would not permit the latter to use Iran for their imperial air communications; and what is more he drove a sharp bargain with the Anglo-Persian Oil Company, almost an adjunct of the royal navy. That company was already paying from £1,000,000 to £2,000,000 a year to the treasury of Iran in royalties; but that was not sufficient for Pahlavi. In 1932 he threatened to close down the company altogether. The British appealed to the League of Nations; but Pahlavi was not to be moved; the company must pay a great deal more. It consented to do so, the royalty was changed from a share of the profits to a base rate per ton, and Iran's share of this new-found wealth increased promptly several hundred per cent.

INDIA

The World War gave a tremendous boost to Indian nationalism. The British lost a great deal of prestige when General Townshend surrendered to the Turks in 1916, and the Indians feared their overlords less than before. In addition, the winged words of President Wilson in regard to self-determination had due repercussion in India. Many thousand native Indian troops were serving on the western front, and Indians back home expected England to show her gratitude for Indian support by at least some concessions in the way of political devolution.

They were not altogether disappointed. In 1917 the British government pledged itself to develop in India "self-governing institutions with a view to the progressive realization of responsible government in India as an integral part of the British empire." After the war in 1919 this promise was implemented by what were called the Montague-Chelmsford reforms. They did four things for India: (*a*) they decentralized the government by giving a wider degree of autonomy to the provinces; (*b*) they introduced into the provinces a new constitutional device known as the dyarchy, whereby representative government was permitted in respect to certain limited governmental functions, that is, elected legislative bodies were placed in full control of the administration of forests, sanitation, and so forth, while more important functions, such as those dealing with justice and finance, remained still under the direct supervision of the governor; (*c*) they greatly enlarged the electorate, both for the provincial and the central legislatures; (*d*) they decreased the proportion of nominated members for the upper chamber of the central legislature (the council of state) so that it was slightly under half, and of the lower chamber (the assembly) so that it was about one-third.

These reforms were not ungenerous. The viceroy still held in reserve great power, and the property qualification remained high; but it surely would have been contrary to British precedent to have gone much further at this time. What really caused trouble in India was not the paucity of reform but rather the Rowlatt Bills and Mohandas Gandhi.

The Rowlatt Bills, in force during the war, suspended guarantees of individual liberty, such as the right of habeas corpus and trial by jury, and made it legal for the government of India to deport agitators without trial. That these bills continued to be in force after the peace created a very poor impression in India and aroused the antagonism of Gandhi, soon to be known as the Mahatma, or Holy One.

That emaciated little Hindu lawyer had distinguished himself many years before the war by leading a strike of Hindu coolies in South

Africa to protest against racial discrimination. He was an ardent pleader for Indian nationalism, but believed that it should be won by non-coöperation and non-resistance, not by force. The foolish British forbade him to travel in certain districts of India and put him in jail when he went there. Their doing so led to instant riots, and in view of the dramatic events connected with them, the specific reforms which the British had introduced received little attention.

For Gandhi had captured the imagination of the Hindu peoples. His teachings were summed up in his doctrine of *satyagraha,* or spiritual non-resistance. To practise it, one must (*a*) boycott all government functions, government schools, and law courts; (*b*) one must boycott foreign-made goods and buy only those produced in India. Thus, and thus only, could *swaraj* (self-determination), be secured.

Now between boycott and physical violence there is no necessary connection; none the less, the two are apt to go hand in hand. So it proved in India. The followers of Gandhi were not content to shun cloth made in England; they made bonfires of it. The result was an increase in rioting. Furthermore, it now happened that the more zealous Sikhs, disciples of the Mahatma, attracted the attention of the world by an exhibition of non-violence. Anxious to recover a certain sacred shrine which the government had decided belonged to certain other Sikhs, they advanced on their temple unarmed. Felled to the ground by the laithis (bamboo rods shod with iron) of the police, they continued for six weeks to practise this painful sort of martyrdom. Gandhi, reproaching himself for all acts of violence taking place in India, pleaded guilty of causing them and accepted a jail sentence of six years gratefully.

Meanwhile, the experience of the Indians with popular elections was not altogether happy. The more ardent disciples of the Mahatma boycotted the elections. Other nationalists, however, participated, and were known as Swarajists, standing for independence. For the time being they professed that they would be satisfied with dominion status; but even that was displeasing to the British, who expected a ten-year trial term of the new reforms before further devolution was demanded. The Swarajists, however, were impatient; to annoy the government they threw out the budget, and to carry on administration the viceroy was forced to certify it on his own responsibility. Legally he could do this; but to the nationalists it was high-handed.

India, indeed, presented a complicated and anarchic picture during the middle 'twenties. The nationalists were divided among themselves as to what should be done. Friction between Hindus and Moslems was rife. The Moslems wanted political representation based on communal creeds, not on numbers, for they were in the minority. Hindus, on the

other hand, having a large numerical majority demanded equal electoral districts. The Moslems were poorer than the Hindus and also
less well educated. On the other hand, they came from fighting stock;
at one time they had conquered India, and they felt competent to do so
again. They laughed at many of the sacred tenets of the Hindu faith.
Every year they were accustomed to kill a cow to celebrate the anniversary of the sacrifice of Isaac offered by Abraham. But according to
the Mahatma the cow "is the poem of pity.... She is the mother to
millions of Indian mankind." Little wonder there was strife in "Congress," as the annual convocation of Indian nationalists was called.

Even the Hindus in that congress did not agree among themselves.
Gandhi was not interested in voting and in contesting the political
control of England in Indian legislatures. He put more and more
emphasis on the resuscitation of ancient Hindu culture by trying to
revive the spinning wheel and by manufacturing *khaddar*, home-woven
cloth. The Indian peasant, he argued, was idle for many months in the
year, and if he would spend his time with handloom and spinning wheel
he would get rid of the moneylender, and India would become economically independent of England. He set the example by spinning virtu-
ously, and soon it became fashionable in nationalistic circles to copy
him. One could even pay one's dues to Congress by spinning a certain
quantity of thread, and quickly this return to the primitive made itself
felt by reduced importations of British cloth.

The British, non-plussed, decided in 1927 to send a royal commission
to India to report on progress (if any) and to make recommendations
for the future. The trial period of ten years for the reforms promulgated in 1919 would soon be up and it would be well if full discussion
preceded any further change. Heading the commission was Sir John
Simon, an English Liberal, who with all the other members was immediately boycotted in India. The Nationalists had no grudge against
Simon; the shout, "Simon, go back," simply meant that they were
indignant that native-born Indians had no representation on the commission. The British were logical; they wanted a unanimous report of
some kind and they knew that it would be impossible to get one if
conflicting Indian opinions were represented on the board of inquiry.
But there are times when tact is more important than logic, and for all
the good it did, the commission might just as well never have sailed
from England. Nevertheless, that commission did make a report; in
guarded terms and with many qualifications, it recommended three
things: (*a*) doing away with dyarchy, which it admitted was a failure,
and the substitution for it of greater Indian responsibility in actual
administration; (*b*) a further enlargement of the suffrage, for there
had been only 5,000,000 Indians given the right to vote by the reforms

of 1919, whereas there were over 250,000,000 people in British India alone; (c) decentralization, to be gained by making the provinces more autonomous and by federalizing the whole peninsula, the native princes to give up their independent status.

This was not at all what the nationalists wanted; before the Simon Commission reported at all, most of them had approved in some degree or other of the Nehru constitution drawn up by Congress, which called for complete dominion status and universal suffrage. Until they could approximate this constitution, they were determined to make life in India unpleasant for the British, and in this they were greatly aided by the example of Gandhi, who undertook a dramatic march to the sea to make salt without the payment of the salt tax, thus symbolizing his contempt for British law. It was very little salt that Gandhi made; but the whole world watched him make it. Soon thousands refused to pay taxes and the jails overflowed with protesting Hindus. Acts of violence also took place which Gandhi repudiated; strikes were numerous; bombs were thrown; and an incipient Communist movement arose, not interested in Gandhi's *satyagraha.*

Back in England Ramsay MacDonald, former pacifist, was prime minister. He still had faith in conferences, and round-table discussion became the order of the day. Let the various Indian groups iron out their own difficulties, was his motto, and three of these round-tables were held in 1930, 1931, and 1932. None of them was successful. The Indian princes came, but they were unwilling to surrender the arbitrary power they still held in their own independent states. The Hindus and the Moslems were unable to agree upon any compromise in regard to the basis of representation. And to add to these dissensions, the Hindus could not agree among themselves, for the outcasts, the "Untouchables," as they were called in India, now became articulate. The Untouchables were the lowest of the low, from the Hindu point of view. They compromised the proletariat in the religious and social scale, and very generally in the economic scale as well. But one of their own number had risen in the world, had been well educated at Columbia University, and had become a lawyer at Bombay. This man. Dr. Ambedekar, was now as vociferous as the Moslems in demanding separate representation for the Untouchables; for otherwise, scattered as they were throughout India, they would be at the mercy of the more numerous caste Hindus. It was a stroke of genius for the British to have invited him. Gandhi, recently out of jail as the result of a hunger strike (the British having made the discovery that India was generally more restless with the Mahatma in jail than out of it), came to the second round-table conference. London was intrigued by his loin-cloth and the fact that he brought his own goats from India; but it speedily discovered that while Indians were willing to worship him as a saint, they were unwilling to follow him as a politician. Neither Gandhi nor any one else could bring about an agreement by general consent. All three conferences failed, and the British shrugged their shoulders. They always knew it would be so! If the Indians could not settle their own affairs then the British Parliament must decide what the government of India should be like.

Whereupon, in 1935, a new constitution was promulgated, drawn up by the British alone and certainly an advance in the direction of dominion status, but still far short of it. The new instrument of government followed along the lines suggested by the Simon report: It decentralized India; abolished dyarchy, making all the cabinet ministers in the provinces responsible to their legislatures; gave these legislatures more power, and permitted over thirty million men and women to elect their membership; reorganized the all-Indian legislature by providing for a council of state with 150 elected members chosen indirectly by the provincial legislatures, as opposed to 100 to be appointed by the native princes (should they choose to enter the Indian federation) and 10 nominated by the viceroy. The lower house was to have 250 members, 125 chosen by the princes, the balance elected by 6,000,000 electors. In both the provincial and national legislature, electoral districts were to be based partly on communal representation and partly on population, thus compromising the Hindu-Moslem impasse.

The constitution looked fair enough but there were jokers in it. These were termed, by the British, "safeguards." The lieutenant-governors, placed over the provinces, were removable by the viceroy but not by an adverse vote of their legislatures, the acts of which they could override if they considered it necessary. There were other safeguards in regard to the army, foreign affairs, and finance, the viceroy possessing enormous residual powers in respect to these vital interests should he choose to exercise them.

This, Congress realized; and within that body there was a strong movement to boycott the new constitution. The radicals who favored this line of action were led by Nehru, a left-wing Indian Nationalist who had become almost, if not quite, as popular as Gandhi. Like the Mahatma, he was a Hindu trained in England in the law, but unlike his famous fellow-Indian, he was not interested in religion, and instead of urging a return to the hallowed traditions of Hinduism as did Gandhi, he favored discarding them. Nehru came from a wealthy family on good terms with the British. Not only did he become a radical Nationalist but he persuaded his father to do likewise, and it was the father, not the son, who drew up the Nehru constitution on behalf of Congress. Both father and son suffered imprisonment for the cause and spent all the family wealth. The younger Nehru served almost as many terms in prison as Gandhi himself, for whom he had intense admiration. But the Mahatma was too willing to compromise, so thought the younger Nehru, who became the recognized leader of the left center in the Congress, the extreme left position being occupied by Communists and acknowledged Socialists.

Gandhi, now approaching seventy years of age, might be regarded as the leader of the right center, then somewhat inclined to coöperate with the British. When the new constitution had first been promulgated he had been very indignant because provision had been made in it for separate communal representation of the Untouchables. His reason for so doing was that it was a disgrace for Hindus to admit that there were such people as Untouchables, that separate representation would prevent their merging with other Hindus. So keenly did he feel about this that he began one of his famous fasts. Again the British did not dare permit his death, for they feared the repercussions it might bring. Therefore they compromised once more, and Gandhi ate. Having won this victory the Mahatma was willing to permit his followers to vote, and they did so.

The Indian Congress being more or less evenly divided between the followers of Nehru and those of Gandhi, partial coöperation with the new constitution was undertaken by a sufficient number of Nationalists to enable them to carry the elections in a majority of the provinces. Since that date (1937) there has been continuous friction and unrest. The new constitution is only partially in force, for to complete federation, native states containing fifty-one per cent of the population of non-British India must first ratify it, a consummation which a majority of the Nationalists devoutly hope will never happen. As for Gandhi, his attitude is enigmatic. In 1939, aroused by an act of signal injustice in a native state, he began still another fast, this time, he said, to the death. It was a dramatic way of calling attention to conditions in the native states, for Gandhi was a clever politician as well as religious prophet. As usual the Mahatma judged rightly; this time he had to fast to dangerous lengths, for he was ninety-eight hours without nourishment. And then Britain gave in; the injustice was remedied by advice of the viceroy, and all that was left of the shriveled little mystic scored another victory over the greatest empire the world has seen since Rome.

Irritation against the British in India is still profound. Half of the famous Indian Civil Service, well paid, hard-working, efficient, was to be manned by Indians not later than 1940; but Congress does not see why there should be any British on that particular pay-roll. They point to the great powers held in reserve by the British viceroy, ap-

Ewing Galloway

The Harbor of Hongkong, Developed Mainly by the British. (See page xvi *ante.*)

pointed by England, to the British control of Indian foreign affairs (one hundred per cent), to the British control of the Indian army, and to huge sums remitted every year to Britain in return for British capital invested in India, and to high taxes. Indian taxation is very low per capita compared with other Asiatic countries; but it is a heavy burden for a teeming population on the border-line of starvation. From the point of view of the Congress, the money thus raised should go to rid the land of illiteracy rather than to support a big army.

The British, of course, have an answer to all of these complaints. Without the investment of millions of pounds of British capital in railroads and irrigation projects, famine would be rife in the peninsula, for the railroad has made it possible to move grain to those districts where there is scarcity, and the irrigation engineer has made possible a greater grain supply. The army is large, but India pays nothing for the royal navy, and a strong defense force is needed on the northwest against Afghanistan with Soviet Russia in the background. Furthermore, without the presence of British troops in that army, what chance would 250,000,000 meek Hindus have against 70,000,000 Moslems? High as taxes are in British India, they are much higher in the native states. A good deal of Hindu poverty is caused by regarding the cow as a sacred animal which can never be killed and which must be fed when worthless, as a religious duty. For the good of the Hindu *ryot* (peasant), ignorant and illiterate beyond measure, knowing nothing of Congress or of those educated Hindus who claim to represent them, the British argue that they must continue to control, in part at least, the destinies of the subcontinent. And for the good of their own pocketbooks, to say nothing of their imperial prestige!

So stood the situation as the second World War broke. Congress immediately offered to back Britain, provided dominion status be instantly granted. The British said that was impossible during the war. What happens next in India is on the lap of the gods.

THE FAR EAST

In the Far East, meanwhile, nationalistic fervors and fevers were even more intense than in Central and Western Asia. The essentially disruptive, anarchic, and volcanic qualities of contemporary nationalism were completely unloosed in this part of the world. The xenophobia which aroused the passions of Turks, Arabs, Persians, and Indians was no less noticeable here than elsewhere, but combined with it there arose such a terrific clash between Chinese and Japanese nationalism that there resulted what the Japanese politely called "incidents" but what the historian calls "war."

A New Conception of the Orient

(From V. Poliakoff's *Europe in the Fourth Dimension*.)

The outbreak of the World War in 1914 in the West was Japan's golden opportunity in the East. At last she was able to revenge herself on the Germans for snatching away the fruits of her victory over China in the nineteenth century; and at the same time she was now free to work her will on China without fear of European interference. Declaring war on Germany, the men of Nippon promptly captured the German colony of Kiauchow, after which they presented in 1915 an ultimatum to the weak and disorganized government of Yuan Shi-kai.

The Chinese yielded to what they considered were twenty-one Japanese demands but what the Japanese ever since have termed the Treaties of 1915, whereby China placed herself pretty thoroughly under the thumb of her island neighbor, ceding to Japan all German concessions in China proper, as well as Russian concessions in Manchuria, while agreeing to accept military and economic advisers from Japan.

The following year Yuan Shi-kai died and chaos dominated the Chinese scene; the radical south revolted from the conservative north; war-lords strove for mastery at Peking, and with fluctuating success one after another sat uneasily on the throne of the Manchus. Before the war was over, China, with the kindly consent of the Japanese, had become one of the Allies. That fact, however, was of little use at the conference table, and China, disgruntled at her inability to get rid of the Japanese stranglehold, refused to sign the Treaty of Versailles. Two years later (1921) at the Washington Conference which we shall discuss later (see p. 286), she was more fortunate; her independence was guaranteed by nine different countries; she was granted the right to increase her tariff; and the Japanese agreed to restore to China the German concessions which they had secured in 1915. But these gains did not stop the spread of anarchy in China, continuous and widespread until the Kuomintang party (southern nationalists) was able to capture Peking in 1929.

Those nationalists were ardent followers of Sun Yat-sen, a capable conspirator but no executive. Before the World War came to a conclusion, he had betaken himself to Canton in the south and had there headed a revolt against the central government. While Dr. Sun lived it met with only local successes, for its leader was more prophet than statesman. In the former rôle, however, he wrote a book of lasting significance to the historian, for it became the Bible of the Kuomintang, and within a decade the most authoritative written word in China.

Dr. Sun's *Three Principles of the People* tries to lay the foundations for a new Chinese society in "nationalism," "democracy," and "social welfare." Individual and family interests must be subordinated to the welfare of the nation—nationalism. The Chinese should never forget that they invented the compass, gunpowder, and a wonderful indigenous architecture of their own; they were just as strong, as intelligent as the peoples of the West, and they must be proud of their past. From the West they should learn the art of government—democracy. That word, to Dr. Sun, was an all-inclusive one, including such concepts as the separation of powers and universal suffrage, and even certain ancient Chinese practices such as civil service examinations, for the West might well profit from Chinese precedents. Then, too, the Chinese must never forget social welfare, which he defines as resting on a social and political platform evolved about one-third from Marxian socialism, one-third from Henry George's land-value theories, and one-third from economic nationalism in respect to protective tariffs. Of these three principles, which was the most important? "Nationalism," asserted the more conservative right-wing members of the Kuomintang; "social welfare," affirmed the left-wing. Seemingly, Dr. Sun sympathized more with the latter, and he entered into negotiations with Soviet Russia, who sent representatives to Canton to drill the Kuomintang army and to capture the Kuomintang mind. They were more successful with the first venture than with the second, for the Kuomintang began to win victories in the field while still torn in regard to ideology.

Dr. Sun died in 1925, honored and revered as the founder of Chinese nationalism, and his mantle descended upon Chiang Kai-shek, a quiet, hard-working, abstemious young soldier, ardent disciple of Sun Yatsen, and commander of the Kuomintang forces. He led the latter to victory after victory as Hankow, Shanghai, Nanking, and Peking fell before his troops. Peking was abandoned and the capital of China was transferred to Nanking. By the end of 1928 the government of the Kuomintang there had been recognized by all the Great Powers and had been admitted to the League of Nations. At last China's main troubles seemed to have ended, for Chiang Kai-shek was a strong and able man, moderate, liberal, devoted to the three principles which were the platform of his party.

There were, however, two obstacles which must first be overcome before China could present a unified front against the foreign capitalist and could call her house her own: (*a*) dissensions in the ranks of the Kuomintang, and (*b*) Japanese ambitions in Manchuria. A part of the Kuomintang, led by its more radical members, among whom Dr. Sun's widow was prominent, was under Soviet influence and rejected Chiang Kai-shek's leadership. At Hankow, well up the Yangtse River it constantly stirred up trouble and virtually threw off its allegiance to Nanking. In Manchuria young Marshal Chang, governor of that province, got in hot water with the Japanese in 1931 so that the latter launched an attack on him which was to prove the beginning of a campaign to conquer a large part of China.

Underwood and Underwood

GENERAL CHIANG KAI-SHEK AND HIS WIFE. (See page xvi *ante*.)

The Japanese were not without legal rights in Manchuria, some of them dating back to the Treaty of Portsmouth, more of them dating to the treaties (or demands?) of 1915. Manchuria had been the original home of the Manchus, who had conquered China, and legally was a part of the Celestial Empire. Nevertheless, within its borders was the Southern Manchurian Railroad, Japanese-owned, and Japan had been granted the right to police that railroad and to develop the economic resources of Manchuria in its vicinity, the Chinese being forbidden to build parallel or competing lines. Japanese colonists also had been granted concessions in the country and Japan had received recognition of extra-territorial rights there which, as interpreted by her, carried with them authority not only to try cases involving Japanese citizens but also to protect the latter by Japanese police.

All these special privileges the Japanese had been able to enforce without too much difficulty after the war, because old Marshal Chang, warlord and governor, had been conciliatory toward Japan. But the elder Chang died in 1928 and his son, the younger Chang, was not only a Chinese nationalist but an adherent of the Kuomintang and of Chiang Kai-shek. As such, he adopted an anti-Japanese policy, trying to prevent Japan from expanding further, interfering with Japanese colonists, and even defying the Japanese military when their activities became too pronounced.

Therefore it happened that there was an "incident." It took the form of an explosion on the Southern Manchurian Railroad, caused, so claimed the Japanese, by the soldiers of Chang. A section of track supposedly was destroyed—supposedly, because the through express passing there shortly after was only a little late at its destination. But the incident was all that was needed. Immediately, the arsenal at Mukden in which slept the soldiers of Chang was rushed by the Japanese, and the Chinese garrison made prisoners, after which Japan proceeded to flood Manchuria with her own troops.

There was no use in China's fighting, and so she appealed to the League of Nations of which both she and Japan were members. That body investigated at length, its committees visiting China, Japan, Manchuria, interviewing both Chinese and Japanese authorities, passing over their testimony to the opposition for rejoinders and surrejoinders, and making a unanimous report signed by a German, an Englishman, an Italian, a Frenchman, and an American, a report accepted by the League (Siam not voting).

This Lytton Report acknowledged that although China held sovereignty over Manchuria that province could not be administered as a part of China since Japan held legal rights there. On the other hand it accused Japan of violating the Nine Power Treaty of 1921, of violating the Briand Kellogg international peace treaty, of violating the covenant of the League of Nations.

Japan already had virtually reduced Manchuria to a Japanese dependency by setting up a puppet ruler, and now in 1932 she re-

COAL PRODUCTION

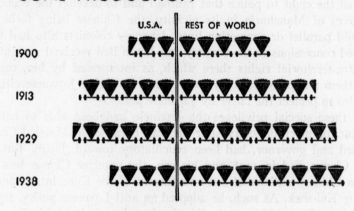

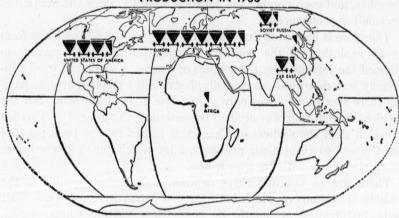

Each symbol represents 100 million long tons

(From Casner and Peattie, *Exploring Geography* [Harcourt, Brace and Co., 1937], courtesy of the Pictograph Corporation.)

nounced the League and all its works, resigning from that body (see p. 285). Manchukuo, she claimed, was an independent country. Did it not have a flag, a capital, even an emperor—no less a person than Mr. Henry Pu-yi, the last Manchu Emperor of China, now restored to a part of his ancient heritage by popular demand? This gentleman had, indeed, been elevated to the peacock throne in Peking at the age of three, only to be driven out in a few years by the Chinese Revolution of 1911. He had lived in exile most of his life, and was a quiet, demure young man about thirty years old when luck and Nippon made him emperor again—a most convenient puppet, so the Japanese thought. Surrounded by Japanese officials and advisers, and by the Japanese army, he was circumspect in behavior—he had to be!

From 1931 to the present there has not been even the semblance of order in the Far East. Russia, England, and the United States all took a hand to some extent in the devil's brew constantly boiling over in that part of the world. Russia, it must be remembered, came close to circling Manchukuo; her maritime provinces bounded that new country on the east, as did Siberia on the north and northwest. Then, too, the Soviets were deeply interested in Outer Mongolia, the northwestern part of China, due west of Manchukuo. Outer Mongolia had become virtually independent of China and established within its steppes was a semi-Communist government in close military alliance with Moscow. From 1936, the date of that alliance, there have been sporadic "incidents" on Manchukuo's western and eastern borders. To separate rumor from fact in regard to them is impossible; but armed encounters have been numerous between Japanese and Russian patrols, and occasional skirmishes have at times assumed the proportion of little battles.

England, too, was concerned, primarily on account of her immense financial interests in the Yangtse Valley radiating out from Shanghai and those centering around Hongkong and Canton, further to the south. With the United States, trade was less an issue, for American investments in China were small compared with those of Britain. On the other hand, American educational institutions had spread out across a large part of China and a great many of the leading Chinese Nationalists had been educated in the United States—facts which drew the American people much closer to the fray than they otherwise would have been.

But the protagonists have been China and Japan. A relatively weak but ever-growing nationalism, that of China, was challenged in one form or another by the most virulent and most concentrated nationalism that the world has ever encountered—that of the chauvinistic Japanese Empire.

In China, Chiang Kai-shek's problem was extremely difficult; at one and the same time he was confronted with an internal Communist civil war and by incessant Japanese nibbling at the frontiers of his country. For a number of years it seemed difficult to discover which of these two dangers he considered the more serious. He was conservative by nature, and by marriage connected with the famous and wealthy Soong family, who, aside from his sister-in-law, the widow of Dr. Sun, believed that Chinese nationalism stood to gain more by accepting loans from capitalistic countries than by relying on hypothetical aid from the Soviets; on the other hand, it was impossible to contend with the Japanese without a united country behind him, and to gain that the Communists must be either conciliated or hunted down and destroyed.

The best Chinese weapon for fighting Japan at first seemed the boycott. Its inauguration in 1931 led to the death of certain Japanese citizens in Shanghai and to the bombardment of that city by the Japanese fleet, followed by a land attack of the Japanese army, said to have involved 50,000 troops. Much to the surprise of the world, the latter were withstood for several weeks by the Chinese Nineteenth Route Army. This army, however, came from South China and received no active assistance from Chiang Kai-shek, who believed it was sympathetic toward communism.

The Japanese were aroused and the militarists apparently gained the upper hand at Tokyo. Their entire country, they realized, could be tucked away in the American state of Montana with room to spare. Much of it was mountainous and could not be tilled. Of mineral wealth, oil, and iron, there was very little. The Industrial Revolution had made such rapid progress in the twentieth century that Japan inevitably would go under without raw materials and without foreign markets. And both were to be found across the narrow seas in China. It would be advisable to procure them while Europe was torn with internal strife, inevitably due, as we shall see, to the march forward of fascism.

The Japanese, therefore, wasted no time. In 1933 they invaded Jehol, an ancient Chinese province southwest of Manchukuo but beyond the great wall of China; it was a rich province and might open the way later to Outer Mongolia. Again Chiang Kai-shek took no active steps in opposition, and the Soviet Bear only growled.

During the next three years Japan stretched out her hand over the five northern provinces of China proper, which included Hopei, wherein Peking was located. Bit by bit these provinces were detached from Chinese sovereignty and drawn into the Japanese net. Finally, in 1937, came a new "incident." Japanese forces at the Marco Polo Bridge within ten miles of Peking lost a private (he came back the next day) and in revenge 35,000 Japanese troops advanced from the sea coast toward that city.

This time Chiang Kai-shek was ready to fight. He recently had gone through strange adventures. The Chinese Communists (they were not really Communists at all, in the Moscow sense of that word, but radical democrats mainly interested in peasant proprietorship and the end of

landlordism) had moved in a dangerous and courageous migration all
the way across China from the low lands of the southeast to the hilly
country of the northwest. Against them Chiang Kai-shek had sent an
army commanded by the young Marshal Chang, late ruler of Manchuria. Then rumor had it that Chang, instead of fighting Communists,
had adopted a friendly attitude toward them. Chiang Kai-shek went

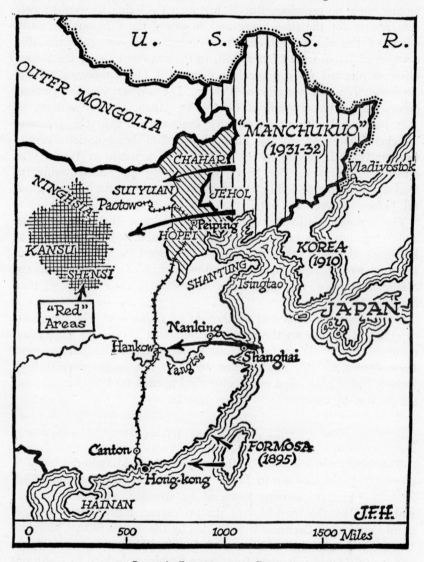

JAPAN'S INVASION OF CHINA

(Reprinted from J. F. Horrabin's *An Atlas of Current Affairs,* by permission of, and
special arrangement with, Alfred A. Knopf, Inc., publishers.)

to investigate. No sooner did this happen than he was kidnapped by Chang, who suggested that Chiang Kai-shek treat the Communists as allies instead of enemies and join with them in driving the Japanese to the sea.

Chiang Kai-shek angrily refused. His wife flew in an airplane to his side, and he returned to Nanking with her and the apologetic Chang, having made no promises. But he had seen the light; he would forget communism for the time being and so would the Communists. Both wings of the old Kuomintang now united with one sole aim, the eviction of Japan from Chinese soil. In the summer of 1937 the Generalissimo plucked up courage; he demanded the withdrawal of the Japanese from the vicinity of Peking. The answer was the prompt occupation of that city and of Tientsin by Japan. The war was on.

It has raged with unabated fury ever since. Again the Japanese attacked Shanghai, but this time Chiang Kai-shek's national army, German-trained, dashed to the defense, and a battle of World War dimensions followed. The Japanese ultimately won, and driving inland up the Yangtse Valley they captured Nanking, the Chinese capital, before the year was out.

The Chinese Nationalists, however, abandoned that city in time, and retreating still farther up the river established their capital at Hankow. The next year the Japanese continued the chase; they captured Hankow; they captured Canton, source of munitions for the Nationalists by way of Hongkong. According to their reckoning they had won the war.

But Chiang Kai-shek had no thought of giving over. He moved his capital still farther up the river to Chungking in western China and encouraged guerrilla warfare against the enemy from within their own lines. Munitions still reached him by a narrow-gauge railroad from French Indo-China, by a new motor road opened up from Burma, and all the way by caravan from Soviet Russia.

RISE OF JAPANESE FASCISM

The speedy victories won by the soldiers of the Mikado did much to speed the rise of fascism in Japan. As in Germany it was semi-socialistic in character, deriving much of its strength from army officers embittered by the hardships of the proletariat from which many of them came; as in Germany it was aided by the discovery that bluff and bluster in foreign policy bore good fruit and brought easy victory; and, as in Germany it grew from roots deeply embedded in traditions of racial grandeur.

The world economic depression of 1930-1933 brought sharp declines in agricultural prices in Japan as elsewhere but no decline in taxation. Japanese farmers sank deeper and deeper into debt. Those who were small landlords were almost as hard hit as their tenants; they were either forced to sell their tiny estates to mortgage banks or else to raise the rent of the miniature farms which they sublet to peasants. The latter were already living on such a narrow margin as to barely keep alive; now they were driven in many instances to sell their daughters into virtual slavery by apprenticing them to mill owners in the big cities. The introduction of cheap competitive farm labor from Korea added to these troubles, and the ground was well laid for sowing seeds of discontent among the soldiers, quite willing to believe that Japan's woes were due to wealthy shipping, manufacturing and banking interests, pretending that they loved Japan and international peace, but with hearts focussed on the pocketbook.

Bluff and bluster in foreign relations worked; that was Japan's experience. The world let her do what she wished in China. One country, and one only, was not easy to deal with—Soviet Russia. But when Japan demanded possession of the Chinese Eastern railroad which crossed Manchuria and was half owned by Russia, she found Stalin willing to sell out at a ridiculously low price. Twice after that she tested Stalin's willingness to fight and twice to her surprise she found him ready to do so. In 1938 the soldiers of the Mikado charged up Changkufing Hill to the south of Vladivostok and just within the borders of Russia's Maritime Province, only to be hurled back with heavy loss. One year later they invaded the Mongolian People's Republic (in military alliance with the Soviets) and after a sharp battle were defeated by the Red army. Russia patently would have to be watched, and presumably on that account Japan joined with Germany in an anticomintern pact in 1936.

But the British and the Americans the Japanese feared not at all; why should they? In 1937 they sunk the small American gunboat, *Panay,* in the Yangtse and shelled the survivors as they sought refuge in the reeds on the river bank. Nothing happened. True, the Japanese government promptly apologized and paid an indemnity, and the Japanese people subscribed some $2,000,000 for the survivors, money paid by us to the Japanese Red Cross. But the Japanese militarists found out what they wanted, namely that we were not greatly exercised by this act of war; and, what is more, we were utterly unwilling to take any joint action with Britain when her gunboat, the *Lady Bird,* was shelled with impunity. Roosevelt was powerless to check the rising power of the Rising Sun. He did refuse to proclaim our neutrality laws as applicable to the Far East, and this he could do since the Japanese had refused to admit that they were waging war in China. But in all other respects he was at the mercy of an isolationist Congress. Japan had violated the Nine Power Treaty which she signed at Washington in 1922, guaranteeing the status quo in the Orient, and the Kellogg Peace Pact which she signed later, together with almost every country on the globe, outlawing war; but when our state department made the slightest move to implement these international agreements it was accused of complicity with "the international intriguers of Geneva," that is, the League of Nations. The isolationists even tried to go farther; they almost succeeded in gaining the approval of the House of Representatives for the Ludlow amendment which would have deprived Congress of the right to declare war except in case of actual invasion of the United States. This was an oblique way of hitting at the President, and was so understood not only in this country but also in Japan. It was an indirect way of saying to all and sundry that it would be fairly safe for venturesome countries to defy the warnings of our chief executive. Yet the amendment was only defeated 209-188.

Meanwhile, without the support of the United States, Britain was as powerless as Roosevelt to curb the predatory Japanese, a fact which they gleefully recognized in 1939 when they blockaded and maltreated beyond the bounds of decency British nationals in Tientsin. All in all, strong-armed methods worked abroad.

And they also worked at home. In the period between the two World Wars no less than five statesmen who urged conciliatory and liberal policies were assassinated by patriotic cutthroats, members of secret Fascist societies, the best known of which was the Black Dragon; and prominent business men like Baron Dan of the House of Mitsui were either murdered or else compelled to hire bodyguards and to wear steel vests, even while playing tennis. These societies, gaining more power, were back of an open rebellion in Tokyo which, led by two young army officers, threatened in 1936 in the name of the Emperor to destroy Parliamentary government completely. The mutineers surrendered and a few were punished. Nevertheless, this mutiny was only suppressed on the surface; it really won the victory, for Parliamentary government (never very strong in Japan) grew steadily weaker. Ever since 1936, militarism has been in the saddle, and a military cabal has been either sub-rosa or openly in control of Japan's destinies.

And it was a fascist militarism, quite similar to German fascism in that both countries tremendous emphasis was laid on traditions of racial glory and queer hypotheses of racial purity. The Japanese claimed to be descended from the Sun Goddess who gave birth to the Japanese Islands and to a parent of the first Japanese Emperor. Since all Japanese are considered relatives of the first Emperor, all Japanese are blood brothers, and all Japanese are divine. In both Japan and

Germany the sacredness of the blood has been mystically elaborated; but in the former country it has not been so essential to twist and to torture anthropological data to prove the impossible. In Japan it is a matter of faith, not one for laboratory analysis. To some historians, and particularly those who like to indict an entire nation, it has always been a matter of faith in Japan, and in a sense they are correct since the animistic aspects of Japanese tradition did not die out completely when Japan adopted western ideas in the late nineteenth century. Presumably, however, if they did not die out, they did die down, so as to be to the better educated Japanese a mere quaint survival. It suited the Japanese fascist to revive this thing, to pump fresh enthusiasm into it. They were altogether successful.

In 1927, a certain Baron Tanaka is said to have presented the Mikado on the behalf of Japanese officers in Manchuria a memorial to the effect that the conquest of Manchuria was a necessary prelude to the conquest of China, that "in the future if we want to conquer China we must first crush the United States." The authenticity of this memorial has been questioned and its existence cannot be proved. But be that as it may, as soon as Japanese statesmen and publicists prattled of the Great East Asia Co-Prosperity Sphere (by which they meant that they intended to make themselves supreme in the Far East while Europe was engaged in the second World War), war between Japan and the United States became inevitable.

CHAPTER XI

FROM RUHR TO PRAGUE (1923-39)

FRANCE had Germany by the throat in 1923. The Ruhr was in her hands, the German mark was tumbling to destruction, and French predominance in Europe seemed assured. It would have needed a bold prophet then to have proclaimed the re-suscitation of the Reich, the challenging of the conqueror within ten years, and the union of Germany and Austria within fifteen—a more powerful empire than that made by Bismarck. Nevertheless, kaleidoscopic changes in international politics brought this about, and in the autumn of 1938 a prime minister of France and a prime minister of England were to plead, and to plead in vain, with a German Fuehrer in South Germany that he withhold his heavy hand from a country created and guaranteed by the Versailles pacts. Rôles were now quite reversed; it was Germany and not France that held the hegemony of Europe!

The factors which underlay this extraordinary reverse were these: the financial settlements made by the Dawes and Young Plans which, unintentionally and indirectly, strengthened Germany enormously; the impotency of the League of Nations; the procrastination of the Great Powers in implementing the disarmament clauses of the Versailles treaty; American isolationists; repudiation of agreements, first by Japan and then by Italy; the superb timing of German foreign policy by Hitler; the Spanish civil war; the unwillingness of France and England to coöperate with one another until a rearmed, confident, and alert Germany was finally planted on the bastions of Czechoslovakia, master now of Central Europe; the fact that there were approximately 80,000,000 Germans in Europe, the largest cohesive national group to be found there if we except Russia; and the social tensions of this period, which affected not only the rise and the achievements of the Fascists and Nazis but also the attitude of the capitalistic democracies toward fascism, many leaders of the democracies shaping their policies on the belief that fascism and national socialism were simply uncouth ways of putting down communism.

FINANCE

The war-weary legions of the French Republic withdrew from the Ruhr Valley in 1924. Seemingly, they had won a victory; they had not been able to operate the industrial plants of Germany but they had forced that country to its knees and to an acceptance of the Dawes Plan, which, in essence, amounted to a kind of international receivership in bankruptcy, whereby Germany would have to pay France huge sums for an indefinite number of years. The details of the plan and of its successor, the Young Plan have been described already. Both plans operated successfully for a season, but owing to one reason alone—the lending of fresh money to Germany. The loans were made partly by the English, more largely by the Americans, childishly believing the fairy stories of their bankers, who, in the lush decade of easy money in the 'twenties, seem to have lost their heads altogether. In addition to several hundred million dollars lent the German government, private investments amounting to some $5,000,000,000 were made in European securities, mainly German, only stopped in 1929 by the orgy of speculation on the New York Stock Market of that year and the subsequent crash. Money began to go round and round in a kind of circle, from England and America to Germany, from Germany to England and France in reparations, from England and France to America in war-debt payments. But always more money stayed in Germany than was paid out! And this money went, as we have seen, toward building new German steamships, new German factories, new German machinery, new German homes and public buildings. From the date of the Dawes Plan, 1924, to the Hoover moratorium of 1931, Germany paid handsomely on her reparation account; but in terms of dollars she received more than she spent. Terrible as was the economic disaster which overwhelmed her in 1923, her complete bankruptcy was not without compensation. By wiping out all internal debt, the Reich was able to start afresh with a new currency, owing no money to her own citizens; but both France and England labored under colossal internal debts inherited from the World War and before it.

THE LEAGUE OF NATIONS

Meanwhile, from the very start, the League of Nations proved an impotent agency for world peace. In dealing with certain weak states it exerted its authority manfully. In a dispute between Turkey and Britain over the oil lands of Mosul there was a League decision in favor of Britain, and Turkey yielded peacefully enough. In a dispute between Sweden and Finland over the Aland Islands there was a

WORLD GOLD RESERVES

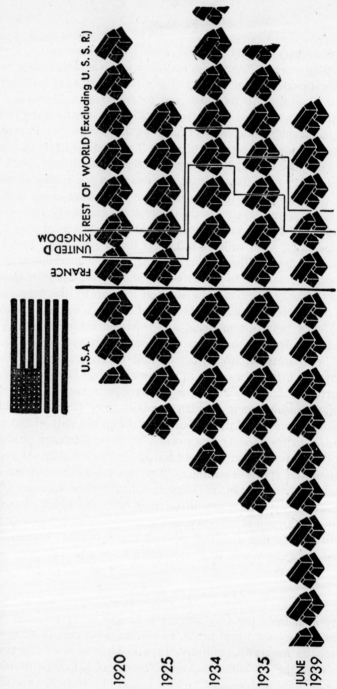

1920

1925

1934

1935

JUNE 1939

U.S.A.

FRANCE
UNITED KINGDOM
REST OF WORLD (Excluding U. S. S. R.)

Each symbol represents 1 billion dollars of old gold content

(From the Pictograph Corporation.)

decision in favor of Finland, and Sweden gave way. And when Yugo-slavia threatened Albania in 1921, talk of sanctions at Geneva stayed the hand of Yugoslavia. The League also kept peace between Greece and Bulgaria, and did useful work in regard to international health, in codifying laws, and bringing about international agreements in regard to opium, the white-slave traffic, and the hours of labor.

But when it came to curbing the will of any Great Power, Geneva failed dismally. Poland seized Vilna in Lithuania, and despite the pro-tests of the League nothing happened. It was not that Poland was a great power, she was not; but Poland was backed by France! Mus-solini, as early as 1923, tested the temper of Geneva, and to his own satisfaction. He bombarded the Greek island of Corfu, killing many Greek citizens—this despite the fact that Greece was a member of the League. The Duce refused to acknowledge that Geneva had any right at all to intervene between Italy and Greece, the plain wording of the Covenant to the contrary.

The disabilities under which the League labored were many, but perhaps the two most prominent were that it had no teeth whereby its decisions might be enforced, and unanimous action on the part of the Council of the League was necessary even to obtain decisions. France was a permanent member of that Council and France was always alert lest the peace settlements of 1919 be weakened. Therefore, Geneva tended to become an agency for perpetuating those settlements rather than for readjusting them.

For two or three years after the invasion of the Ruhr it seemed pos-sible that the machinery of the League might be so changed as to make that body a real agency to insure real peace. Scarcely had the ink dried upon the bankers' agreement (the Dawes Plan) than the French and British governments made a brave effort to stop the gaps in the Cove-nant and to outlaw war. They did succeed in getting the League to accept what was called the "Geneva Protocol" which gave teeth to the Council of the League, enabling it to compel arbitration, "to forbid mobilization, or to impose an armistice." This protocol defined the aggressor in specific terms and provided for outlawing him. At last France had what she wanted, security. And England agreed to give it to her.

But before Parliament ratified the protocol, Ramsay MacDonald was out as prime minister and Baldwin was in. The British Tories would have none of the protocol. Austen Chamberlain, brother of Neville, was British foreign secretary, and he scented commitments which he was unwilling for his country to make. The chief agency for enforcing the future decisions of the League would be, in his opinion, the royal navy, for even if the method of enforcement took the mild form of economic sanctions, it would be sea power in the last analysis which would enforce them. England, therefore, decided to keep her fleet to fight her own battles, and consequently the protocol never was ratified.

Despite this drawback, the cause of international peace guaranteed by a league made headway. England, following the policy of Pitt in Napoleonic times, was willing to make local commitments and so, too, it seems, were France and Germany. In 1925 Stresemann, the German foreign secretary, Austen Chamberlain for England, and Briand for France met at Locarno in Switzerland. From this conference, which was a very friendly one, emerged the Locarno treaties by which Belgium, England, France, Italy, and Germany guaranteed the existing frontiers between Belgium and Germany and those between France and Germany. The demilitarization of Germany for fifty kilometers east of the Rhine was agreed to, and a permanent place on the Council of the League of Nations was to be given Germany. That country also agreed to arbitrate any disputes she might have with Poland and Czechoslovakia. She reserved the right to seek peaceful changes in her eastern frontier, but her western one she accepted as permanent. In case there should be a flagrant violation of these sacrosanct boundaries in the West, there was to be immediate action taken by the signatories; in case of doubt the Council of the League was to determine what should be done.

With the signing of the Locarno treaties the world breathed easier. There were, of course, a number of problems yet unsolved; there was as yet no guarantee of Europe's eastern boundaries, for although everyone promised not to go to war over them, that was not very specific; there was no assurance that Germany's permanent seat on the Council would carry with it colonial mandates; there was no time limit set for Germany's payments under the Dawes Plan; and, possibly even more important, there was no strengthening of the machinery of the League of Nations, aside from the presence of Germany on that body, and no indication that the pledges given and taken at Versailles in regard to future disarmament would be implemented. A local and regional pact had been drawn up, and an important one. That was all.

Within five years dark clouds settled down again upon Europe. One of them was the disastrous and complete failure of Geneva to function in a Far Eastern dispute, resulting in Japan's resignation from the League. Another was the equally disastrous and equally complete failure to bring about disarmament, resulting in Germany's withdrawing from the League, which, from now on, despite the subsequent adhesion of Russia, grew gradually less and less influential.

The sudden flooding of Manchuria in 1931 by Japanese troops we have already described (see p. 271). Almost instantly China complained to the Council of the League, which called upon both China and Japan to withdraw their soldiers from the disputed areas. Japan refused, asserting that negotiations and a settlement must come first. Weeks were spent in argument and finally a suggestion of Japan's was accepted, the sending of a commission of the League to the Far East.

In the interim came the Japanese attack on Shanghai, and immediately China made a new appeal to the Council and, when that body did nothing, to the Assembly. Fifty nations attended the 1932 meeting of the Assembly which appointed a committee of nineteen to deal with the Shanghai incident. Its report called for the withdrawal of the Japanese troops from Shanghai, and Japan complied.

The commission of the League sent to the Far East reported this same year. It disputed some of the Chinese claims but leaned very heavily against those of Japan, called for the recognition of Chinese sovereignty (with limitations) in Manchuria, and for the strict enforcement of three treaties: the Covenant of the League of Nations of which both Japan and China were members, the Nine-Power Treaty of the Washington Conference of 1922, and the Kellogg-Briand Pact of Paris of 1928, whereby war was denounced ultimately by almost every country in the world as an instrument of national policy.

The Committee of Nineteen now swung into action, asking for a conciliation commission on which both Russia and the United States were to be represented. Japan refused to accept this offer, whereupon the committee reported to the Assembly against the actions of that country in the Far East in no uncertain language, recommending that all nations should refuse to recognize the Japanese puppet state of Manchukuo. The League accepted the report and Japan withdrew from Geneva. She had torn up the Covenant and nothing happened! Reliance upon the Covenant of the League of Nations had proved useless in a real emergency. In the few years intervening before the second World War it was to prove so again and again.

DISARMAMENT

Number four of the fourteen points had been quite specific in regard to disarmament. "Adequate guarantees," it said, "given and taken that national armaments will be reduced to the lowest point consistent with domestic safety." But in regard to Germany alone had any such guarantees been enforced; the German army had been reduced to 100,000 men and the German navy had been rendered negligible. But how about the other signatories of the Versailles Treaty?

They did do something in regard to naval disarmament in the Wash-

A COMPARISON OF THE NAVAL TONNAGE OF THE MAJOR POWERS

		BATTLESHIPS	AIRCRAFT CARRIERS	CRUISERS	DESTROYERS	SUBMARINES	TOTALS
BRITAIN	BUILT	16 / 514,550	5 / 91,900	62 / 446,415	219 / 285,808	48 / 50,570	1,389,243
	BUILDING	7 / 265,000	6 / 138,000	23 / 158,500	?	30 / 20,260	581,760? / 1,971,003?
UNITED STATES	BUILT	15 / 464,300	6 / 134,800	37 / 328,975	153 / 210,910	102 / 102,060	1,241,045
	BUILDING	10 / 390,000	5 / 125,800	21 / 206,000	57 / 104,950	40 / 59,050	885,800 / 2,126,845
JAPAN	BUILT	10 / 301,400	6 / 88,470	39 / 262,565	119 / 154,948	66 / 90,863	898,246
	BUILDING	6 / 240,000?	2 / 30,000?	0 / 17,000?	4 / 6,800?	9 / 4,000?	327,800? / 1,226,046?
GERMANY	BUILT	7 / 135,580	1 / 19,250	4 / 28,000	20-50 / 36,000-90,500	70-130 / 42,000-78,000	306,080
	BUILDING	3 / 115,000	1 / 19,250	8 / 66,000	?	?	200,250? / 506,330?
ITALY	BUILT	6 / 164,488	0	20 / 145,918	125 / 128,954	105 / 80,735	520,095
	BUILDING	2 / 70,000	0	14 / 56,344	12 / 15,200	22 / 24,955	166,499 / 686,594

ESTIMATED PLANE STRENGTH OF THE POWERS

GERMANY	BRITAIN	ITALY	JAPAN	UNITED STATES
14,000-27,000	12,000-15,000	4,000-7,000	4,000-7,000	5,000

(From the New York *Times*, September 8, 1940.)

ington Conference of 1921-22. Britain, the United States, Japan, France, and Italy agreed there to set a ratio for their capital ships at 5: 5: 3: 1.75: 1.75—the ratio to be set in the order of countries named. There was to be no new construction of battle-ships for ten years, and after that date Britain and the United States were to be allowed only a total tonnage of 500,000, Japan of 300,000, and France and Italy of 175,000 respectively.

To bring about this modest limitation, all the signatory powers made sacrifices except Italy. That country was so far short of 175,000 tons and so far behind France in naval equipment that to be placed upon an equality with her Latin neighbor was no hardship for the Italians. The French, on the other hand, saw objections, and refused to agree until the conference applied the ratio only to battle-ships. It was very largely a matter of prestige with the French; they were not building any battle-ships at the time, and were not likely to exceed the 175,000 ton limit anyway. Submarines, however, were another matter; and for them and other small craft they would not accept the ratio.

For the Japanese it was likewise a matter of prestige. Their pride was hurt at accepting a lower ratio than that for the British and the Americans. On the other hand they secured some concessions. They won the right to complete a new battle-ship under construction; and the Americans and the British agreed not to build naval bases within striking distance of the Japanese homeland.

It was not easy for the British to yield parity to the Americans, or to any one else for that matter. Still, two monster British battle-ships were nearing completion and Britain was permitted by the treaty to finish them. With these two ships, capable of sinking anything afloat, she was still mistress of the seas. The Americans, meanwhile, offered to scrap battle-ships which they had commenced to build but which were far short of completion. This was their contribution to world peace.

Even less successful were the conferences held at Geneva in 1927 and at London in 1930. The purpose back of the first was to extend the ratios of the Washington Conference to smaller craft, that of the second to accomplish the same end, and also to provide for the continuation of battle-ship limitation, the earlier treaty running out in 1931. Both conferences were failures. At the first a lively quarrel broke out between American and British admirals as to the size of cruisers. The Americans, having few naval bases, insisted on large cruisers but few in number; the British, well-equipped with naval bases but having a large mercantile marine to protect throughout all the seven seas, wanted small cruisers but many of them. The quarrel was renewed in 1930, this time primarily between France and Italy. The two countries wrangled long and loud, the Italians demanding complete equality with the French in small ships as well as large, the former country unwilling to grant it unless Britain agreed to a Mediterranean Locarno guaranteeing the status quo in that sea. This, Britain would not give unless the United States was willing to commit herself by something more than words to the cause of world peace. At this suggestion the Americans were indignant. They had proposed in 1927 a formal renunciation of offensive war which had been signed willingly enough between 1928 and 1932 by almost every nation (the Kellogg-Briand Peace Pact). What more than this could any one ask of America?

The conference broke up, to meet again in 1930 in London. All that was accomplished then was a highly tentative agreement between the big three naval powers—England, Japan, and the United States—to retain the old ratio (with minor concessions to Japan) for five more years; but even this agreement was contingent upon France and Italy not exceeding their old allotment of tonnage.

And in 1935 even less progress was made. Japan quit this final naval conference in high dudgeon, and so did Italy. The remaining three countries—Britain, the United States, and France—came to a temporary understanding in regard to the size and armament of heavy cruisers and in regard to gun calibers. But the time limits set by the earlier treaties had now elapsed and the tide of human affairs was already setting toward the second World War. One year later Germany was to tear up the Locarno pact which she had signed of her own volition, and German troops would be back again on the Rhine!

Meanwhile, there had been no progress at all in disarmament on land. The League of Nations did nothing in regard to this all-important question until 1926, and then only by the appointment of a commission to consider drafts presented by the British and French governments. The commission could come to no specific agreement. Countries with conscript armies objected to counting their reserves as "effectives"; countries like Germany and England wished to have the reserves included in the total armed force allowed. Some countries, like England and France, were willing enough to reduce expenditures, but countries like the United States where the military budget was high in proportion to the number of enlisted men wanted to reduce the number of soldiers rather than lower the expense of supporting them. The French reverted time and again to the necessity of an international force to compel the observance of such disarmament as should be agreed upon, for the French did not trust the Germans, and above everything else they were concerned about their own security. The "have not" states—such as Italy, Germany, Hungary, and Bulgaria—wished to remake the map of Europe, or at least to modify existing boundaries as part of a scheme for general disarmament. The "haves"—France, Poland, Czechoslovakia, Rumania, and Yugoslavia—preferred to "freeze" European boundaries as they stood, and only to disarm with some assurance that they could retain their wartime gains. In consequence it was not until 1932, fourteen years after the war, that the League finally summoned a world conference on a vital matter which should have been tackled ten years earlier.

Some sixty nations were represented at this conference which, if we include adjournments, lasted for a year and a half. It was a heart-rending affair, since at times it almost seemed as though an agreement could be reached. The Russians professed themselves quite willing to disarm altogether, if the other nations would only do so; the Americans, first under Hoover and then under Roosevelt, withdrew to some extent from their post-war isolationist policy and said that they would be willing to consult as to violations of the Kellogg-Briand Pact of Paris, even if they would not bind themselves to enforce it. The British were eager that aerial warfare be placed under the ban, with a caveat in regard to distant and desolate regions like Afghanistan where the possession of planes made much easier their task of maintaining the Pax Britannica. The French even agreed to a German army equal to their own in Europe, with the caveat that sufficient colonial troops be given to the Tricolor for service in Africa and Asia. Even the Germans finally intimated that they might be willing to wait a few years before insisting on full equality, provided they were permitted to have immediately a limited number of tanks and planes as an indication of good faith and ultimate equality. Now at last it seemed possible to rid the world of at least one nightmare.

When, indeed, the British presented a detailed plan showing how the sum total of men under arms in Europe might be reduced by 450,000, although adding to the armed force of Germany, Austria, Hungary, and Bulgaria 177,000 men, and when the Germans accepted the British plan on principle, hopes ran high.

Suddenly, then, Hitler ordered his representatives back from the conference and withdrew Germany from the League of Nations. He appealed to the German nation for a vote of confidence. He had done his best, he said, to preserve peace, but he would no longer submit to the humiliation of his country. His action was endorsed overwhelmingly at the polls as we have seen (see p. 172), and in the next year the German budget for armaments was published—an increase of three hundred per cent for aircraft (forbidden altogether by the Versailles Treaty) and an increase of over fifty per cent for the army. Disarmament was dead in Europe!

And why? One answer may be found in a table, prepared by the

Carnegie Endowment for International Peace, which shows the following figures in millions of dollars for military and naval purposes:

Country	1914	1931	Percentage
Britain	375	535	+42
France	348	455	+30
Italy	179	258	+44
Japan	95	232	+142
Russia	447	579	+30
Germany	463	170	—60

Geneva had dallied too long with this question, so the Germans thought, and perhaps Geneva really intended to continue the humiliation of Germany by insisting on a far too lengthy trial period. That such presumably was intended would seem to be a fair interpretation placed upon the legalistic phraseology of Sir John Simon, British foreign secretary. Perhaps also Hitler had secret intimation of possible support in the future from Mussolini; perhaps he realized that a quick election on this issue in Germany might endear him so greatly to his German *Volk* that it would be worth while simply from the point of view of domestic politics. At any rate, disarmament was dead; Germany was rearming.

American Isolationists

The rearmament of Germany was a danger signal and so recognized in Europe; but in America Hitler's withdrawal from the League scarcely created a ripple. The reaction against Wilsonian idealism as shown by the 1920 election of Harding grew stronger during the period between the two wars. True, in regard to the Far East we were willing to bring pressure (apart from the boycott and armed force) to preserve the open door in China, and in everything that concerned disarmament, particularly naval, we took a lively interest. We were even willing to have an "observer" present at Geneva to represent the American viewpoint. But throughout this entire period (1920-1939) we refused to make any commitments which might involve us in action, and as the war-clouds gathered in the late 'thirties the United States drew more and more within herself, absorbed in her own domestic crisis, confident that nature protected her by a broad ocean on the east and an even broader one on the west.

The indifference of the United States to the growing power of Nazi Germany was due to many causes but prominent among them were two: we felt that we had been generous and kind to our late allies both in the war and in the settlement of their war debts and we thought them ungrateful; we also harbored the naïve belief that future wars could be voted down, prevented, by merely agreeing not to fight, as though war was a kind of disease, like intemperance, and that taking the pledge might ward off its recurrence.

During the first World War and the armistice period, European governments borrowed from that of the United States $10,338,000,000, and concerning repayment there was much dispute. The British, sagacious in matters of finance, proposed a general cancellation all around; they owed us between four and five billion dollars and they offered to cancel a larger sum owed them by France, Germany, and other countries if we would cancel their indebtedness to us. We rejected their proposal, partly because we considered England's word as good as her bond, partly because we saw in it an effort to tie reparation payments to war debts. Instead, we signed a contract with the British on the basis of reducing interest from five to three per cent, payments to stretch over a period of sixty-two years, and we signed similar agreements with our other debtors, in all cases cutting the interest charges way below three per cent, but in every instance demanding and receiving (on paper) full repayment of principal.

We thought ourselves very generous; Europe thought us avaricious. There was something to be said for both points of view. Most of the money had been loaned before the armistice and when the loans were originally made they were not thought of as ordinary commercial transactions; they were popularly regarded, even in the United States, as part of our contribution to the war effort. We were at war with Germany, and until our soldiers could be trained and sent into battle the Allies would hold the line, aided by our money. Now we wanted it all back!

The only way our former allies could pay us was by gold, by goods, by services, or by getting the money out of Germany. A large share of the world's gold was already in American banks (soon to be buried in the ground in Kentucky), and it was impossible for our debtors to pay in gold. Our high tariff, raised much higher after the war, made it impossible for them to pay in goods. Payment by services rendered would have been possible had we welcomed British and French workmen in our factories; but that solution would have created unemployment in America. The only possible way remaining was to have our debtors pay over to us what they first must garner in from the Germans. But we stoutly insisted that reparations from Germany were none of our affair. We not only did not ask for reparations for ourselves; we considered our former allies greedy, forcing the defeated enemy to pay unjust reparations. Our former allies said, "The money we get from Germany we pay to you. Uncle Sam is the greedy one; he insists on making the Germans sweat." The Americans refused to ac-

UNCLE SAM'S TONIC TALK.

Uncle Sam. "MY POOR DEAR FRIENDS, WHAT HAVE YOU LEARNT FROM THE GREAT WAR? NOTHING!"

Chorus of poor dear Friends "OH, SIR! AT LEAST WE'VE LEARNED WHAT WE OWE TO YOU."

(*Punch*, March 31, 1936. Reprinted by permission of the proprietors of *Punch*.)

knowledge that this was so; they pointed to the secret treaties made during the War for which they were not responsible, to incessant European broils subsequent to that conflict, to huge sums wasted in rearmament, to their own modest demands made on Germany as evidence of their own moral worth.

These debt settlements made bad blood between Europe and America. Calvin Coolidge put it bluntly when he said, "They hired the money didn't they?" It was not so simple: debt contracts running for generations are apt to be voided, since grandchildren are not concerned about debts incurred by their grandfathers, and currencies are apt to fluctuate in value; thus, when the British pound dropped from $4.86 to $4 the British discovered that although they had paid us several hundred million dollars they owed us more in terms of their own currency than before they paid anything at all. To the significance of these facts we were blind, and then as the years passed and the European countries one by one defaulted (except Finland) the ire of Americans at European bad faith mounted higher and higher until in 1934 Congress passed the Johnson act forbidding American loans to foreign governments already in default on payments due the United States.

Meanwhile we celebrated the "outlawing of war" by the Kellogg-Briand Peace Pact, drawn up during the administration of President Coolidge and signed in 1929 by his successor, President Hoover. The original impetus for this unusual document came from Aristide Briand, Premier of France, who thought a public declaration of eternal peace between the United States and France might be useful. The idea was taken up with enthusiasm in the United States and enlarged so as to include all countries. As amended by us it became a general international agreement whereby the signatories (and practically every country in the world signed it) renounced war as an "instrument of national policy" and agreed that all disputes "of whatever nature and of whatever origin" were to be settled by pacific means. The pact was ratified by the United States Senate by practically a unanimous vote.

This Kellogg Pact was our principal contribution to world peace during the hectic years before 1929. As a gesture of friendliness to all the world there was, perhaps, something to be said for it. Since, however, there were no provisos in the pact for its enforcement, the evangelical warmth with which we greeted it was open to question, and herein lay a genuine danger; it led too many Americans to clothe themselves and their country in the righteous garments of peace at far too easy a price.

When the world entered the depression of the 'thirties President Hoover, like a good business man, proposed a one-year moratorium

on all international debts. One year later the Lausanne agreement
virtually ended reparations. Our newspapers were delighted at this
magnanimity displayed toward Germany; but when they discovered
that our allies were only willing to forgive Germany provided we for-
gave them, they were horrified. Hoover, however, realized that there
was a real connection between reparations and war debts whether we
were willing to acknowledge it or not, and he was not unwilling to reopen the debt question at a world economic conference to be held in
London. But before it met, Roosevelt succeeded Hoover, and the
former commenced his long presidential career by siding with the
economic isolationists, thus torpedoing the London conference in 1933.
The President, hypnotized by his theory of the commodity dollar, instructed our representatives to have nothing to do with any program
which led to any international stabilization of currency, a bad omen,
indeed, for future relations between countries. Without such action
there was no sense in holding the conference and it shortly closed its
sessions.

Toward the end of his first administration the President realized
that peace was being rapidly undermined, and ably assisted by Cordell
Hull, secretary of state, did his best to align the United States with
those powers trying to stay the storm cloud of fascism then rising fast
in both Europe and Asia. But he, himself, was blocked by an isolationist Congress. Thus, in 1935 the United States Senate refused to
ratify the World Court Treaty, a most innocuous treaty whereby under
carefully worded reservations the United States agreed to join the
Permanent Court of International Justice. The treaty had been ac-
ceptable to the Senate nine years earlier with five reservations, and of
these, four had been approved *in toto* by the League of Nations. The
fifth had been modified, toned down, and put in formal shape by Elihu
Root. There apparently was no good reason now why the United States
should refrain from joining the other countries of the world in this
limited coöperative enterprise, and few thought that this treaty, endorsed as it was by the President, could fail to pass.

But now isolationists within Congress and without beat old patriotic
tom-toms, once more chanting the Declaration of Independence and
George Washington's Farewell Address. The world court, they said,
was a child of the League and anything sired at Geneva in their eyes
was anathema; the World Court was a political, not a judicial body
and had so shown itself in the decision against Germany in the matter
of an Austro-German customs union (*anschluss*); and people of foreign
origin with unpronounceable names (Senator Huey Long's argument)
might come to sit in judgment on legal disputes concerning the United
States.

In vain was it argued that under the treaty the United States retained the option of resigning from the court if she did not think it advisable to submit to it a case concerning this country. The isolationists still insisted that danger lurked in the treaty. Father Coughlin, radio demagogue, denounced it; lukewarm senators changed their minds; the opposition was noisy, also malignant; and the treaty failed to receive the two-third vote required under the Constitution.

An even more striking illustration of isolationist strength was the way in which Congress tied our country up in so tangled a web of neutrality legislation as to deprive the Executive of much needed liberty of action. We not only forbade the export of arms and ammunition to all nations at war, irrespective of who was the aggressor, we also turned our face completely against the historic American doctrine of the freedom of the seas, supplanting it by a new doctrine, "cash and carry." No longer did we propose to protect our American ships, our American goods, or even our American citizens upon the ocean lanes. What we fought for in the first World War we now renounced. In case of war we would sell only for money paid down and for delivery on this side of the Pacific or Atlantic.

The League of Nations was supposed to enforce peace by inaugurating sanctions, penalties laid down, economic or otherwise, against predatory powers. American foreign policy also envisaged peace, for America at least, by a theory quite different. Our position during the second half of the 'thirties was aptly described by Senator Thomas when he said, "The primary object of sanctions is to stop or prohibit war. The primary object of our neutrality is to keep America out of war. The sanction theory is based upon the acceptance of a moral attitude that war is bad, that it is of universal concern and therefore should be prohibited. The neutrality theory does not consider the moral question nor does it accept the idea of wars being a matter of universal concern. War is not condemned by the law; it is merely assumed to exist. Our neutrality's purpose is one of expediency."

This frank statement in some respects comes close to representing average conviction in the United States. It is somewhat unfair to the isolationist majority. They did not consider "expediency" their watchword; instead what was in their minds was the golden dream of American tradition that this country had been set apart by the Almighty as a haven of refuge from the wickedness of the old world and as a home for the free, the brave, the energetic folk who had cast off forever the effete fetters of Europe. The slogan, "The Yanks are not coming" was not yet posted on American billboards but it was deeply imbedded in the psychology of isolationist America.

In two respects only were the President and Secretary Hull able to dent the prevailing isolationist sentiment. One concerned Latin America. Although Europe was much closer to us than South America, both as regards geography and economic interests, the American people were not opposed to what was called "hemispheric solidarity." Public opinion, decidedly hostile to Roosevelt in all that concerned collective security in Europe, welcomed the President's search for it in Latin America. Roosevelt went to Buenos Aires in 1936 to urge inter-American solidarity, and in 1938 Cordell Hull secured a declaration whereby the Latin American countries joined the United States in favoring joint consultation in case war threatened. Isolationists were quite agreeable to coöperation with South America. They were also willing to spend money on the navy. A few were ardent pacifists and regarded the construction of even a new submarine as a step toward war. But the country at large would not listen to them. The navy was popular, and the President, a big navy man, had no difficulty in procuring funds to augment our fleet.

Europe seemed far away to most Americans. So thoroughgoing, indeed, was reaction in this country against Woodrow Wilson's idealism that many Americans thought on the flimsiest of evidence that our entry into the first World War had been due to hard-boiled munition manufacturers, crafty bankers. Americans were interested in Europe, but at a distance. We were highly critical of the ineptitude of the League of Nations in the Ethiopian crisis, but we had no intention of doing anything ourselves; we denounced the weak-kneed acquiescence of France and England when confronted by the rape of Austria, but we did not regard that dastardly act as our affair; we were wildly indignant at Chamberlain and Bonnet for selling the Czechs down the river, but that America was in any way responsible for Munich never occurred to us. By the middle 'thirties most Americans were too engrossed, anyway, with the industrial depression at home, to take more than an academic interest in Europe, a fact not displeasing to those three desperado countries, Germany, Italy, and Japan.

The International Scene (1934-39)

During the next six years (1934-39), the remaining bulwarks of European peace were swept away, one by one. All the major countries of Western Europe played at cross-purposes with one another, and charges of double-dealing and treachery reverberated back and forth between Berlin, London, Rome, and Paris. "*Homo homini lupus*—man is a wolf to his fellow-man," said the cynics, pointing to treaties broken almost before the ink dried on the parchment, and to bold words no sooner spoken by bewildered statesmen than repudiated by fatuous qualification and contradictory act. With the single exception of the first year, the tide set steadily against the democratic powers, England and France, and in favor of the fascist countries, Germany and Italy. The cynical observer was prompt with his explanation: British Tories and French bourgeois, fearing above everything else the shadow of the Soviet, were willing to jettison the League of Nations and the cause of international peace in the vain hope of protecting their own pocket-books by an ultimate war between Nazis and Russians from which they themselves would be delivered. The accusation is questionable. It can only be defended by drawing up an indictment based on a priori hypotheses, by using historical data for the purposes of a lawyer's brief. There is no such clear trail to be found in the diplomatic labyrinth of these perplexing and confused years. In summing them up, about all we may truthfully say is this: Hitler and Mussolini, leaders of the "have-not" bloc of nations, found by 1935 that they could play ball with each other by alternating pressure on the democracies. The latter, wedded to the status quo, suspicious of one another's good faith (as were Hitler and Mussolini), unwilling to acknowledge harsh truth until directly under their noses, began a disorganized and almost panic-stricken retreat before fascist advance, until Adolf Hitler, in March, 1939, entered the Czech city of Prague at the head of his armed forces, there proudly to prophesy the rebirth of the Holy Roman Empire of the German Nation, the ghost of which (supposedly) had been finally buried by Napoleon in 1806.

Only during the first year was there a temporary check to the forward march of the German Cæsar. The Nazis overreached themselves when they tried to gain Austria in 1934 by a blundering coup d'état which succeeded only in killing Dollfuss and in enraging his friend and champion Mussolini. The Duce was not yet willing to have the swastika fly in Vienna, and Hitler did not dare aid those Austrian Nazi cutthroats who broke into the chancellery and slaughtered in cold blood Austria's diminutive Christian Socialist dictator.

It is true that direct evidence is lacking that connects the German Fuehrer with that vile act. But the German Nazis could not well have been uninformed of Austrian Nazis on Bavarian soil, who had used the radio for a year past to foment revolution in Austria. They must have known of plans to invade that country from Germany at the very moment when the state radio in Vienna, which the insurgents in Vienna had captured, proclamed the downfall of the Dollfuss régime.

In 1935 the German star was in the ascendant. In January came the plebiscite in the Saar which united that valley with the Reich. Within two months followed the proclamation of universal military service in Germany. France and England fumed at this repudiation of

Versailles. The former country sounded out Russia for a mutually defensive pact and signed one in May, 1935. The latter tried to make the best of a bad situation by a unilateral bargain with Hitler. The realistic British knew a *fait accompli* when they met one. Germany had built two pocket battle-ships, as she was entitled to by the Versailles Treaty. Now Britain agreed to her repudiation of that treaty in regard to naval construction, provided Hitler would promise not to build a fleet more than thirty-five per cent as strong as Britain's.

The French were not pleased by this act on the part of their sister democracy. If the Germans built to within thirty-five per cent of the British they would have a larger fleet than France, a fact not forgotten by the French when there were intimations a year or two later that France was reluctant in assisting the British to maintain sanctions against Mussolini in Abyssinia.

But Germany's greatest triumph lay ahead. On Saturday, March 7, 1936 (the Fuehrer was said always to choose Saturdays for his thunderbolts because of the British habit of week-ending), Hitler announced that German troops were crossing the Rhine. "We have no territorial demands to make in Europe," said Hitler, "but the Russian menace is intolerable, and France has broken the Locarno treaty by making a defensive pact with that country."

France had done no such thing. There was nothing in the Locarno Treaty which forbade a defensive pact similar to that made between France and Russia in 1935; and even if there had been room for differences of opinion on that point, the signatories of Locarno had pledged themselves to arbitrate questions which might arise in the future concerning that treaty. Locarno had been freely entered into by Germany and had been guaranteed by her as well as by France, England, Italy, and Belgium.

Hitler had no legal justification for violating this treaty, and to do so was an extremely risky act. His army was still small and not well trained; and France could easily without aid from outside have driven his troops, only 90,000 at the end of a week, back fifty kilometers east of the Rhine where the Germans had promised to keep them. Only the year before, in 1935, Italy, France, and England at a meeting at Stresa in Italy had formally rebuked Germany for rearming, and Italy was supposed to be very angry at the German threat against Austrian independence at the time of the Dollfuss murder. No wonder that Schacht, the German finance minister, Neurath, the foreign secretary, and Blomberg, commander of the German army, advised against Hitler's rash adventure.

But the Fuehrer had an uncanny hunch that no one would challenge him. Had not the British made a bargain with Germany whereby they had insured their naval supremacy? He did not think that they would fight to keep German soldiers away from the Rhine. Italy was already in difficulties over her Abyssinian expedition and there were questions of oil sanctions aired at Geneva; he might be of use to the Duce in regard to these. There remained only France; and with the French alone he was willing to take a chance.

France hesitated and was lost. The Czechs were in alliance with her and would have hit Germany from the south as she struck from the west. It was her golden opportunity, and all she did was to explode verbal bombs! This grave infringement of the Locarno pact most certainly would have to be referred to Geneva, so she said, and when the League acted, then France would act. General mobilization was too expensive at this time, in the opinion of the French. Their frugality was ill timed. Needless to say, the Germans remained, and nothing happened except many and violent protests on the part of almost everybody, the Germans being loudest of all, saying that they would be perfectly willing to retire fifty kilometers east of the French boundary if the French would retire fifty kilometers west of it.

Mussolini and Abyssinia

Japan defied Geneva and departed from the League in 1933; Germany did likewise in 1934. It was now the turn of the Duce to defy that august body. He had done so in 1923 without let or hindrance, and he thought it fairly safe to do so again in regard to Abyssinia.

That country, like Italy, was a member of the League, but it was a wild, barbaric land without means of self-defense; and it was flanked besides by two low-lying coastal Italian colonies, Eritrea on the Red Sea and Italian Somaliland on the Indian Ocean. The two colonies were not worth much, but they might serve as pincers between which Abyssinia might be squeezed and conquered, and thus a sizable empire found for Italy.

Mussolini knew that the League (as such) would not be apt to prevent him. It had already been greatly weakened by the successive withdrawals of Japan and Germany, and the only interference with his schemes of conquest that he might encounter would come from Britain and France. The former country, he estimated, would be the more difficult to deal with. She might suspect him of ulterior designs, the extension, for instance, of an Italian empire all the way across the Nile and Egypt whereby Libya (Tripoli) and his new conquests might be united; she depended somewhat on the waters of the Blue Nile for irrigation of the Sudan and would do so more in the future. A British-constructed dam had been projected for Lake Tana, the headwaters of the Blue Nile, and Tana was in Abyssinia; furthermore, the mistress of the seas was still mistress of the Mediterranean, and an Italian empire to the east of that sea might tempt the Italians to challenge Britain's control of her route to India.

France, of course, would also object, but he was not afraid of France. The tiny French colony of Obok, or French Somaliland, on the Red Sea, lay between the two Italian colonies, and from Djibouti, its capital, ran the only railway to Addis Ababa,, the capital of Abyssinia. The conquest of Abyssinia might threaten the French colony and most certainly would involve readjustments in regard to the railway. Furthermore, there had been friction for many decades between France and Italy over Tunis, and a successful Italian campaign in Abyssinia might make the French fear lest the Italians, on conquest bent, might turn west from Libya as well as east, and take Tunis in their stride.

But France, the Duce knew, had her hands full with a revived Germany. So had Britain, too, for that matter, but Britain's frontier did not run side by side with that of Germany on the Rhine, and Britain had less to fear from hostile Germans in the near future than had France. The British and the French did not see eye to eye on the German menace. There was an influential body of British opinion in favor of coming to terms with Hitler, an opinion which was soon to make itself felt in the Anglo-German naval agreement of 1935. The German Fuehrer had proclaimed after the return of the Saar Valley that he had no further ambitions in the west, but the French did not believe him. With the French concerned first with Germany, the Duce thought that he was fairly safe in attacking Abyssinia.

There is some reason to believe that he intended to attack that country as early as 1933, but it was 1934 before frontier clashes occurred between the tribesmen of the Negus of Abyssinia, the King of Kings, and Italian soldiers in the hinterland of the Italian colony of Eritrea. Ethiopia (to use the new name coming into vogue for Abyssinia) appealed to the League; but Mussolini sent reinforcements to his troops and signed a treaty with the French. The latter did not give the Duce a free hand in Ethiopia, but the treaty with Italy did indicate a certain nervousness on the part of the French and a desire to come to terms with the energetic Duce. By this treaty France ceded to Mussolini a very large acreage in the hinterland of Libya, mostly worthless, while at the same time she granted privileges to Italian settlers in Tunis.

Meanwhile, the League delayed acting on Ethiopia's complaint. An arbitration commission appointed by Geneva decreed with the wisdom of Solomon that no one was responsible for the frontier incident, since it took place in a region where both contestants believed themselves fighting on their own land. Then France and England offered financial aid to Italy in developing the economic resources of Ethiopia, and they got the ruler of that doomed country to consent to this projected exploitation. But this did not please the Duce; he said that he was going to annex part of Ethiopia and that he was determined to set up a protectorate over the rest of that country.

Committees of the League now tried to bring about a compromise

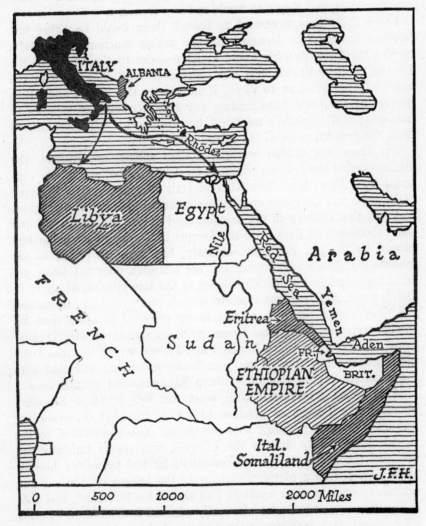

ITALY AND THE RED SEA (1936)

(Reprinted from J. F. Horrabin's *An Atlas of Current Affairs,* by permission of, and special arrangement with, Alfred A. Knopf, Inc., publishers.)

of some sort; but while they talked the Duce acted. In 1935 he began an invasion of Ethiopia both from north and south, and in the autumn captured Adowa, the scene of Italy's debacle in 1896. Geneva now plucked up courage; the council of the League denounced Mussolini as the aggressor and so reported to the Assembly, where by a vote of fifty-one to three, sanctions were invoked—Austria, Hungary, and Albania alone supporting Italy. The fifty-one countries agreed that they would withhold from Italy money, munitions, and necessary raw materials, and they also would not buy from her.

For a short time it seemed as though there would be either war between Britain (the foremost country urging sanctions) and Italy, or else the latter country would knuckle under to the wishes of the League. A large British fleet was concentrated off Alexandria in the eastern Mediterranean to close, if necessary, the Suez Canal, thus preventing the Duce from sending any reinforcements or supplies to Ethiopia; and England's mightiest battle-ships lay off Gibraltar, to close the western gates of the inland sea.

But there was neither war nor Italian submission. Instead, the Italians defied the League, advanced on Addis Ababa, and finally captured it in May, 1936. The King of Italy was proclaimed Emperor of Ethiopia and the entire country was annexed to Italy. The conquest had cost that country in the neighborhood of one billion dollars and some thousands of lives. And the League of Nations once again had proved its futility. England, not Italy, had been compelled to eat humble pie. And why? Presumably the historian does not know yet what happened in the British cabinet in the late autumn of 1935. In October Mr. Baldwin was resolute enough and promised "no wavering." No sooner, however, was he safely returned to office than his foreign secretary, Sir Samuel Hoare, made an agreement with Premier Laval of France, by which England and France agreed that the Duce might annex large parts of northern Ethiopia, become entrusted with the economic exploitation of southern Ethiopia, and assume even a kind of veiled protectorate over what was left of Haile Selassie's kingdom, the League of Nations to act as "a kind of consulting specialist, or more probably as a mortician." The implication, to the British Labor party and to the Liberals, was plain: Baldwin had betrayed the cause of collective security; he had permitted himself to be reëlected on a platform supporting the League of Nations and sanctions; once in office again he had shown his real hand, and that of the class-conscious Tories who really admired Mussolini, by offering up Ethiopia as a sacrifice to the Duce and dynamiting the League. Instantly there was hue and cry raised against Baldwin, and this time not by the Laborites and Liberals alone. The Prime Minister, in evil odor with many of his own Tories, yielded before the storm. Sir Samuel Hoare resigned and Anthony Eden, a great advocate of Geneva and of sanctions, succeeded him.

The government intended to continue sanctions; so it said. But it

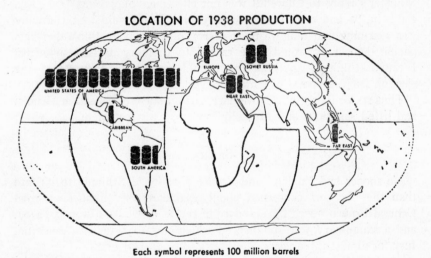

WORLD PRODUCTION OF OIL

U.S.A. | REST OF WORLD

1900

1913

1929

1938

LOCATION OF 1938 PRODUCTION

Each symbol represents 100 million barrels

(From Casner and Peattie, *Exploring Geography* [Harcourt, Brace and Co., 1937], courtesy of the Pictograph Corporation.)

did so half-heartedly, the necessary supply of oil not being cut off. The Duce did not worry; the Germans would soon give the British more serious things to worry about than Ethiopia, and so he pushed his soldiers forward until by the spring of 1936 Addis Ababa was in their hands.

During the interval Hitler occupied the Rhineland and unilaterally tore up Locarno, a menace which struck home to France, which had no intention whatever of risking a war with Italy over Ethiopia. The British knew that they could hold the Mediterranean against the Duce; but how about the North Sea; and the German airplanes as an additional liability in war if they chose to check the German Fuehrer's forward march?

The Germans were rearming with lightning-like speed. From 1933 to 1936 inclusive it was estimated that they spent some $7,500,000,000 on rearmament, and a large part of that sum on new airplanes. Britain might control the sea but she was well behind in the air race. Winston Churchill, carefully analyzing the British air force in the autumn of 1936, estimated that there were at home only 960 first-class planes. The Germans, he asserted, had over 1,500. Churchill was an alarmist and a Cassandra, said the government, and Britain could depend somewhat on the French air fleet. But the numerical superiority of the combined air fleets over the German was not great, and German planes were much newer. The facts were that Germany was spending money on rearmament at a much faster rate than Britain, and the Prime Minister's reply to Churchill was not effective. "Supposing," said Mr. Baldwin, "I had gone to the country (1933) and said that Germany was rearming and that we must rearm, does anybody think that this pacific democracy would have rallied to that cry at that moment? I cannot think of anything that would have made the loss of the election from my point of view more certain."

Thus spoke Baldwin in November, 1936. Four months earlier Geneva had lifted sanctions and Mussolini's victory was complete.

SPAIN

No sooner had England and France abandoned Ethiopia to its fate than they became concerned about Spain. In the summer of 1936 General Franco raised the standard of revolt, as we have seen (p. 236), and a sanguinary war commenced which was to rage with unabated fury for almost three years.

At times it almost seemed as though this civil war were an international one, or about to become so. The Italians and the Germans supported Franco, both morally and physically. They sent him supplies, munitions, airplanes, and also men—the Italians an expeditionary force, the Germans air pilots and technicians. The Russians, on the other hand, forwarded a number of planes to the hard-pressed Spanish Republicans during the first part of the conflict, and from Britain, France, the United States, and elsewhere many thousand volunteers, for the most part Communist sympathizers, dashed to the fray, forming an international brigade which did yeoman service fighting against Franco and his rebels.

The Spanish Republicans (the Loyalists) fought against terrific odds, and had they received half as much assistance from the outside world as did Franco and his Fascists, they would have won. Even as it was, the medley of Spanish leftists who composed the Republican or Loyalist armies put up the only real fight waged in all Europe against triumphant fascism between Hitler's advent to power in 1933 and the second World War of 1939. Even if the French, British, and Americans had only permitted the Loyalists to buy arms in the open market, they might still have kept the Fascists at bay. But this opportunity was denied them. A strict embargo was maintained against the Republicans, but no such embargo, except on paper, prevented the free flow of arms to Franco and the Fascists.

Why was this so? The French government was leftist under Blum, and why could not the popular front in France support the popular front in Spain? It certainly was not to the interest of any Frenchman to have Italian armies south of the Pyrenees in friendly collaboration with German airmen, nor to have Italian troops in the Balearic Islands menacing the French communication with Algeria. The British foreign policy was directed by Tories; but the latter by tradition were supposedly imperialistic, and the extension of German and Italian influence was scarcely a favorable augury for the British Empire. Presumably, both Italians and Germans would be paid somehow by Franco. There were the Straits of Gibraltar for the British to consider, to say nothing of Port Mahon in Minorca which might readily fall into Italian hands, a *point d'appui* in the western Mediterranean similar to Malta in the eastern; there were the Spanish copper and iron mines which the British might not care to have under Hitler's control. Why, then, should England and France turn their backs on cries for aid from stricken Spain and give, as they did, a completely free hand to Hitler and to Mussolini?

Two reasons would seem to have motivated France—fear of Germany and advice from England. Blum, the premier, had just taken office and had a first-class domestic crisis to deal with (see p. 191). He knew that his country was far from united, that there were discordant elements in his Popular Front threatening its dissolution any moment, that his country was in no mood for challenging both Germany and Italy, that those two countries were already collaborating with each other in Spain, that France could not possibly survive another war with Germany without the active assistance of Britain, and that in this emergency it was necessary to let England take the lead. The

British motivations were somewhat different. The Conservatives in control of Downing Street disliked all radicals in general and Communists in particular. They considered the Spanish Civil War an ideological struggle in which there was so much to be said on both sides that there was nothing to be said for intervening on behalf of either. They wanted a stable government in Spain with which they could do business, and the various leftist alliances which formed the Loyalist majority they suspected would prove unstable. The Loyalists might claim to be merely Republicans, but the British Tories saw communists and anarchists of every stripe and description allied with them, and the fact that the Pope had publicly blessed Franco's cause made them perhaps unduly suspicious of his Spanish enemies. Then, too, Russia was supporting the Loyalists, and the British tradition, with the exception of 1907-17, had been Russophobe for over a century. Lenin and Stalin had been bitter in their jibes against British imperialism, and Russian policy had been orientated too long against the British Empire for British Tories to regard the friends of Soviet Russia with a friendly eye. Neither Hitler nor Mussolini had gone so far as the Russians in abolishing the very foundations of bourgeois society, namely, private property, and possibly they were less dangerous in the long run than Moscow. The British Tories were not prepared to sacrifice the national interests of Britain for their own class interests, but they did tend to identify their class interests with those of the nation. They longed for appeasement, the end of war, the lowering of taxes, and the unity of western Europe against the Soviets—if such were only possible. Whether they went so far as to tell Blum that England would not support him if he got in trouble with Hitler over the Spanish situation is a matter of conjecture. The facts are that Blum visited London, made a favorable impression there, returned to France, and then put on a strict embargo on all arms exported to either side in Spain.

To do so was scarcely to preserve neutrality. By international law the Loyalists, as the official government of Spain, had a right to buy arms in foreign countries, whereas Franco's régime was legally only a rebellion and was not entitled to buy arms. Consequently, the British, the French, and the Americans who placed an interdict on the sale of all arms must be said actually to have taken sides with the Spanish Fascists, no matter how far their sympathies lay with the other side.

Italy and Germany, meanwhile, recognized Franco's government as the legal government of Spain and sent him arms and men. They did, it is true, preserve a semblance of neutrality, since they agreed to join with twenty-five other nations in adopting a policy of non-intervention. All twenty-seven countries prohibited volunteering for the Spanish war,

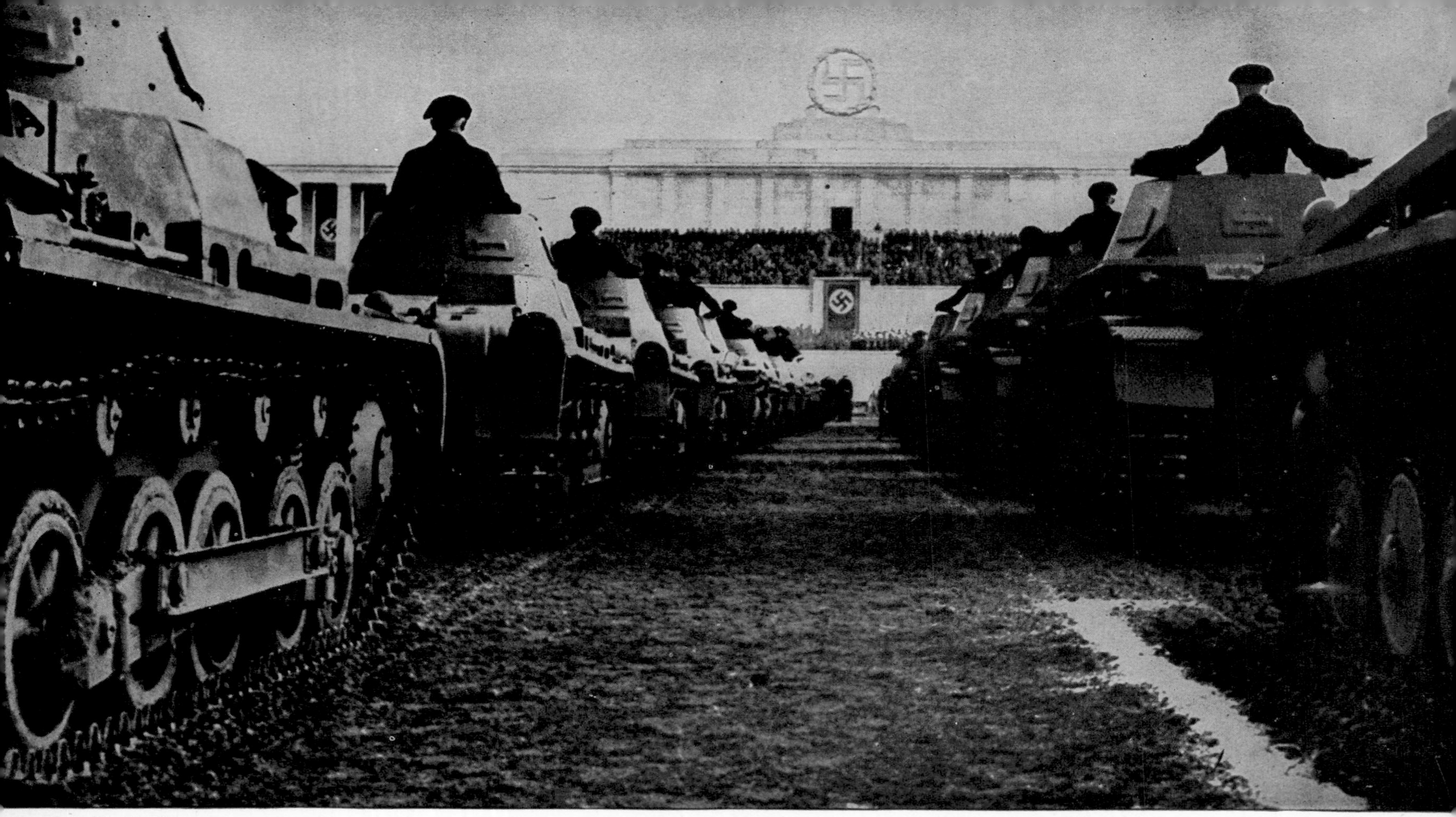

Wide World Photos

and an international committee meeting in London supported an international blockade of Spain to be carried out by the British, French, Italian, and German navies.

The blockade was a farce; neither Germany nor Italy paid any attention to it and both seceded from the international committee, only to return. A number of British and Russian freighters were sunk by submarines, supposedly of Italian origin, and for a brief period the international horizon looked very dark. There were threats from England and the submarining ceased. But not so the flooding of Spain by Italian volunteers. England and France tried to get Italy to withdraw her nationals, but Italy hedged, claiming that she could not enter any conference in regard to Spain without the inclusion of Germany, and that belligerent rights should first be extended to Franco. Later in the year 1937, when Franco's victories in northwestern Spain seemed indicative of ultimate conquest, Italy and Germany said they would be willing to consider "token withdrawals," provided they were made by both sides. Hitler and Mussolini were testing their weapons.

The fatal year 1938 dawned with democracy in retreat everywhere before advancing fascism. Baldwin had been succeeded in 1937 as prime minister by Neville Chamberlain, more prone even than his predecessor to make concessions. Chamberlain was determined to appease both Hitler and Mussolini, and this meant the sacrifice of his foreign secretary, Anthony Eden. The latter had acted reluctantly at Geneva as England's agent in removing sanctions against Italy; but he was determined that he would not give way in regard to Italian soldiers in Spain. Chamberlain thought otherwise and took Italian negotiations in his own hand. Eden resigned, a hero to Liberals and Laborites, and to many of the Tories as well, although party discipline kept them from going into the lobby with the opposition. The Duce was delighted and promptly signed an agreement with England on April 16, pledging the withdrawal of Italian troops from Spain *after* the termination of the war. One day earlier Franco reached the sea, thus cutting Loyalist Spain in two halves. That the war could continue in the Iberian peninsula for another year seemed beyond belief.

AUSTRIA

The downfall of Eden synchronized with the end of Austrian independence. Hitler's timing had been perfect. He had supported Mussolini tacitly in Ethiopia and openly in Spain; it was now his turn, and the pay and the prey was Austria. The English and the French had not been without intimation of the Fuehrer's dash to the Danube. Rapprochement between the two dictators of Central Europe had

SINBAD THE SAILOR.

(*Punch*, July 15, 1936. Reprinted by permission of the proprietors of *Punch*.)

become more and more pronounced during the preceding autumn. The Duce was welcomed with pomp at Berlin. Shortly afterward he proclaimed his adherence to an anti-Comintern pact between Germany and Japan, which seemed to prophesy a political alliance between the three Fascist states. And as the year closed, Rumania seemed on the verge of joining the Fascist parade with a pro-Fascist premier. Early in 1938, Hitler announced that Germany would not forget her racial comrades who were persecuted in other lands. He mentioned 10,000,-000 of them—and nearly 7,000,000 were in Austria. He then reorganized the German high command, dismissing certain conservative generals and appointing in their place officers said to be more amenable. Nazi agitation increased visibly in Austria, and a Nazi plot was unearthed whereby a legion of exiled Nazi agitators was to march on Austria from nearby Germany to save their country from the Red menace. Schuschnigg, successor to the martyred Dollfuss, feared the worst and fled to Rome to beseech the Duce to protect Austria as he had done four years earlier, when the Italian army at the Brenner Pass had led Hitler to disavow the Nazi revolt which killed Dollfuss. But this time the Duce gave the Austrian no encouragement.

Then Schuschnigg received an invitation from Hitler to attend him at Berchtesgaden, the favorite residence of the Fuehrer, in Bavaria. Here he was berated for many hours by an angry Hitler and presented with an ultimatum. He must release all Nazi prisoners in Austria; he must give Austrian Nazis full political rights; and he must appoint two Nazis to his cabinet. These were Germany's minimum demands.

Schuschnigg hurried back to Vienna and made another desperate attempt to talk to Mussolini. The latter could not be located. The Chancellor then capitulated. With the streets full of recently imprisoned Nazis and with a Nazi in the cabinet in command of the police, it was the beginning of the end. The Chancellor made belated overtures to the Socialists shot down by Dollfuss, but it was too late. In despair Schuschnigg bethought himself of a national plebiscite on Austrian independence, full of tricky provisions whereby he might be assured of a tremendous majority. Hitler forbade the plebiscite and demanded that Schuschnigg resign or face invasion. There was no help to be had from without in this month of March, 1938. France was in the midst of a ministerial crisis and had no government; in London the German ambassador, Ribbentrop, was supposedly laying the foundations for an Anglo-German entente; and in Italy the Duce had gone skiing. Schuschnigg resigned, as per order, but that did not stop the Germans. The new Austrian chancellor requested Hitler to march in and restore order. The Fuehrer generously acceded. His triumph in the land of his forefathers was complete. After April, Austria no longer existed as a state, 99.75 per cent of its inhabitants approving by a popular plebiscite its incorporation into the Third Reich as the *Ostmark*.

Thus there came to an end another of the provisos of the Versailles pacts—Austrian independence. And the Fuehrer had broken his word once again. In 1934 he had promised to respect Austrian independence, and in 1938 he had promised Schuschnigg that if the latter yielded to the German ultimatum he would reaffirm his promise. Both promises were broken. Whether the majority of Austrians preferred annexation to Germany in 1938 we shall never know. Presumably the older Austrians did not, presumably the younger Austrians did, if we may judge from the way in which Schuschnigg attempted to rig the projected plebiscite which was never held. France and England pretended to be deeply shocked. Chamberlain said he was shocked. There were even whispers of what the half-buried League might do. In Czechoslovakia, now surrounded on three sides by Nazi Germany, there were those who recalled Hitler's words of the previous January in regard to ten million racial comrades. Seven of the ten millions had been redeemed by Austria's annexation, including those unfortunate Austrians who happened to be Jews, Slavs, and Magyars. Roughly speaking, there were three and a quarter million Germans in Czechoslovakia; could it be that they were the remaining racial comrades in captivity?

CZECHOSLOVAKIA

The Czechs had watched with anxious eye, as well they might, the submergence of their southern neighbor in the German Reich. Not only did they have Nazis to the north of them and Nazis to the south of them, but within their own border was a clamorous German minority, the redemption of which might be sponsored any day by Adolf Hitler. That minority had received more consideration than that given to any other minority in the post-war world. It had full parliamentary representation and equal educational opportunities—in fact, there were more German secondary schools in Czechoslovakia in proportion to the population than there were schools for Czechs. On the other hand, that German minority had just cause for complaint: Public officials were generally Czechs; and minor officials, such as postmen and ticket agents, were apt to pretend that they could not understand German. The great estates in Czechoslovakia before the war had been owned by German landlords who were dissatisfied with the compensation paid them when the lands were subdivided after the war among the peasants. More important yet, the condition of the German workingmen in the industrial districts was deplorable. The Czechs were not responsible for the world economic depression of the nineteen-thirties, but they might have been more generous in the relief given to the stricken areas. At one time there were nearly a million unemployed in this little country, and over half were Germans!

Until 1935 most of the Germans in Czechoslovakia coöperated with the Czechs in carrying on parliamentary government, but in that year Konrad Henlein's *Sudetendeutsch Partei,* intransigent and disaffected, captured sixty per cent of the German vote. This party, the S.d.P., was not originally allied with the German Nazis. It did, however, stress certain German principles: hatred of democracy, devout obedience to a Fuehrer—Henlein—and racial particularism. The S.d.P.'s demands now increased, one of them being "full liberty for Germans to proclaim their Germanism and their adhesion to the ideology of Germans," and another a demand that Czechoslovakia should renounce its treaties with France and Russia, the former calling for the military support of the Third Republic should Germany threaten invasion, the latter promising Russian aid, provided France aided the threatened state first. Neither of these demands could safely be granted by the Czech majority; to accede to the first would invite open propaganda against democracy in a democratic state; to accede to the second would make Czechoslovakia defenseless in case of attack.

War was narrowly averted in the month of May, 1938. A frontier incident resulted in the death of two Germans; Hitler promptly cut off negotiations with the Czechs and hastened troops to the border. Czechoslovakia as promptly mobilized and rushed 400,000 men to the German frontier. France affirmed her support of Czechoslovakia and that meant that Russia must follow suit. Britain agreed to support France, and Hitler withdrew his troops.

But he did not change his intentions, nor did the Czechs their resolution to fight for their country. What did take place during the four succeeding months was the betrayal of Czechoslovakia by France, aided and abetted to no little degree by England.

It is very difficult to fathom what lay behind French and British policy in the crisis of September, 1938. Mile by mile the two governments gave way to Hitler's threats and bombast, until finally there was nothing left of Czechoslovakia except a completely disillusioned and discouraged little rump of a country, which could not fight if it wanted to, and which was occupied without a shot by the Fuehrer the following spring.

Czechoslovakia was by no means defenseless in the summer of 1938. She had a good army, a mountainous frontier, defended by a Maginot line reputed stronger than even the famous line of that name in France. Near Prague were the strategic Skoda munitions works, the largest in all Europe, owned by a resolute people, protected not simply by their natural frontiers but by the pledged word of France. In addition, Czechoslovakia was a member of the Little Entente, and both Yugoslavia and Rumania were sworn to aid her. True, Yugoslavia might stand aside for fear of Mussolini, and Rumania was not a dependable ally. But the Rumanians presumably would at least permit the passage of Soviet troops through their territory to aid the Czechs if they were attacked. With France, England, and Russia behind them it seemed improbable that Mussolini would give any active aid to Hitler in order that the latter might occupy Prague.

Nevertheless, the British and the French between them opened the mountain passes to the Bohemian plain, permitted Nazi troops to pass through unopposed, and thus made sure of a war in which they would not have Czechoslovakia as their ally, and Hitler would have Skoda.

The feeble and inept behavior of Britain and France during the last six months of 1938 is incredible. It began to be in evidence when the British sent Lord Runciman to Prague as a kind of unofficial adviser to the Czechs. The Czechs did not ask for him; they did not want him; but they were afraid that if they did not accept him Britain would wash her hands altogether and persuade France to do likewise. Chamberlain had blown neither hot nor cold. He had refused a definite guarantee of Czechish independence, but at the same time he had intimated that British policy was not to be interpreted as one of nonintervention under all circumstances. Plainly, they had better accept Runciman.

The Czechs, urged on by his lordship, now offered generous concessions to the S.d.P. and Henlein. They agreed to a cantonal division of Czechoslovakia on the Swiss model. "All nationalities should share proportionately in all state offices and in state enterprises, monopolies, institutions and other organizations." Autonomy in all local matters was assured the Sudetendeutsch, and a large sum of money was to be granted for their economic relief.

This was fair enough, but not sufficiently fair for the London *Times*. It proposed that Czechoslovakia cede its border districts to Germany. The *Times*, of course, was not an official organ of the British government, but the Nazis had good reason to believe that it flew the Chamberlain kite. Hitler took the cue. A few days later, September 12, he addressed a huge meeting of Nazis and said that he intended to come instantly to the relief of his oppressed racial comrades in Czechoslovakia and announced simultaneously that the most impregnable defenses ever built by man were being rushed to completion on the western frontier of Germany.

On September 13 there were uprisings among the Sudeten Germans (acknowledged later by Runciman to have been stirred up by Nazi agitators) and the instant reply of Beneš, President of Czechoslovakia, was to proclaim martial law. One day later Chamberlain announced that he would go by airplane to consult with Hitler.

This was to be the first of three trips by air to Canossa which the Prime Minister of England was to take—successive steps, all of them, in humiliating subservience to the will of the German dictator. The first flight was to Berchtesgaden, where he was told by Hitler that Germany insisted on the instant inclusion of the Sudeten Germans in the Third Reich, even at the cost of a general war. Time would be given Chamberlain to consult with his ministers; no other concession was offered.

What was to be done? The British cabinet was divided; so was the French. The Premier of France and his foreign secretary flew to London and a decison was reached without consulting Prague. Czechoslovakia was told by England and France that she must deliver "the districts mainly inhabited by the Sudeten Germans" to Germany. If this was done there would be guarantees of her future independence.

This was selling the pass, for the districts to be ceded lay along the frontier where the Czechs had their fortifications. England and France were now offering Hitler all that he demanded. Beneš and his cabinet begged for reconsideration. Czechoslovakia had, they said, a treaty of arbitration with Germany. Why not invoke it?

Runciman, meanwhile, made his formal report. It proposed not only to give Germany all that Hitler had demanded but a little more, for he suggested not only that parts of Czechoslovakia be ceded Germany but also that the rump which remained should renounce all treaties of defense with other countries, suppress all anti-German agitation, and enter into close economic relations with the Reich.

The Runciman report was followed by sharp insistence at Prague on the part of the French and British ambassadors that Beneš agree to the Anglo-French proposals. Beneš asked that the demands be given him in writing; he was refused. Would the Czechs yield or not? If France fought on their side they had a good chance, but even so there were German divisions to the south of them in Austria and their own Maginot line was in the North. They would, in any case, be subject to a severe bombardment from the air. But France had now repudiated her word, and without France, Russia was under no obligation. Beneš and his colleagues decided to yield—with the understanding, they said, that Britain and France would guarantee the future independence of what was left of their country, and that the land transferred to Germany would not be occupied by German troops until the new frontiers had been delimited.

Whereupon followed Chamberlain's second flight to Canossa, this time to the little German town of Godesberg. To his surprise he found Hitler in a towering rage. The German army was going to march on October first, roared the Fuehrer, and nothing could stop it. There might be "subsequent corrections" in the boundaries suggested, and perhaps plebiscites. But Germany was going to take by force what was hers by right and would listen to no one. Hitler presented Chamberlain with a map showing what districts Germany was going to annex immediately, and Chamberlain received it, agreed to present it to the Czechs without recommendation, and flew back to London.

The Czechs indignantly rejected the Godesberg ultimatum, the British mobilized their fleet, the French their army. It looked like war. Trenches were dug in London streets, tanks and trucks rolled through Berlin on their way south, and gas-masks were distributed in Paris. The British foreign office gave categorical assurance to France that Britain would come to her assistance if she took military action against Germany in the event of that country's invading Czechoslovakia—a much stronger guarantee than Britain gave France on August 2, 1914. Seemingly, Hitler must give way or the second World War would break.

The Fuehrer gave no indication of yielding. Within five days his Germans were to march. He had no claims, he said, against Poland or France. "After the Sudeten German question is regulated," he asserted, "we have no further territorial claims to make in Europe." But October first was the deadline, and to prove that he meant business, German divisions were concentrated on the Czech frontier, and German workmen labored day and night on the "Westwall." To frighten the democracies he even took another step: "German action" (whatever that meant), he told the British ambassador, would commence the next day at 2 P.M., namely, on September 28.

The democracies, on the other hand, did give signs of yielding. The French newspapers deliberately minimized as unofficial the British guarantee of standing by France; and Chamberlain, in a most ambiguous speech, showed that he was of two minds—he spoke of Czechoslovakia as a "far-away country" for whom it seemed almost impossible that England would be fighting, and the general tenor of his remarks in the House of Commons sounded more like Hamlet than Pitt or Palmerston. Then, just as the last sands were running out of the hour-glass, the Fuehrer, at the request of Mussolini, postponed mobilization twenty-four hours and invited Daladier and Chamberlain to a conference with the Duce and himself at Munich.

Chamberlain accepted, and for the third time made a journey to Canossa. This Munich Conference was still another victory for the dictators. Czechoslovakia was an uninvited onlooker as the four statesmen carved up that unhappy country in accordance with the Godesberg ultimatum. Minute concessions of no importance were made by which England and France might save face. Four zones were to be occupied by the Germans "in four rapid bites instead of one." A fifth zone was created in which there were supposed to be plebiscites. "But the final result was worse for the Czechs than Godesberg would have been."

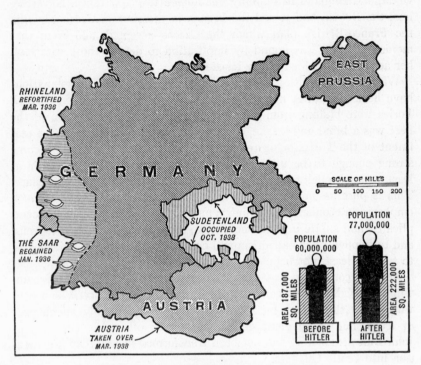

ACCRETIONS OF GERMANY, 1933-38
(Courtesy of the New York *Times*.)

The international commission supposedly in control of plebiscites was a farce. The Germans took what they wanted, marched to within forty miles of Prague, and absorbed about 750,000 Czechs in the new Germany. As they did so the Poles invaded Teschen, annexing about 80,000 Poles and 120,000 Czechs. Hungary then advanced on the helpless Czechs from the south, crossed the Danube, took Bratislava, and would have divided Ruthenia and perhaps Slovakia with Poland had she been permitted to by the all-powerful Germans. The latter, together with the Italians, decided everything. All French and British guarantees vanished into thin air.

"I return from Germany," said Chamberlain to cheering thousands, "bringing peace with honor." He brought back neither. Peace the Prime Minister might have envisaged, but how about honor?

We are too close to these events to write now with assurance of the motives which underlay them. Perhaps some day history will show that the French were more to blame than the British, for it was France, not England, that guaranteed the independence of Czechoslovakia, and England had simply guaranteed to help France. Nevertheless, the British had joined the French in pressing on Czechoslovakia the Franco-British plan which the Czechs accepted, and from that moment Britain was bound by implication to defend those who took her advice and yielded at her insistence.

Why did the British give way all along the line? Several explanations have been offered. A number of journalists asserted that the British Tories were bluffing from the beginning, that the mobilization of the fleet was a blind and a fake, carried on to deceive the simple, the real intent of the Tories being to support Hitler so that he might become strong enough to be ultimately victorious over Soviet Russia, or at least strong enough to act as their agent in staving off the Red menace. This is pure assumption and a rather silly one, for it lays too much emphasis on economic determinism and suggests an altogether too complicated and subtle a plot. The Tories, after all, were British citizens, and to impugn their patriotism and common sense without evidence is, to say the least, not being historically minded.

Another conjecture was that Britain was profoundly pacifistic, unwilling to fight in any cause which did not directly concern land over which flew the Union Jack. In this there was probably an element of truth, but not a great deal. Pacifistic or otherwise, the sons of John Bull presumably had not been transformed in less than a generation into gentle Quakers.

Two other reasons for Chamberlain's stand come closer to the truth. He knew that, arrogant and boastful though Hitler might be, he had a good talking point in demanding the inclusion of Sudeten Germans in the Reich on the grounds of self-determination. Bohemia had been a part of the old Austria, not a part of the old Germany, but that could not offset altogether the argument for self-determination. Might not Hitler be content with just annexing Germans? Perhaps there was a possibility that he would be! And finally, and perhaps most important of all, was the military argument. Russia was an uncertain factor. The Soviets were said to have promised 200 airplanes for the defense of Czechoslovakia, but on the border of that country were 1,000 German planes that probably would sweep over it before France, England, and Russia could do anything. Stalin had but recently put to death so many generals that Chamberlain might well have questioned the importance of any help Russia might provide, even if she honored her treaty with France. The French were well prepared with their Maginot line for defense, but how could they reach Czechoslovakia to rescue that country from Hitler's maw? And if the French could not, how about England? His first duty was to secure the safety of his own country. He

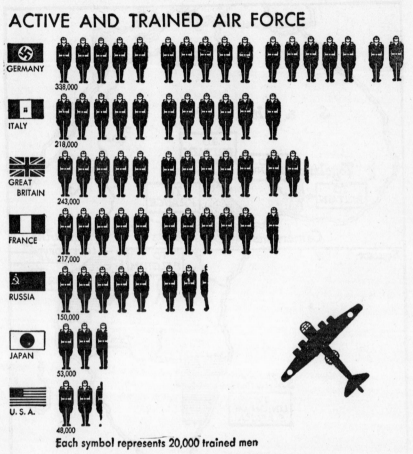

ACTIVE AND TRAINED AIR FORCE

Each symbol represents 20,000 trained men

AIR FORCE STANDINGS IN NOVEMBER, 1940
(Courtesy of the Pictograph Corporation.)

knew that Germany was better prepared for air battles than Britain, and it is possible that he had reliable information that the Reich had a two-to-one superiority in the air. Could he afford to risk a war under such circumstances? Possibly Hitler was bluffing; but on the other hand, possibly he was not. Chamberlain's rôle in this affair certainly was not brilliant, but that does not necessarily mean that it was absurd. Perhaps he had some right to feel that Baldwin and MacDonald were more responsible in the long run than himself, for it was they who neglected for so many years to make ready against the day when no argument could prevail against Hitler's lawless will unless backed by superior force.

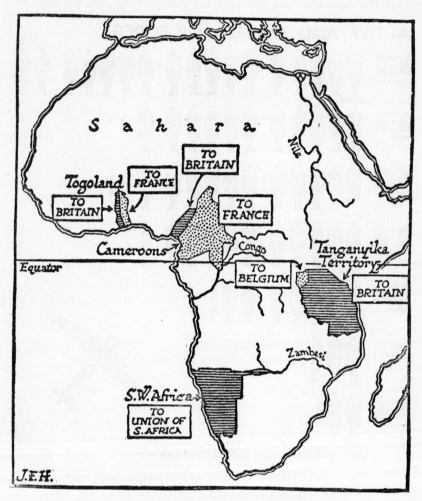

GERMANY'S LOST POSSESSIONS IN AFRICA (1919)

(Reprinted from J. F. Horrabin's *An Atlas of Current Affairs*, by permission of, and special arrangement with, Alfred A. Knopf, Inc., publishers.)

The triumphant Germans, meanwhile, had won two astonishing diplomatic victories in less than six months, since without any fighting at all not only Austria but also the mountain bastions of Bohemia lay in their hands. Hitler had solemnly pledged himself to go no farther, but he had not the slightest intention of keeping his word. Having swallowed somewhat more than one-third of the area of Czechoslovakia, and somewhat less than one-third of the population, he was still greedy for more. What was left of the Republic of Czechoslovakia soon found that it was independent in name only and that it must look to Berlin for guidance. The Germans demanded and obtained a corridor across the country for a military highway; they demanded and obtained the right to decide on the destinies of Slovakia and Ruthenia, not only in respect to government but also in respect to how much land should be ceded to Poland and Hungary. And when Hacha, the last president of the republic, protested against Germany's highhanded interference, he, like Schuschnigg, was summoned to Hitler's presence.

His going to Germany was a formality. Even before he reached Berlin, the German army had started south again. Hacha, berated and browbeaten by Hitler, signed away the independence of his country, and almost simultaneously with his so doing, the Germans entered Prague, none resisting. A few snowballs were thrown at the Teutonic invader; that was all. Czechoslovakia was made a German protectorate, and Hitler could boast of adding still more military booty, to say nothing of much needed gold, to Germany's store.

In somewhat characteristic vein, he boasted of other things and especially of the first German Reich which had been born again. That German Reich had been the Holy Roman Empire, reaching far across the Rhine into France and across the Alps into the heart of Italy. Mussolini knew this as well as Hitler, knew that Milan and Florence had been part of that Reich. The Duce said nothing, but one suspects he made note of these new boasts of the German Fuehrer. It was not tactful for Hitler to speak thus.

And he spoke of other things as well, this fateful month of March, 1939. It was not self-determination that Hitler emphasized now, but rather the idea of a German *Lebensraum,* a living space, which he was now in process of gaining for the Third Reich. How large was that living space to be, and where beyond Czechoslovakia was it to be extended? Always until March, 1939, there had been explanations of Nazi diplomacy based upon the iniquity of Versailles and of the violations by the Allies of the sacred right of self-determination. But the demise of Czechoslovakia could not thus be explained. Quite evident it now seemed to thoughtful men that, unless Hitler was stopped somewhere by force, a large part of eastern Europe would fall speedily under his control. And after that, what about Alsace-Lorraine, and French, Belgian, Dutch, and British colonies; and, for all anybody knew, the coast of the English Channel?

CHAPTER XII

SECOND WORLD WAR

THE occupation of Prague made war well nigh inevitable. Up to that event there was always a chance, though a slim one, that Hitler would be content with his many victories; from now on it was evident to all but the blind that the Nazis were bent on further conquest. Always hitherto they had been able to advance the argument that their successive victories had simply united to the Reich good Germans who longed for a common fatherland. That argument no longer held. The Czechs were not Germans, and the brutal and unprovoked attack on their country in March, 1939, seemed conclusive evidence that Hitler would not stop until the entire continent lay under his thumb—and perhaps not then! Presumably Poland might well be his next victim, but after Poland, what country? It might be Russia; but there were those in London fully aware that Britain administered former German colonies; and there were those in Paris who remembered the ominous words in *Mein Kampf*, "The German people's irreconcilable and mortal enemy is and remains France."

In the spring of 1939, therefore, France and England increased their military preparations, drew closer their political ties, sought allies. They struck alliances with Poland and Turkey; they guaranteed to march to the aid of the former if she were invaded by Germany; they joined the latter in a mutual defense pact to preserve the status quo in the eastern Mediterranean; they promised unilateral protection to Greece and Rumania; and they invited the Soviets to join them in a defense pact against German aggression.

Joseph Stalin pondered deeply. He hated and distrusted Hitler; he also hated and distrusted Chamberlain. If the Germans drove through Poland or across the Baltic states and attacked Russia, guarantees were needed of armed support from France and Britain. But suppose those two countries failed him at the last hour; suppose they consented to a second Munich whereby Poland fell a prey to Germany and the Wehrmacht stood on the borders of the Ukraine? France and England had ignored Russia in 1938; Stalin had not been invited to Munich; the protests of his representative, Litvinoff, had been ignored at Geneva; the two western powers had abandoned, apparently, the

320

whole idea of collective security. There seemed to be more than an even chance, so Stalin thought, that they would not be displeased at a German-Russian war from which they would stand aloof.

The inept and temporizing character of Franco-British diplomacy did much to heighten his suspicions. Chamberlain three times had flown to Germany to placate Hitler, and Chamberlain, accompanied by Lord Halifax, secretary of state for foreign affairs, had visited Mussolini; but to Moscow at the height of the crisis the British had accredited as their special envoy an under-official of the foreign office, without prestige, without authority.

Nevertheless, Stalin stood ready to make a hard and fast military alliance with France and Britain, provided that it included not only guarantees for Poland but for all six small countries on the western Russian frontier, Finland, Estonia, Latvia, Lithuania, Poland, and Rumania; guarantees not only against external but also against internal aggression. What this latter meant was clear enough to Stalin. He proposed to ward off and to prevent Fascist propaganda and revolt from within, such as had given Hitler his excuse for invading Czechoslovakia.

These guarantees the British and French were unwilling to give. They feared, and perhaps justly, a Soviet advance in the region of the Baltic, and they argued that the Baltic countries did not want a Soviet guarantee. They would guarantee Poland and Rumania alone; but Stalin thought an attack by the Germans on Russia might readily be staged through the Baltic countries, and he held out for their inclusion in any pact.

Germany, meanwhile, claiming that she was being encircled, and flushed with her bloodless victory of March pounced upon the tiny area of Memel on her northeastern border, hitherto administered by Lithuania in the name of the League of Nations, and made demands on Poland for the return of Danzig to the Reich, together with a strip of land across the Polish Corridor. As she did so Hitler denounced his ten-year peace pact with Poland, proclaiming that the treaties just made by that country with the western democracies had broken friendly relations between Germany and Poland. Likewise for good measure he denounced Germany's naval treaty with Great Britain.

At the other end of the Axis was Italy. The Duce, not to be outdone, let forth a tremendous blast against the follies of democracy and peace, invaded Albania, and annexed that country to Italy.

The spring of 1939 had been hectic, the summer more so. None could tell just what was happening in Moscow.

Then in late July the French and British sent a military commission to Moscow. Despite many clear warnings from a number of authoritative sources that Stalin might bargain with Hitler, it did not go by air-plane; it took a slow steamer and did not reach Moscow until August 10th. Immediately it encountered a snag. The Russians were willing to fight the Germans in Poland provided the Red army was permitted to defend Poland's western boundary. But neither the Poles nor the western allies would accept this qualification. If the Russians were once in Poland, who could or would evict them? On the other hand, from the Russian viewpoint, if the Red army was to fight the Nazis it did not intend to wait until the latter swallowed Poland and were on the Russian border.

Stalin, in the meanwhile, determined not to be caught napping. If the anti-Nazi powers would not do business with him, he would do business with the Nazis. It would be a risky thing to do, but to wait longer was also risky. So it came about that on August 23rd the Nazi foreign minister, Von Ribbentrop, was welcomed in Moscow, and one day later a Soviet-German non-aggression pact was signed, the two contracting powers agreeing that for a period of ten years they would "refrain from any violence, from any aggressive action, and any attack against each other, individually or jointly with other powers."

The Brief Polish Campaign

This act gave the green light to the Nazis in Poland and in Germany the government-controlled press unleashed a slashing attack on that country, accusing her not only of refusing all concessions but of mal-treating Germans within her borders. The Polish question must be settled immediately, said Hitler. He would be content with the return of Danzig to the Reich and the ownership of a super-corridor across the Polish Corridor, in other words with a strip of territory one kilo-meter wide, sufficient for four railways or motor roads; but that strip must be German. Polish lines of communication north and south must go over or under this strip.

Hitler pressed the Poles hard; and as he did so the Japanese created a diversion by blockading the port of Tientsin, where the British had granted sanctuary to several Chinese whom the Japanese accused as being assassins. British citizens were stripped naked by Japanese sentries, but England did nothing. The royal navy was needed at home. England was determined that there should not be a second Munich. In the summer the skies darkened over Poland. Poles were persecuted in Germany, according to the Polish newspapers; Germans were brutal-ized in Poland, if the German press was to be believed. Hitler outdid himself in truculence; he would negotiate no longer with the Polish ambassador; the Poles must send a plenipotentiary to Berlin, pre-

BEGINNING OF WAR

(Courtesy of *Newsweek* Magazine.)

sumably their prime minister, to accept a German ultimatum, else Germany would act.

In vain did the French and British ambassadors at Berlin assure the Fuehrer that they would investigate fully and carefully German charges made against the Poles. Hitler would not listen to them, asserting that it was none of their business, that he had no quarrel with western Europe, that England and France had no right to intervene in Polish-German controversies. German troops were concentrated on the Polish border and south of it in Slovakia, supposedly an independent country. Then, to frighten the western democracies still further, Hitler published in triumph a ten-year non-aggression pact with Soviet Russia, his old enemy. Germany was secure now on the east; let the two democracies to the west beware!

The Germans, set on forcing the issue, on August 31 presented the British ambassador (they refused to have any dealings with the Polish ambassador) with a peace proposal in sixteen points which considerably enlarged their demands on Poland. Not only were Danzig and the extraterritorial traffic zone to be annexed, but also there were to be plebiscites whereby the Germans hoped to add the entire Polish Corridor to the Reich. The Poles, unwilling to sign on the dotted line, were not unwilling to negotiate. But Hitler refused to wait longer. On September 1, without declaration of war, the German armies invaded Poland, Hitler asserting that he had waited two days for the Poles to submit, that Germans were being mutilated by Polish mobs, and that the preceding night Polish troops had fired across the border.

Within one month Poland was conquered. England and France declared war on Germany on September 3, but did nothing to stave off annihilation of their ally, aside from scattering propaganda pamphlets over the German country-side. The very first day of September saw Warsaw bombed three times and German armies advancing on doomed Poland from four different points. So swift was the German onrush by motorized divisions on land and by squadrons of planes in the air that the Poles never had a chance. While optimistic prophets in London and Paris predicted that French and British planes would soon be shuttling back and forth across Germany to Polish air-fields to refuel and return, those very air-fields were wrecked by German bombs, and Polish planes were destroyed on the ground. The famous Polish cavalry was helpless against the German *panzer* (armored) divisions. Brilliant sunshine baked the Polish plain, and the rain upon which the Poles depended to make their fields a sea of mud failed to materialize. By the middle of the month all of Poland's important cities (except Warsaw) were in German hands and the Polish government had begun its flight toward the Rumanian frontier.

The Poles fought bravely; they simply were not equipped for modern war. Here and there, scattered Polish divisions thrust vigorously at the encircling Germans; at the Danzig Westerplatte and at Warsaw they made notable stands. The civilian population of Warsaw turned out en masse to dig trenches around their capital, and the Warsaw radio alternated martial music, defiance of the enemy, and appeals to the world for succor as German planes droned overhead, reducing the proud city to a mass of ruins.

Then, on September 17, came an invasion of Poland by the Soviet army. The Polish government, so the Russians said, no longer existed, and Soviet forces were needed to restore order and to rescue peasants from oppression. Caught between the Germans and the Russians, Poland collapsed. Warsaw, that shell of a city, bombed and burning in a dozen places, held out until the end of the month. On October 1 the Germans occupied what was left. Russian and German armies met as Russia and Germany divided Poland between them, the lion's share of the booty in economic resources going to the Reich, the eastern marshes and the Polish Ukraine falling to Russia. Thus within one month perished Poland, a country of 50,000 square miles and 35,000,000 people.

Nazi Germany and Soviet Russia were in accord. Their non-aggression pact now was supplemented by another agreement, the opening paragraph of which struck an ominous note. "In the case of the war's being continued," it read, "joint consultations will take place between the German and Soviet governments on the subject of necessary measures." Just what did that mean? The rest of this pact simply provided for lines of demarcation in Poland and for economic coöperation between the two signatories, Russia agreeing to supply Germany with raw materials in exchange for manufactured goods. From the German point of view this economic accord by itself seemed sufficient guarantee of victory; if the Germans could depend on the Soviets for oil and food, what more was necessary!

Meanwhile, on the western front the French and British were almost immobile. The former wrested a few square miles from the enemy in the region of the Saar and the Moselle; the latter contented themselves with the worldwide seizure of German shipping and with setting up again the blockade of Germany as in 1914. During the autumn, the German submarines proved effective in sinking a considerable number of British merchant vessels, also one airplane carrier and a large battleship, the *Royal Oak*. These victories were offset in December in the South Atlantic when the German pocket-battleship *Graf Spee* crept into Montevideo after an eighteen-hour engagement with three British cruisers, later to be sunk by her own crew rather than fall into British hands. Aside, however, from these maritime encounters, there was little action on the high seas.

For the first six months the war in the west was remarkably quiet. The bulk of the British regular army, upward of a quarter of a million men, was transported to France without mishap and went into winter quarters. In both France and England the idea seemed to hold that the war could be won by simply exhausting the economic life of the enemy. It would not be necessary to fight; all one had to do was to wait! The Germans in turn seemed perfectly willing to wait. They did stage a counterattack in the late autumn to win back that tiny sector of Germany occupied by the French in September; but this once accomplished there were for the time being no large movements of troops on either side. There were occasional flights of German planes over France and Britain, and of British and French planes over Germany; but these, aside from the sporadic bombing of the British naval base at Scapa Flow, primarily were for observation purposes, and only a scattering number of planes were shot down. British children evacuated from London gradually slipped back again. Life was uncomfortable during the long, record-breaking cold winter of 1939-40, but as the months passed with little happening, the war almost seemed unreal.

Russia Attacks Finland

All but in one country—Finland. Here there was a war within a war, Finland against Russia. No sooner did Stalin occupy eastern Poland and agree with the Germans in regard to the Polish loot than he stretched out his hands to the Baltic states. Three of them, Estonia, Latvia, and Lithuania, were too feeble to offer resistance and almost immediately agreed to cede land to the Soviets for naval and air bases. Not so with Finland. The Finns had fought hard for their independence and had won it in 1920 from Red Russia. Now when Stalin sought to whittle it down by demands for Finnish territory the little republic refused to accede. To fight Russia might be madness but even that was better than surrender.

Throughout November negotiations continued. The Russians pressed the Finns hard. They asked for a rectification of their frontier at Petsamo, a port on the Arctic Ocean belonging to Finland, for six islands commanding the approaches to Leningrad, for a naval station at Hängo, and for a considerable stretch of Finnish territory on the southeastern frontier where Finland's boundary was only twenty miles away from Leningrad. That distance, so the Russians said, made it possible for the Finns to bomb a large Russian city from their own forts, an intolerable situation. If the Finns would yield to these demands, then the Soviets would be conciliatory and offer territorial compensation.

AT IT AGAIN!

(Messner, in the Rochester *Times-Union*, August, 1940.)

The Finns would not yield. Thereupon the Russians, asserting that they were in danger of Finnish attack (they outnumbered the Finns 50 to 1), commenced an undeclared war, dropping bombs on Helsinki, Finland's capital, on November 30.

The world expected that Finland speedily would be overrun by the Russian steam-roller; but the world was mistaken. From the 1st of December, 1939, to March 12, 1940, the Finns put up an astonishing resistance, only to capitulate when their vastly outnumbered soldiers, without ammunition and without sleep, could fight no more.

History has on record no braver epic than this. The Russians swept into Finland along several different routes. They tried to conquer north Finland near Petsamo; they tried to cut across the narrow central section or waist of that underpopulated country, thus severing the north from the south; and they advanced on both sides of huge Lake Ladoga on the southeast, endeavoring to storm the main Finnish defenses, the Mannerheim line, which stretched across the Karelian peninsula from Lake Ladoga to the Gulf of Finland.

In every direction the Finns beat them off. There was only a handful of Finns; but their country was two-thirds the size of France and was said to contain 65,000 lakes, while the land between was covered for the most part with dense forests where roads were few and poor. The athletic Finns, skilful on their skis and well-nigh invisible in their white clothing against the background of their frozen country-side, mowed down the invaders from numerous ambushes; they dug traps for Russian tanks; they placed and set off dynamite under the ice; they broke the Russian lines of communication and captured thousands of the enemy.

Aside from the Karelian peninsula, immediately in front of Leningrad, the Russians had only one approach to Finland, a railway 800 miles long which stretched from Leningrad all the way north to the Murmansk coast and at no great distance from the Finnish frontier. This railway was easy to raid. The Finnish air force, as might have been expected, was unable to cope with the air armada let loose by the Russians; but on the other hand a number of planes were sent to Finland by France, England, Sweden, and even Italy, and the Finns were not helpless in the air. Furthermore, Finland was almost exclusively an agricultural country, and outside of Helsinki and Viborg there were few towns worth bombing.

The Soviet army, meanwhile, proved extremely inefficient, particularly during the early stages of the war. The army purge of 1937 had resulted in the execution of three out of five field-marshals; and all of the eight general officers who court-martialed them had since been shot. It was estimated that no less than 30,000 officers of the Red army had thus been disposed of, and in consequence the morale of the Russian troops was poor. So also was the equipment; the soldiers were clad in flimsy cotton uniforms and thin boots; the fighting was in subzero weather; they never had seen skis; their tanks, huge and cumbersome, broke down in swamps, were surrounded, isolated, captured. Not until Russia threw the best of her fighting men into the war in 1940 was she able to make headway.

The Finns got a great deal of sympathy from the outside world but, apart from Sweden, little actual aid. It was impossible to reach Finland except either through the arctic wastes south of Petsamo or across Norway and Sweden; and the Germans made it abundantly clear to the Scandinavian countries that they would not permit French and British expeditionary forces to cross Scandinavia. The Germans were not sympathetic toward Russia; but the major source of iron ore for Germany came from northern Sweden and they were determined not to risk having that region overrun by Allied troops. The British had sent the Finns considerable supplies of munitions, and volunteers also made their way in civilian clothes to Finland; but no expeditionary force actually was sent.

Then came a final massed assault by the Russians on the Mannerheim line. Throughout February an incessant rain of steel blasted away its concrete fortresses and wave after wave of Russian tanks drove at the defenses. The number of fresh Russian troops was inexhaustible, but for the Finnish regiments no more men were available. Finland, therefore, with inevitable collapse staring her in the face, yielded to all of Russia's demands, made peace in the middle of March, and commenced evacuating the choicest part of what had been Finnish soil, the Karelian peninsula. From it some 400,000 Finns, more than one-tenth of Finland's population, packed their scanty possessions and moved westward into what was left of their country.

Thus far there had been two victors, Russia and Nazi Germany. England and France seemed semi-paralyzed with inaction. In the former country Neville Chamberlain, firm in declared purpose but sluggish in act, was still prime minister. That the situation was highly critical and that his own country was well-nigh unprepared for "total war" he never seemed to realize. At the very commencement of the war the Germans began strict rationing of not only food but clothing; not so in England. In Germany not only was there no unemployment but actually a scarcity of labor; in England after five months of war the number of the unemployed had only diminished slightly. The British enforced a strict blackout in their cities and called to their colors their young men. But the necessity of operating their factories day and night and of throwing all they had into military preparation for total war, while there was yet time, did not dawn upon the government. Only Winston Churchill, pugnacious head of the royal navy, had sufficient imagination and foresight to know that the Germans were implacable and ferocious foes who had not yet begun to fight.

So likewise was it in France. General Gamelin, generalissimo of the Allied armies, was reputed Europe's ablest soldier, and the French army reputedly was the best in Europe. The Maginot line, from Switzerland to the Belgian frontier, was regarded as impregnable. The Belgians, supposedly, were much better prepared for war than in 1914, and the Belgian army was mobilized and on guard. If the Belgians were attacked they would be instantly supported by a well-trained Anglo-French army. Military experts spoke of the day of offensive war being over, and the French were determined not to sacrifice their diminishing man-power by a useless and costly offense. There was the living example of what happened to Poland; but the Poles had been caught napping, so thought the French, and they were not regarded as scientific fighters anyway. And so in Paris there were even less precautions taken than in London. The French made scarcely a pretense of rationing either food or clothing. They stamped down rigorously on the Communists, established a strict censorship of the press, and increased the hours of labor. But they were as confident of ultimate victory as the British—a victory to be won without shedding much blood!

Both French and British were deceived, perhaps, by the international situation. Between them they had several billion dollars in assets available for expenditure in America, and the friendly attitude of the United States to their cause was a great encouragement. In October, 1939, the United States lifted the embargo on the export of munitions and airplanes to warring countries, thus deliberately changing its avowed policy of neutral isolation to one of acknowledged aid to the Allies; and whatever superiority in the air was possessed by the Nazis it was thought would be overcome within a year by the importation of American planes.

There was, of course, danger of Italian intervention on the side of Germany; but this the Allies discounted. Mussolini was constantly proclaiming that his alliance with Hitler held; but the Italians certainly hated the Russians and feared their possible advance in the Balkans. After all, Mussolini's threats might be nothing more than blackmail, a bid for concessions in return for neutrality. The Allies were chary of interfering too much with Italian commerce, and when the seizure of Italian coal ships enroute from Belgium to Italy brought sharp protest from the Duce the British yielded and released the ships. But then, Italy was for many months no major problem. With the Suez Canal and Gibraltar in British hands, and Franco-British naval control of the Mediterranean secure, there was nothing Italy could do. She would scarcely risk an invasion of the Lombardy plain which might easily be launched from the French Alps. To be sure her nuisance value to Germany was considerable, since her warlike gestures made it necessary that the French keep a large army on the Franco-Italian frontier; but that was all.

THE GERMANS CONQUER DENMARK, NORWAY, HOLLAND AND BELGIUM

Aside from Portugal, the only one of the small neutral states in Western Europe having nothing to fear was Spain. Franco owed much to Mussolini and Hitler, but on the other hand, Spanish fascism with its strong Roman Catholic flavor had been even more opposed to communism than German fascism, and the Soviet-Nazi pact was much criticized in Spain. That country at first was really neutral, by necessity if not by choice. The wounds of civil war had scarcely begun to heal and seemingly Spain was permanently out of the conflict.

Scarcely another small country in Europe had this comforting assurance. The Swiss, armed to the teeth and standing guard in their narrow valleys, were for the time being relatively safe from invasion, but this was not true of either Holland or Belgium. Those lowland countries had good cause for worry. Ever since the days of Cæsar, Belgium had been the cockpit of Europe, and since the Maginot line did not extend south of Belgium, a dash through Belgium was an obvious strategem for the Nazis. On the other hand, if the major German aim was the immediate defeat of Britain, then Holland also was a prize worth having, since the Dutch sea coast would be invaluable for submarine and airport bases.

The defenses of Holland and Belgium later proved feeble, both from the point of view of morale and of armament. There were numerous Nazi sympathizers in the two countries and active Fascist propaganda. On paper the Low Countries had a combined military force of over 600,000 men, but it was lamentably weak in matériel—tanks, planes, and anti-aircraft guns. The Dutch and the Belgians were very nervous during the winter months of 1940 and tried their best to preserve strict neutrality—no easy matter, since the British asserted that their protests against the sinking of their ships by German submarine and German mine were feeble, and since the Nazis denounced them for the mildness of their resistance to the strict rationing of their imports imposed by the British fleet.

Of all the small states, the one which had suffered the most from the war had been Norway. Ship after ship of the Norwegian mercantile marine had been destroyed by Nazi mine and submarine while plying between British and Norwegian ports. There was nothing the Norwegians could do about it except put their shipping under the protection of the British convoy system, which the Germans claimed would be unneutral. Norway, indeed, had legitimate complaint against both Germans and British. A British destroyer boldly entered Norwegian territorial waters to rescue British seamen from a Nazi prison ship, and the British constantly interfered with German shipping threading its way down the coast of Norway with the much prized iron ore of Sweden which, when the Baltic was frozen in winter, reached Germany via the Norwegian port of Narvik, far north within the Arctic circle.

Then, with the coming of the spring, war came to Norway with sudden fury. On April 8 the British announced that they had mined the approaches to Narvik, despite the fact that these were within Norwegian territorial waters. One day later Germany invaded Norway.

To reach that country the Nazis were compelled to occupy Denmark, which they did in one day, the Danes offering no resistance. Less than one year earlier the Nazis had signed a non-aggression pact with Denmark. But they did not hesitate to violate it. They were eager to swallow two countries in one bite—Denmark and Norway—and they succeeded.

The very day the Germans swept across the Danish plain, small picked detachments of the German army seized Oslo, Norway's capital, and her only important ports—Stavanger, Bergen, Trondhjem, and Narvik. Only a few thousand men proved necessary for this undertaking, 1,500 being sufficient to secure Oslo. By various routes the Germans came—some by sea, some by transport planes, some disembarking from German merchant ships anchored innocently alongside Norwegian wharfs, while some were already within the country in disguise.

The Norwegians, taken by complete surprise, honeycombed by Nazi propaganda, and ill equipped for war, were not able to put up much resistance. Here and there, Norwegian detachments fought bravely, and effectively. A Norwegian mine-sweeper sank a German cruiser and so did a land battery, and in the mountains hastily assembled militia (the Norwegian army was scarcely more than militia) retarded the German advance.

But there was treachery in Norway. Some Norwegians, dubbed "fifth columnists," welcomed the invaders, and among them were officers in the army. The German plans had been prepared in great detail, long before the British mine-laying at Narvik, and everything ran like clockwork. On the very first day all the Norwegian air-fields were occupied by Germans and the tiny air force of Norway was of no use at all. So completely taken by surprise were the Norwegians that their king, pursued by Nazi troopers in four auto-buses, barely escaped capture.

Nevertheless, for two weeks or so it looked as though the Allies might successfully come to Norway's rescue. From Denmark to southern Norway across the Skagerrak was a distance of some seventy miles, and Britain was less than twice as far away. Theoretically, with Britain in command of the seas it should have been easier to land larger bodies of Allied troops in Norway than of Nazi soldiers. To many commentators Hitler's coup seemed a rash adventure, even more rash than the great Napoleon's invasion of Spain.

But the facts were that the Germans commanded the air if not the sea, that they did not need many troops, that at the start they had secured all the available ports at which any large number of troops could be disembarked easily. The British navy did score a real although minor success in sinking some German ships in the Skagerrak; but it proved difficult for the British to operate successfully in those near-by waters, with the German submarine beneath and the German airplane overhead, and after all it was not necessary for the Nazis to transport many men by water. Speed counted far more than numbers, and needed reinforcements were sent by passenger airplanes.

It was a difficult task to dislodge the German invader, and one beyond the none too brilliant British war office. At Narvik the British had their greatest success when their battleship *Warspite*, veteran of Jutland (see p. 60), did break into Narvik fiord, there to sink seven German destroyers. And this most northern port of Norway, far away from German reinforcements, ultimately was captured by the Allied besieging army, only to be evacuated in early summer, as the German advance in the Low Countries and in France made it necessary for Britain to recall all soldiers available for the defense of their island home.

The Allies could not well fight the Germans from Narvik; too many miles of well-nigh trackless forest intervened between that arctic port and the more inhabited parts of Norway. Therefore an expedition against Trondhjem was decided upon. This Norwegian port, at the head of a long and winding fiord opposite Yorkshire, could not well be approached directly because of fear of German mines, even though there were only a handful of German soldiers within the city. The plan was to assault the port from the land, and for that purpose the British landed 12,000 men in two divisions, one to the north and one to the south. Ships could not attack forts.

These two expeditionary forces had to disembark on open beaches and were ill supported by light artillery and anti-aircraft guns. What was more serious, they were practically without planes, for the Germans had the landing-fields in their possession. Nevertheless, the British advanced boldly, seeking to join their forces and encircle Trondhjem. As they did so the Germans moved swiftly to succor their detachments in that city. Scattered Norwegian units attempted to hinder the swift moving German motorized detachments, but German speed and German efficiency were at their best. On April 30 the German advance units had made contact with the German garrison of Trondhjem. Three days later the British took to their boats which lay north and south of the city they had hoped to capture. It was a humiliating evacuation; nevertheless, since landing-fields could not well be devised overnight in Norwegian valleys, and since frozen lakes could not be depended on for planes, it may have been the wisest course to take.

To conquer Poland took five weeks; now within less than a month Denmark and Norway (aside from the half-frozen Narvik) followed Austria, Czechoslovakia, and Poland down the Nazi maw. With Denmark gone, the British lost an important source of food; with Norway gone, the British lost not only supplies of fish and timber but were confronted by German airmen within striking distance of northern England and Scotland; and in addition the coastline of Scandinavia, indented with deep fiords, provided ideal lurking places for the submarine. A consolation prize for Britain was the Norwegian mercantile marine, the larger part of which was at sea.

For a few days the Nazis rested. There were ominous troop concentrations on the borders of Holland, Belgium, and Switzerland, but none knew where the next blow would fall. In Parliament there was angry debate. Men asserted that the Norwegian fiasco might have been prevented, that a bold assault on Trondhjem fiord by the navy would have captured the city, that Chamberlain was inept, supine. A vote to censure his government failed, but so heavy was the cut in its usual majority and so many were the abstentions that Chamberlain handed in his resignation.

Instantly he was succeeded by Winston Churchill, first lord of the Admiralty. A short time before it seemed impossible that Churchill ever would become prime minister. For many decades a stormy petrel in Parliament, he had numerous enemies. He had been a Tory, a Liberal and a Tory again without qualm or misgiving; he had served in many cabinets, holding the home office, the treasury, and twice the naval portfolio. Trenchant in speech and with pen, he was thought somewhat too brilliant and too erratic to head a cabinet; he had been responsible for the Dardanelles expedition in the first World War, and that had failed (see p. 48). His constant prophecies of approaching disaster in the years immediately preceding the second World War had made him persona non grata to those Tories who like Chamberlain believed in appeasement. Now Britain applauded him.

As England changed her prime minister, Germany struck again, this

WINSTON CHURCHILL WITH SIR DUDLEY POUND IN LONDON (1940). (See page xviii.)

time at the Netherlands and Belgium. On May 10 the Nazis invaded the Low Countries and Luxembourg, claiming that they did so only to forestall an Allied invasion. Simultaneously, they came by air and by land. Within five days the Netherlands, always at their mercy, was completely conquered. The Dutch resisted as well as they could; but their airplanes were few, their country flat and tiny, and many Netherlanders were fifth columnists, National Socialists, and Dutch Fascists who aided the seizure of vital points by the Germans. The latter dropped down from the skies by parachutes; they came by the thousand in transport planes; they crossed flooded areas in rubber boats; they bombed the airports and almost captured Queen Wilhelmina before she could flee to England. Futile resistance soon ceased, but not until a large part of the city of Rotterdam had been reduced to smoldering ruin by aerial bombardment.

Belgium, also invaded May 10, was able to withstand the Nazis only a few days longer. The first line of Belgian defense went down almost without a fight, but the second line, following the course of the Meuse River and the Albert Canal from the French frontier to Antwerp on the Scheldt, was stoutly defended, with the hope that the oncoming French and British reinforcements might enable the Belgian armies stationed there to withstand the German attack.

On the second day of the invasion that hope died, as the Germans captured the bridgeheads of the Albert Canal, stormed the great fortress of Eben Emael, outflanked the Belgians, and drove at Brussels. Within one week they had not only occupied that city but, pushing south, had pierced the French defenses in the Ardennes forest (the little Maginot line), opening up a sixty-mile gap in northeastern France between Montmédy, the northern end of the Maginot line proper, and the French fortress of Maubeuge to the west.

THE FALL OF FRANCE

Neither in 1870 nor in 1914 had the Germans advanced with such speed. Yet they were to keep on with relentless violence and in uninterrupted success for the rest of May and most of June, two months during which Belgium and France were to be conquered and the Third Reich to become master of continental Europe, apart from Soviet Russia.

For convenience' sake the German victories of the next six weeks may be summarized under two battles—the Battle of Flanders and the Battle of France. But such description is purely arbitrary. There was fighting all the time, continuous correlated movement of troops, airplanes, tanks, a continuous, unremitting slicing forward of irresistible Nazi power, a continuous retreat of baffled, broken-up, and out-maneuvered Allied armies.

The first of these so-called battles, that of Flanders, began with the German break-through of the little Maginot line and ended on June 2 with the miraculous escape from the beaches of Dunkirk of four-fifths of the British expeditionary force. Sometimes it is spoken of as the Battle of the Pockets, due to the way in which the onrushing Germans segregated by flanking movements large sections of the Allied forces.

What took place was this: The Germans dashed through the gap they had made at Sedan in the little Maginot line, pressed forward with all speed with tanks and planes until they reached Soissons on the Aisne. Then, instead of keeping on toward Paris as in 1914, they wheeled toward the right in the direction of the English Channel, their idea in so doing being to cut off the Allied armies—French, British and Belgian, upward of a million men, which were retreating slowly down the sea coast in western Belgium—from the French armies to the south.

Seemingly it was impossible to stop this destructive process. At the apex of it was the tank and airplane, and not until they opened the way did the artillery and the infantry follow. The weather was dry and clear, and so rapidly did the German tanks push forward that frequently they became isolated from supporting columns. But the French artillery was too light to destroy the huge German tanks, few of which fell into French hands and the roads were cluttered with fleeing civilians, Belgian and French, a fact which sadly impeded Allied resistance but aided the German advance, since the German *stukas*, low-flying dive-bombing planes, struck mercilessly at civilians and soldiers alike.

Speedily the German scythes swept on down the valley of the Somme toward Peronne, scene of desperate fighting in the first World War, and cut down Amiens, a key railway junction never captured in that conflict; then cut through to Abbeville, only a few miles from the Channel, and sweeping toward the north reached Boulogne. The exultant Germans, not stopping, kept on to Calais and, finding that town stoutly defended, swept around it, almost reaching Dunkirk. A million Allied soldiers apparently had been surrounded.

There were for the latter three possibilities: to cut through the German lines of communication, not as yet very wide or strongly held, along which the German armies were driving in; to surrender; or to escape by sea to England.

On paper the first possibility seemed feasible. In less than a week the German lines had been so distended by the great, huge arc which they formed that a simultaneous thrust by the Allies on the Channel and by the main French armies before Paris might have pierced it, thus creating a pocket or pitfall whereby the German armies, which had passed the point of piercing and which had reached the Channel at Abbeville, would be severed from the main German forces and in turn be in danger of segregation and forced surrender.

Why was this not done? Gamelin had been removed as Allied generalissimo and Weygand, pupil of Foch and hero of the first World War, now in command, was expected any moment to commence this counterattack. Instead of doing so, he began hastily to dig trenches and to form a new line of defense. Possibly he considered that essential to protect Paris; possibly, and more likely, owing to the confusion created by the sheer audacity of the German thrust, and by the activity of German fifth columnists in France, he was unable to concentrate his troops. Yet every hour this counterattack failed to materialize saw the German lines of communication strengthened by German artillery and German infantry.

Then, whatever chance the Belgian, French, and British armies at the Channel had of piercing the German lines and joining forces with the French armies to their south went begging when the Belgian king surrendered. His army, upward of a half-million men, was in sorry plight, its ammunition spent, its food supply gone, almost to the last biscuit. King Leopold's men held the left wing of the Allied forces, and if they were out of the combat apparently there was nothing to prevent the Germans in Belgium from pushing on until they joined hands with the German army advancing eastward along the Channel. The French and British had come to Belgium's succor at the request of the Belgian King and he was under deep obligation to them. On the other hand, could he fight longer? To do so, he thought, would simply result in sacrifice of life.

The Belgian lines covered a distance of thirty miles which instantly had to be covered by the hard-pressed British. The result was that the latter lost contact for the time being with parts of the French army, several divisions of which were cut off by advancing German columns. What was left of the French army joined with the British, and these Allies, closing their ranks, pressed close together along the sea coast at Dunkirk, where it seemed improbable that more than a few thousand could be conveyed across the Channel.

Then out of the jaws of death and gates of hell over 335,000 French and British soldiers were rescued. From the end of May to the fourth of June the Royal Navy and the Royal Air Force, aided and abetted by all kinds of miscellaneous sea-faring folk, worked at this task. The skies were darkened by planes as the R. A. F. and German planes engaged in one unceasing duel; German artillery sprayed the beaches with its shells; German submarines and motor-launches, equipped with torpedo tubes and rapid-firing guns, swarmed out for the kill; and the German infantry threw itself "on the ever narrowing and contracting appendix within which the British and French armies fought."

The British would not use their battle-ships in these too narrow waters, but every available light cruiser and destroyer was commandeered, as well as innumerable other craft. Over 200 naval warships took part, and three times as many other vessels. No one will perhaps ever know just how many, since with complete unanimity the owners of yachts, tugs, fishing-smacks, motor-boats, river steamers, and barges aided in it. Anything afloat that could carry men was used. Only one narrow pier at Dunkirk, constantly bombed by the Germans, was available, and over this poured a steady stream of men. Soldiers by the thousand waded into the shallow waters off the beaches and stood up to their armpits waiting for a friendly hand. Old men past sixty and young boys of fifteen worked together in hauling them into lifeboats. Almost every one in southeastern England connected in any way with boats and shipping took part.

Day and night the work continued; back and forth the impromptu ferries plied; and on one day alone over 60,000 half-starved Soldiers of the King reached home in safety.

The evacuation was unparalleled in military annals, and the total loss to the British army was but 30,000, but little over ten per cent. Nevertheless, the very fact that there had to be evacuation made it a disastrous British defeat. Left behind in France and in the hands of the Germans were over 1,000 heavy pieces of artillery, vast stores of munitions, food, gasoline. For the time being, Britain's scarcity of war matériel was appalling, and a militant foe, flushed with victory, held Scandinavia, Holland, Belgium, and the Straits of Dover.

Not since the days of Bonaparte had Britain been in such evil case. Churchill, while praising his fighters, did not minimize the issue. Said the Prime Minister in the House of Commons: "We shall defend our island whatever the cost may be; we shall fight on the beaches, landing grounds, in fields, in streets, and on the hills. We shall never surrender, and even if, which I do not for a moment believe, this island or a large part of it were subjugated and starving then, our Empire beyond the seas, armed and guarded by the British fleet, will carry on the struggle until in God's good time the New World, with all its power and might, sets forth to the liberation of the Old."

Dark as the Allied cause was, it speedily grew darker. The Germans did not hesitate a minute. While the world wondered whether they would instantly "sail for England" or try to destroy France first, the Nazi legions embarked on the latter course. On June 5, the day after

Churchill's speech, the superbly mechanized armies of the Third Reich attacked the French in an offensive that stretched from the northern end of the Maginot line all the way to the mouth of the Somme at Abbeville—the Battle of France had begun.

This time, instead of concentrating on one break-through, the Germans hit at four different places; they rushed westward across the Somme into northern Normandy; they hit south from Amiens straight toward Paris; they crossed the Aisne farther east for a drive down the Oise River toward the French capital; and still further east they commenced the encirclement of the Maginot line.

Everywhere they met with victory. For a brief moment it looked as though they might be foiled by the new tactics of Weygand. That general, copying German precedents in 1918, made no attempt at holding a rigid line but let the German tanks through the first French defenses and tried to lead them into carefully concealed traps. But all that Weygand did was to retard the enemy slightly. The Germans now were using 1,500,000 men, nearly 100 divisions, and the French were outnumbered in the field two to one, since large numbers of their best troops were either isolated in the Maginot line or guarding the Italian frontier. The line of battle extended over 200 miles and so swiftly drove the Germans that the breaking French had no time to gather their forces to counterattack.

Soon it was all over. As the German armies drew close to Paris for their final battle, Italy declared war on France and England. The Duce said the time had come to break the Mediterranean prison in which Italy was confined, to strike a blow at the "pluto-democracies," and to fulfill his alliance with Hitler. Whatever his reason, one fact remained: on the Franco-Italian frontier were 400,000 Italian troops ready to attack France from a new quarter. Italy was to be in at the death.

The latter was not unduly prolonged. On June 1 the Germans marched into an undefended Paris and three days later Marshal Pétain, at the head of the French government which was now at Bordeaux, asked for an armistice. On June 22 it was granted, and the French armies surrendered, the Germans occupying France to the Loire, the Italians having advanced a few miles in the French Alps and along the Riviera.

The Battle of France had ended. Like that of Flanders it was a quick, decisive victory for the invader. The French had been no more successful than the Poles in defending their country; and why?

Certainly one important reason was the subversive activity of the Nazi fifth column. France was betrayed as well as defeated. It had long been flooded with Nazi agents pretending to be tourists or salesmen or sometimes refugees from Nazi oppression. Now, during the war, wearing the uniform of the French staff, they gave contradictory orders, signaled German planes, aided German parachutists, spread rumors of defeat and disaster, demoralized the civilian population and paralyzed military action.

The people were none too united for war. French Communists, subsequent to the Nazi-Soviet pact, encouraged desertions and acts of sabotage, and French Fascists gave aid to the enemy. Many Frenchmen felt that the British were not too wholeheartedly in the war, and the evacuation of the latter from Dunkirk was held by some as evidence that England neither could nor would assist France further.

More important, probably, in the long run were the mistakes in preparedness of the French. As in 1870, their military reputation stood much higher than facts warranted. Their best tanks surpassed those of the enemy, but these were not ordered into battle. This was not true of their planes. The French high command had been caught napping by the sheer audacity of the German thrust and had erred sadly in permitting its armies to be separated, a situation that might have been avoided had the first French army, together with the British, retreated promptly to the south as the Germans broke the little Maginot line at Sedan. Open wars of maneuver had gone forever, so French and British strategists were persuaded. They believed that the first World War had demonstrated that defense had grown so strong that a quick and successful offense was impossible. Deluded by this falsehood, the French had no time to readjust their ideas to realities before the Germans were in Paris.

The armistice granted by the Germans paralleled in many ways that earlier armistice of November 11, 1918 (see p. 94). It was signed in the same railway carriage and at the same spot where the Germans surrendered in the first World War. Its terms were equally harsh, and in one important respect even more so. Not only were the French to give up all their military supplies and equipment and to pay for the cost of occupation, but more than half of France was to be occupied by the triumphant Germans, including the entire Atlantic sea coast from the Belgian border to that of Spain. Concerning the ultimate disposal of this occupied territory nothing was stipulated. Even the Italians, who signed a separate armistice with France a day later, were content to wait until the war was over before receiving the jackal's share of booty.

The Germans had reason to think that the war was over. To be sure, the British had retrieved most of their troops, but the greater part of their war matériel had been left behind in France, munitions and gasoline now in German hands. A few days before the armistice Churchill had begged the French government to flee to North Africa, promising political union with the British Empire and a joint fight for victory. The offer had nearly been accepted; it failed by but one vote in the French cabinet. But the French, like the Germans, thought the war at an end, and the aged Marshal Pétain, who had assumed control of the government with dictatorial powers in the midst of the crisis, believed it his duty to come to such terms as he could with the enemy.

Fortunately for Britain, the Germans were in no condition to start an immediate invasion of that hated island. The disarmament of France had to be completed and vast military preparations made at the Channel ports before that happy event could be announced. Consequently there came a lull in hostilities which, apart from various intermittent air attacks on British ports and British shipping, was to last the greater part of the summer.

The second half of 1940 was to prove in some ways almost as dramatic as the spring and early summer of that year. To Britain there came a most extraordinary rebirth of national energy and fighting spirit, amid trials and tribulations unexperienced since the days of the Conqueror. In the Far East, Japan, thirsting for the colonial possessions of France and the Netherlands, threw in her lot—part way that is—with the Axis powers. In the Near East the war spread rapidly. Here Egypt was invaded by the Italians, Rumania invaded first by Russians and then by Germans, and finally Greece was invaded by Italy. And what perhaps was most important of all, the United States came closer and closer to the brink of conflict.

BRITAIN FIGHTS ON

But first the British scene: England was not only stunned; she was bitterly disappointed at her ally's withdrawal from the war. If Pétain had only transferred his government to Morocco it would have been safe from the Germans except for a possible air attack, so the British thought. Furthermore, the large French army in Syria would also be safe, and with the French army in Tunis threatening Italian Libya on one flank and with the British in Egypt on the other, any Italian offense in North Africa could be checked. Churchill had promised to carry on the war from Canada if England should be subjugated; why should the French be less determined?

What disturbed the British more than anything else was the future of the French fleet. The armistice terms provided that it should be interned for the war, except for a few patrol boats for the French colonies, and the Germans promised not to make use of the French navy against France's ally. German, French, and Italian navies might

WITHIN ONE YEAR!

(Courtesy of *Newsweek* Magazine.)

readily cripple British sea power, and in that eventuality the war would indeed be lost.

Thereupon the British, most reluctantly, decided they must act. The French fleet was scattered; part of it was in British harbors, part in home ports, part at Alexandria in Egypt, with the British squadron stationed there, part in the Pacific and in the West Indies. But the larger part lay off the French North African port of Oran, and to it steamed three of Britain's largest warships and numerous lighter craft. Their commander delivered an ultimatum to the French admiral; he must either join forces with him against the Germans or sail to British ports or cross the Atlantic to dismantle his ships there, or else the British would use force to prevent the French ships from falling into German or Italian hands. The French elected to fight rather than yield; the British opened fire and sank or disabled three French battle-ships, a seaplane carrier, and two destroyers. One battle-ship, badly crippled, escaped, together with some lighter craft, to Toulon. The French squadron at Alexandria, meanwhile, agreed to dismantle and the French ships in British ports surrendered without much fuss, some of the sailors agreeing to continue the fight on the British side. One great French battle-ship stationed at Dakar was put out of action by a surprise attack, and here and overseas some French naval vessels were seized. Of the very considerable French navy, only a few scattered units remained (for the most part at Toulon), and the British breathed easier.

This naval activity ushered in the month of July. Otherwise it was to prove a comparatively quiet month. There were vast threats of the invasion of England in the German press, but aside from renewed activity on the part of German submarines and aircraft hovering under and over the English Channel, the war was not pressed. Despite the fact that the entire coast of France was in German hands, the British managed to send their merchant ships through the Channel. There was a great increase in the number sunk, and the British lost several destroyers of which they had all too few, but they were able to keep the Channel open. What is more, they could claim by the end of the month that despite all losses since the commencement of the war the total tonnage of their mercantile marine had increased, since large numbers of Norwegian, Danish, Dutch, and Belgian ships were now under their control.

The only marked successes of July, curiously enough, were won without bloodshed by Stalin. That wily Russian seized this moment to annex to the Soviet state Lithuania, Estonia, and Latvia, the three little Baltic states which he had already cowed into granting naval bases to the Soviet. Bessarabia also was demanded from Rumania and obtained without a fight, and together with it the Russians took part of Bukovina for good measure. The Germans and the Italians did not dare protest at these aggrandizements of their eastern neighbor and the British were not disappointed by them. The left-wing British labor leader, Sir Stafford Cripps, now represented his country at Moscow, and it was hoped that through his agency a wedge might be inserted between the Nazis and the Soviets.

Meanwhile, England girded herself for battle on her own soil. At last the British were fully awake to their own danger. They made an armed camp of their island. To its strength were added certain Polish detachments, many French soldiers under General De Gaulle, recognized by the British as the head of "Free Frenchmen" who would continue the fight, and over 100,000 soldiers as well from Canada, New Zealand, and Australia.

There were men enough, over 1,000,000 under arms, but the immediate danger lay in civilian coördination and in war matériel. Almost overnight England was transformed. Parliament placed every man and every shilling at the disposal of the government. Arrests were made of all suspects; possible landing-fields for enemy planes were blocked by concrete pillars and trenches; home guards were organized to watch for parachutists; and factories worked day and night turning out planes, guns, shells.

Fortunately for the British, the Germans were so occupied in coalescing their continental gains that it was a good six weeks after the fall of France before they were able to strike at England with force. Intermittent air raids continued during that time on British seaports, and the R. A. F. struck back as far as it was able on Nazi-controlled French air bases, but it was September before the Nazi power really showed itself.

The Nazis then struck straight at London, their bombers swooping across from Calais and swarming up the Thames valley. Their planes came in squadrons of 100 or more at a time, first by day and then by night, and kept on doing so for weeks at a time. Occasionally there would be a lull, a day or two with scarcely an alarm. Then would follow renewed raiding. In September it was directed mainly at London, but as the autumn wore on it extended elsewhere—to Bristol, Southampton, Liverpool, and other shipping centers, to the Midland cities of Coventry, Birmingham, and Manchester.

Early in the air war the R. A. F. was able to strike down a great many of the invading planes, for the latter flew mainly then by daylight, seeking definite targets such as docks, railway yards, manufacturing plants. But when the Germans switched to night attacks it was not so easy for the R. A. F. or the anti-aircraft gunners to locate the foe.

Wide World Photos

Hitler Addressing the Reichstag Just After the Outbreak of War. (See page xvi *ante*.)

Wide World Photos

THE BRITISH LION GOES UP OVER TRADED AMERICAN DESTROYERS. (See page xvi *ante*.)

In the summer the British had looked forward to the short winter days as partial protection against the *Luftwaffe* (air force) of General Göring. But now with night attacks the autumn and winter season made it all the harder for the harassed islanders.

The damage done by the Luftwaffe was extensive. First would come a squadron of planes to unload incendiary bombs to start fires which would serve as beacons; and then successive waves of bombers would follow. Thousands of houses were destroyed, in many cases their inhabitants buried beneath the debris. Docks, churches, hospitals, factories, whole city blocks were left in ruins. The home of the rich (fortunately for the morale of the Londoners) were struck quite as often as the homes of the poor. Bombs fell upon St. Paul's cathedral, Buckingham Palace, and a dozen other historic landmarks of London. A considerable part of the city of Coventry was wiped out of existence, and if half of the German claims in regard to Birmingham and Liverpool should afterward be substantiated, property damage in those cities would be comparable in extent to that suffered by stricken Coventry.

Meanwhile, the R. A. F. struck back with all its power at Germany. Its principal targets were shipping centers and the industrial Ruhr, but from time to time it bombarded Berlin and even Turin in Italy. The R. A. F. was under a double disadvantage: the number of its bombers was slight in comparison with the Luftwaffe, and Berlin was far distant. German planes had but a short journey with their cargo of death, but British planes because they traveled far had to go lightly loaded, and so the damage they wrought on Berlin in 1940 was more psychological than material.

The Germans could report great material success, but one thing they had not been able to accomplish: they had not "softened" the fighting spirit of the British. Rather they heightened it. Crowded into congested and unsanitary bombproof shelters and in the London subway, snatching a few hours' sleep here and there, the citizens of London responded superbly to the German challenge. The killed and seriously wounded numbered several thousand a week while the raids were at their worst, but after all, this was recognized as only a very slight proportion of London's many millions of inhabitants, and the latter, regarding themselves as real soldiers (as they were), kept their thumbs up, working like beavers to clear their streets of debris and to "carry on."

And the best proof that this was so may be found in the fact that the Nazis continued to postpone their threatened invasion. It is of course possible that on one or two occasions, as rumor has it, they actually filled their barges and transports with troops, only to have these vessels destroyed before sailing by the accurate bombing of the

R. A. F. But the chances are they never tried at all, since they were aware, despite their published air victories, that British morale was high and that they had not yet come within striking distance of gaining a mastery of the air over their proposed victim.

As a matter of fact, serious as were the air raids over British cities, they were far less serious than the ever-increased activities of the German submarine. Bad as the situation had been in 1917, it threatened to become much worse in 1941. In the former year the U-boat bases were confined to the narrow shore line of Germany and of Belgium. In 1941 the entire sea coast of Norway, Denmark, Germany, the Netherlands, Belgium and France (as far as the Channel and the Atlantic were concerned) was now at Germany's disposal. Forth from their innumerable lairs now crept the Nazi submarines, not one at a time as formerly but hunting in packs like wolves and assisted by planes of wide cruising area, serving as eyes for the submarines.

The sinking of vessels flying the Union Jack jumped up to dangerous proportions and early optimism gave way to genuine alarm. More civilians thus far had lost their lives than had British soldiers, in England; but after all civilians could, if they must, adjust themselves to sleeping underground. But the war would be lost if cargoes could not be delivered, cargoes of food as well as of munitions. And what made the British worry more than anything else was that the royal navy, gravely deficient in destroyer strength at the war's commencement, had suffered severely in this category of ships, many destroyers having been sunk and many more laid up for repairs because of damage from the air.

Fortunately for the British, they had a warm friend in President Roosevelt, who did not hesitate by a stroke of the pen to deliver to the British Admiralty in September fifty over-age American destroyers in return for naval bases in the Atlantic and Caribbean.

The agreement was as follows: Great Britain presented two of the eight bases, those in Newfoundland and Bermuda, as a free gift. The other six, those in Jamaica, St. Lucia, the Bahamas, Trinidad, Antigua and British Guiana, were in payment for the destroyers. All eight bases were to be leased to the United States for a period of ninety-nine years, free from rent.

Congress was in session at the time but the President did not consult that body. Arming himself with an opinion handed down by his attorney general as to the validity of the transaction, he acted with speed and secrecy, and certain of the destroyers were already on their way to a Canadian port before America knew of their transfer to the British flag. Nevertheless, there was only scattered criticism in the United States, partly because the "destroyer deal" was an extraor-

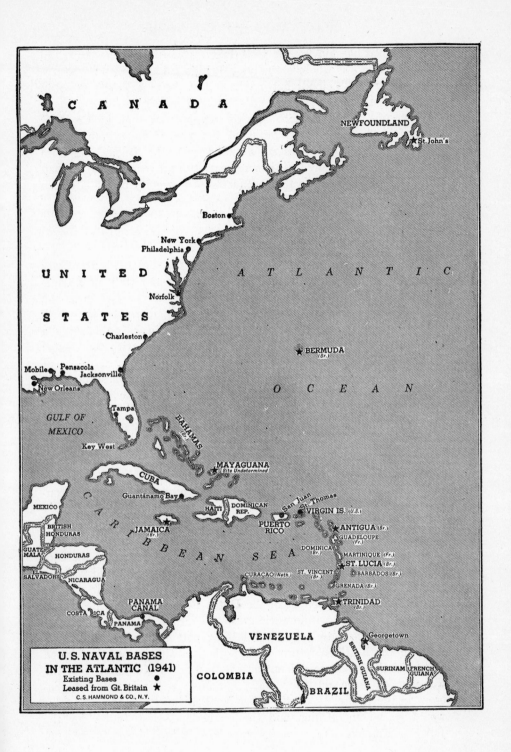

U. S. NAVAL BASES
IN THE ATLANTIC (1941)
Existing Bases ●
Leased from Gt. Britain ★
C. S. HAMMOND & CO., N.Y.

dinarily good bargain for the United States, partly because American public opinion was wholeheartedly on Britain's side.

The destroyers helped; but by the end of the year Britain stood in need of even more naval assistance, and particularly in need of more cargo vessels. Over 3,000,000 tons of shipping was sunk by Germany during the first fourteen months of the war, if we are to include Belgian, Dutch, and Norwegian shipping flying the Union Jack. With British yards producing less than 1,500,000 tons a year, and with small likelihood of speeding up that production, the gravity of the situation became more and more apparent.

JAPAN JOINS THE AXIS

On September 27 an important victory on the diplomatic front was won for the Axis when Japan joined Germany and Italy in a triple alliance whereby Japan recognized the leadership of Germany and Italy in establishing a "new order" in Europe, in return for which Germany and Italy recognized Japan's leadership in establishing a "new order" in "Greater East Asia." In accordance with the treaty: "if one of the three contracting powers is attacked by a power at present not involved in the European war or in the Chinese-Japanese conflict" then the other two powers must assist "with all political, economic and military means."

Ostensibly this was a thrust against the United States, since that country and Russia were the only nations which could well be called powers not already engaged in the conflict, and since Article 5 in the treaty expressly stated that its terms "do not in any way affect the political status which exists at present between each of the three contracting parties and Soviet Russia."

Why this treaty? The reasons motivating Japan are easy to fathom. Angered by the Russo-German neutrality pact on the eve of the war, Japan had stood warily to one side during the first year of the conflict, waiting to see who would win. Now she felt she could wait no longer. The Japanese longed for French Indo-China; their mouths also watered at the thought of the Dutch East Indies, so ripe and so rich a prize almost within their grasp. Victorious Germany was now willing to concede to Japan the leading part in organizing a "new order in the East" in return for hypothetical aid against the United States. If the Japanese did not accept now and if Germany won the war without their aid, they might not find the Nazis quite so generous in the future. If, on the other hand, Britain won the war there would be no Indo-China and the Netherland East Indies for the Japanese Empire.

The Japanese were as yet far from winning their war in China; new victories somewhere were needed, and that right speedily, to stiffen the morale of the Japanese people, poverty-stricken and burdened with terrific taxation. The British had agreed to a temporary closing of the Burma Road which wound its way through mountain passes to Chungking, capital of the Chinese Republic; but it was possible for the Chinese to get supplies via Indo-China and also overland from Russia. To sign this pact would protect Japan's western front from possible military attack by Soviet Russia and would bluff the Americans. So, presumably, argued Konoye, the premier of Japan.

Just what Germany and Italy hoped to gain is not quite so evident. Clearly the alliance meant that Germany was now granting Japan the hegemony if not ownership of lucrative colonial pickings which the Nazis had hoped to secure for themselves in Asiatic seas. Probably it meant an insurance policy taken out against the United States, a policy which Germany might hope to cash in on later by causing the United States to keep her fleet in Pacific waters. Also, and very probably, it was a bait to the Soviet. Let the latter join the new triple alliance and there would be "new orders" and *Lebensraumen* for all the allies: the Far East for Japan; India, Afghanistan, and Iran for Russia; the Mediterranean for Italy; western Europe, central Africa, and perhaps South America for the Nazis!

If this latter was the main Nazi motive, it failed of accomplishment. The Russian foreign secretary, Molotov, came to Berlin and engaged in long conversations. But nothing apparently eventuated except protestations of neutrality and good will. The Russians were said to have advanced claims too extensive for the three allies to accept, claims which involved territorial concessions in eastern Asia at Japan's expense. What actually took place was a closely guarded secret. But Russia did not sign the pact and the three allies had to be content with the adherence, as we shall note later, of Rumania, Hungary, and that pygmy creation of Nazi Germany, Slovakia.

For the time being, the diplomatic adherence of Japan to the Axis accomplished little. It gave the Japanese an easy entrance into northern Indo-China, which they occupied with very faint protests from the defeated French government of Pétain—located at Vichy in unoccupied France, supposedly independent, but entirely at the mercy of the Nazis who had incarcerated in Germany over 1,000,000 French soldiers. But it also led to action on the part of the United States which took the form of an embargo on certain highly desired war matériel and an official warning to all Americans to withdraw from Japanese-controlled China. The United States even went further: she extended financial aid to the embattled Chinese Republic and encouraged Britain to reopen the Burma Road in order that war supplies might be rushed to Chungking and Chiang Kai-shek. The Japanese did not take these rebuffs kindly. On the other hand, there was lit-

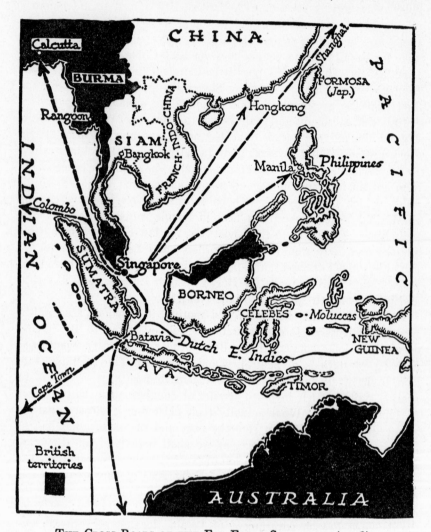

THE CROSS-ROADS OF THE FAR EAST—SINGAPORE (1938)

(Reprinted from J. F. Horrabin's *An Atlas of Current Affairs*, by permission of, and special arrangement with, Alfred A. Knopf, Inc., publishers.)

tle they could do about it. The American fleet stationed at Hawaii was superior to their own, and presumably the great British naval depôt at Singapore would be open to it in case of emergency. The Japanese army had bogged down in China, and certainly no help was immediately available from Germany and Italy. Therefore the Japanese government did nothing, but the Japanese press boasted loudly of Japan's Monroe Doctrine for eastern Asia and that the dawn of Nippon's greatness would soon come.

THE NEAR EAST

Meanwhile, in 1940 the war spread to the Near East. The Balkan states had no desire to be drawn into the conflict. Nevertheless it was almost impossible for them to avoid it, partly because within their borders were raw materials much sought after by the Germans, like oil and foodstuffs, partly because they lay between the triumphant Axis and lands subject to British and French overlordship, such as Syria, Lebanon, Palestine, Egypt, and countries still farther distant, such as Iraq and Iran.

Of the five Balkan countries, three leaned toward the Allies, one might be said to be at first almost completely neutral, and one leaned somewhat toward the Axis. The Turks were both anti-German and anti-Italian. They were not, however, anti-Russian, and the defense pact which they had signed with the Allies before the war and which they had strengthened after its advent specifically excluded action against Russia. Yugoslavia and Greece also were pro-Ally in sympathy, not so much because of fair liberty as for fear of Hitler. The Yugoslavs had neither forgotten nor forgiven the unwillingness of the Italians to aid Serbia during the first World War, nor Italian determination to control the Adriatic. The same held true of Grecian memories of Mussolini's earlier bombardment of Corfu (see p. 283). To both of these Balkan countries the Italian annexation of Albania in 1939 was an ominous warning. Rumania was more or less equally poised between the conflicting powers. She asked nothing of her neighbors but she feared them all; feared Hungary (rapidly becoming a satellite of Berlin), for Hungary would demand the return of Transylvania; feared Bulgaria, from whom she had taken the Dobruja after the Second Balkan War (see p. 31), feared Soviet Russia lest that country should invade Bessarabia, a czarist possession in 1914. What Rumania wanted was to be left alone, and therefore she played Germany and the Allies against each other, hoping for the best. Bulgaria alone somewhat favored the Axis, for the status quo displeased her mightily and she held grudges against all her neighbors.

Meanwhile, in the Near East one other country, theoretically independent, hoped against hope to stay out of the war. Egypt was an ally (as far as the law went) of England. But the alliance had been part of the bargain whereby Egypt had won recognition of her independence, and since British troops were in Egypt to guard the Suez Canal, the independent status of Egypt seemed only a nominal affair to many Egyptians.

To act as a counterweight against an Axis offensive in the Near East, and possibly to organize a thrust of their own, directed against Germany's back door, the Allies had stationed relatively large armies in that region, the British components of which were located in Egypt and Palestine, the French in Syria and French Somaliland. Before the fall of France this seemed good strategy. If the Italians should strike east from Libya against Egypt and the Suez Canal, they would be caught between two fires—between the French in Tunis and the British in Egypt. Should the Italians in Ethiopia move against the Nile Valley or the Suez, they would be exposed to a flank attack from French Somaliland. The French and British warships between them easily controlled the Mediterranean. Their influence would, it was believed, give sufficient weight to the Allied cause to maintain at least the status quo in the Near East.

And doubtless the Axis powers would have hesitated long before launching an offensive there, had not the fall of France altered the situation so completely. That event encouraged Stalin to occupy and to annex both Bukovina and Bessarabia, a *fait accompli* which the Axis scarcely dared challenge; it also made shaky (on paper at least) British naval dominance of the Mediterranean, and even more shaky Britain's grip on the Suez Canal.

Even before Italy was in the war she proceeded to augment her already large forces in Libya and to prepare an offensive against Egypt. During the summer of 1940 the Italians started their march against Egypt from Libya, and invaded British Somaliland from Ethiopia, easily conquering that sandy waste south of the Red Sea. And as they did so, they pushed westward from Ethiopia into the northern Sudan and southward into the outlying districts of Kenya. The hard-pressed British were indeed in danger and had, for the time at least, but one ally upon which to depend—the weather, since campaigning in Egypt and in the Egyptian Sudan is extremely difficult in the summer.

Then, as the Italians struck at the southern sections of the Near East, the Germans laid their heavy hands upon Rumania. The Russian occupation of Bessarabia and Bukovina almost instantly reverberated in Bulgaria, which threatened now to seize the Dobruja, and in Hungary, which mobilized for a thrust at Transylvania. Whereupon Germany acted, compelled the Rumanians to give up the northern half of Transylvania to Hungary and to cede the southern third of the Dobruja to Bulgaria.

This dismemberment infuriated the Rumanians, who considered King Carol responsible for their calamities. That unfortunate monarch fled from his country, abdicating on September 5. Young Michael, his son, became a puppet ruler, doing the bidding of the Iron Guard, a Rumanian Fascist organization which his father had, on occasions, opposed and, also on occasions, placated. The Germans, under pretext of preserving order and preventing the British from blowing up Rumanian oil-wells, sent larger and larger bodies of troops to Rumania and finally forced that Balkan state, together with Hungary and Slovakia, - to join the all-Fascist alliance of which Japan, Italy, and Germany were the charter members.

Rumania now was lost to the democracies, and with the coming of autumn Egypt was invaded with apparent success by the Italians from Libya, who reached Sidi Barrani on the Mediterranean littoral without serious opposition. For some reason, perhaps the water supply, this offense soon bogged down, but as it did so the Italians on October 28, struck at Greece through Albania.

To the surprise of almost every one the Greeks flew to arms with apparently all the spirit of ancient Hellas; they drove the Italians out of northern Greece; they followed after them, forced them into precipitate retreat, and by December a large part of southern Albania was in Greek hands. Throughout that month and January, 1941, Greek victories continued. The snow lay heavy on Albanian hills but the dogged Greeks continued slowly but persistently to carry hill after hill at the point of the bayonet until, by February 1, 1941, they had not only reached the Adriatic but were within seven miles of Valona, Italy's strongly fortified and much prized port on the Albanian coast.

The British, meanwhile, rendered the Greeks valuable assistance by air and by sea; they attacked the Italian fleet at anchor at Taranto and severely damaged several of its larger units; they steamed into the Adriatic and bombarded Albanian seaports; and they established themselves snugly on the island of Crete. Nor did this aid to the Hellenes interfere with a most dashing offense against the Italian land forces in Africa. In December the British army in Egypt, strongly reinforced by Australians and supported by "Free French" troops, swept across the desert and ferociously attacked the Italians at Sidi Barrani. That town capitulated and some 30,000 Italians surrendered. The British offense continued without let-up, this time in Libya. Bardia, the Italians' strongly fortified port in eastern Libya, bombarded by land and by sea, capitulated in early January, 1941, and the British, having bagged some 40,000 additional prisoners, swooped down on Tobruk, another Libyan port still farther to the west, running up their total number of prisoners to approximately 100,000. Nor did they stop. Striking across the desert, they soon were before Derna, which they stormed as the month drew to a close. They now were no less than 145 miles west of the Egyptian frontier. Some 100 miles beyond lay Bengazi, next to Tripoli, Libya's most important city. A long way to go; but in modern warfare, tanks and planes travel fast, and fortunately for the British there was at Derna a superb water supply. If they could only capture Bengazi, all of Eastern Libya (ancient Cyrenaica) would be lost to Mussolini.

As 1941 opened, the Italian dreams of turning the Mediterranean into a *mare nostrum* seemed faint, very faint indeed, since the British kept on rolling westward, not only taking Bengazi in early February but advancing far beyond it to El Agheila, well along the sea coast road to Tripoli. It was evident to all that Britain would soundly thrash the Italians in Libya and perhaps elsewhere unless Germany took prompt action. This Hitler realized, and soon German airmen came pouring into Italy. In January the famous *stukas* began striking at Malta and at the British convoys in the Middle Sea, doing more damage in one day than Italian planes in six months of war.

The United States on the Brink of War

The Greeks and the British had defeated the Italians, but the latter had never been anything more than the tail of the Nazi wolf. The German armies still dominated the land mass of western Europe. Nothing could prevent their occupation of that part of France still ostensibly "free." Their legions might continue southward through the Iberian peninsula to besiege Gibraltar or to plunge west into Portugal. Sweden and Switzerland lay at their mercy; and, if the Nazis chose to risk the enmity of Stalin, Bulgaria, Greece, and Yugoslavia might be conquered with comparative ease. Until the German armies were defeated there was scant likelihood that the Nazi grip upon conquered territory would relax. Here and there a daring Dane, Norwegian, Netherlander, Belgian, Pole, Frenchman, or Czech might try as an individual to sabotage the Nazi régime or escape to the British flag; but so long as Rumanian and Russian oil flowed to Germany, so long as Swedish and French mines produced iron-ore for German smelters, and so long as the conquered peoples were compelled to share their food supply, as well as everything else, with the victors, there was no chance for revolt succeeding, within the Reich or without.

This the British fully realized. They could not by themselves defeat the Germans; their only hope of ultimate victory depended upon America. To that country Britain looked primarily for food, munitions, planes, and shipping, since without them Britain could not even ward off disaster. Grueling as was the destruction of British cities, it was not as serious as the loss of cargoes. Life underground in bomb-proof shelters is not impossible, even in northern latitudes, but to continue to fight without food and without the implements of war is impossible. No matter how extensive were their food reserves, the British knew their larder would be empty in the near future if their life-line across the Atlantic broke. And no matter how well stocked that larder, it would be of no use whatever once air supremacy over Britain was won by the Luftwaffe and maintained by it.

And so, with the coming of 1941, it became evident to the clear-sighted on both sides of the Atlantic that the United States, and the United States alone, could stave off German triumph. The Americans with their tremendous resources could, in conjunction with British efforts, surpass the German plane production by 1943—if they tried hard enough! The American mercantile marine (9,000,000 tons), plus those European vessels interned in American ports which flew the Dutch, Belgian, Norwegian, French, German, and Italian flags (158 in number), should offset submarine sinkings. Some or all of these ships Britain urgently needed. And if the Americans should be willing to turn over to the Royal Navy another fifty destroyers to guard the sea-lanes, so much the better.

What would America do? That country was closer to war in January, 1941, than most Americans realized, but still far from entering it as a declared belligerent. Informal war against Germany to all intent and purpose had seemed assured early in the contest when Congress authorized the sale of munitions; but from active armed conflict Americans were averse. The presidential election (1940) gave relatively little clue as to American opinion in this matter. Both the major candidates favored aid to Britain without stint; but both also promised that American boys would not fight in Europe. A formula, "all aid short of war," seemed to represent average American opinion.

It is, however, always easier to invent a formula than to implement it. Billions of dollars had been voted by Congress in 1940 for national defense; conscription had been adopted; and a "two-ocean navy," presumably invincible in both the Atlantic and the Pacific, had received Congressional approval. Suppose the British said their need called for every available American plane; in what situation would that leave the armed forces of the United States? This single difficulty was met by the President in assigning fifty per cent of all new government planes to Britain, thereby presumably inserting the adjective "reasonable" between the words "all" and "aid." But who was to decide on what was "reasonable," the President or Congress; and did such aid involve unlimited credit? The Johnson Act forbade loans to nations defaulting on previous loans, and Britain had defaulted. Would it be necessary to repeal the Johnson Act; was Britain's financial need really pressing; was it desirable that more naval vessels be given to Britain, with or without a quid pro quo; could the United States open its ports to British warships, take over German shipping in American ports, release these ships to Britain, and at the same time avoid war with Germany?

There was no doubt where the President stood. In December, 1940, at a press conference he suggested the possibility of a lease-lend program whereby help to Britain could be instantly granted. This he followed up by a radio address in which he suggested that in case of fire one lends one's garden hose to one's neighbor, expecting that it be returned, but not trying to sell the hose first. Then, apparently satisfied with the reaction of public opinion, Roosevelt went further and in his annual message to Congress on January 6, 1941, did not hesitate to speak as follows:

Let us say to the democracies: "We Americans are vitally concerned in your defense of freedom. We are putting forth our energies, our resources and our organizing powers to give you the strength to regain and maintain a free world. We shall send you in ever-increasing numbers, ships, planes, tanks, guns. That is our purpose and our pledge."

Followed then a bill in Congress to grant to him almost unlimited, as well as unprecedented, powers in placing the material resources of the country in the scale against Germany. The bill was fought stubbornly by non-interveners, who insisted that America had little to fear from a victorious Germany; that if the Germans could not invade England across the Channel it was absurd to be alarmed at the specter of Germany invading the United States; that democracy and all that went with it would perish in this country if it became involved in the war; and finally that opening American ports for the repair of British naval vessels, the seizure of foreign shipping in American ports in order to supply British needs, and the convoying of American ships to England by the United States navy were, in fact, acts of war.

These arguments were variously met. The more intelligent interventionists did not stress the likelihood of a Nazi invasion of the United States but sketched a situation wherein South America fell under Nazi influence, thus leaving the United States isolated in a hostile world, confronted by totalitarian states across both oceans, and subjected to subversive propaganda from all sides. Democracy here, they held, stood or fell with democracy elsewhere: the Fascist-molded states had won hitherto because the democracies had failed to support one another. As to whether such support as they proposed to give Britain was an act of war or not, that was an academic matter. The Nazis, in the President's words, "did not wait for Norway or Belgium or the Netherlands to commit an act of war. Their only interest is in a new one-way international law which lacks mutuality in its observance and therefore becomes an instrument of oppression." The United States, by implication, then, was under no obligation to regard "international law" as binding in dealing with an outlaw nation such as Hitler's Germany. The case for intervention was tersely put by Roosevelt in one sentence: "Those who would give up essential liberty to purchase a little temporary safety deserve neither liberty nor safety."

The bill, introduced into Congress on January 10, 1941, became law, with certain modifications, on March 11. To many it meant a last desperate effort to keep America out of the conflict by turning that country into an arsenal for Greece, China, and particularly Great Britain; to others it meant that the full military and naval strength of the United States would inevitably be used to destroy the armed strength of Germany; and that, as in 1918, America would arrive like Blücher at Waterloo before the coming of the night.

CHAPTER XIII

FROM LEND-LEASE TO TUNISIA

THE spring and summer of 1941 made it evident that America must do something more than to lend and to lease, if the Axis was to be defeated. The long shadow of Nazi enslavement darkened Balkan skies before the United States made her economic commitments to the Allies, and by midsummer a series of German victories carried the swastika to the Aegean and came close to driving Britain out of the Mediterranean.

The Germans cared nothing for the Italians; but it did not suit their purpose to let them be exterminated by British and Greek armies in Libya and Albania. If that happened, German prestige in Turkey and the Balkans, to say nothing of the entire Arab world, would be lessened. Berlin knew full well that there was no unity among the Balkan peoples, jealous as they were of one another. A blitzkrieg in the Balkans against the Greeks not only would rescue the Italians but also might pay good dividends, both economic and psychological, for Germany. Perhaps the threat of war, combined with economic and diplomatic pressure, might enclose the entire Balkan peninsula in the Nazi net. If not, well, Germany could spare a few armored divisions; Russia would be displeased, but the Soviets would not dare to interfere, and the same held true to an even greater degree for the Turks. If Britain chose to jeopardize her army by assisting Greeks, so much the worse for her; a British expeditionary force in the Balkans would drain England's strength in Libya and in Egypt, and if this happened it might prove possible to drive the British not only headlong out of Greece but also out of Africa.

For months past, Nazi troops had poured into Rumania, ostensibly to protect that country. On March 1, 1941, they crossed from it into Bulgaria and within one day they clicked their heels in the streets of Sofia. Thus two out of five Balkan states went down without a fight. Beyond Bulgaria lay Turkey and Greece. Both countries threatened to resist, but British troops already had landed in Greece and the Germans decided to leave Turkey alone for the time being. How to get at the Greeks? The frontier between Greece and Bulgaria was mountainous and the Germans hesitated. They could hit at Greece more readily through Turkey in Europe but they did not want to put the wily Turk to the test, not yet. Better it seemed to them to engulf Yugoslavia first, and then to flow through the Vardar Valley to inundate both Greeks and Britons from the north.

Yugoslavia, that triune kingdom of Croats, Serbs, and Slovenes, was in a serious dilemma. If she resisted, the Croats within her borders might mutiny; if she yielded, the more numerous Serbs who hated the Germans might revolt. Prince Paul, the regent, tried to dodge; he signed a pact with Germany on March 24th which admitted German technicians to Yugoslavia and gave to Hitler the right of transit across his country to munition and hospital trains. But now the Yugoslavian army under Serbian officers revolted, overturned the government of the regent, raised young King Peter, not yet eighteen, to the throne, and defied the Germans. The latter did not hesitate: on April 6th they invaded both Yugoslavia and Greece.

THE BALKAN CAMPAIGN OF 1941

The campaign thus initiated was to last slightly less than a month. The Yugoslav mobilization necessarily was slow, since Yugoslavia was not blessed with many railroads or motor cars. On paper there should have been some 900 planes, but they were of antiquated design, and of armored divisions the army had none. A German arc of 1,000 miles stretching from Austria through Hungary, Rumania, and Bulgaria ran parallel with two-thirds of the Yugoslav frontier. All the Nazis had to do was to keep the Greeks and British occupied on the Bulgar-Greek frontier while they launched several convergent attacks on Yugoslavia. The most important of these struck like lightning at the Vardar Valley from Bulgaria, thus cutting off the greater part of Yugoslavia from her allies. The German wedge now fanned out north and south, while units of it going west joined hands with the harassed Italians in Albania. Meanwhile, Belgrade fell before a German rush from the north. The oncoming Germans, with new light-built tanks for mountain warfare, with trained parachute troops supported by two of Germany's six air fleets and some 3,000 planes, were irresistible. There was nothing the smitten Yugoslavs could do except fall back into their western mountains. In a sense they were in a worse plight than in the first World War, for then at least succor awaited them in their winter of crucifixion, 1915-1916, if they could reach the Adriatic. But now that sea was infested with Italians. At Sarajevo the Yugoslav army made its last stand. Here it was trapped, in part by aid given the enemy by treacherous Croats. On April 16th, it lay down its arms. There was nothing left of Yugoslavia now unless scattered bands of guerilla fighters in remote valleys could be said to represent her.

The Greeks were next on the German slaughter list. Although they held the Wehrmacht back on the Bulgarian frontier by furious fighting, they could do nothing to stem the Nazi offensive down the valley of the Vardar. Germans, streaming down that spacious valley, captured Salonika, where the Vardar flows into the sea, and thus the Greeks in the east were isolated from their main army. As this happened, the 57,000 British troops sent to their assistance, for the most part Australian and New Zealand Anzacs, fell back slowly to Mt. Olympus, the eastern pivot of the last feasible defense line if Greece was to survive. Here they held out right stubbornly until the Germans, breaking Greek resistance further west, threatened to outflank them. The British now retreated across the flat Thessalian plain, harassed by a murderous assault from the Luftwaffe which the feeble squadrons of the R.A.F. could do little to check. The Anzacs kept their ranks intact and managed for three days to hold the pass at Thermopylae against six German divisions. But this they did, not so much to help the Greeks, who had already told them on April 21st that nothing more could be done, as to make possible their own debarkation. Again, the royal navy did its part, and from tiny ports and scattered beaches it managed to rescue 44,000 exhausted British soldiers. A second Dunkirk.

By May 1st all was over. The Greeks who had fought to the last ounce of endurance lay prostrate under German and Italian rule, for Mussolini, Hitler's lackey, claiming his share of victory, was permitted to police Athens. Yugoslavia was hung, drawn, and quartered. Croatia fell to Italy, the Banat to Hungary, and that part of Macedonia formerly in Yugoslavia was thrown to the Bulgars. The Germans took what was left. A German army rested on its laurels in Belgrade, and only the most courageous and most daring of the Serbs fled to the hills with their rifles. As for Britain, this was just one more disaster.

Crete and Libya

There were others to follow in this spring of 1941. Both in Libya and in Crete the British were to undergo defeat, and at home to stave off starvation and destruction by the narrowest of margins.

The Nazis had their eye on Africa as well as on the Balkans. For a long time they had been training men in Germany for desert warfare, conditioning them to excessive heat, preparing them with Teutonic thoroughness for what they must contend against in Africa. This German Afrika Korps, commanded by General Rommel, a strategist of the first rank, they despatched to Tripoli. With its armored tanks it became the spearhead of the Axis army, the Italians under Rommel's orders being left the minor function of consolidating land won by the more warlike Nazis.

Rommel struck out at El Agheila on March 21st, and then and there began the retreat of Wavell's Britishers all along the weary, dusty coastline of Cyrenaica over which they had so recently driven the Italians. The British had advanced rapidly; their retreat was even more rapid; past Benghazi, past Derna, all the way to Tobruk. They clung so doggedly to that wretched seaport that the Afrika Korps was not able to dislodge them. Leaving it besieged, Rommel drove the British further east, past Bardia and into Egypt. He then halted to capture Tobruk, for he did not dare leave his flank exposed. In vain, however, did the Germans roll their tanks forward against the British lines. Reinforced constantly by sea, the tenacious Britons retained their useful toehold on the African coast, and Rommel, far now from his base, was compelled to give over further advance.

This Libyan setback did not cost the British many lives, nor was the terrain lost of great strategic value. The same could not be said of Crete. Thither the Greek government had retired after the German occupation of Athens; thither had gone the greater part of the British expeditionary force rescued from the Grecian fiasco. Crete had much to offer; it protected both Palestine and the Suez; it threatened Italian communication with the Dodecanese Islands. It should and could be defended; so thought the British.

But once again they underestimated Hitler's men. Before they knew it, German paratroopers began dropping from the skies all over Crete, thousands of them. They came by air, in transport planes, in gliders towed by transport planes, ten or twelve men to a glider, equipped with radio sets, machine-guns, fully prepared to fight. The Nazi air superiority was marked; the British had no fighter planes competent to drive off the Nazis; bombers flying at low levels, raked the British with machine-guns and soon rendered untenable their hold on Crete. The German attack began on May 20th. There was no halting it. Within ten days, evacuation became inevitable. It was a third Dunkirk. Nearly half the British troops were killed or taken prisoner. Four cruisers and six destroyers were sunk, a battle-ship crippled. It was a sad day for Britain. What now could stop victorious Nazidom from spreading further east, to Syria, to Palestine, to Iraq?

IRAQ AND SYRIA

As the Nazis drove the British out of Grecian valleys and pried loose their grip on Crete, they noted with great glee events in Baghdad. Rashid Ali Beg Gailani, former premier of Iraq, a disgruntled Anglophobe and in contact with Von Papen at Ankara, deposed by force the pro-British regent who acted for the six-year-old king. Britain had secured the admission of Iraq in 1930 to the League of Nations and Britain had recognized the independence of Iraq; nevertheless by treaty she was authorized to maintain troops in Iraq, to guard imperial communications, and more especially the precious oil-fields. And now, as Britain reinforced her slender garrison at Basra at the head of the Persian gulf, Rashid Ali besieged a large British airport at Habbaniah, sixty-five miles east of Baghdad, and besought the aid of Germany. Throughout the month of May the British and the pro-German Iraqi engaged in desultory warfare. Habbaniah was unfortified, and to defend it the British had to fly both men and artillery in from Basra. If the Iraqui won, if they once succeeded in cutting the pipe-line to Haifa in Palestine, the plight of the royal navy and of the R.A.F. in the eastern Mediterranean would be serious. Fortunately the Germans were so heavily engaged this month in Crete that they were unable to help Rashid Ali except by flying in a few planes from Syria; fortunately, also, many Arabs revolted against Rashid Ali. By the end of the month his inglorious rule was over and the former regent was back on the throne.

The planes which the Germans sent to Iraq had been flown from French bases in Syria, and the excuses offered by the French governor there, who had been appointed by Vichy, were very flimsy. The British felt they could take no chances; a German occupation of Syria was by no means impossible, and once nested there the Nazis could put pressure on Turkey from the south, on Palestine from the north, and on Iraq from the west. Only part of the oil from Mosul went to Haifa; the pipe-line bifurcated and a great part of it flowed to the sea at Tripoli in Syria, an invaluable source for the Luftwaffe whose technicians and ground personnel already were said to have taken over the Syrian airdromes. The British decided to strike. Conjointly with the Free French troops of General De Gaulle they crossed from Palestine into Syria on June 8th. The allied columns moved slowly, for there was no desire to fight Frenchmen. The Vichy régime in Syria put up something more than a token resistance, but the French soldiers in Syria were ill equipped, and many of them were De Gaullists at heart. By June 28th, Damascus fell and immediate danger was over.

THE THREAT NEARER HOME

Clearly it had been an Axis spring; and not in the Near East alone. The Luftwaffe had been turned loose once more on Britain, this time to focus primarily on British ports. Eight raids on Plymouth in April left that city a smoldering mass of ruins, more battered in 1941 than Coventry in 1940. Eight nights in succession the Nazis blasted at Liverpool's docks. Hull, Newcastle, Bristol, Portsmouth, and even Belfast were visited by Nazi airmen who also were not forgetful of London, giving that city the most savage pounding it received during the entire war.

Upon the high seas the U-boats took heavier and heavier toll of British shipping. In April 589,273 tons were sunk, this the peak month since the war commenced. Ships were lost at three times the rate of construction in British and American shipyards; and food and war matériel piled higher and higher on American and Australian docks. The food ration was cut in Britain and her margin of safety grew appreciably less. The German subs were prowling further and further afield, far south of the equator and up and down the coast lines of the Americas and Africa.

The picture was not altogether one-sided. In the Mediterranean the Italians felt the weight of British armor when three of their heavy cruisers and presumably a battle-ship and numerous lighter craft were sunk. Moreover throughout the spring their Ethiopian empire faded into dust when Addis Ababa fell, as did one by one their pockets of resistance in northeast Africa. Also German victories of April and May were marred somewhat by the sinking of their finest battle-ship, the *Bismarck,* after a long and exciting chase by the most powerful units of the British fleet. Nonetheless, the over-all picture was highly favorable to the Axis. The Balkan peninsula was under their thumb, all of it, to do with as they wished. The southeastern door to Europe was shut and bolted. There would be no second front there to worry about for months or years to come. And in Greece, in Crete, in Libya, they had administered a most sound drubbing to their most dangerous foe, Great Britain, whom they continued to bomb constantly from the air and partially to strangle on the oceans.

HITLER INVADES RUSSIA

When German armies invaded France in 1940 Russia saw her chance and took it; she ordered Rumania to cede to her Bessarabia and northern Bukovina. The former province had been Russian territory before the first World War and Russia had never acquiesced in its loss. Bukovina had been part of the old Austrian empire and never had been Russian. Its population, however, was predominantly Ukrainian and Stalin thought there was no time like the present for uniting all Ukrainians under the Soviets, whether in Bukovina, Poland, or Russia. In 1940 he gauged the situation correctly: the Nazis were not consulted about this enlargement of the Russian frontiers and the Nazis were sulky; but the Nazis did not interfere.

A month or two later, after France had fallen and England seemed about to fall, the Nazis were not so conciliatory toward Soviet ambitions in the southeast. So Stalin discovered when he put renewed pressure on Rumania. This time the Nazis took action in a supposedly Russian sphere of influence without consulting him. They carved Rumania according to their own plans, presenting part of Transylvania to Hungary, the Dobrudja (formerly Bulgarian territory) to Bulgaria, granting what was left a guarantee of territorial integrity backed by the immediate presence of German troops.

It was now Stalin's turn to be conciliatory; he had miscalculated German strength and had neither wished nor expected such a speedy and overwhelming German triumph in the west. With Germany supplying the Finns with numerous planes and fresh ammunition in the autumn of 1940, the Russian decided to be circumspect; they scrupulously delivered to Germany the goods called for by their trade agreement of 1939; they sent Premier Molotov to Berlin late in 1940 to return Von Ribbentrop's visit of the preceding year. It was not a pleasant visit for the Russian, since he discovered that his country was expected to join the Axis, as had Rumania and Slovakia. This Stalin would not do; he had no intention of duplicating Mussolini's fateful career and playing second fiddle to Hitler. The Germans hinted that Russia might receive territory in Iran and Iraq, in return for concessions in the Ukraine. But the Russian negotiators backed water fast. They suspected that sooner or later the Nazis would attack the Soviets.

Stalin knew that Russia was ill prepared for war, but he also knew that Hitler distrusted and hated him as much as he did Hitler. And so he made his preparations. He signed a peace pact with Japan (still in force in Sept., 1943) thus temporarily at least insuring Russia against war on two fronts; he lengthened the work-day from seven to eight hours; he made it a crime against the state to be more than twenty minutes tardy at the factories; he shunted nearly a million boys and girls into trade schools for special training in mechanical pursuits; he speeded production in war matériel; and he gave orders that many vital war industries in Moscow, Leningrad, and elsewhere should dismantle their machinery and reassemble it east of the Urals.

Meantime the Soviet chieftain tried by diplomacy to stave off Nazi attack. For a short time he apparently toyed with the idea of assisting the Yugoslavs, for he signed a treaty of friendship with them on the eve of their war with Germany and he upbraided the Bulgars for their subservience to the Nazis. But caution proved the better part of valor.

To curry favor with the Germans he refused recognition any longer to the Belgian and Norwegian embassies and he gave it to the pro-German rebels in Baghdad. And finally in May, 1941, he dismissed the ministers of Greece and Yugoslavia.

In that same month Rudolf Hess, designated by Hitler in case of death as his successor, flew solo to Britain on a secret mission. Whether it involved a plan for peace between Britain and Germany if the former would guarantee the latter a free hand against the Soviets we can only guess. But this much can be affirmed: by June, Hitler had determined to smite the Russians, that is, if troop concentrations have any significance. The Rumanians mobilized on the Russian border; the Nazi soldiers who had conquered Greece were ordered to the Polish frontier; to Finland the Nazis despatched German units, artillery and tanks; and the Luftwaffe, withdrawn largely from the west, was concentrated in the east, its squadrons flying over Russian territory on reconnaissance flights.

Then without warning on June 22nd the Nazi legions crossed the border and there was war with Russia! The most gigantic duel in recorded history now had opened. Never before had so many million men been hurled so savagely at one another; never before had there been a battle line of 1,800 miles across which so many armies lunged. Tanks ripped holes in opposing lines and syphoned through to widen salients. And then, the pincer movements; planes droning overhead and dropping death amid the ack, ack of the anti-aircraft guns; pockets of resistance, now large, now small, contracting, expanding, encirclements, escapes, the trapper sometimes trapped; a constant fluid war of movement; a ruinous scene of hell on earth which Lucifer himself could not surpass. And all this made possible of articulation and control by a new invention of resourceful man, the pocket radio.

The Germans had a plan of campaign, brilliant in design, brilliant in execution, which suited well their temperament and their superb military skill. The "Blitzkrieg" tactics so successfully applied two years earlier in Flanders were to be repeated. The Nazis aimed at Moscow, but it was neither this river nor that town that was their main objective. The Russian armies were their quarry, and these they proposed to run down and to exterminate before cold weather came, by wide open maneuvers across wide, level plains. Dive bombers and tanks, speed and force would encircle the Slav, enfold him in unexpected pockets, and then crush and slay the ponderous red giant. And this the Germans almost did in 1941, but not quite; and once again in 1942, but not quite.

For the Russians, too, had a plan, one suited to their temperament, their tradition, their climate. It was very simple: to keep their armies intact no matter how much ground they yielded. A hundred thousand square miles was less important to them than their armies. Space, time, and winter weather, Russia's ancient allies, had served her well against the Swedes in the eighteenth century, against the French in the nineteenth. The Russian defense was one in depth, not ordinary depth but Russian depth. Stalin proposed to contest the frontier lightly, to lure on the enemy, to depend on guerilla action to harass his communications, to hammer away at his flanks, and above all to be patient under defeat, conscious that new Russian armies, and still more new Russian armies, given time, would hurl themselves at the Hitlerites and expel them from Sovietland.

As might have been predicted, 1941 was a year of German victory. In little more than three weeks the Luftwaffe destroyed a considerable part of the Russian planes before they even left the ground, the German tanks penetrated the Stalin line of frontier defense, and the German infantry was in Smolensk with Moscow only two hundred miles away. To have covered two-thirds of the distance to the Russian capital in twenty-six days was good going, particularly if the German claim to have surrounded and to have annihilated two Russian armies in a great circle six hundred miles around be given only partial credence. Nevertheless, the war was still young and the road to Moscow was no open highway.

It was now midsummer and the Nazis looked forward hopefully to the conquest of Moscow. But the Russians had just begun to fight. Already they had ruined by fire and by dynamite their bridges, railways, power houses, water mains, dwellings; and now they counter-attacked all along the line, warily, intermittently, avoiding encirclement. The series of sanguine battles which followed one another in quick succession in central Russia are known collectively as the Battle of Smolensk, although for the most part they took place to the east of that strategic rail center and at some distance from it. The spearhead of the German advance reached Vyazma, northeast of Smolensk and only one hundred miles from Moscow; it penetrated to Bryansk to the southeast, athwart the Moscow-Kiev-Odessa railroad. But the Russian lines were elastic; they bent but did not break.

Long before German pressure on the central front slowed down it was felt in the Ukraine in southern Russia and at Leningrad in the north. The black earth of the Ukraine, the mineral wealth of the Donets basin, and the rich oil-fields of the Caucasus lured on the Nazis. From early August to late November they kept advancing. By-passing Kiev, they raced for the Black Sea coast and reached it; they then dived at Kiev from the east, and that capital of the Ukraine fell into their hands. All through October Teutonic victory-waves flowed east and

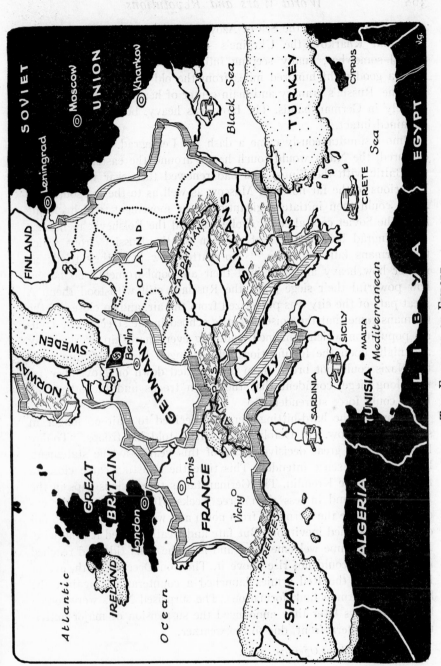

The Fortress of Europe
(Courtesy of the New York *Times*.)

south. They swept to the Sea of Azov; they submerged Stalino on the Don and Kharkov, the Ukraine's second largest city. Then they abated somewhat, finally seeping into Rostov at the mouth of the Don, a good eight hundred miles from the old Russian frontier. The Ukraine, Russia's granary and main center of heavy industry was now entirely in German hands. The blow was heavy. but the Red armies remained intact.

Almost simultaneously came a dash for Leningrad. That city once captured, the Nazis would touch hands around the eastern shores of the Baltic with the Finns, who had renewed their war with Russia. Victorious to the far north of Moscow as well as to the far south, the Nazis could then initiate a gigantic pincer movement, which closing in on the Soviet capital could choke and end the Bolshevik menace.

"Leningrad became the first position on the Russian front which the Germans failed to take." [1] No matter how hard they tried; no matter how heavy and sustained their air bombardment; no matter how powerful their siege guns, the Russians still withstood them. A great part of the city was pulverized from the air, and so close did the Germans come that the noise of battle echoed in the streets. The civilian population which remained, enduring every hardship, worked day and night upon the fortifications which ringed their city. And since the Nazis could not break them they settled down on November 1st to a long siege, confident that their own troops and the advancing Finns could force surrender.

Meanwhile the hard-hitting Germans decided to wait no longer in subduing Moscow. On October 2nd Hitler told his troops, "To-day begins the last great decisive battle of this year"—a true statement, but not in the sense intended. This time the swastika came close to floating over the Kremlin. The German tanks tore vicious gaps in the Russian lines and in less than three weeks Moscow was nearly encircled. On came the Germans, from north and west and south. The fall of Moscow seemed inevitable. But fate and weather ruled it otherwise. In November came welcome snow and ice. The Nazi tide had reached its apogee but could not rise above it. Then on December 6th, eve of Pearl Harbor, the Red armies launched a counterattack against the half-frozen German tank formations. The surprised Nazis were forced back; two days later they announced the suspension of major activities on the eastern front, due to the weather.

[1] Werner, *The Great Offensive*, p. 74.

The United States Closer to the Brink

"Give us the tools and we will finish the job," thus spoke Churchill in 1941 as the American public debated the pros and cons of lend-lease. The implication to many was that Britain did not need the armed intervention of the United States. But did "give us the tools" mean give them to us in America, or deliver them to us in England?

The majority of Americans would avoid "a shooting war," yet that same majority was determined that the Nazis must not win. To find an intermediate way between lend-lease and war was difficult, but the President found it. To order the American navy to convoy trans-atlantic cargoes meant "shooting"; but how about patrols instead of convoys? There is no difference, cried the isolationists; but in this they erred somewhat. To use the President's analogy, a patrol on the high seas had the same function as a scout on the western plains: not to fight but warily to watch, and instantly to report the presence of hostile Indians. Warships on patrol would do the same, would look for submarines, those "rattlesnakes of the ocean," and send word by wireless of their whereabouts. If British naval units picked up said messages and acted thereon, that did not mean war, or did it?

By April 11th our navy was on patrol duty and on April 25th the President said that patrol would be extended, if necessary, to "all the Seven Seas." Two days after, the day the Germans entered Athens, Churchill addressed his faithful House of Commons. "When you come to think of it," he said, "the United States are very closely bound up with us now. . . . When I said ten weeks ago: give us the tools and we will finish the job, I meant, *give* them to us: put them within our reach—and that is what it now seems the Americans are going to do." The situation in the Near East is perilous but what of it? "Nothing that can happen in the east is comparable with what is happening in the west." And Churchill ended, quoting Clough:

> And not by eastern windows only,
> When daylight comes, comes in the light;
> In front the sun climbs slow; how slowly!
> But westward, look, the land is bright.

Through the spring we drifted toward war with Nazi Germany; we occupied Greenland to forestall Hitler there; British warships limped into our drydocks to have their war wounds treated, unquestionably an unneutral act on our part; and, May 21st, the *Robin Moor,* an American ship far from the prescribed war zone, was sunk in the South Atlantic, unquestionably an act of war on the part of the Reich. Technically we were still at peace but more thoughtful isolationists, realizing the inevitable, were resigning from America First Committees, and more did so when President Roosevelt announced July 7th that our troops had landed in Iceland.

THE ATLANTIC CHARTER

On August 16th the President of the United States and the Prime Minister of England made rendezvous off Newfoundland. While their naval and military staffs took common council the two chief magistrates drew up and signed the Atlantic Charter, a document reminiscent of Wilson's fourteen point in proposing general principles for future guidance. Both statesmen proclaimed that they opposed "aggression, territorial or otherwise"; that "they desired to see no territorial changes that do not accord with the expressed wishes of the people concerned"; that "they respect the right of all peoples to choose the form of government under which they will live"; that they favored "access on equal terms to the trade and to the raw materials of the world"; that they wished to secure for all nations "improved labor standards, economic advancement and social security"; that "after the destruction of Nazi tyranny" a peace should be established which would guarantee "to all men, in all lands" the chance to live "in freedom from want and fear"; that the high seas be free for all; that the use of force be abandoned; and that "a permanent system of general security is essential."

This charter, of course, was not binding; it was not an alliance; it stated the ideal goal toward which both countries meant to strive. British public opinion would have welcomed an alliance between Britain and America and was disappointed that the Atlantic Charter did not go farther. But would such an alliance have been ratified by the United States Senate? Roosevelt and Churchill were practical and experienced politicians; and both were confident that time, tide, and Nazi Germany would soon bring such hopes to happy fruition.

Nor were they disappointed. On September 4th the United States destroyer *Greer* was fired on by a German submarine. The *Greer* escaped, but promptly the President stated that henceforth the navy "would shoot on sight." On October 17th the U. S. destroyer *Kearney* was badly mauled in fighting a German submarine, and shortly after, the destroyer *Reuben James* was sunk. These acts of war brought congressional repeal of neutrality legislation which had forbidden the arming of merchant vessels and their entry into combatant harbors. But the vote in the House of Representatives was only 212 to 194 in favor of such repeal and this was on November 13th, less than a month before Pearl Harbor. Pacifists and non-interventionists were still nu-

Philip Gendreau, N. Y.

MEDIUM TANKS ROLLING OFF THE ASSEMBLY LINE IN DETROIT

Photograph by U. S. Army Signal Corps

FRANKLIN DELANO ROOSEVELT

merous in America. Yet to many it seemed that we had been at war since the sinking of the *Robin Moor*, or at least since the "shoot on sight" order.

THE UNITED STATES ENTERS THE WAR

December 7th, and all doubts were removed; America was in the war.

Relations between the United States and Japan had been increasingly strained since 1931. Our refusal to recognize the Japanese puppet state of Manchukuo and our steadfast sympathy with China led the militarist statesmen of Japan to conclude that they must either abandon their ambition to rule East Asia or fight the United States.

The dispute was not primarily economic. Our trade with China was limited and our capital invested there comparatively small. But Americans had educated many Chinese, built missions, schools, universities, hospitals in China, and for a long time had been annoyed, not merely with Japan's outrageous behavior toward China but also with themselves for doing nothing effective to prevent it.

In July 1939 the United States gave the requisite six months' notice that it intended to denounce its commercial treaty with Japan, due to expire in January, 1940. The Japanese were furious, also somewhat alarmed. The United States was their best customer and from us they imported much war material, particularly scrap iron and high octane gas. Why should America act thus? Our ambassador at Tokio, Mr. Grew, told them the blunt truth. "The people of the United States," he said, "resent the methods which the Japanese armed forces employ in China today and what appears to be their objective."

Unfortunately, when the trade treaty expired we did nothing; the Japanese continued to buy American oil, scrap iron and other war matériel. They therefore concluded that we cared more for dollars than for China. Just why, indeed, we made this gesture without implementing it is difficult to fathom; perhaps we wanted to discourage Japan from joining the Axis, as she did in 1940; perhaps we did not want her driven toward the conquest of the East Indies; or perhaps we did care more for dollars than for China.

Meanwhile we advanced loans and credits to the Chinese whereby they could purchase tools of war. But how could these be imported? There were only two feasible routes—one by rail through French Indo-China; the other by the Burma Road, a steep and twisting motor highway from railhead in Burma to Chungking in far western China, a road handmade by Chiang Kai-shek's people with pick-axe, crow bar and wheelbarrow. The first route the French promptly sealed, for impotent Vichy dared not defy the Japanese ultimatum to do so. Britain in 1940 knew she had no chance to defend Hongkong without aid from America, and very little with it. Therefore she, too, gave way, and that summer agreed to close the Burma Road for three months.

The British held no cards and could do no otherwise; but this was not true for the Americans. We could stop shipment of vital war matériel to Japan, and this we gingerly began to do by restricting export of scrap iron and gasoline. In September, Japan joined the Axis and shortly after the United States advised her citizens in Japan to return home. Whether this act of ours stayed Japan's hand, or whether the cautious Nipponese were waiting the results of German air assault on Britain one cannot say but the Burma Road was reopened in November without incident.

For some months Japanese policy remained uncertain. Japan might have sailed south and seized the Dutch East Indies, taking French Indo-China, Hongkong, Malaya, Singapore, and the Philippines en route. But Japan was not sure of Russia; and with that traditional foe on friendly terms with Germany, threateningly close to Japan and snugly dug in at Vladivostok, perhaps it was as well to see what diplomacy might win.

And so Matsuoka, secretary for foreign affairs, visited first Berlin, then Moscow, signing a non-aggression pact with Stalin. The absorption of French Indo-China followed, the French, in June, 1941, granting military bases and the right to troop transit. Thereupon soldiers of Japan were rushed to the Thai border, thus putting pressure on Thailand to accept Japanese domination, or else! As Churchill broadcast in August, "They stretch their grasping hand into the southern seas of China. They snatch Indo-China from the wretched Vichy French. They menace by their movements Siam. They menace Singapore, the British link with Australasia, and they menace the Philippine Islands under the protection of the United States. It is certain that this has got to stop."

Who was to stop it, and when? Both Britain and the United States froze Japanese credits this fateful summer of 1941, thus ending trade relations with Nippon; the Dutch East Indies, absorbing courage from the two democracies, grew recalcitrant about selling Tokyo more oil; and there was much talk of the A.B.C.D. powers (America, Britain, China, and the Dutch East Indies) acting in unison: but China was otherwise engaged and so was Britain; only a handful of Netherlanders were in the East Indies; the native peoples were not organized for defense; and that left the United States as the solitary lion in the path of aggressive Japan.

The American public had been so engrossed with the European

drama that it had not paid much attention to the Far East, and President Roosevelt had been careful since the outbreak of the war scarcely to mention Japan in his public addresses. With one war menacing us in the Atlantic we preferred avoiding another in the Pacific, and the state department did its best to delay an outbreak there. But our government remained adamant in helping China; it extended lend lease to that country; it permitted an American officer to organize a Chinese air service; it despatched a military mission to Chungking; and it continued to protest the boa-constrictor engorgement of Indo-China.

Few dreamed the Japanese might attack us. After three years invasion of China and with a million soldiers stationed there, it surely would be the height of folly for Japan to engage America. We little realized the bitter hate and scorn with which we were regarded in Tokyo, or how the war lords had hynotized their people in regard to their divine ancestry and the equally divine mission of Japan. What we thought was that Tokyo probably intended to absorb Thailand; and few Americans cared much about that remote nation. Once secure in Thailand Japan might then invade Burma to close the Burma Road. But why cross that bridge until we came to it; it was not nearly as exciting a topic as the siege of Leningrad or Mr. Roosevelt's Atlantic patrols.

And so when the Konoye cabinet fell in October, 1941, and militarist General Tojo became premier, Americans were not much concerned. Nevertheless, until that month, the Japanese had not decided "whether Japan should reach an agreement with the United States at the cost of considerable concessions, or should pursue her immutable national policies by lining up with Germany under the Axis alliance. The final domestic show-down had now come, and there could be little doubt of the outcome. "Konoye was through...."[2] War was close at hand.

On November 5th Tojo announced that he was sending Kurusu as a special envoy to the United States. His *peace* mission in all probability was but a screen behind which Japan made ready her lightning stroke of December 7th, and so Churchill saw it when he warned Tokyo on November 12th that if war came between Japan and the United States, Britain would be at war with Japan "within the hour." Americans, however, were more optimistic. Kurusu doubtless would tempt us to abandon the Chinese, and this we would not do; but possibly he had some compromise to offer; perhaps he came just to hurry Hitler so that he would speed the war on Russia which was not then as decisive as Japan had hoped.

Kurusu suggested a modus vivendi, with the United States acting as

[2] Otto Tolischus, *Tokyo Record*, p. 269.

mediator in the Sino-Japanese War. The President agreed under certain conditions to act as "introducer" but not as "mediator"—a subtle
distinction to avoid offending China. Kurusu then proposed on November 20th to evacuate southern Indo-China as soon as an agreement
was signed with the United States, and all of Indo-China on the conclusion of general peace in the Far East. We were to cease our aid to
China and withdraw our economic sanctions against Japan, which
meant, if we sold Japan oil and the tools of war she agreed to use them
against China and not against us.

We countered with a note withdrawing the President's offer to act
as introducer, reaffirming continued aid to China and proposing that
Japan withdraw from China and resign from the Axis. If Japan would
do this we would remove all restrictions on exports to Japan and help
that country stabilize its currency. In other words, Japan was to drop
war and go back to work. The Japanese reply was handed to Mr. Hull
on the afternoon of December 7th. All this was superfluous; torpedo
planes and fighter escorts blazoned with the rising sun of Japan were
already dropping bombs on our naval base at Pearl Harbor.

JAPANESE VICTORIES

Our carelessness in Hawaii was inexcusable. More than ten days before our commanders there had been advised that war might break at
any instant, yet few precautions were taken, not even the elementary
one of coördinating naval and military intelligence. The navy took it
for granted that the aircraft warning system operated by the army was
functioning all the time, and would give adequate advance notice of
the approach of enemy planes; but the army only operated this system
three hours a day. The army took it for granted that the navy kept
constant watch by long distance reconnaissance flights; but the navy
patrolled to the south only, and the Japanese came from the north. The
army had one chance to save the day and muffed it; a soldier experi-
menting after hours with the aircraft detector heard the approaching
Japanese planes only to be told by his superior that they were American flying fortresses. The navy also had its chance; a full hour before
the attack it sank an enemy submarine just off Pearl Harbor but gave
no general alarm.

Down swooped Japanese planes upon our motionless aircraft, an
excellent target, since to prevent sabotage they were lined up in close
formation, wing to wing. Having destroyed at one blow most of our
planes the Japanese airmen made for our warships and caught them
at anchor. The crews did what they could with their anti-aircraft
batteries, but a battle-ship at anchor, unsupported by planes, is help-

less, and in a few minutes five of our battle-wagons were either sunk or badly crippled, to say nothing of the loss of other craft.

Three days later the *Prince of Wales* and the *Repulse,* two of the Royal navy's best and biggest ships, were sent to the bottom off the coast of Malaya by Japanese torpedo planes and bombers. The British admiral in command took a chance, and lost. Without air escort he steamed north to intercept a Japanese convoy, trusting to murky weather to screen him from air attack. He missed the convoy, turned south again, and instead of returning to Singapore decided to investigate another Japanese landing. The weather suddenly cleared and down upon the huge ships swept the Japanese planes. The British put up a stiff fight for three hours; but the Japanese got their quarry.

These two naval disasters were catastrophic. The Japanese army was well trained, needing little food, fanatically patriotic, hardened by years of war in China; but without command of the sea even that army could not approach the Philippines or the Dutch East Indies, much less Singapore. United, the Anglo-American fleets would have controlled the seas off Asia; but now the rising sun of Japan shone far and wide across those waters.

Throughout December we took a severe drubbing, as did our British allies. Almost simultaneously the enemy struck at Singapore, Hongkong, Guam, Wake Island, the Philippines. We had recently sent to Manila many new planes. Parked in rows, wing to wing, precisely as at Pearl Harbor, most of them were caught on the ground before dropping a bomb. Guam, located in a veritable nest of Japanese islands and (thanks to Congress, still unfortified) succumbed after four days. The 378 marines on Wake held out heroically until December 23rd, sinking with their light shore batteries two destroyers and a cruiser. Two days later Hongkong, battered by artillery and dive bombing and with its water supply exhausted, surrendered to Japan. Within one week after Pearl Harbor the Japanese army had landed in force in Luzon, both north and south of Manila, thus forcing the evacuation of the Philippine capital. Our army retreated according to plan with its Philippine allies into the wild and mountainous peninsula of Bataan, to fight on for months, hoping against hope for succor that could not come.

If the Japanese had struck only at the Philippines we would, of course, have gone to war, for we had pledged the independence of those islands. But the voices of isolationist and pacifist would have risen high in lamentations for the death of our soldiers, sailors, and marines in lands far away. Now all such internal wrangling ceased. The Americans were angry; all of them. And as the casualty list lengthened they became more so.

The United States declared war on Japan; Germany and Italy declared war on us; Churchill flew the Atlantic to consult with Roosevelt. The world-wide issue now was joined. The United Nations (in 1917 it had been the Allies) signed on January 1, 1942, a military alliance. China, the Chinese Republic, Britain, and the United States, plus governments in exile (Luxemburg, Holland, Belgium, Norway, Greece, Yugoslavia) plus also the Central American and Caribbean republics and India made up the original list. Russia remained at peace with Japan. But the "phoney war" of 1939 was global war in 1942

The Swarming Japanese: Bataan

For a good half year the United Nations saw their enemies win victory after victory, east and west, on Russian plains and African deserts, in the jungles and swamps of southeastern Asia, and among the clustered islands of the East Indies. Nippon paid a heavy price in ships and men, but on her swarming fighters came until they were near to Australia, until they had swallowed Burma, cut the Burma Road, and reaching the Indian Ocean threatened India.

The honor of withstanding them longest is ours, for we did not surrender Bataan until the 9th of April, nor our rocky island of Corregidor in Manila Bay until the 7th of May. There were few American troops in the Philippines, but despite loss of the Flying Fortresses destroyed there we had two main advantages. One was the terrain. Corregidor was strongly fortified; it could be approached only by sea or air, and deep within its bowels was a huge tunnel the length of a city block, sufficiently wide to permit two ambulances to pass abreast, and with lateral tunnels on either side. Corregidor seemed a safe refuge from Japanese bombing and artillery fire. So long as our flag flew over it the enemy was not safe in Manila; and so long as our artillery could fire from it we could protect to some extent our troops on Bataan, only four miles away. Bataan was a natural fortress; its precipitous hills and deep ravines, covered by jungle growth, and its relatively narrow neck made penetration difficult.

Equally important was the loyal support of our Filipino allies. The Filipino Scouts, hardy, agile, well disciplined, proved themselves as good as any soldiers; and the regular Filipino army, largely without training, acquitted itself with distinction. Even the aboriginal Negritos joined in lustily, capturing Japanese stragglers and bringing them into the American lines in bamboo cages. The wise policy of Philippine independence bore good fruit; had it not been for these allies we could have done little to stave off the enemy.

In mid-January, 1942, the Japanese made a major assault on the

American lines, and again in early February. And on both occasions they were driven back. None could gainsay their reckless courage: they charged into nests of machine-guns without faltering; they hurled themselves on barbed wire, electrically charged, and stuck there, making of themselves a living bridge over which poured their reserves; they dangled like monkeys from tree tops; they fought by night and day. Death had no terrors for the men of Nippon.

Even so, Bataan's 40,000 defenders, mostly Filipinos, could have held out had it not been for lack of air support, food, and matériel. After January 1st, MacArthur never had more than five military planes, all old models, continuously damaged and repaired with great difficulty. Four antique civilian planes, called "the bamboo fleet," because held together by splicing them with bamboo and bits of wire, were his service of supply, and the Bamboo Fleet could do little to replenish drugs, spare parts, and food, even if Corregidor could have spared them its stores. The defense grew weaker from malnutrition, malaria, dysentery, beri-beri, and hookworm. And as this happened the Japanese changed commanders and resolved to end American resistance no matter what price was paid. Soon our outnumbered men could get no sleep. There was no intermission, no relief; for there were not soldiers enough to spell the half-starved malaria-stricken men in the front-line fox holes. Driven back to the sea some few were evacuated to Corregidor by motor torpedo boats, and some, challenging the sharks, swam four miles to the island where our flag still flew. What remained of the ammunition was destroyed and the flag of Nippon flew over the peninsula of Bataan.

General MacArthur, complying with the command of the President, had left by motor boat and submarine to renew the war as commander-in-chief of the United Nations in Australia. General Wainwright, his successor, continued American resistance on Corregidor until May. His men were sick, half-starved, cooped up underground, their island refuge shaken day in and day out by Japanese bombs. Before long the enemy made good a landing. Resistance being futile, Wainwright surrendered.

SINGAPORE

Meanwhile, in February, Singapore had fallen. That populous and wealthy city was a strong bastion of empire, but only as a naval base. Millions had been spent solely to ward off attack by sea. In January, 1942, aside from a cruiser and a few destroyers there was no fleet to defend. The gun emplacements faced seaward, for Singapore was an island as well as a city, and the need of an army base had not been foreseen. Surely the Malay peninsula, nine hundred miles long, a grotesque geographical appendix, was a strong wall to landward—and so it would have been with sea and air supremacy.

The British had over 70,000 troops to defend Malaya and Singapore, but their naval strength was puny, their air force utterly inadequate. Even so, if their troops had been trained for jungle fighting (which was not the case) and if the Malays had been given Commonwealth citizenship (or even the promise of it) and trained to fight, the story of Singapore would have been different.

At Singapore there were British regiments famous for tropical warfare of the nineteenth-century variety celebrated by Kipling, the hollow square beating off the Fuzzy Wuzzies. In all the Far East the British had nothing comparable to our Filipino Scouts. The Malays were not treacherous, nor had they been ill treated by the British raj, which had left them under their native sultans. But the Malays simply did not consider it their war.

Worst of all was the plane shortage. "In Malaya and Singapore the Japanese command of the air changed gradually from superiority to an almost unchallenged superiority."[3] Then the British were doomed. Reconnaissance in jungle fighting is practically impossible except from the air. As soon as the British tried to establish a base they were photographed from the air and bombarded from it. Week after week the Imperials fought without sighting a friendly plane.

The Japanese fought this brief, incisive, and completely victorious campaign with astonishing skill and foresight. Their shock troops, carefully selected and better paid than the average soldier, were the snipers. Especially trained in tree climbing, in remaining motionless for hours, in camouflaging themselves to look like leaves, the snipers dropped hand grenades on the British by day and, to give the illusion of attack, set off firecrackers by night. Japanese troops were everywhere; they were lightly clad and carried no heavy equipment; they lived on hard rice cake impregnated with meat; they needed no fire; they were prepared for every emergency, with rubber sneakers in place of shoes, with bicycles for jungle paths, with collapsible boats for jungle streams, with chemicals to purify muddy water.

The British army was a land force; that of the Japanese was amphibious, traveling by boat and barge, sometimes by river, sometimes by sea, forcing its way along roads or through rubber plantations, forever getting in the rear of the baffled British and cutting off detachments. The Japanese tanks were light but far superior to the British armored cars, some of which dated from 1918. Excellent, too, were the Japanese paratroopers, skilled in signaling with the radio, adept at ambush. And so the British land army, almost as large as the

[3] G. Weller, *Singapore Is Silent*, p. 615.

invading force, according to the Japanese larger, never had a chance. Defeated in skirmish after skirmish, in foray after foray, it staggered back to the tip of Malaya, crossed the causeway to Singapore, blew up the bridge behind it, and thought to hold Singapore until help came.

The Americans still held Corregidor; the British still held Malta; but Singapore was too big; there were forty miles of coastline and the Straits of Johore were easy to cross, particularly in the west where the water was shallow and where reedy swamps and shallow streams on the Singapore side invited Japanese infiltration. There were no underground caverns as on Malta or man-made tunnels as on Corregidor. Fighting was in the open, and from the pitiless skies poured down the Japanese bombs. The British did their best to send reinforcements, even endangering their Eighth Army in Egypt by so doing. Planes arrived, but too late, for the Japanese had already infiltrated through the marshy shorelands of the west and had repaired the dynamited causeway. With the enemy in command of both sea and air a Dunkirk was impossible. After a thirty-day siege came the surrender—the most humiliating in British army annals and, historically speaking, the most significant since Saratoga.

BURMA

Burma in many ways repeated Malaya and Singapore, the soldiers of the rising sun bobbing up where least expected; the Imperials baffled and confused, fighting back blindly, strafed from the air, losing contact with their own detachments, cut off from retreat, poorly led by officers whose ingrained contempt for "natives" was costly.

The Burma campaign synchronized with Malaya and Singapore and lasted longer, but only because Burma was of large area and it was impossible to push all the British to the sea. Nevertheless, the outcome was soon a foregone conclusion. At the outset the British, by taking a long chance, might perhaps have made it otherwise. They never had many troops in Burma; but if they had united them in December, 1941, and had pushed boldly into Thailand it is barely possible they could have dammed the Japanese flood until reinforcements came from India and from China, alarmed at the menace to the Burma Road. But instead of this the Imperials remained on the defensive; and during the early campaign the soldiers of Chiang Kai-shek were forbidden to enter Burma.

For a long time that country had been a neglected ward of the Empire, the Burmese complaining that they had no land communication with India, owing to the pull of shipping interests, and that their pleas for self-government were without effect. The Japanese took full advantage of this disaffection; their spy system in Burma was well organized, their promises of independence for Burma loud and emphatic. British propaganda could hardly have been worse; it promised nothing apart from protection; it did not even try to enlist the Burmese to defend their own country. Keep cool and trust us, was the British slogan; and in consequence as fast as the Japanese won victories just so rapidly did the Burmese lose their respect for British arms. Long before the campaign closed the Burmese were actively aiding the invader by providing food, by acting as guides, and occasionally by fighting at his side.

The main Japanese objective was Rangoon at the mouth of the Irrawaddy where extensive lend-lease cargoes waited transshipment to Mandalay. Once Rangoon fell the Burma Road would be bottled up, the Chinese life-line severed, and the Japanese could attack the oilfields far up the Irrawaddy.

January 15th the invasion started and it took the Japanese over two weeks to cut through the tangled jungles on the Thailand border, to ward off attacks by the R.A.F. and American flyers, to capture Moulmein opposite Rangoon on the Gulf of Martaban. Once there they fanned out, crossed the broad and shallow Salween (three miles wide at its mouth), and circled around to the north of Rangoon. Meanwhile, detachments slipped across the Gulf in small boats to strike at Rangoon from the south and west. The city became impossible to hold and its evacuation in early March was a military necessity.

During the next two months the Japanese swarmed north up the Irrawaddy, the Sittang, and the Salween, driving before them the British and the Chinese, who had finally been welcomed as allies. Numerous and isolated engagements took place between invaders and defenders; the former, wary in frontal attack but swift in movement, appeared with monotonous regularity from nowhere to block roads, to bomb tanks, and to worry and harass the exhausted soldiers of Britain and China; the latter kept on retreating toward the borders of India, the foothills of the Himalayas, and to the far southeastern corner of China, dynamiting oil wells and burning lend-lease matériel as opportunity offered.

The retreat became a rout. The British, burdened with mechanized equipment utterly unsuitable for a terrain of interlaced swamps and forest, abandoned their tanks and scurried on toward India. Most of them made it. The Chinese under the American General Stilwell came near being caught. They had stayed, perhaps, too long in central Burma and the Japanese had already cut off their retreat over the Burma Road by penetrating northeast from Thailand. The problem which confronted this fifty-nine-year-old American general was to press north faster than the Japanese could outflank him. Plans laid for so doing were countermanded by the commander-in-chief of the Chinese army. Radio communication with Chungking was interrupted, and the Chinese forces in Burma widely scattered. Stilwell succeeded in extricating some Chinese and British soldiers and miscellaneous civilians by a march of wild adventure and diversified hardship which deserves well the attention of future historians.[4]

For months to come refugees straggled into India. Fed from the skies by British planes, with swamps under their feet as often as dry land, plunging blindly where trails were not even blazed, many lost their way and perished; how many died will be forever unknown.

JAVA AND AUSTRALIA

"The fall of Singapore opened the battle for Australia," thus spoke the Prime Minister of Australia in the middle of February, 1942. But the battle for Java had first to be fought. Java was the key island of the East Indies. Although not the largest, it was, owing to its tea and coffee, rice, quinine, manganese, and oil, the most prosperous. On Java was the capital of the Dutch empire in the East, also a not inconsiderable naval base and what would have been a not inconsiderable air force had Britain and America time to deliver the planes they promised. Java once in Japanese hands, northwestern Australia lay open to invasion; contrariwise, as long as Allied planes could be based on Java the Japanese occupation of Singapore and the Philippines was menaced from the south.

To defend Java the Dutch had a hastily drilled army of 100,000 natives, not too reliable, some 400 planes, mostly obsolete, a few cruisers, none very large, and a number of destroyers and submarines. Add to this our own Asiatic squadron (which had left the Philippines in the nick of time) of one heavy cruiser together with a number of destroyers and submarines, a British cruiser, an Australian cruiser, and some lesser British craft, all under the command of a Dutch admiral, and it is evident that prospects were not promising.

The Japanese took few chances; their game was to isolate prey before devouring it. In December, 1941, British North Borneo with its oil-fields fell to their attack, and in January the eastern coast of Borneo and the island of Celebes. Delayed by continued British resistance at Singapore, the Japanese spread further east, taking the northern coastline of New Guinea in their stride and landing a force at Rabaul in New Britain, thus planting the flag of the rising sun well to the northeast of Australia. Then came direct action toward Java down

---

[4] For an excellent account, see J. Belden, *Retreat with Stilwell*.

through the Macassar Straits. This time the Japanese were driven back, American and Dutch submarines dealing heavy damage to their destroyers and transports.

The check was momentary; no sooner did Singapore fall than the Japanese made good their conquest of Sumatra, thus closing off Java to the west; and as they did so they occupied Portuguese Timor to the east, and after that Bali on Java's eastern tip. It was now late in February, and as the invaders prepared their armada for Java the United Nations' motley fleet boldly challenged the navy of Japan.

The fleet gave as good as it took and possibly sunk a Japanese tonnage equal to its own; but the Battle of Macassar Straits sealed the fate of Java. Only a few Allied ships survived this two-day sea fight, and when these tried later to escape almost all were sunk. Of our Asiatic fleet only four destroyers finally cut their way out.

On now came the Japanese hitting at Java from east, west, and center. Their transports drew close to shore, and then, just above the water line great doors opened and out came motored barges. On reaching shore these barges dropped gangways, and dashing pell-mell over them came the little yellow men with bicycles, motorcycles, the lightest of tommy-guns and artillery. It was Bataan, Singapore, and Burma over again, with one difference. In Java were many well-paved roads over which the Japanese scooted so rapidly that their conquest made record time. They landed on February 28th and by March 9th, aside from isolated fighting in the mountains, it was all over.

Then began the battle for Australia, an island-continent in area approaching the United States and with population centered in the far south and southeast. There were Australian air bases on the southeastern shores of New Guinea (Papua) at Port Moresby, and also at Darwin in north central Australia. But Darwin was 1,700 miles from Adelaide, capital of South Australia, and most of the distance there was naught but trackless desert. In 1940 the Australians had rushed a railroad to Darwin, and that city and Port Moresby, with the help of the Americans, they determined to hold.

The Japanese though persistent were cautious. Before trying invasion they tried to soften Port Moresby and Darwin by frequent air raids. Perhaps they were not even certain whether to keep on to the southeast or to advance westward. During April they attacked Ceylon and sank British ships in the Indian Ocean. Possibly the course of empire ran that way; and having Vichy under the yoke they might try the same manoeuvre in Madagascar. While they were making up their minds, the British landed in Madagascar and American planes bombed Tokyo from carriers. This challenge to their homeland may have decided the Japanese to veer to the southeast against both Australia and

America, for the Americans were now rushing to help their allies "down under."

So it happened that during the first week in May a great concentration of Japanese shipping was seen in the Coral Sea, which separated northeastern Australia from the Solomon Islands. The Japanese objective was plain: abandonment of the invasion of North Australia and a bold bid toward Sydney and Melbourne, heartland of the continent. Could the Japanese land near those cities in force and hold their lines of communication, Australia would be lost to us. And not Australia alone. Going further east they could pounce upon New Caledonia where we had a base, and this meant severing the American-Australian life lines. South of New Caledonia was New Zealand. The prospects for Japan were truly imperial.

But now Japan met her first major reverse in six months of war. A task force of the United States navy met the oncoming Japanese in the Battle of the Coral Sea and compelled Japan to withdraw. It was a fight unparalleled in naval history, a battle not only at huge distances but also by planes. No battle-ship, apparently, was engaged by either side: but Japan did lose two airplane carriers to one of ours, and her loss in cruisers and destroyers was heavier. For the time being the Japanese would have to be content with their enormous and swiftly won conquests of millions of square miles, millions of people across 3,000 miles of ocean.

Rommel Routs the British

The Allies fared no better amid the sand dunes of Libya than in the archipelagoes of the South Seas. Their African prospects in December, 1941, were bright; but so alarming was the tale of disaster from the Far East that few rejoiced over British advance in Africa. Nevertheless the Eighth Army was repeating in late 1941 its victories of 1940, covering the old ground once more, by-passing thousands of Axis troops in Halfaya Pass and compelling them to surrender, hoisting the Union Jack again over Bengazi, driving back the Axis forces even farther than the Italians in the earlier year, this time one hundred miles beyond Bengazi, all the way to El Agheila, where Rommel, protected by the sea on one flank and by salt marshes on the other, stayed his retreat. But 1942 reversed all this; and disaster so serious overtook the overconfident Britons that as fast as their sun of empire sunk in the Far East almost as rapidly did it sink in North Africa.

Throughout all January, 1942, and for many weeks after, the Axis plastered Malta with incessant bombing, presumably as a screen behind which their transports could move freely from Italy to Tripoli.

Thousands of fresh troops were added to the Italo-German army in Libya under that wolf of desert warfare, General Rommel, also many new high-powered field guns, self-propelling, which could outshoot the light British field artillery, and many new tanks of the Mark IV model, a better tank than any thus far shipped to Egypt from America or England.

Optimistic Britons were of the opinion that Rommel would be dug out of his new lair; but it was Rommel who hit first, so hard, and so skillfully, at the end of January, that in little more than five months he threw the British back 360 miles to the Egyptian border and, breaking through, kept on halfway to Alexandria.

His campaign was superb; he not only had better tanks but knew how to concentrate them to best advantage; he caught the British off center by feints to the wasteland in the south as he kept on with his main offense along the seacoast; he outflanked and outwitted his enemy so fast that over and over again their food, their oil, their ammunition, their tanks fell into his hands. His own tanks he repaired on the spot without dragging them off to the rear and the tanks he captured he repaired likewise. Sloshing swastikas upon their turrets he turned them back against the British lines; and in odd moments he delivered lectures on desert strategy and tactics to captured British officers.

The British, exhausted by their rush from east to west, now had no time to rest as they were rushed back faster even than they had come. For a brief season in May it looked as though Rommel might be held; he was far from his supply line and every week that passed the British came closer to their own. Thanks to American and British matériel rushed around to Egypt through the Red Sea they were now nearly equal to the Germans in tanks and probably superior in the air: but Rommel was a genius in the art of war and he led the overconfident Ritchie into ambush. Out of 300 tanks, 230 were lost. And without tanks one does not win desert battles.

A painful decision confronted the British; their main army must retreat to the Egyptian border but should they, or should they not, leave their garrison in Tobruk? They had only recently landed fresh supplies there at tremendous sacrifice in shipping, and in that much battered port they had 25,000 men. Tobruk had withstood one long siege, and as long as the Union Jack flew above its low ramparts Rommel's advance would be endangered. The decision was to hold Tobruk: but now before the garrison could sow mines properly the German panzer divisions were upon them. In some ways what followed was even worse than Dunkirk, Crete, Greece, or Singapore. A very few managed to escape by sea; the remainder died or were made prisoners; and the piled-up war matériel came in very handy for Rommel.

That master of war gave his enemy no breathing space; by the end of June he was deep in Egypt. If he once reached Alexandria, then Cairo and the Suez were at his mercy and the British fleet would be compelled to abandon the eastern Mediterranean or risk being bottled up in it. Once at Suez, the shadow of the swastika would darken the entire Middle East. At this very moment the Wehrmacht was striking across the Ukraine toward the Caucasus. Rommel's army was the southern prong of a gigantic pincer movement, the northern prong of which was approaching the Volga and the Caspian. The two prongs might close in northern Persia.

To throw Rommel back the British put in everything they had: soldiers from Iraq, Palestine, and Syria, green troops from England, and equally green Americans handling a few American lend-lease tanks. The R.A.F. flew to the rescue, aided and abetted by American airmen. It was nip and go: but much Nazi matériel en route to Rommel was reported sabotaged in the Balkans, and he was held at El Alamein, seventy miles west of Alexandria, the last available defensive position between him and his objective. El Alamein was on the sea and forty miles inland from the Quattara Depression of sand so soft as to make tank warfare impossible. But forty miles left ample room to maneuvre, and on July 1st a panzer spearhead broke through the British lines. It was driven back by almost superhuman counterattack and Rommel was stopped. The Nazi tide in the Near East had reached its perigee; but who could then be sure of that?

RUSSIA: THE SECOND NAZI OFFENSIVE, 1942

Throughout the winter of 1941-42 the Nazis went defensive in Russia, withdrawing much of their army and depending on strategic fortresses to hold the furious Russians back. Out around these fortresses were fortified villages like the quills of the hedgehog, and to strike through to the center of a hedgehog or to encircle it point by point and compel surrender was costly business. Yet all winter long that was the main Soviet endeavor. It had a certain measure of success and by spring the Nazis had been worried out from some of their "hedgehogs"; neither Leningrad nor Moscow were threatened as seriously as in December. But that was all.

The Red army fought through long winter months with abandon; its soldiers endured sub-zero weather better than did the enemy; they were better clad; and the Russian inferiority in tanks, noticeable in the summer of 1941, was now ended. From their factories beyond the Urals came new tanks, "white mammoths," as they were called by the Germans, huge brutes of fifty tons, which the Red tankmen drove at the Germans with ferocious skill through great snowbanks, across frozen lakes and rivers. The ice groaned and bent beneath their weight but the winter-wise Red soldiers put down timbers, covered them with water so they froze and made precarious roadways like frozen pontoons. Time and again they surprised startled Nazis, cut deep behind German lines, and looked forward hopefully to a major German defeat. It never came. "Hedgehogs" might be surrounded, but their garrisons were supplied with food by plane. There were not enough of the white mammoths, not enough of their "little brothers," English tanks sent to Russia and manned by Russians. The Red cavalry performed prodigies of valor; so did the Red ski troops; so did the Red paratroopers. The Nazis suffered horribly, as Hitler acknowledged. But reinforced in February they held most of their hedgehogs. Staraya Russa, Vyazma, Bryansk, Orel, Kursk, Kharkov were still in their hands by the spring of 1942. The Russians at most had retaken but 20 per cent of the invaded lands and the invaders were in good shape to try again.

This time the Nazis must not fail. They had now been at war two years and a half, and now with the United States a foe, with the R.A.F. hampering their production, it was essential that 1942 see all Europe under their yoke. They had underestimated Red armies once; they would not do so again.

Very carefully they made ready a concentrated drive south and east, a surge to carry the swastika to the Black Sea, the Caucasus, and to the Volga whereby they would obtain precious oil for themselves and also deprive the Russians of it, thus ending all danger from "White Mammoths." Once Soviet oil was theirs it would make little difference how many planes Britain and America shipped their communist ally. If Germany held Stalingrad on the Volga, lend-lease matériel which was seeping into Russia via Persia and the Caspian would be blocked. If once she dominated the Black Sea she would have the Turks at her mercy. With Bulgar-German forces close to Istanbul, and with a victorious German army on their eastern frontier, the Turks could be persuaded (or compelled) to open the gates of Anatolia. What chance then of Syria or Palestine remaining under British occupation?

For many months, beginning in May, 1942, German victories came in such quick succession that almost every day fresh disaster overwhelmed the Red armies. Within two weeks the Wehrmacht penetrated 150 miles further east than in 1941. Timoshenko tried a counterattack which only briefly stayed the grey-green flood. Sebastopol, under siege all winter, resisted stubbornly. But the Germans were not to be denied. They could not use their tanks effectively among the jagged hills which ringed that seaport but their artillery and their Luftwaffe blasted the

THE RUSSIAN FRONT, SUMMER, 1942

(From Brown and Herlin, *The War in Maps: An Atlas of New York Times Maps*
[Oxford University Press], by permission of the publishers.)

city into ruins, and their infantry, assisted by Rumanians, completed the conquest. It took three weeks of hand-to-hand fighting before they forced their way into the town, and even after that the Russians did not give over. They fought from street to street, from house to house, retreating to their few ships gathered in the harbor. It was a kind of Russian Dunkirk.

Meanwhile in the eastern Crimea the Kerch peninsula had already fallen to the Nazis and just beyond the narrow straits lay the Caucasus. The Nazis were not quite ready for adventure there; an army of several hundred thousand needs room in which to operate, and to secure it the German steam roller moved steadily and relentlessly in June across the eastern Ukraine, pushing the Russians back beyond the Donetz River.

Then at the end of June, 1942, came the final rush for oil and glory. Behind the Donetz lay the Don, sweeping in a majestic arc far to the east before flowing into the sea at Rostov. To force a crossing of the Don, to seep through the rich lands of the Don basin, to conquer Rostov at the river's mouth, to cross the Kerch Straits and invade the Caucasus took the greater part of the summer.

Timoshenko, Russian commander, traded space reluctantly for time. He was outnumbered, far inferior in equipment, and under orders on no account to risk encirclement; but he did something more than make a token resistance as the Nazis thrust their "iron fists" (a new term representing tank infiltrations much more heavily supported by infantry and artillery than the tank blitzkrieg tactics of 1940 and 1941) now here, now there. Early in July the Germans were across the Don; by the middle of the month they had cut the railroad from between Stalingrad and the Donetz, thus severing the northern from the southern Russian armies; and by the end of the month they were attacking Rostov at the Don's mouth from the east. Early in August the Maikop oil-fields which produced seven per cent of Russia's oil fell to the invader, whose rate of advance in the Caucasus was rapidly accelerated as the Russians withdrew their tanks and depended for defense on cavalry. Meanwhile by the middle of August the entire Don Bend was in German hands and by the 31st a Nazi panzer division shoved into the outskirts of Stalingrad.

The German press freely and officially prophesied the capture of that city in September and there were few outside Russia who had any other expectation. Unlike Bataan or Sebastopol, Stalingrad had no natural defenses. It stretched north and south along the west bank of the Volga for twenty straggling miles, and between it and the victorious Germans was open steppe with a few low-lying hills. The Nazis had superiority in numbers, in tanks, and especially in the air, assailing the city with a thousand planes. They held the west bank of the Volga both north and south of Stalingrad; they had cut all rail communication; no reinforcements could reach the Russians except by water; and German planes hovered over the river. The prospects of making Mother Volga the eastern boundary of Hitler's Thousand Year Reich seemed exellent.

Nevertheless, as week followed week and the war swung into its fourth year the Nazis failed to nail their conquest down. They drove their tanks again and again into the heart of the city; they blasted tall new factories and turned residential quarters into shambles; they took house after house, street after street, and even reached the Volga. But always the Red army fought back. Houses and factories became debris; but behind crumbling walls and shattered cement crawled Red army men with machine-guns, bayonets and knives, careless of death. The very destruction the Germans wrought helped the defense against them, for the streets of Stalingrad choked with collapsed buildings stopped the ingress of German tanks. Sometimes the Nazis would clear an entire city block, but always was there danger of losing it next day. Yet the Germans dared not lift the siege. So long as the Soviets held here on the western bank of Russia's greatest river any further drive to the Caspian would fail by a Soviet flank attack.

As for the Russians, their Stalingrad was the sign and symbol of the 1917 revolution. Stalin had ordered it defended to the death and so long as their flotilla on the Volga could shell Nazi outposts, so long as fresh troops could seep into their city across Mother Volga under friendly shelter of the night, the cursed Nazis were deprived of their prey and Red Russia lived.

Midway, Aleutians, Guadalcanal

In the summer of 1942 the outlook for the United Nations would have been bleak indeed but for the Pacific. There, in the far North among the fogbound Aleutians, in the central Pacific at Midway, 1,304 miles west of Hawaii and 1,185 east of Wake, as also at Guadalcanal in the Solomon Islands in the South Pacific, the Americans took the war to their foes.

The most important of these engagements was the Midway battle. As in that of the Coral Seas opposing warships never sighted one another and offensive fighting was entirely by plane. Early in June some eighty vessels under the rising sun ensign—battle-ships, carriers, cruisers, destroyers, transports—converged on American-held Midway. This was no reconnaissance in force. Clearly the Japanese intended, if victorious here, to attack Hawaii. But the Mikado's soldiers never

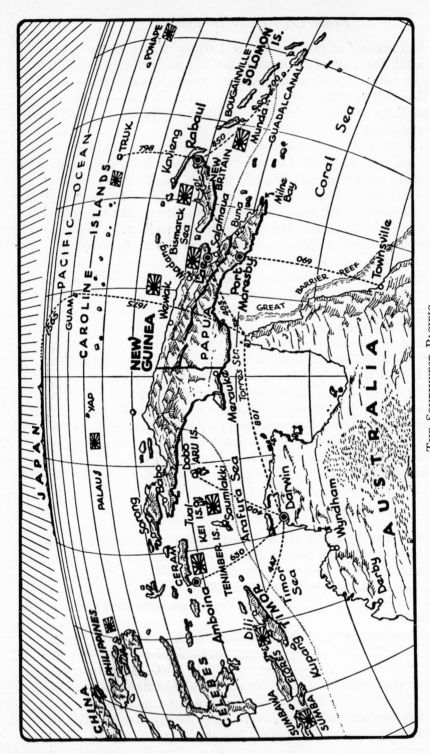

The Southwest Pacific

(From Brown and Herlin, *The War in Maps: An Atlas of New York Times Maps*.
[Oxford University Press], by permission of the publishers.)

landed on Midway. Land-based bombers of the army, navy planes from carriers, navy flying boats intercepted the Japanese fleet and it sought safety in flight. Action continued for four days. The loss of American planes was heavy, five out of six in one sortie, eight out of sixteen in another, and fifteen out of fifteen in a third. The Japanese also sank our carrier, the *Yorktown*. But their own losses were far more serious, four carriers being sunk, two heavy cruisers, three destroyers. We also wiped out 275 planes, messed up several battle-ships, cruisers, and lighter craft. Midway was a happy augury for the future, particularly heartening in the destruction of carriers, a type of craft in which the enemy's navy hitherto had beeen predominant.

Along with the raid on Midway came a Japanese thrust at Dutch Harbor, our base in the eastern Aleutians, that chain of islands stretching a thousand miles and more across the North Pacific from Alaska well-nigh to Kamchatka in Soviet Siberia. Dutch Harbor, at the eastern end of the chain, was lightly defended, its fortification as yet incomplete. Planes based there could easily raid Alaska, make possible an invasion of continental America.

Again the Japanese came on in force with two carriers, two cruisers, three destroyers. Their fighters and bombers outclassed the few planes we had at Dutch Harbor and probably would have won the day had not the American army surprised them. Sixty miles west of Dutch Harbor lies Umnak Island and upon it two months earlier we had laid steel landing mats for planes. From this secret base in the fog our army Warhawks swooped down upon the foe—and from west of them. Confused by this attack from ambush, the invaders broke and fled. They stopped in retreat to capture Kiska, 672 miles from Dutch Harbor, and Attu, still further distant at the Aleutians' western tip. Hence our North Pacific victory was incomplete. But for the time being Alaska, Canada, and our northwestern states were clear of enemy bombers. Conversely, as long as Kiska and Attu remained in their hands, Nippon was similarly protected.

Two months later there was discouraging news from the South Pacific. Despite the Battle of the Coral Seas the Japanese were still set upon the conquest of Australia. They strove persistently to capture Port Moresby on the southeastern side of New Guinea; their forces fanned out steadily from the northern Solomons southeastward along the thousand-mile length of that archipelago and built an airfield on the large island of Guadalcanal in the southern Solomons. Their objective was evident—cutting the American life-line to Australia. And this we had to protect by an offensive-defensive at Guadalcanal.

On August 7th our marines, protected by a naval air task force, landed on Guadalcanal and on the nearby islands of Tulagi and Gavutu.

They surprised the enemy on Guadalcanal, captured the airfield, renaming it Henderson Field. On Gavutu they ran into a hornet's nest,
the Japanese defending their caves with reckless courage, dying to a
man. On Guadalcanal the surprised Nipponese rallied to the attack. So
did the Japanese navy. Smashing into our task force on August 8th, it
sank three heavy American cruisers and one Australian. Our transports,
however, escaped destruction, and our marines, heavily reinforced, beat
off the Japanese on land.

Throughout August and September the enemy did its best to dislodge the marines, strafing from the air and shelling from the sea
the narrow and confined area which they had won, only about seven
miles along the coast by four or five in depth. On the island there was
endless fighting. Japanese troops, continuously reinforced at night by
fast destroyers, proved worthy antagonists. Few were captured; many
died. So also was it with the marines, who found the hot miasmic air,
the malaria, and insect life of Guadalcanal quite as unpleasant as the
soldiers of the Mikado. Time after time the latter returned to the fray,
supported by naval carriers, destroyers, and battle-ships; time after
time they were repulsed. The flag still flew over Henderson Field, and
from it rose American bombers to harry Japanese ships and bomb
Japanese installations. The yellow tide of conquest still lapped these
shores but whether it had passed its peak and was now receding was
anybody's guess.

Air Raids and Submarines

In 1942 the war in the air encouraged the United Nations. There
was no proof as yet that the Luftwaffe was outclassed in Europe, since
a large part of Goering's fleet was heavily engaged on the eastern front;
but German assaults on Britain did peter out, while British attacks on
Germany, and upon armament factories, docks, and railroads in the
German occupied lands began to tell heavily against the Nazis.

There were more allied raids than before; there were many more
planes to each raid; and the bombers were much heavier, huge Stirlings,
great four-motored Lancasters, and 300 planes often in a single raid.
The British focussed on the Ruhr and on industrial Germany; they
lambasted Cologne in one night with 3,000 tons of bombs carried
by over 1,000 planes; they spread afield; they flew to Augsburg in
southern Germany and destroyed Diesel engines being fabricated for
submarines; they flew to the distant Baltic ports of Rostock and
Lubeck, wiped out docks, shipbuilding yards, aircraft factories, doing
more damage to those ancient cities than the Germans ever did to
Coventry. And they found time to smash as well at French factories

in the suburbs of Paris itself, fabricating war matériel for the conqueror.

Upon the high seas, however, it was a different story. The menace of the submarine grew greater, not less, during 1942. The ways of British, Canadian, and American shipyards creaked and groaned as new ships slid into the water, and before they could be towed to dock new keels were laid. Even so, construction did not keep pace with sinking and at the end of the year the tonnage of the United Nations was down by approximately a million tons. Submarines were not only more numerous, they were much larger. Slipping out from hangars of thick reinforced concrete conveniently located on the Atlantic coast of France, they scoured the Seven Seas, sank cargo ships in the St. Lawrence, bombed tankers in the Caribbean, lay in wait for Suez-bound convoys in the South Atlantic, for Russian convoys in the Barents Sea, for food supplies en route to Malta, and in the mid-Atlantic, relatively safe from Allied planes they hunted in great packs watchful both day and night for any straggler that fell out of line or was disabled.

The loss of life among merchant seamen ran inordinately high, and highest of all on the convoy route to Murmansk. Nazi subs were reinforced here by Nazi planes based on Norway, and sub and plane between them raised havoc with this all-important life-line to the Soviets. How many ships were sunk on this route in 1942 remains unstated but it was an open secret that sometimes a third or even a half or more of the heavily laden vessels went down in these icy waters. The best swimmers here had little chance to live. The dice were loaded against seamen on rafts and lifeboats. Zippered suits of rubber might keep out water but did not keep out cold. Escorting craft dared not delay for errands of mercy; their duty was to the convoy. The Nazi planes skimmed the water, sank lifeboats, and the convoy steamed ahead. Tanks lashed on decks broke loose and caromed back and forth, clumsy crates of airplane parts did likewise. The air was thick with fog and bombs and geysers, and across the lead-grey sea torpedoes sped. But some ships got through; planes and tanks and food from America and Britain did reach the Red army.

AUTUMN, 1942

The war swung into its fourth year, and almost everywhere the Axis still was winning. The Hitlerites had one foot in Stalingrad and looked hopefully to sweeping up the Volga valley to roll in on Moscow from the east. They were already deep within the Caucasus, the Maikop oilfields had been won, and Nazi advance units were progressing steadily along the western shoreline of the Black Sea toward Batum. On the east the Axis' chances of forcing its way through Daghestan to Baku were slight, but the Nazis might slip around the snow-clad mountains of that wild and sparsely settled province and following the shoreline of the Caspian penetrate to Baku, there to quench the thirst of their war machines with endless Soviet oil. Over the Caspian, then, soon would fly the Nazi banner, and the southern supply line from the United States to Russia would be severed. If necessary, northern Persia could be taken, and Turkestan. Perhaps a junction could be effected with Japan in Afghanistan or in the Pamirs. The prospects were enticing.

In Egypt, Rommel was halted at El Alamein. But Alexandria was only sixty miles away, a glittering prize. Nothing favored the British except terrain, and their badly battered Eighth Army only recently had been outwitted and outflanked by military wizardry which might well outwit and outflank them again. One more deceptive infiltration, one more successful ruse, and the entire delta of the Nile with Cairo at its apex was at Rommel's mercy.

India, meanwhile, seethed with rebellious unrest and the victorious Japanese, engorged with Burma, were at her borders. The leaders of the Indian National Congress, exasperated by the evident unwillingness of British authority to implement promises of self-government after the war by trusting Congress with any important share in the prosecution of it, actively engaged in fermenting "non-violent resistance," that is, promoting strikes, discouraging enlistment, spreading defeatism. Gandhi, whether prophet, saint, or politician (the Axis cared not which) implied that he was not unwilling to negotiate with Japan. And communication between China and India was now ended except for a trickle by transport plane over high mountains.

The entire East Indies lay quiescent under Japanese authority. The northern coastline of New Guinea was in Japanese hands and Port Moresby on the southern shore in grave danger. Everywhere north of Australia the Japanese swarmed. The Americans, it is true, had won a great mid-Pacific victory at Midway and had driven back an armada aimed at Hawaii and Alaska, had won a toehold on Guadalcanal. But this was most precarious, a single airfield only, surrounded by a jungle infested with Japanese soldiers, constantly under attack from their land-based planes in the northern Solomons and at Rabaul, still further north in New Britain Island. The southward expansion of Japan toward Australia and New Zealand was blocked for the time being, and that was all.

In Western Europe, meanwhile, there was no second front, nor any near prospect of one. In August a reconnaissance in force met with bloody rebuff at Dieppe on the French coast. The participants were mainly Canadian and more than half were killed or wounded. After this, it seemed obvious that no second front could be established in 1942, not without too frightful a loss of life. Yet Stalin kept on insisting that there must be one. Churchill flew to Moscow to pacify him. The British are sea animals, he explained, the Russians land animals. The latter must be patient. But still the Russian chieftain was dissatisfied; he did not think the British and Americans were doing their fair share to win the war.

The United Nations fought for time as well as victory; time to convert America into the arsenal of democracy promised by Roosevelt; time to make the tools with which to make the ships, the planes, the tanks that would beat Hitler down; time to build factories, and homes for men and women to work in them; time to assemble raw materials, to train craftsmen, chemists, soldiers, technicians; time to transport overseas millions of men from Canada and the United States with arms and food; time to equip and drill these forces, and to pile up in Britain vast reservoirs of all things necessary for offensive war.

If America was the arsenal of democracy, Britain was its warehouse. The average Englishman ate less now than formerly, but his health was better; his house, if he had one, was damp and cold, but his spirits were high. He knew it was not so bad as in 1940 when England faced the Nazi storm alone; his island now was an armed camp, and with every passing month became more crowded with fighting men. The worst, he sensed, was over. Sometime, somewhere, somehow, the measure of the Axis would be taken.

The Axis, on the other hand, was not so confident as in 1940. The English were still in the war, and now there were Russians and Americans in as well! The conquered countries would not support the new order. The name of Hitler's Norwegian viceroy, Major Quisling, was a hissing and a byword to all the world. Norwegians refused to enlist for the crusade against bolshevism; they turned their backs on German soldiers, put poison in fish canned for the German army, stood by their bishops, ministers, and teachers who refused to follow Quisling's orders, and escaped when possible to England.

So likewise was it in Denmark, the Netherlands, Belgium, Luxemburg, France, Czechoslovakia, Poland. Fines, exactions, court-martials, starvation, death—they made no difference. The terrorism of the gestapo met with sullen bitterness, secret sabotage, sporadic assassination. When "Hitler's hangman," Heydrich, was killed in Czechoslovakia and the Nazis slew every male adult in Lidice, the wrath of the Czechs but mounted higher. In Yugoslavia's mountains the breath of freedom never died, and every outlying German garrison knew it must keep constant watch or else, perchance, be slaughtered. In London, General de Gaulle still kept the Tricolor flying, and by ones and twos and threes his Free French forces were augmented, as young lads slipped through the German lines to join him. There were many accidents in French factories; trains were derailed, bridges mysteriously blew up, cars were set afire, and German soldiers died. The French respected old Marshal Pétain, who had signed the armistice with Hitler, but Pierre Laval, the Nazi stooge, was anathema in France as was Quisling in Norway. A scattering few were found to fight bolshevism, and Frenchmen agreed to work in Germany that French prisoners of war might be delivered from German concentration camps; but the great majority, as near as may be ascertained, watched dumbly as their goods and chattels, machinery, horses, cattle, even grain were passed over the border into Germany. They were helpless and knew it; but collaborate with Hitler they would not.

Three years of war had not turned Nazi victims into Nazi slaves, nor had it convinced Chinese that Japan was sincere in her grandiloquent proclamation of the "Great East Asia Co-Prosperity Sphere." In this, and in their fast accumulating stores of war matériel, lay the major hope of the United Nations. But the latter knew that time works two ways. Blood and flesh, heart and sinew cannot resist forever, and hope delayed grows sick and dies. If the war was not to drag out interminably, if there were to be any Poles, French, Dutchmen, and Belgians left alive, far sturdier blows against the Axis must be struck than had thus far been delivered.

NOVEMBER VICTORIES

The autumn of 1942 was to bring sweet revenge for 1940, for 1941, for 1942. In the month of November alone, the Axis suffered defeat after defeat, of such colossal magnitude as to change the entire complexion of the war. In Africa, Europe, and in the South Seas the story was the same. By the end of the month the United Nations could list these victories: Rommel routed in Egypt and in Cyrenaica; French Morocco and Algeria occupied by British and American troops; the collapse of the German offense in Russia, which Hitler had promised would entrench the Axis on the Volga; and a new defeat of the Japanese navy in the South Seas, together with the drowning of thousands of soldiers headed for the reconquest of Guadalcanal.

When General Montgomery and his British Eighth Army struck at El Alamein at the end of October, he did so with superb superiority of artillery, tanks, planes. Most of his new matériel had reached Egypt via the long sea route around Africa, much of it American. Montgomery's army was mixed, pure British units, New Zealanders, men of Australia, long accustomed to desert war, men of South Africa, Punjabis, Sikhs, and other Indian warriors, a few Americans, most of them tankmen or airmen.

This time the British made no tactical errors; their infantry prodded up the land mines left by the retreating foe before the tanks made massed attacks and while the R.A.F. protected their countrymen from the skies. The Afrika Korps withdrew swiftly but with skill. Between themselves and the advancing British they placed their Italian Allies who surrendered in droves. Past all the old landmarks flowed the retreating German tide, past Tobruk, Derna, Bengazi with its useful harbor, around the bend of Cyrenaica, back to the salt marshes of El Agheila. For the first time since the war began the church bells pealed in England. As Churchill told his public: "We have now 100 Italian generals and 300,000 of his (Mussolini's) soldiers in our hands as prisoners of war."

As Montgomery's artillery barked at El Alamein an Anglo-American expeditionary force bound for Northwest Africa was on the high seas. Plans had long been laid in great detail for the occupation of Morocco and Algeria, and it was hoped that the French garrisons there, upwards of 100,000 men, would welcome our arrival. For the most part they did so. As we landed at Algiers only a few shots were fired. At Oran, 130 miles west, there was more serious resistance. And at Casablanca on the Atlantic coast of Morocco there was, for a time, stiff fighting. It was necessary for us to land tanks both east and west of that city and begin siege operations. Meanwhile off the harbor the French battle-ship, *Jean Bart,* opened fire on our fleet and had to be destroyed before the French gave over. Fortunately the mysterious Admiral Darlan in Algiers, the North African representative of Marshal Pétain, decided to join us and gave orders to end resistance.

The American general, Eisenhower, commander-in-chief of the expeditionary force, immediately recognized Darlan as head of the civil administration and for this was violently criticized. Darlan's previous career had been that of a bitter Anglophobe, and since he had yielded from time to time to Nazi pressure most Englishmen and many Americans considered it undesirable that we should have any dealings with him. But Darlan, as our enemy, could cause us no end of trouble; and as our friend he could, and did, render possible our occupation of a great empire in record-making time.

His collaboration with us gave Hitler an excuse for occupying all France and for seizing the French ships at Toulon. The French army did not resist but Hitler lost the fleet. As the Nazis reached Toulon, their planes filling the skies, the French blew up their vessels! Meanwhile the British First Army, along with American detachments raced for Bizerte and Tunis. These two seaports in the French Protectorate of Tunisia were five hundred miles from Algiers and less than a hundred from Sicily, too great a handicap. The Germans got there first by air and sea, and in superior numbers. The Allies, within twelve miles of their goal, were driven back.

The redoubtable Russians also took the offensive this month of November, all the way from Leningrad to Stalingrad. For this Stalin had carefully prepared all summer, and when his hammer blows fell the Nazi troops gave way everywhere. Instead of capturing Stalingrad before snowfall, as Hitler had promised his people, 300,000 desperate Germans and Rumanians before and within that ruined city found Russian forces slowly closing in around them from north and south. Besiegers became the besieged. Farther south in the Caucasus trapped and widely scattered divisions of the mighty German host now sought safety in retreat. Back in Germany dreams of the gushing oil from Baku faded fast; instead came memory of last year's trials on Russian steppes and forebodings lest another and a worse year was in store.

Nor was this all! The Japanese suffered a double setback in the South Seas. Just as Hitler prophesied the fall of Stalingrad to his own men and the capture of Port Moresby in Papua by his yellow allies, the nimble Nipponese infiltrating through the jungle and over the Owen Stanley range of mountains were driven back by MacArthur's Australian-American fighters. And better yet, the American Admiral, Halsey, won in mid-November a victory almost as decisive as that scored at Midway. On November 13-15, the Japanese advanced in full strength to recapture Guadalcanal. The battle was sanguine, this time not at long distance or by planes alone. The enemy lost a battle-ship, perhaps two, five cruisers, six destroyers. We lost two cruisers, six destroyers. But in addition, we sank eight out of twelve transports heavily loaded with troops, presumably drowning some 20,000 men. Four more transports were later found beached near Henderson Field, the troops in them perhaps landed in Guadalcanal. Danger to that base was not over but at least Japanese reconquest was not imminent.

WINTER, 1942-43

In all three major theatres of war, in the Asiatic and Pacific area, in Africa, and in Russia the United Nations kept on winning. The Japanese made little headway in China and were subject there to continuous and effective, if somewhat meagre, air raiding; a Japanese army in Papua (eastern New Guinea) was exterminated and Papua cleansed of the invader; in Africa the British Eighth Army, still in pursuit of Rommel, this time went beyond El Agheila, captured Tripoli, cleared the Axis entirely out of Libya, penetrated southern Tunisia; and in Russia the greatest victory thus far of the United Nations was won at Stalingrad.

The major fighting in the Southwest Pacific took place in Papua, where some 1,500 Japanese troops tried to force their way across high mountains to attack Port Moresby. These Japanese were in retreat and a somewhat larger force of Americans and Australians was driving them back to their base at Buna on the northern shore of Papua. Absence of roads and the necessity of transporting all food, ammunition, and supplies by hand or by airplane made progress slow; and the further our soldiers dipped north over the Owen Stanley mountains and the closer they got to Buna the slower the drive became. Slowly we closed in on the trapped Japanese. Reinforcements were sent them from their island bases farther north; but these were wiped out by our airmen. The fighting was carried on by every ruse known to the jungle. Thick undergrowth made visibility only possible a few feet ahead, and underneath was soggy ground in which fox-holes filled with water. We inched forward; we drove wedges in between Japanese detachments; we isolated them in pockets; and these one by one we exterminated. To do this was the work of weeks.

There would have been no Buna victory had it not been for our air force which not only kept the foe at bay but flew jeeps, artillery and munitions to our men. And now our flyers did even more. In the Bismarck Sea they intercepted a Japanese fleet bound for New Guinea and destroyed it. Three light cruisers, 7 destroyers, 12 transports, and 102 planes were lost to the enemy. Out of 136 of our planes that took part in this naval battle in which the United States used not a single warship, 132 of our planes returned in safety.

The North African winter campaign would have ended in stalemate had it not been for General Montgomery and his British Eighth Army. Early in the winter it was at El Agheila, still in pursuit of Italians and Germans. The closer the latter got to their main base at Tripoli the shorter became their lines of communications; conversely the further the British shoved ahead the more difficult became theirs. Nevertheless, the British were not held up long at El Agheila. By the time their artillery was ready to clear a passage, and their engineers had exploded mines and booby traps, the Afrika Korps was in full retreat. Montgomery pushed on. Beyond lay Tripoli, capital of Libya, a good seaport, well defended from encircling hills. But the Germans did not choose to hold it, and Italians could not. A brief skirmish and Italy's

African empire was fallen. In thirteen weeks the Eighth Army had chased the enemy 1,300 miles, the longest drive in history. On went Montgomery. The retreating Germans panted after the security of the Mareth line in French Tunisia, and Montgomery followed them there. To breach these strong fortifications was a first-class military action as Montgomery well knew, and the Eighth Army halted.

Elsewhere in North Africa the situation was more complicated. There was the problem of logistics, how to supply an army of approximately 200,000 with food and guns, tanks and planes, from bases as far distant as England and the United States, with submarines lurking in the ocean pathways; how after the matériel once reached Africa to distribute it to fighting men often hundreds of miles from the port of debarcation. The U-boat war was at its height and tankers were sunk, even if troop ships arrived safely; yet without gasoline there was no campaigning. Railways in North Africa were few and in disrepair; in some instances they had to be rebuilt and locomotives and freight cars imported from America.

Then, too, there was the political problem; who was to govern the restless, seething population, part French, part Arab. It had been solved temporarily by putting Darlan in authority; but Darlan was promptly assassinated. The men under him had been of Vichy and in consequence bitterly anti-British. Though not pro-German they were undemocratic, loyal to Pétain alone. They hated de Gaulle and his "Free French" who had done so much to keep alive the fires of French resistance; and the Free French replied in kind.

The only common denominator available seemed to be General Giraud, an officer reputed as patriotic as de Gaulle himself. Giraud had not been a party to the fall of France. Imprisoned by the Germans in 1940, he had escaped from Germany and been taken to North Africa by a British submarine. Giraud succeeded Darlan as the head of French administration in North Africa; but the Free French would not acknowledge his leadership and bitter feud continued.

Another problem was what use to make of the North African French army. That force was ready to fight, but its equipment was far outdated and to supply it with modern weapons was not easy. Units had opposed our landing and many officers were regarded as still under Vichy influence. The French should prove useful in driving the Germans out of Tunisia. But what particular rôle could or should be given these new allies of ours in the campaign to come?

And finally there was the military problem itself. Germans and Italians had entrenched at Bizerte and Tunis and behind these two cities were fortifying a range of hills from which it would be difficult to oust them. They had already forced back the British First Army, and American and French contingents, inexperienced in war. If we were not careful we might be caught between Axis troops rolling down from Tunis and the Afrika Korps, rolling up from the Mareth line. Our lines of communication were far extended, stretching all the way from Casablanca in Morocco to Tunisia. The railway from Casablanca ran closely parallel with the borders of Spanish Morocco. It would not do to leave that vital link unprotected.

To solve these and other problems of United Nations' strategy Roosevelt and Churchill conferred in mid-January at Casablanca. They declared conjointly that there would be no terms given any Axis nation except the grim acceptance of unconditional surrender; they agreed on certain measures toward that end; and de Gaulle and Giraud shook hands before the camera, a reconciliation formal rather than genuine.

Meanwhile Hitler insisted that his bridgehead in Africa be held, and Axis reinforcements flowed into Tunis and Bizerte. All over Tunisia the weather was atrociously bad and for a large part of the winter the war was reduced to patrol action. Then it flared up suddenly and with startling reverses for the Americans.

On February 11th the Nazi army poured through Faid Pass at the eastern end of the American sector. Tanks and dive bombers seemed to come from everywhere, and all at once. We took quite a beating, retreating to Kasserine Pass, surrendering some 4,000 square miles of territory. We were even driven out of the Kasserine, and that meant serious business, for if the Germans gained control of the plateau region beyond, they might encircle the British First Army to the north and drive the United Nations back into Algeria. This was our baptism of fire, and apparently we were caught with equipment too light, with poor air support, and inferior tactics. We tried to rescue detachments which could not be rescued; we fell into traps and got what was coming to us.

Then the very next week we held and defeated the Wehrmacht. That drubbing had served us well. Our army functioned like a well-oiled machine. Stuka bombers were something to laugh at; our artillery fire was excellent; and the hitherto triumphant Nazis retreated through the Kasserine Pass with their tails between their legs. Eisenhower was quoted after our initial defeat as saying, "Our boys will fight better now they are mad."

STALINGRAD

The Fuehrer's New Year's message to his folk was not cheerful. The best he could say about the eastern front was that the winter there could not be worse than the preceding one. He erred. In January and

February, Stalin's armies hurled themselves with such terrific and unrelenting force upon the discouraged Nazis as to free Leningrad from its besiegers, draw tighter and tighter the noose around twenty German divisions trapped at Stalingrad, and on February 2nd to compel the half-starved and abandoned soldiers left there to surrender.

There had been time enough to withdraw these divisions and sufficient warning during the Autumn that fatal consequences would follow if they were not withdrawn. Only the conceit of a paranoiac would have abandoned them to their fate. Early in January they were cut off completely by a ring of Red armies, and beyond that ring a second was in process of formation, and beyond that a third. And now as the Red soldiers closed in for the kill it was the turn of the Nazis to dig for shelter in the ruined cellars of Stalingrad and to feed as the Russians had on horse meat, when and if it could be found. Their only contact with the outside world was by plane, and that too intermittent to provide sufficient food and ammunition, much less reinforcements. Nevertheless they stuck it out, and did so until over half had been exterminated.

Germany was thrown into consternation. "Europe is in mortal peril," cried Goebbels. "Only Germany can save Europe now. The onrush of the steppes against our venerable continent has broken out this Winter with a violence overshadowing all human imagination." European civilization would be defended in total war which the Nazis would wage. If they were to do the fighting the least the rest of Europe could do was to labor in the common cause. His words speak volumes.

Stalingrad was the greatest single blow the Germans took thus far in the war, but the sum total of their 1943 defeats exceeded it in gravity. Rostov at the mouth of the Don was recaptured. Leningrad after a siege of over a year was set free and rail communications restored. One after another famous German hedgehog positions yielded to the Red armies. Even Kharkov, now in ruins, was won back. It began to look as though the entire Ukraine might be freed and the Nazis driven out of the Caucasus. But their lines of supply were excellent. The winter proved mild; the mud of early Spring thaws brought the Russian offensive to a halt. In early March the Germans started a counteroffense of their own which succeeded in recovering Kharkov, and they also retained control of the western tip of the Caucasus and the lower valley of the Kuban River. These victories, however, were slight comfort for the loss of over a million troops and much good land upon which Germany had relied to feed her people.

The Axis Expelled from Africa

Autumn victories over the Axis had cautiously been hailed by Churchill as "the end of the beginning." And now as winter turned to spring one could somewhat confidently write of "the beginning of the end." The tide had been slow in turning but by the middle of May it had run out a good six months, and there was rejoicing in the camp of the United Nations.

A second front clearly was impossible until Tunisia was won, and as winter ended that task seemed formidable. In northern Tunisia the Germans and Italians were safe behind a range of jagged hills and in the south they held the Mareth line against Montgomery. Their weakest point was the elongated corridor which led to the Mareth line, but it was protected by the sea on one side and by deep gorges and ravines on the other. Both French and Americans had tried to break through here in the neighborhood of Faid Pass and had been rolled back. Could they have done so they would have split the Axis forces in two. Conversely, so long as Montgomery's Eighth Army was on the other side of the Mareth line the United Nations' armies remained split.

Montgomery tried to crack the Mareth line, failed, then deployed his New Zealanders and the Free French who had crossed the Sahara to join him, into the desert at his left. These sturdy warriors circled around the Mareth line way to the northeast thus compelling the outflanked Afrika Korps to abandon their fortifications and to follow the coastal plain toward Tunis. Montgomery lunged after them as fast as his engineers could dig up land mines left by the capable Germans, who now had steadily retreated some 1,600 miles from El Alamein.

By these maneuvres the Axis armies were forced back into northern Tunisia in an area somewhat smaller than Connecticut. They could not adopt defense in depth, for they were held too close to the Mediterranean; yet they had a long line to defend, well over one hundred miles. Their front wound like a snake around mountainous crags which their artillery commanded, and it was thought they might hold out many weeks, perhaps longer, if reinforcements could be gotten in from Sicily.

In less than a fortnight, however, the Italians and Germans were surrendering in tens of thousands. What took place was roughly as follows. As Montgomery swept north along the seacoast the British First Army and the French closed in on the now shrinking Axis lines, leaving the Americans apparently far to the rear. For several days there was no report of their whereabouts as they were being shifted rapidly behind the lines of communication of the British First Army and at right angles to it to a critical sector opposite Bizerte. As formed now

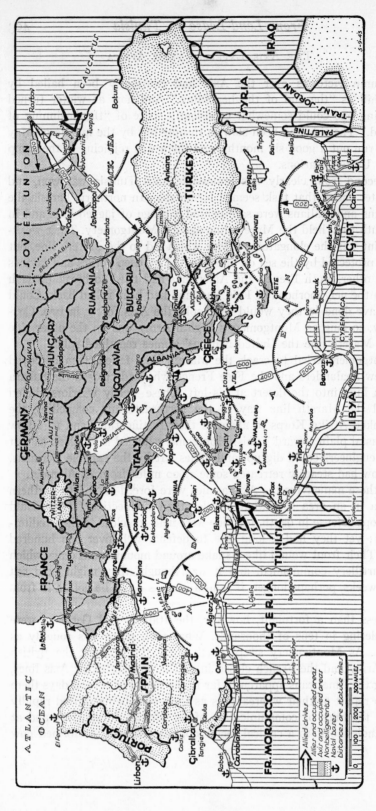

THE AFRICAN APPROACHES TO EUROPE
(Courtesy of the New York *Times*.)

the Allied line ran from northwest to southeast thus: French Moroccan troops faced Bizerte on the Mediterranean, then came the Americans, the British First Army, the main body of the French, and the British Eighth Army.

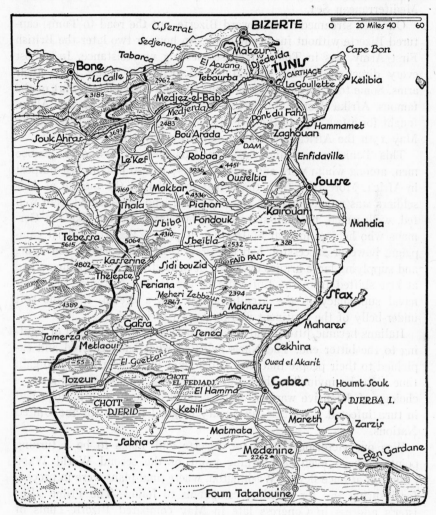

TUNISIA

(Courtesy of the New York *Times*.)

The American assignment was important; it was to pry open the mountain gateway at Mateur, leading to Bizerte. To do this it was necessary to storm three hills, the key one, Hill 609, defended by as good troops as Germany had, and in a region so rough that mules were used for trucks. In the face of heavy machine-gun fire the Americans stormed this hill with hand grenades and at the point of the bayonet. Beyond they could see Mateur, now defenseless, and farther beyond shimmering in the sunshine the white houses of Bizerte and the blue Mediterranean Sea.

Our men streamed down toward Bizerte, cut the road to Tunis, captured Bizerte without further fighting. An hour or two later the British First Army was in Tunis, likewise meeting no resistance. In almost every direction German and Italian detachments threw down their arms. Some took refuge on Cape Bon but soon surrendered. Part of the famous Afrika Korps, by-passed by the quick dash of the Allies, fought for a few days in the hills. By May 8th victory was assured; by May 15th the African resistance ended everywhere.

This Tunisian campaign cost the Axis dear. It lost over 300,000 men, among whom were 266,000 prisoners; it also lost its last outpost in Africa. More than that, the defeat proved that the morale of Axis soldiers was much impaired, since the men who surrendered were well fed, well armed, not half-starved and hopelessly beaten like the Germans who held so long at Stalingrad; it proved that the U-boat campaign, however successful, had not prevented their enemy's conveying and supplying large armies overseas; it proved that air supremacy had at last shifted from the Luftwaffe to the United Nations; that Axis naval supremacy in the Mediterranean was a dream, that the soft under-belly of the continent was now open to invasion.

Italians became jittery and talked alternately of peace and of fighting to the bitter end. The Nazis belittled what had occurred and explained to their people that they had fought in Tunisia merely to gain time to make invincible their Europa fortress. The Maginot line psychology of defensive warfare which bedeviled the French in 1940 had in turn infected the Nazis, an augury of good fortune for the United Nations.

Was our victorious battle for Bizerte and Tunis to be a turning point, perhaps even *the* turning point of the second World War? Churchill at once flew to Washington, where final plans were in process for insuring and for speeding campaigns to follow. The Prime Minister's address in Congress late in May compared Bizerte-Tunis of 1943 to Gettysburg of 1863 but warned that though the grey tide of the Confederate army never rose so high again, two years passed and thousands died before the victors came to Appomattox.

Finis.

READING LIST

Bibliographies

ALLISON, W. H. and others [eds.], *A Guide to Historical Literature* (1931).
GOOCH, G. P., *Bibliography of European History 1918-1939* (1940).
LANGER, W. L. and ARMSTRONG, H. F., *Foreign Affairs Bibliography* (1933).

Source Readings

Contemporary Civilization Source Book, Part II, published by the Columbia University Press (1941). Excellent.
COOK, A. N., *Readings in Modern and Contemporary History* (1937).
LANGSAM, W. C., *Documents and Readings in the History of Europe Since 1918* (1939).

Surveys

CHAMBERS, F. P., GRANT, C. P., and BAYLEY, C. C., *This Age of Conflict* (1943).
BENNS, F. T., *Europe Since 1914*, 5th edition (1941).
HAINES, C. G. and HOFFMAN, R. J. S., *The Origins and Background of the Second World War* (1943).
LANGSAM, W. C., *The World Since 1914*, 5th edition (1943).

Periodicals Found Most Useful

Annals of the American Academy of Political and Social Science.
Annual Register.
Foreign Affairs.
Foreign Policy Reports (Published by the Foreign Policy Association, too numerous for separate mention).
International Conciliation. (Monthly publication of Carnegie Endowment.)
Political Science Quarterly.

CHAPTER I

ANTECEDENTS OF THE FIRST WORLD WAR

(a) Cultural and General

BINKLEY, R. C., *Realism and Nationalism, 1852-1871* (1935).
COLUM, M. M., *From these Roots, the Ideas which Have Made Modern Literature* (1937).
CROCE, B., *History of Europe in the Nineteenth Century* (1933).
HAYES, C. J., *A Generation of Materialism, 1871-1900* (1941).

LASKI, H. J., *The Rise of Liberalism* (1936).
LUCAS, F. L., *The Decline and Fall of the Romantic Ideal* (1936).
MacCAFFREY, C., *History of the Catholic Church . . . 1789-1908*, 2 vols. (1910).
McGIFFERT, A. C., *The Rise of Modern Religious Ideas* (1915).
MEADE, G. H., *Movements of Thought in the Nineteenth Century* (1936).
RANDALL, J. H., *Making of the Modern Mind*, rev. edition (1940).
ROBERTSON, J. M., *History of Free Thought in the Nineteenth Century* (1929).
ROUTH, H. V., *Toward the Twentieth Century: Essays in the Spiritual History of the Nineteenth* (1937).

(b) *Economic*

ASHLEY, A. J., *The Progress of the German Working Class in the Last Quarter of a Century* (1904).
COLE, G. D. H., *A Short History of the British Working Class Movement*, Vol. II, 1848-1900 (1926).
EDWARDS, G. W., *The Evolution of Finance Capitalism* (1938).
EMDEN, P. H., *Money Power of Europe in the Nineteenth and Twentieth Centuries* (1938).
FAY, C. R., *Life and Labour in the Nineteenth Century* (1920).
HOBSON, J. A., *The Evolution of Modern Capitalism*, rev. edition (1926).
LAIDLER, H. W., *History of Socialist Thought* (1927).
KUCZYNSKI, J., *Labour Conditions in Western Europe, 1820-1935* (1937).
NUSSBAUM, F. L., *A History of the Economic Institutions of Western Europe* (1933).
ORTEGA Y GASSET, J., *The Revolt of the Masses*, Eng. trans. (1932).
SÉE, H. E., *Modern Capitalism, Its Origins and Evolution* (1928).
WILSON, E., *To the Finland Station* (1940).

(c) *Imperialism and Diplomacy*

BEAZLEY, C. R., *The Road to Ruin in Europe 1870-1914* (1932).
BÜLOW, B. VON, *Memoirs*, 4 vols. (1931-32).
CLARK, G., *The Balance Sheets of Imperialism* (1936).
CHURCHILL, R. P., *The Anglo-Russian Convention of 1907* (1939).
DICKINSON, G. L., *International Anarchy 1904-1914* (1926).
DURHAM, M. E., *The Sarajevo Crime* (1925).
FABRE-LUCE, A., *The Limitations of Victory* (1926).
FAY, S. B., *The Origins of The First World War* (1931). Important.
GREY, SIR E., *Twenty-five Years, 1892-1916*, 2 vols. (1925).
HALDANE, VISCOUNT, *The Autobiography of Richard Bordon Haldane* (1929).
HELMREICH, E. C., *The Diplomacy of the Balkan Wars, 1912-13* (1938).
HOBSON, J. A., *Imperialism, A Study*, 3rd edition (1938).
KAUTSKY, K., *The Guilt of William Hohenzollern* (1920).
LANGER, W. L., *The Diplomacy of Imperialism 1890-1902*, 2 vols. (1935).
LICHNOWSKI, PRINCE K. M., *Heading for the Abyss* (1928).
MONTGELAS, COUNT M., *The Case for the Central Powers* (1925).
MOON, P. T., *Imperialism and World Politics* (1926).

OWEN, D. E., *British Opium Policy in China and India* (1934).

PALÉOLOGUE, G. M., *An Ambassador's Memoirs,* 3 vols. (1924-26). French Ambassador to Russia.

PORTER, C. W., *The Career of Théophile Delcassé* (1936).

FRIBRAM, A. F., *Austrian Foreign Policy 1908-1918* (1923).

——, *England and the International Policy of the European Powers 1871-1914* (1931).

RENOUVIN, P., *The Immediate Origins of the War* (1928).

SCHMITT, B. E., *The Coming of War,* 2 vols. (1930). Important.

——, *Triple Alliance and Triple Entente* (1934). Brief but excellent.

SCHOEN, W. E., *The Memoirs of an Ambassador* (1922). German Ambassador to the Third Republic.

SCHWEITZER, A., *On the Edge of the Primeval Forest* (1922).

SETON-WATSON, R. W., *Sarajevo, A Study in the Origins of the Great War* (1926).

SONTAG, R. J., *European Diplomatic History 1871-1932* (1933).

CHAPTERS II AND III

THE FIRST WORLD WAR

ABBOTT, G. F., *Greece and the Allies, 1914-1922* (1922).

ANDRASSY, COUNT J., *Diplomacy and the War* (1921).

AHMED (ENIM), *Turkey in the World War* (1930).

ARTHUR, SIR G. C. A., *The Life of Lord Kitchener* (1920).

ASHMEAD-BARTLETT, E., *The Uncensored Dardanelles* (1928).

ASQUITH, H. H., *Memoirs and Reflections, 1852-1927,* 2 vols. (1928).

ASTON, SIR G. G., *The Biography of the Late Marshal Foch* (1929).

BAERLEIN, H., *The Birth of Yugoslavia,* 2 vols. (1922).

——, *The March of the Seventy Thousand* (1926). Exploits of the mutinous Czech soldiers.

BAKER, R. S., *Neutrality 1914-1915* (1935). Vol. 5 of the author's *Life of Woodrow Wilson.*

—— and DODD, W. [eds.], *The Public Papers of Woodrow Wilson,* 6 vols. (1925-27).

BENÉS, DR. E., *My War Memoirs* (1928).

BERNSTORFF, J. VON, *My Three Years in America* (1920).

BOWMAN-MANIFOLD, SIR M. G. E., *An Outline of the Egyptian and Palestine Campaigns, 1914 to 1918* (1922).

BRUSILOV, A. A., *A Soldier's Notebook* (1930).

BUCHAN, J., *A History of the Great War,* 4 vols. (1922).

BUCHANAN, SIR G., *My Mission to Russia* (1923).

BUNYAN, J. and FISHER, H. H. [eds.], *The Bolshevik Revolution 1917-1918* (1934).

CALLWELL, SIR C. E., *Field Marshal Sir Henry Wilson,* 2 vols. (1927).

——, *The Life of Sir Stanley Maude* (1920).

CAPEK, K. [ed.], *Masaryk Tells His Story* (1935).

CHAMBERLIN, W. H., *History of the Russian Revolution,* 2 vols. (1935).

CHARTERIS, J., *Field Marshal Earl Haig* (1929).

CHESTER, S. B., *Life of Venizelos* (1921).

CHURCHILL, W. S., *The World Crisis, 1911-1918*, 4 vols. (1923-27).
CLARKSON, G. B., *Industrial America in the World War* (1923).
CORBETT, J. S., *History of the Great War Naval Operations*, 4 vols. (1920-28).
CRUTTWELL, C. R. M., *A History of the Great War, 1914-1918* (1934).
CZERNIN, O., *In the World War* (1920).
DAHLIN, E., *French and German Opinion on Declared War Aims, 1914-1918* (1933).
DANIELS, H. G., *The Rise of the German Republic* (1928).
DANIELS, J., *Our Navy at War* (1922).
DAVISON, H. P., *The American Red Cross in the Great War* (1919).
DENIKIN, A. J., *The Russian Turmoil* (1922).
DENNET, T. and FULLER, J. V. [eds.], *Papers Relating to the Foreign Relations of the U. S.; Supplements: The World War* (1928).
DEWAR, G. A. B., *Sir Douglas Haig's Command*, 2 vols. (1923).
DONIVILLE, C., *Submarines and Sea Power* (1919).
DUMBA, K., *Memories of A Diplomat* (1932). Austrian Ambassador at Washington.
FALKENHAYN, E. von., *General Headquarters and Its Critical Decisions* (1919).
FISHER, J. A., *Memories and Records*, 2 vols. (1920).
FLORINSKY, M. T., *The End of the Russian Empire* (1931).
FOCH, F., *Memoirs* (1931).
FORSTNER, G. G. VON, *The Journal of Submarine Commander von Forstner* (1917).
FROTHINGHAM, T., *The Naval History of the World War* (1926).
————, *The American Reinforcement in the World War* (1927).
FULLER, J. F. C., *Tanks in the Great War* (1920).
FÜLÖP-MILLER, R., *Rasputin: The Holy Devil* (1928).
FRADKIN, E., *Chemical Warfare* (1929).
GALET, E. J., *Albert, King of the Belgians, in the Great War* (1931).
GERARD, J. W., *My Four Years in Germany* (1917). American Ambassador at Berlin.
GIBBONS, H. A., *Venizelos* (1923).
GIBSON, R. H. and PRENDERGAST, M., *The German Submarine War, 1914-1918* (1931).
GIOLITTI, G., *Memoirs of My Life* (1923).
GLAISE VON HORSTENAU, *The Collapse of the Austro-Hungarian Empire* (1930).
GLEAVES, A., *A History of the Transport Service* (1921).
GOLOVINE, N. N., *The Russian Army in the World War* (1931).
GUICHARD, L., *The Naval Blockade* (1930).
GOLDER, F. A. [ed.], *Documents of Russian History, 1914-1917* (1927).
GWYNN, S. [ed.], *The Letters and Friendships of Sir Cecil Spring-Rice*, 2 vols. (1929). British Ambassador at Washington.
HAMILTON, SIR I., *Gallipoli Diary*, 2 vols. (1920).
HARBORD, J. G., *The American Army in France* (1936).
HARPER, J. E. T., *The Truth About Jutland* (1927).
HAYES, C. J. H., *A Brief History of the Great War* (1926).
JÁSZI, O., *The Dissolution of the Hapsburg Monarchy* (1929).
————, *Revolution and Counter-Revolution in Hungary* (1924).

JELLICOE, J. R., *The Grand Fleet, 1914-1916* (1919).
JOFFRE, J. J. C., *Personal Memoirs*, 2 vols. (1932).
LAWRENCE, T. E., *Revolt in the Desert* (1927).
LIDDELL HART, B. H., *A History of the World War, 1914-1918* (1935).
——, *Colonel Lawrence: The Man Behind the Legend* (1934).
LIGGETT, H., *Commanding An American Army* (1925).
LIMAN VON SANDERS, O., *Five Years in Turkey* (1927).
LLOYD GEORGE, D., *War Memoirs of David Lloyd George*, 4 vols. (1933-34).
LUTZ, R. H. [ed.], *The Causes of the German Collapse in 1918* (1934). A translation of German documents.
MADELINE, L., *Foch* (1929).
MAVOR, J., *The Russian Revolution* (1928).
MAXIMILIAN, PRINZ VON BADEN, *The Memoirs of Prince Max of Baden*, 2 vols. (1928).
MERCIER, D. J., *Cardinal Mercier's Own Story* (1920).
MILLIS, W., *Road to War: America, 1914-1917* (1935).
MILIUKOV, P. N., *History of the Second Russian Revolution* (1920).
NOWAK, K. F., *The Collapse of Central Europe* (1924).
PAPOUSEK, J., *The Czechoslovak Nation's Struggle for Independence* (1928).
PALMER, F., *Newton D. Baker*, 2 vols. (1931).
PERSHING, J. J., *My Experiences in the World War* (1931).
PILSUDSKI, J., *The Memories of a Polish Revolutionary and Soldier* (1931).
RALEIGH, W., *The War in the Air*, 2 vols. (1922-28).
REDLICH, J., *Emperor Francis Joseph of Austria* (1929).
RODZIANKO, M. V., *The Reign of Rasputin: An Empire's Collapse* (1927).
ROSENBERG, A., *The Birth of the German Republic, 1871-1918* (1931).
ROSS, E. A., *The Russian Bolshevik Revolution* (1921).
SCHEER, R., *Germany's High Sea Fleet in the World War* (1920).
SEYMOUR, C. [ed.], *The Intimate Papers of Col. House*, 4 vols. (1926-28).
——, *Woodrow Wilson and the World War* (1922).
——, *American Neutrality, 1914-1917* (1936).
SIMS, W. S., *The American Navy in the War* (1920).
TIRPITZ, A. VON, *My Memoirs*, 2 vols. (1919).
TOWNSHEND, SIR C., *My Campaign in Mesopotamia* (1920).
TOWNSHEND, M. E., *The Rise and Fall of Germany's Colonial Empire, 1884-1918* (1930).
TRACHTENBERG, A. [ed.], *Lenin: Toward the Seizure of Power*, 2 vols. (1932). Lenin documents prior to the Revolution of 1917.
TROTSKY, L., *The History of the Russian Revolution* (1934).
WALSH, E. A., *The Fall of the Russian Empire* (1928).
WAVELL, COL. A. P., *The Palestine Campaign* (1928).
WHITLOCK, B., *Belgium, A Personal Narrative*, 2 vols. (1919). The American Ambassador to Belgium.
WHEELER-BENNET, *The Forgotten Peace—Brest-Litovsk, Marde, 1918* (1939).

CHAPTER IV

PEACE TREATIES AND THEIR AFTERMATH (1919-1923)

ABBOTT, G. E., *Greece and Her Allies, 1914-1922* (1922).

ADAM, G., *The Tiger: Georges Clemenceau* (1930).

ALMOND, N., and LUTZ, R. H. [eds.], *The Treaty of St. Germain* (1934).

BAKER, R. S., *Woodrow Wilson and the World Settlement*, 3 vols. (1922-23).

BARUCH, B. M., *The Making of the Reparation and Economic Sections of the Treaty* (1920).

BASSETT, J. S., *The League of Nations; A Chapter in World Politics* (1928).

BENTWICH, N. DE M., *The Mandates System* (1930).

BERGMANN, C., *The History of Reparations* (1927). A statement of the German position.

BIRDSALL, P., *Versailles Twenty Years After* (1941). Favorable to Wilson.

DEÁK, F., *Hungary at the Paris Peace Conference* (1942).

DODD, W. E., *Woodrow Wilson and His Work* (1932).

DONALD, SIR R., *The Tragedy of Trianon* (1928).

DICKINSON, T. H., *The United States and the League* (1923).

FOLEY, H. [ed.], *Woodrow Wilson's Case for the League of Nations.* Extracts from presidential speeches.

GERIG, B., *The Open Door and the Mandates System* (1930).

HASKINS, C. H. and LORD, R. H., *Some Problems of the Peace Conference* (1920).

HOUSE, E. M. and SEYMOUR, C. [eds.], *What Really Happened at Paris: The Story of the Peace Conference 1918-1919 by American Delegates* (1921).

HOWARD, H., *The Partition of Turkey* (1913-1923). Excellent on Sevres Treaty.

HOWARD-ELLIS, C., *The Origin, Structure and Working of the League of Nations* (1928).

KEYNES, J. M., *The Economic Consequences of the Peace* (1920).

LANSING, R., *The Peace Negotiations, A Personal Narrative* (1921).

LICHTENBERGER, H., *Relations between France and Germany* (1923).

———, *The Ruhr Conflict* (1923).

LODGE, H. C., *The Senate and the League of Nations* (1925).

LLOYD GEORGE, D., *The Truth about Reparations and War Debts* (1932).

MARBURG, T., *Development of the League of Nations Idea*, 2 vols. (1932).

MARGALITH, A. M., *The International Mandates* (1930).

McFADYEAN, SIR A., *Reparations Reviewed* (1930).

MILLER, D. H., *The Drafting of the Covenant* (1928).

MOLONY, W. O., *Nationality and the Peace Treaties* (1934).

MORLEY, F., *The Society of Nations* (1932).

NICHOLSON, H., *Peace-Making, 1919* (1933). Important.

NOWAK, K. F., *Versailles* (1929).

NOEL-BUXTON, E. and CONWELL-EVANS, T. P., *Oppressed Peoples and the League of Nations* (1922).

PALMER, F. BLISS, *Peacemaker, the Life and Letters of General Tasker Howard Bliss* (1934).

QUIGLEY, H. S., *From Versailles to Locarno* (1927).
RAPPARD, W. E., *The Geneva Experiment* (1932).
ROSE, A., *Germans and Poles in Upper Silesia* (1919).
SCHIFF, V., *The Germans at Versailles* (1930).
SETON-WATSON, R. W., *Britain and the Dictators* (1938). Good on Versailles Treaty.
SEYMOUR, C., *The Intimate Papers of Colonel House*, 4 vols. (1926-28). Valuable.
STEGEMAN, H., *The Mirage of Versailles* (1928).
TARDIEU, A., *The Truth about the Treaty* (1921).
TEMPERLEY, H. W. V. [ed.], *A History of the Peace Conference at Paris*, 6 vols. (1920-24). Invaluable.
TOYNBEE, A. J., *The World after the Peace Conference* (1925).
———, *Survey of International Affairs* (1920-23).
WAMBAUGH, S., *Plebiscites Since the World War*, 2 vols. (1933).
WRIGHT, Q., *Mandates under the League of Nations* (1930).

CHAPTER V

THE UNION OF SOVIET SOCIALIST REPUBLICS (U.S.S.R.)

ARNOT, R. P., *Soviet Russia and Her Neighbors* (1927).
BALDWIN, R. N., *Liberty under the Soviets* (1928).
BARBUSSE, H., *Stalin: A New World Seen through One Man* (1935).
BATSELL, W. R., *Soviet Rule in Russia* (1929).
BEAUCHAMP, J., *Agriculture in Soviet Russia* (1931).
BORDERS, K., *Village Life under the Soviets* (1927).
BRAILSFORD, H. N., *How the Soviets Work* (1923).
BRAZOL, B. Z., *The Balance Sheet of Sovietism* (1922).
BUKHARIN, N. and PREOBRAZHINSKY, E., *The ABC of Communism* (1922).
CHAMBERLAIN, W. H., *Russia's Iron Age* (1934). Good but disillusioned.
———, *Soviet Russia* (1931). Valuable.
COATES, C. H., *The Red Theology in the Far East* (1927).
COATES, W. P. and ARMED, Z. K., *Intervention in Russia, 1918-1922* (1935).
———, *The Second Five-Year Plan of Development of the U.S.S.R.* (1934).
COUNTS, G. S., *The Soviet Challenge to America* (1931).
CUDAHY, J., *Archangel: The American War with Russia* (1924).
DAVIES, J. E., *Mission to Moscow* (1941). Important.
DAVIS, K. W., *The Soviets at Geneva* (1934).
DENIKIN, A. I., *The White Army* (1930).
DENNIS, A. L. P., *The Foreign Policies of Soviet Russia* (1934).
DUNN, R. W., *Soviet Trade Unions* (1924).
DURANTY, W., *Duranty Reports Russia* (1934). Impartial, vivid.
EASTMAN, M., *Since Lenin Died*, 1925.
EMHARDT, W. C., *Religion in Soviet Russia* (1929).
FARBMAN, M. S., *Bolshevism in Retreat* (1923).
FÜLÖP-MILLER, R., *The Mind and Face of Bolshevism* (1928). Especially recommended.

GOLDER, F. and HUTCHINSON, L., *On the Trail of the Russian Famine* (1927).

GRAVES, W. S., *America's Siberian Adventure* (1931).

GUEST, L. H., *The New Russia* (1926).

GURIAN, W., *Bolshevism: Theory and Practice* (1932).

HARPER, S. N., *Making Bolsheviks* (1931).

——, *The Soviet Union and World Problems* (1935).

HECKER, J. F., *Religion and Communism* (1935).

HINDUS, M. G., *Humanity Uprooted* (1928).

——, *Red Bread* (1931).

——, *The Great Offensive* (1933). The agricultural revolution.

HOOVER, C. B., *The Economic Life of Soviet Russia* (1931).

IAKHONTOV, V. A., *Russia and the Soviet Union in the Far East* (1931).

JOHNSON, H., *The Soviet Power* (1940). Highly laudatory.

KRUPSKAIA, N. K., *Memoirs of Lenin* (1930).

LAWTON, L., *The Russian Revolution, 1917-1926* (1927).

——, *An Economic History of Soviet Russia*, 2 vols. (1932).

LEVINE, I. D., *The Man Lenin* (1924).

——, *Stalin* (1931).

LITTLEPAGE, J. D. and BESS, D., *In Search of Soviet Gold* (1938).

LYONS, E., *Assignment in Utopia* (1937).

MARCU, V., *Lenin* (1928). Recommended.

MASLOFF, S. S., *Russia after Four Years of Revolution* (1923).

MAYNARD, SIR C. C. M., *The Murmansk Venture* (1928).

MILIUKOV, P. N., *Russia Today and Tomorrow* (1922).

NEARING, S., *Education in Soviet Russia* (1926).

NEWSHOLME, A. and KINGSBURY, J. A., *Red Medicine: Socialized Health in Soviet Russia* (1933).

POPOV, N., *Outline of the Communist Party of the Soviet Union*, 2 vols. (1935).

PRICE, G. M., *Labor Protection in Soviet Russia* (1928).

ROCHESTER, A., *Lenin on the Agrarian Question* (1942).

SCOTT, J., *Behind the Urals* (1942). Excellent account of Magnitogorsk.

SPINKA, M., *The Church and the Russian Revolution* (1927).

SMITH, J., *Woman in Soviet Russia* (1928).

STEWART, G., *The White Armies of Russia. A Chronicle of Counter-Revolution and Allied Intervention* (1933).

STRONG, A. L., *The Soviets Conquer Wheat* (1931).

TROTSKY, L., *My Life* (1930).

——, *The History of the Russian Revolution*, 3 vols. (1934).

——, *The Real Situation in Russia* (1928). Anti-Stalin.

——, *The Revolution Betrayed* (1937).

VERNADSKY, G. V., *Lenin, Red Dictator* (1931). Hostile.

WEBB, S. and WEBB, B., *Soviet Communism: A New Civilization*, 2 vols. (1936).

WICKSTEED, A., *My Russian Neighbors* (1934).

YARMOLINSKY, A., *The Jews and Other Minor Nationalities Under the Soviets* (1929).

CHAPTER VI

ITALIAN AND GERMAN FASCISM

(a) *Italy*

BINCHY, D. A., *Church and State in Fascist Italy* (1941).
BOLITHO, W., *Italy under Mussolini* (1926).
CRESSWELL, C. M., *The Keystone of Fascism* (1929).
FINER, H., *Mussolini's Italy* (1935). Recommended.
GOAD, H. E., *The Making of the Corporative State* (1932).
HAIDER, C., *Capital and Labor under Fascism* (1930).
JOHNSON, H. J. T., *The Papacy and the Kingdom of Italy* (1926).
KING, B., *Fascism in Italy* (1931).
MATTEOTTI, G., *The Fascisti Exposed* (1924).
MEGARO, G., *Mussolini in the Making* (1938). Good for the Duce's early
 years.
MUSSOLINI, B., *My Autobiography* (1928). Disappointing.
NITTI, F., *Bolshevism, Fascism and Democracy* (1927). Former Premier.
———, *Escape* (1930).
RAWLINS, C. D. and CARPENTER, H. C. A., *Economic Conditions in Italy*
 (1930).
SALVEMINI, G., *The Fascist Dictatorship in Italy* (1927).
———, *Under the Axe of Fascism* (1936). Hostile.
SCHNEIDER, H. W., *Making the Fascist State* (1928). Good.
———, *The Fascist Government in Italy* (1936).
SILONE, I., *The School for Dictators* (1938). Satirical.
VILLARI, L., *Italy* (1929). Favorable.

(b) *Germany*

ANGELL, J. W., *The Recovery of Germany* (1929).
ARMSTRONG, H. F., *Hitler's Reich: The First Phase* (1933).
BISCHOFF, R. F., *Nazi Conquest through German Culture* (1943).
BRADY, R. A., *The Spirit and Structure of German Fascism* (1937).
BRUNET, R., *The New German Constitution* (1922).
BUTLER, R. D. O., *The Roots of National Socialism* (1941).
CHILDS, H. L., *The Nazi Primer* (1938). Translation of an influential text-
 book used in Hitler's Germany.
COAR, J. F., *The Old and New Germany* (1924).
CURTIS, J. S., *An Appraisal of the Protocols of Zion* (1942).
DANIELS, H. G., *The Rise of The German Republic* (1928).
DAWSON, SIR P., *Germany's Industrial Revival* (1926).
DEUEL, W. R., *People under Hitler* (1942).
DODD, W. E., JR. and DODD, M., *Ambassador Dodd's Diary* (1941).
DORPALEN, A., *The World of General Haushofer* (1942).
DOUGLAS, P. F., *God Among the Germans* (1935).
EBENSTEIN, W., *The Nazi State* (1943).
FEDER, G., *Hitler's Official Program and its Fundamental Ideas* (1934).
FOERSTER, F. W., *Europe and the German Question* (1940).

GUILLEBAUD, C. W., *The Works Council. A German Experiment in Industrial Democracy* (1928).

HAMBURGER, L., *How Nazi Germany Has Mobilized and Controlled Labor* (1940).

HEIDEN, K., *A History of National Socialism* (1935).

———, *Hitler* (1936).

HERMAN, S. W., JR., *It's Your Souls We Want* (1943). Excellent, and despite the title a judicial inquiry into Nazi religious ideas.

HITLER, A., *Mein Kampf* (1933). Reynal and Hitchcock. Unexpurgated edition.

———, *My New Order* (1941). Collected speeches.

HOETZSCH, O., *Germany's Domestic and Foreign Policies* (1931).

HOOVER, C. B., *Germany Enters the Third Reich* (1933).

JÄCKH, E., *The New Germany* (1927).

KOSOK, P., *Modern Germany: A Study in Conflicting Loyalties* (1933).

LAUTERBACH, A. T., *Economics in Uniform* (1943). A careful study.

LENGYEL, E., *Hitler* (1933).

MARCUS, J. R., *The Rise and Destiny of the German Jew* (1934).

MARX, F. M., *Government in the Third Reich* (1936).

MILLER, D., *You Can't Do Business with Hitler* (1941).

NEUMANN, F. L., *Behemoth: The Structure and Practice of National Socialism* (1942).

OLDEN, R., *Stresemann* (1930).

QUIGLEY, H. and CLARK, R. J., *Republican Germany* (1928). Thorough.

REED, D., *The Burning of the Reichstag* (1934).

RHEINBABEN, R., *Von Stresemann, the Man and the Statesman* (1929).

SCHULTZ-PFAELZER, G., *Hindenberg* (1931).

SCHUMANN, F. L., *The Nazi Dictatorship* (1935). Able.

SUTTON, E. [ed.], *Gustav Stresemann, His Diaries, Letters, Papers* (1935).

STRAUSZ-HUPÉ, R., *Geopolitics* (1942). Valuable.

SWEEZY, R., *The Structure of the Nazi Economy* (1941).

ULLSTEIN, H., *Rise and Fall of the House of Ullstein* (1943).

WETERSTETTEN, R. and WATSON, A. M. K., *The Biography of President Von Hindenberg* (1930).

WAGNER, L., *Hitler, Man of Strife* (1942).

WHITTLESEY, D. and others. *German Strategy of World Conquest* (1942). Geopolitics as taught in Hitler's Reich.

YBARRA, T. R., *Hindenberg, the Man with Three Lives* (1932).

CHAPTER VII

FRANCE AND ENGLAND BETWEEN TWO WARS

(a) *France*

BARTHELEMY, J., *The Government of France* (1924).

BROGAN, D. W., *France under the Republic* (1940). Authoritative.

CLEMENCEAU, G., *In the Evening of My Thoughts*, 2 vols. (1929).

GWYNN, D. R., *The Catholic Reaction in France* (1924).

HAYES, C. J. H., *France: A Nation of Patriots* (1930).
HUDDLESTON, S., *Poincaré: A Biographical Portrait* (1924).
MACDONALD, W., *Reconstruction in France* (1922).
MOULTON, H. G. and LEWIS, C., *The French Debt Problem* (1925).
OGBURN, W. F. and JAFFÉ, W., *The Economic Development of Post-War France* (1929).
SIEGFRIED, A., *France: A Study in Nationality* (1930).
STOKES, R. L., *Leon Blum: Poet to Premier* (1937).
TABOUIS, G., *They Called Me Cassandra* (1942).
THOMSON, V., *Briand, Man of Peace* (1930).
WERTH, A., *Which Way France?* (1937).
WOLFERS, A., *Britain and France Between Two Wars* (1940).

(b) *England*

BATTEN, E., *National Economics for Britain's Day of Need; the Solution of the Unemployment Problem* (1926).
BREBNER, J. B. and NEVINS, A., *The Making of Modern Britain* (1943). Excellent brief sketch of British History.
CHURCHILL, W. L. S., *The Aftermath* (1939). Last volume in *The World Crisis* (1918-1928).
———, *While England Slept: A Survey of World Affairs, 1932-1938* (1938).
CLYNES, J. R., *Memoirs*, 2 vols. (1937).
COLE, G. D. H., *A Short History of the British Working Class Movement* (1927).
DIBELIUS, W., *England* (1930). Comprehensive German analysis.
FYFE, H., *The British Liberal Party* (1928).
GRAVES, R. and HODGE, A., *The Long Week End* (1941). Social history of the period between the World Wars.
GREENWOOD, G. A., *England Today* (1922).
HEATON, H., *The British Way to Recovery* (1934).
HILL, A. C. C., JR. and LUBIN, I., *The British Attack on Unemployment* (1934).
LAWRENCE, F. W. P., *The Gold Crisis* (1931).
LEE, J., *This Great Journey* (1942). Superb autobiography of the daughter of a coal miner.
MALLET, SIR C. E., *Mr. Lloyd George: A Study* (1930).
MASTERMAN, C. F. G., *England After the War* (1922).
NICHOLSON, H., *Curzon The Last Phase 1919-1925* (1934).
PEEL, G., *The Economic War* (1930).
PRIESTLEY, J. B., *An English Journey* (1934). The depressed areas. Excellent.
SIEGFRIED, A., *England's Crisis* (1931).
SNOWDEN, P., *Autobiography*, 2 vols. (1934).
STEED, H. W., *The Real Stanley Baldwin* (1930).

CHAPTER VIII

THE BRITISH COMMONWEALTH AND EMPIRE

AMERY, L. C. M. S., *The Empire in the New Era* (1928).
BAKER, P. J. N., *The Present Judicial Status of the British Dominions in International Law* (1929).
BARNOUW, A., *Languages and Race Problems in South Africa* (1934).
BEASLEY, P., *Michael Collins and the Making of New Ireland* (1926).
BOVEY, W., *Canadien, A Study of the French Canadians* (1933).
COOK, A. N., *British Enterprise in Nigeria* (1943).
DAWSON, R. M., *The Development of Dominion States, 1900-1936* (1937).
DILLEY, M. R., *British Policy in Kenya Colony* (1937).
ELLIOT, W. Y., *The New British Empire* (1932).
FITZPATRICK, B., *The British Empire in Australia* (1941).
GOOD, J. W., *Ulster and Ireland* (1919).
GWYNN, D., *De Valera* (1933).
———, *The Irish Free State, 1922-1927* (1928).
HALL, H. D., *The British Commonwealth of Nations* (1920).
HALL, H. W., *Australia and England: A Study in Imperial Relations* (1934).
HALL, W. P., *Empire to Commonwealth* (1928).
HARRISON, H., *The Neutrality of Ireland* (1942).
HEALEY, T. M., *Letters and Leaders of My Day*, 2 vols. (1929).
HOFMEYER, J. H., *South Africa* (1931).
HOLE, H. M., *The Making of Rhodesia* (1926).
HUXLEY, E. J., *White Man's Country: Lord Delamere and the Making of Kenya*, 2 vols. (1935).
KEITH, A. B., *The Governments of the British Empire* (1935).
KNAPLUND, P., *The British Empire 1815-1939* (1941). The best general account.
MILLER, E. H., *Strategy at Singapore* (1942).
MORRELL, W. P., *New Zealand* (1935).
MOSS, W., *Political Parties in the Irish Free State* (1933).
NADEL, S. F., *Black Byzantium; The Kingdom of Nupe in Nigeria* (1943).
NEWMAN, E. W. P., *Great Britain in Egypt* (1928).
NEUENDORFER, G., *Studies in the Evolution of Dominion Status* (1943).
O'BRIAIN, B., *The Irish Constitution* (1929).
PAUL-DUBOIS, L. and GILL, T. P., *The Irish Struggle and Its Results* (1934).
PHILLIPS, W. A., *The Revolution in Ireland, 1906-1923*. Prejudiced but full account.
RAPHAEL, L. A. C., *The Cape-to-Cairo Dream* (1936).
REITZ, D., *Commando* (1929). Recollections of one of General Smuts' right-hand men.
SMITH, A. N., *Thirty Years: The Commonwealth of Australia*, (1901-1931) (1934).
SIEGFRIED, A., *Canada* (1932).
SYMONS, M. T., *Britain and Egypt: The Rise of Egyptian Nationalism* (1925).

TINLEY, J. M., *The Native Problem in South Africa* (1942).
TALBOT, H., *Michael Collins' Own Story* (1923).
WOOD, F. L. W., *Constitutional Development of Australia* (1933).
YOUNG, G., *Egypt* (1927).

CHAPTER IX

THE LESSER STATES BETWEEN TWO WARS

ALASTOS, D., *Venizelos: Patriot, Statesman, Revolutionary* (1942).
APPONYI, COUNT S. and others, *Justice for Hungary* (1928).
ARMSTRONG, H. F., *The New Balkans* (1926).
———, *Where the East Begins* (1929).
ASHMEAD-BARTLETT, E., *The Tragedy of Central Europe* (1923).
ATCHLEY, T. W., *Finland* (1931).
BAREILLES, B. and others, *Albania and the Albanians* (1920).
BASCH, A. and DVORÁTEK, J., *Austria and Its Economic Existence* (1925).
BAUER, DR. O., *The Austrian Revolution* (1925).
BEARD, C. A. and RADIN, G., *The Balkan Pivot: Yugoslavia* (1929).
BORKENAU, F., *The Spanish Cockpit* (1937). Pro-Republican.
BUELL, R. L., *Poland, Key to Europe* (1939). *Excellent.*
BUJAK, F., *Poland's Economic Development* (1926).
BULLOCK, M., *Austria, 1918-1936: A Study in Failure* (1937).
BRANDT, J. A., *Toward the New Spain* (1933).
CABOT, J. M., *The Racial Conflict in Transylvania* (1926).
CLARK, C. W., *United Rumania* (1932).
CHESTER, S. B., *Life of Venizelos* (1921).
CRABITÈS, P., *Beneš* (1934).
CRANE, J. O., *The Little Entente* (1931).
DEAKIN, J. B., *Spain Today* (1924).
DEVEREUX, R., *Poland Reborn* (1922).
DONALD, SIR R., *The Polish Corridor and its Consequences* (1929).
DYBOSKI, R., *Poland Old and New* (1926).
EDDY, C. B., *Greece and the Greek Refugees* (1931).
FELINSKI, M., *The Ukranians in Poland* (1931).
GEDYE, G. E. R., *Heirs to the Hapsburgs* (1932). The succession states.
GERMAINS, V. W., *Austria Today* (1932).
GIBBONS, H. A., *Venizelos* (1923).
GILLIE, D. R., *Joseph Pilsudski* (1931).
HARDY, C. O. and KUCZYNSKI, R. R., *The Housing Program of the City of Vienna* (1934).
HOLLAND, C., *Czechoslovakia: The Land and Its People* (1931).
JÁSZI, O., *Revolutions and Counter Revolutions in Hungary* (1924).
KROFTA, K., *A Short History of Czechoslovakia* (1934).
LAFFAN, R. G. D., *Jugoslavia Since 1918* (1929).
MACARTNEY, C. A., *The Social Revolution in Austria* (1926).
MACHRAY, R., *Poland, 1914-1931* (1932). Good.
MENDIZABEL, A., *The Martyrdom of Spain* (1938). Judicious.
MURRAY, K. M., *Wings over Poland* (1932). The war against the Soviets.
McBRIDE, R. M., *Finland and Its People* (1925).
MITRANY, D., *The Land and the Peasant in Rumania* (1930).

PATTERSON, E. J., *Pilsudski, Marshal of Poland* (1935).

PATTON, K. S., *Kingdom of the Serbs, Croats and Slovenes: Commercial and Industrial Handbook* (1928).

PEERS, E. A., *The Spanish Tragedy, 1930-1936: Dictatorship, Republic, Chaos,* 2nd edition (1936). Excellent.

POPOVICI, A., *The Political Status of Bessarabia* (1925). Pro-Rumanian.

RUTTER, O., *The New Baltic States and Their Future* (1925).

SALTER, C., *Try-Out in Spain* (1943). Journalistic but vivid.

SENCOURT, R., *Spain's Ordeal: A Documented History of the Civil War* (1940). Pro-Catholic and nationalist.

SETON-WATSON, R. W. [ed.], *Slovakia, Then and Now* (1931).

SHEEHAN, V., *Not Peace but A Sword* (1939). Graphic first-hand account of the Civil War in Spain.

SÖDERHJELM, H., *The Red Insurrection in Finland, 1918* (1920).

VAN CLEEF, E., *Finland: The Republic Farther North* (1929). Recommended.

WUORINEN, J. A., *Nationalism in Modern Finland* (1931).

YOUNG, G., *The New Spain* (1933).

ALVAREZ, DEL VAYO, *Freedom's Battle* (1940). The Spanish civil war from the Republican angle.

CHAPTER X

ASIA DURING TWENTY YEARS OF ARMISTICE, 1919-1939

(a) *Near and Middle East*

ALI SHAH IKBAL, *Kamal: Maker of Modern Turkey* (1934). A Persian estimate.

ALLEN, H. E., *The Turkish Transformation* (1935). Stresses social changes.

ANDREWS, C. F., *Mahatma Gandhi's Ideas* (1930). Important.

ANDREWS, MRS. F. F., *The Holy Land under Mandate,* 2 vols. (1931).

ANSTEY, MRS. V., *The Economic Development of India* (1931). Recommended.

ARMSTRONG, H. C., *Turkey and Syria Reborn* (1930).

———, *Grey Wolf: Mustapha Kemal* (1933).

ANTONIUS, G., *The Arab Awakening* (1939). Indispensable.

BEAUCHAMP, J., *British Imperialism in India* (1934).

BENTWICH, N. DE M., *England in Palestine* (1935). Good.

CHIROL, SIR V., *The Occident and the Orient* (1924).

COUPLAND, R., *The Cripps Mission* (1942).

DUNCAN, A., *India in Crisis* (1931).

DUTCHER, G. M., *The Political Awakening of the East* (1925).

ELLISON, G., *Turkey Today* (1928).

FOSTER, H. A., *The Making of Modern Iraq* (1935). Excellent.

FULLER, J. F. C., *India in Revolt* (1931).

GANDHI, M. K. and others, *Young India 1919-1922* (1923). The non-co-operative movement.

———, *Young India, 1924-26* (1927).

———, *The Story of My Experiments in Truth,* 2 vols. (1927-8).

GRANOVSKY, A., *Land Settlement in Palestine* (1930).

HANNA, P. L., *British Policy in Palestine* (1942).

HOCKING, W. E., *The Spirit of World Politics* (1932). Confined to the Near East.

HOSKINS, H. L., *British Routes to India* (1928). Excellent.

HYAMSON, A. M., *Palestine: A Policy* (1942).

LAWRENCE, T. E., *Revolt in the Desert* (1926).

MAIN, E., *Iraq* (1935).

MAYO, K., *Mother India* (1927). To be read with caution but contains some valuable information not readily available elsewhere.

MEARS, E. G., *Modern Turkey* (1924). Recommended.

McCALLUM, E. P., *The Nationalist Crusade in Syria* (1928). Excellent.

MILLSPAUGH, A. C., *The American Task in Persia* (1925).

MUZUMDER, H. T., *Gandhi the Apostle: His Trial and His Message* (1930).

NEHRU, J., *India and the World* (1936). Essays by the Indian Nationalist leader.

———, *Toward Freedom, the Autobiography of Jawaharlal Nehru* (1941). Important.

———, *The Unity of India; Collected Writings* (1937-1940).

RAJAGOPOLACHAR, C. and KUMARAPPA, J. C. [ed.], *The Nation's Voice* (1932). Selected speeches of Gandhi.

RANGA, IVER, C. S., *India in the Crucible* (1928).

READ, M., *The Indian Peasant Uprooted* (1931).

REVUSKY, A., *Jews in Palestine* (1936). Good on economic aspects.

SAMUEL, M., *On the Rim of the Wilderness* (1931). Jewish-Arab problem.

SPENDER, J. A., *The Changing East* (1926). Good on India and Egypt.

STEIN, L., *Syria* (1926). Analysis of social problems.

STOYANOVSKY, J., *The Mandate for Palestine* (1928). Legalistic.

TOYNBEE, A. J., *Survey of International Affairs, 1925*. Part I: "The Islamic World since the Peace Conference" (1927).

WRIGHT, Q., *Mandates Under the League of Nations* (1930).

YOUNGHUSBAND, SIR F. E., *Dawn in India* (1931).

(b) *The Far East*

ABEND, H., *Ramparts of the Pacific* (1942). On the eve of Pearl Harbor.

BAU, M. J., *Modern Democracy in China* (1924).

———, *China and World Peace* (1928).

BISSON, T. A., *Japan in China* (1938).

BLAKESLEE, G. H., *The Pacific Area* (1929).

BORTON, H., *Japan since 1931* (1940).

BROWN, A. J., *Japan in the World of Today* (1928).

BUSS, C. A., *War and Diplomacy in Eastern Asia* (1941).

CARLSON, E. F., *The Chinese Army* (1940).

CHIANG KAI-SHEK, Generalissimo, *Messages during China's Six Years of War, 1937-1943* (1943).

CLARK, G., *The Great Wall Crumples* (1935). Recommended for China.

CLOSE, U., *The Revolt of Asia* (1927).

CLYDE, P. H., *A History of the Modern and Contemporary Far East* (1937).

CROCKER, W. R., *The Japanese Population Problem* (1931).

DENNERY, E., *Asia's Teeming Millions* (1931). Population problem.

DOLSEN, J. H., *The Awakening of China* (1927).

ETHERTON, P. T. and TILTMAN, H. H., *Manchuria, the Cockpit of Asia* (1932).

FLEISHER, W., *Volcanic Isle* (1941). Authoritative account of Japan on the eve of Pearl Harbor.

HINDMARSH, A. E., *The Basis of Japanese Foreign Policy* (1936).

HOLCOMBE, A. N., *The Chinese Revolution* (1930). Excellent.

HUDSON, G. F., *The Far East in World Politics* (1939).

HSU, L. S. [comp.], *Sun Yat Sen, His Political and Social Ideas* (1933). Extracts from sources.

KAWAKAMI, K. K., *Manchukuo, Child of Conflict* (1933). Pro-Japanese.

KEETON, G. W., *The Development of Extraterritoriality in China*, 2 vols. (1928). Authoritative.

KENNEDY, M. D., *The Changing Fabric of Japan* (1930).

LATTIMORE, O., *Manchuria, Cradle of Conflict* (1935). Indispensable.

LIN YU-TANG, *My Country, My People* (1936). Excellent for China.

MACNAIR, H. F., *China in Revolution* (1931). Excellent.

MILLS, L. A., *British Rule in Eastern Asia* (1942).

MOORE, F., *With Japan's Leaders* (1942).

MOULTON, H. G. and KO, J., *Japan* (1931). Good analysis of economic problems.

PEAKE, C. H., *Nationalism and Education in Modern China* (1932).

PEFFER, N., *China, the Collapse of a Civilization* (1930).

POLLARD, R. T., *China's Foreign Relations 1913-1931* (1933).

RASMUSSEN, O. D., *The Reconquest of Asia* (1934). Anti-Japanese.

SAITO, H., *Japan's Policies and Purposes* (1935). Pro-Japanese.

SHARMAN, T., *Sun Yat-sen* (1934). Excellent.

SNOW, E., *The Battle for Asia* (1941).

————, *Red Star over China* (1939). Superb account of Chinese Red Army.

STIMSON, H. L., *The Far Eastern Crisis* (1936).

SUN YAT-SEN, *The Three Principles of the People* (1927). Invaluable.

TAKEUCHI, T., *War and Diplomacy in the Japanese Empire* (1935).

TANIN, O. and YOHAN, E., *Militarism and Fascism in Japan* (1934). Valuable.

VAN DORN, H. A., *Twenty Years of the Chinese Republic* (1932).

VINACKE, H. M., *A History of the Far East in Modern Times* (1941). Excellent.

WILLOUGHBY, W. W., *Foreign Rights and Interests in China*, 2 vols. (1927).

WOO, T. T. C., *The Kuomintang and the Future of the Chinese Revolution* (1928).

WU CHAO CHU, *The Nationalist Program for China* (1929).

YAKHONTOFF, V. A., *Russia and the Soviet Union in the Far East* (1931).

YOUNG, A. M., *Imperial Japan, 1926-1938* (1938).

CHAPTER XI

FROM RUHR TO PRAGUE (1923-1939)

(a) *General accounts*

GATHORNE-HARDY, G. M., *Short History of International Affairs* (1938).
LEE, D. E., *Ten Years, the World on the Way to War* (1942).
SCHUMAN, F. L., *Europe on the Eve* (1939).
————, *Night Over Europe* (1941).
SETON-WATSON, R. W., *Britain and the Dictators* (1938).
WHITAKER, J. T., *We Cannot Escape History* (1943).

(b) *More Specific Studies*

ALEXANDER, F., *From Paris to Locarno* (1928).
ANGELL, J. W., *Financial Foreign Policy of the United States* (1933).
ARMSTRONG, H. F., *When There Is No Peace* (1939).
AULD, G. P., *The Dawes Plan and the New Economics* (1927).
BEARD, C. A., *The Idea of National Interest and the Open Door at Home* (1934).
BERGMAN, C., *The History of Reparations* (1927).
BERDAHL, C. W., *The Policy of the United States in Respect to the League of Nations* (1932).
BLOCK, K., *German Interests and Policies in the Far East* (1940).
BUELL, R. L., *The Washington Conference* (1922).
CECIL, LORD ROBERT, *A Great Experiment* (1941).
CHAMBERLAIN, N., *In Search of Peace* (1939). Speeches by the British Prime Minister. Invaluable.
DAWES, R. C., *The Dawes Plan in the Making* (1925).
DEAN, V. M., *The Quest for European Peace* (1936).
DUTCH, O., *Thus Died Austria* (1938).
EINZIG, P., *Appeasement Before, During and After the War* (1942).
————, *The World Economic Crisis* (1931).
ENGELY, G., *The Politics of Naval Disarmament* (1932).
EPPSTEIN, J., *Ten Years' Life of the League of Nations* (1928).
FRASER, H. F., *Foreign Trade and World Politics* (1926).
FUCHS, M., *Showdown in Vienna: The Death of Austria* (1939).
GARRATT, G. T., *Gibraltar and the Mediterranean* (1939).
————, *Mussolini's Roman Empire* (1938).
GORDON, M. S., *Barriers to World Trade* (1941).
GRISWOLD, A. W., *The Far Eastern Policy of the United States* (1938).
HAMILTON, T. J., *Appeasement's Child: The Franco Régime in Spain* (1943).
HEIDEN, K., *One Man Against Europe* (1939). An indictment of Hitler's foreign policy.
HIGHLEY, A. E., *The First Sanctions Experiment* (1938).
HOWLAND, C. P., *American Foreign Relations*, 3 vols. (1928-30).
JACOBS, A. J., *World Peace and Armaments* (1931).
KUCZYNSKI, R. R., *American Loans to Germany* (1927).
LENNHOF, E., *The Last Five Hours of Austria* (1938).

MACARTNEY, H. H. H. and CREMONIA, P., *Italy's Foreign Policy, 1914-1937* (1938).

MADARIAGA, S. DE, *Disarmament* (1929).

——, *Reality and Myth in Modern Spain* (1942).

MARTELLI, G., *Italy Against the World* (1938).

MATTHEWS, H. L., *Two Wars and More to Come* (1938). The Spanish Civil War; somewhat pro-loyalist.

MILLER, D. H., *The Peace Pact of Paris* (1925).

MOULTON, H. G. and PASLOVSKY, L., *War Debts and World Prosperity* (1932).

MOWAT, R. B., *Europe in Crisis* (1936).

NEVINS, A., *The United States in World Affairs* (1942). Good summary.

RAPPARD, W. E., *The Geneva Experiment* (1931).

RAUSCHNING, H., *The Voice of Destruction* (1940). An important analysis of Hitler by one who was close to him.

ROBBINS, L., *The Great Depression* (1936).

RÖPKE, W., *International Economic Dislocation* (1942).

SCHACHT, H., *The End of Reparations* (1931). By Germany's financial wizard.

SETON-WATSON, R. W., *Munich and the Dictators* (1939).

——, *From Munich to Danzig* (1939).

SHOTWELL, J. T., *On the Rim of the Abyss* (1936).

——, *War as An Instrument of National Policy* (1929).

——, and DEÁK, F., *Turkey at the Straits* (1940).

SIMONDS, F. H., *The A.B.C. of War Debts* (1933).

——, *American Foreign Policy in the Post-War Years* (1935).

SMITH, R. M., *The Day of the Liberals in Spain* (1938). Excellent account of the Spanish Republic.

SPROUT, H. and SPROUT, M., *Toward A New Order of Sea Power* (1940). Masterful study.

STAMP, SIR J., *Financial Aftermath of the War* (1932).

TAYLOR, G. E., *America on the Pacific* (1942).

TAYLOR, E., *The Strategy of Terror* (1940).

VILLARI, L., *The Expansion of Italy* (1931).

WEBSTER, C. K. and HERBERT, S., *The League of Nations in Theory and Practice* (1933).

WERTH, A., *France and Munich, Before and After Surrender* (1939).

WHEELER-BENNETT, J. W., *The Disarmament Deadlock* (1934).

——, *The Wreck of Reparations* (1933). Excellent.

WOOLF, L. J., *Britain and the War Debts* (1933).

ZIMMERMAN, A., *The League of Nations and the Rise of Law* (1936).

CHAPTERS XII AND XIII

THE SECOND WORLD WAR

A Few of the More Worthwhile Contemporary Books

AGLION, R., *The Fighting French* (1943). The story of the Free French.

BELDEN, J., *Retreat with Stilwell* (1943).

CHURCHILL, W. L. S., *Blood, Sweat and Tears* (1941). Speeches of the British Prime Minister between May, 1938 and February, 1941.
———, *The Unrelenting Struggle* (1942). Speeches of the British Prime Minister from Nov., 1940 to Dec. 30, 1941.
CARR, E. H., *Conditions of Peace* (1942).
CURIE, E., *Journey Among Warriors* (1943). Particularly good for Russia and China.
DAVIES, R. A. and STEIGER, D., *Soviet Asia: Democracy's First Line of Defense* (1942).
FORD, C., *Short-Cut to Tokyo* (1943).
FRIED, H. E., *The Guilt of the German Army* (1942).
GUDME, S., *Denmark, "Hitler's Model Protectorate,"* (1942).
HERMAN, F., *Dynamite Cargo* (1943).
HOOVER, H. and GIBSON, H., *The Problems of Lasting Peace* (1942).
HÖYE, B. and AGER, T. M., *The Fight of the Norwegian Church against Nazism* (1943).
LASKI, H. J., *Reflections on the Revolution of Our Times* (1943).
LIDDELL HART, B. H., *This Expanding War* (1942).
LEONHARDT, H. L., *Nazi Conquest of Danzig* (1942).
MARCHAL, T., *Vichy: Two Years of Deception* (1943).
MASSOCK, R. G., *Italy from Within* (1943).
McINNIS, E. W., *The War, First Year* (1940).
———, *The War, Second Year* (1941).
———, *The War, Third Year* (1942). Three excellent accounts of the military campaigns in general outline.
MICHIE, A. A., *The Air Offensive Against Germany* (1943).
MOOREHEAD, A., *Don't Blame the Generals* (1943).
PEPPER, N., *Basis for Peace in the Far East* (1943).
POLIAKOV, A., *White Mammoths* (1943). Russian tanks in action.
RAPPART, W. E., *The Quest for Peace* (1943).
ROMULO, COL. C. P., *I Saw the Fall of the Philippines* (1943). By a Filipino officer attached to MacArthur's staff. Excellent.
SALTER, C., *Tryout in Spain* (1943).
SCOTT, J., *Duel for Europe* (1942). Hitler *vs.* Stalin.
SHIRER, W., *Berlin Diary* (1941). Authentic and valuable for an understanding of Germany, 1934-1941.
SMITH, D., *America and the Axis War* (1942).
SMITH, H. K., *Last Train from Berlin* (1942).
STRABOLGI, LORD, *Singapore and After* (1942).
STREZETELSKI, S., *Where the Storm Broke* (1942).
TOLISCHUSS, O. D., *They Wanted War* (1940).
———, *Tokyo Record* (1943). The best of the contemporary books on Japan.
TORRES, H., *Pierre Laval* (1941).
TOYNBEE, A. J., *Christianity and Civilization* (1940).
TREGASKIS, R., *Guadalcanal Diary* (1943).
TUTAEFF, D., *The Soviet Caucasus* (1942).
WATSON, B., *Miracle in Hellas: The Greeks Fight On* (1943).
WELLER, G., *Singapore is Silent* (1943).
WERNER, M., *Battle for the World* (1941).
———, *It is Later than You Think* (1943 edition).

WERNER, M., *The Great Offensive* (1942).
WHITE, W. A., *They Were Expendable* (1942).
WILLKIE, W., *One World* (1943). Excellent.
WRIGHT, Q., *A Study of War*, 2 vols. (1942).
VÓYETEKHOV, B., *The Last Days of Sevastopol* (1943).

INDEX